The South Returns
to Congress

The South Returns to Congress

Men, Economic Measures, and
Intersectional Relationships, 1868–1879

Terry L. Seip

Louisiana State University Press
Baton Rouge and London

Designer: Albert Crochet
Typeface: Linotron Trump Medieval
Typesetter: G & S Typesetters, Inc.
Printer: Thomson-Shore, Inc.
Binder: John Dekker & Sons, Inc.

LIBRARY OF CONGRESS CATALOGING IN PUBLICATION DATA

Seip, Terry L.
　The South returns to Congress.

　Bibliography: p.
　Includes index.
　1. United States—Economic policy—To 1933.　2. United States—
Politics and government—1865–1877.　3. United States. Congress—
History.　4. Legislators—Southern States—History.　5. Reconstruction.
6. Sectionalism (United States)　I. Title.
HC105.7.S44　　1983　　　328.73'073'0975　　82–4654
ISBN 0–8071–1052–3

To the memory of two fathers
Leslie Grant Seip
and Raymond Lee Sejkora

Contents

Maps

Tables

Acknowledgments

I am indebted to a good many institutions and individuals for their assistance in the preparation of this study. I wish to acknowledge the generous help of manuscripts librarians and staffs at the Alderman Library, University of Virginia; the Baker and Houghton libraries, Harvard University; the Barker Texas History Center, University of Texas; the Henry E. Huntington Library; the Indiana State Library; the Library of Congress and National Archives; the Massachusetts Historical Society; the Middleton Library, Louisiana State University; the Mississippi Department of Archives and History; the North Carolina State Archives; the Perkins Library, Duke University; the South Carolina Department of Archives and History; the South Caroliniana Library, University of South Carolina; and the Van Pelt Library, University of Pennsylvania. Milo B. Howard, Jr., and Virginia Jones of the Alabama Department of Archives and History, Thomas A. Smith of the Hayes Presidential Center, Phyllis E. McLaughlin of the Iowa State Historical Department, and the full staff of the rich Southern Historical Collection at the University of North Carolina deserve special mention, for they drew my attention to collections I might have otherwise overlooked and they frequently went out of their way to accommodate my requests.

The late T. Harry Williams of Louisiana State University originally suggested the topic and provided reassuring and provocative direction as my dissertation advisor. Like his other students, I will sorely miss his stimulating counsel and company. I owe him a considerable debt, as I do William J. Cooper, Jr., who has given generously of his time and offered needed encouragement and indispensable advice over the past few years. I have also profited greatly from the comments and suggestions of William C. Harris, James E. Sefton, John L. Loos, Carl V. Harris, and Philip J. Avillo, Jr., who read parts of or the whole manuscript at some stage in its evolution. Jean H. Baker and John Kent Folmar offered a useful commentary on a paper based on the manuscript which I gave at the Southern Historical Association convention in 1977. George C. Rable not only shared his thoughts on research materials but cheerfully labored through an early draft and offered an incisive critique which improved the manuscript immeasurably.

My colleagues at the University of Southern California have been a constant source of encouragement; special thanks are due John A. Schutz, Edwin J. Perkins, and Steven J. Ross, who gave me thoughtful suggestions on an early draft of the manuscript. In addition, the University of Southern California provided essential computer time, and a Louisiana State University Dissertation Year Fellowship, grants from the Warrick Memorial Fund at LSU, and a Haynes Summer Fellowship from USC helped finance several research trips through the South and East. I would also like to express my appreciation to cartographer David L. Fuller, who drew the maps with care and facility. Finally, it has been my pleasure to work with three skilled and accommodating editors at Louisiana State University Press: Beverly Jarrett, Martha Hall, and John Easterly. Those who have contributed so generously to the completion of this study, of course, bear no responsibility for what remains—that belongs to me.

My greatest debt is owed to my wife Patricia, who patiently spent long hours over the past decade at the calculator, keypunch, and typewriter and continuously provided love and encouragement, and to Jeremy, Brandon, and Ginger, three marvelous individuals who entered our world at various stages of this study and kept the two of us in touch with reality.

The South Returns
to Congress

Introduction

This study examines the careers of the 251 men who represented the
South in Congress during Reconstruction with the primary aim of
understanding them as members of political parties, representatives
of regional interests, and products of the chaotic political world of
the postwar South. Neither the region nor the era has suffered from
a lack of scholarly attention. The civil rights revolution of the 1960s
sent students with new attitudes toward blacks and Radical Republicans scurrying back to examine the South during the first Reconstruction. The result has been a revisionist onslaught—a plethora of
state and local studies displaying the complexity and diversity of the
Reconstruction experience. Neglected in this scholarly deluge, however, are the southern congressional delegations, the critical link between the South and Washington. The senators and representatives
offer a revealing cross section of southern political leadership and
provide a broad range of individual perspectives for examining some
of the central questions in Reconstruction historiography.

The bitter struggle between President Andrew Johnson and Congress over the requirements for readmission delayed the Southerners' reappearance in Washington a full three years after Appomattox.
It was not until June, 1868, that Congress overrode Johnson's veto
and seated six southern delegations, but the process of restoring the
four remaining states to the Union spanned another two years. Virginia, Mississippi, Texas, and Georgia satisfied congressional requirements in early 1870, and the South finally attained full representation when Georgia Senator Homer V. M. Miller took his seat in
February, 1871—just eight days before the end of the Forty-first Congress and ten years after the secession winter of 1860–1861.

The decade after 1868 was as dramatic and significant for the South as the previous one. The region was represented in Congress to a considerable extent by Republicans—a northern-imposed, alien leadership in the eyes of most white Southerners. The atmosphere and tempo of Washington had changed remarkably since the antebellum years—to one southern gentleman, the nation's capital had become a "rather crude place . . . and the Congress and Society was about as tough a set as one cares to see."[1] The Senate and House of Representatives had emerged from the immediate postwar years as a more dynamic and forceful branch of government. The party of Lincoln now dominated the legislative branch; a new Massachusetts-Ohio Republican axis had replaced the old New York–Virginia Democratic axis of the prewar period. In addition to changes in institutional procedures, a new set of names dotted the leadership ranks and a host of new issues occupied congressional attention. But at least one feature of the late antebellum years remained unchanged; despite the frequently heard rhetoric of reconciliation, sectional antipathy remained sharp.

Thrust into this uneasy atmosphere were 251 southern senators and representatives—themselves the products of a highly charged political environment in a region struggling to adjust to a new and in many ways unfamiliar order in American life. The key to the new order, of course, was black suffrage and the subsequent emergence of a southern Republican party. Had a casual observer compared the southern congressional delegations of the late 1860s with those of a decade earlier, he might well have concluded that the section had undergone a startling transformation. The Southerners appearing in the Fortieth Congress during the summer of 1868 were certainly a different breed of men than those who had resigned their seats during the winter of secession. Absent were such familiar personalities as James M. Mason and Robert M. T. Hunter, Jefferson Davis and Albert Gallatin Brown, Howell Cobb and Robert Toombs, and others prominent in the late antebellum congresses. In their places sat the new representatives of a momentarily altered South. Of the forty-five Southerners seated in the Fortieth Congress, forty-two were Re-

1. R. T. W. Duke, Jr., "Recollections, 1853–1926" (Typescript in Alderman Library, University of Virginia, Charlottesville), 199.

publicans. Over half of these were carpetbaggers, the variously motivated Yankees who had decided to settle in the postwar South; the
remainder were scalawags, who, in the conservatives' parlance, were
little better than traitors to their race and section. Providing the primary electorate and soon to send representatives of their race were
the blacks, the third and most unsettling element of what conservatives referred to as the "unholy triumvirate" of the Reconstruction
South.

Republicans dominated the region's delegations through the elections to the Forty-third Congress in 1872. With the exception of
South Carolina, where Republicans remained entrenched, the most
dramatic change in the fortunes of the party occurred in the congressional elections of 1874. The Democratic gains of that year, which
included control of the House, reflected a renewed party organization
after the Liberal Republican debacle of 1872. But the Republicans,
faced with the scandals of the Grant administration and economic
depression touched off by the Panic of 1873, fared poorly nationwide.
In the South, Republican factionalism, waning northern support for
reconstruction, and the conservatives' use of intimidation and violence reduced southern Republican seats in the House from 57 percent to 26 percent as a result of the 1874 elections, and to 12 percent
in 1876. Only four Republicans out of a delegation of sixty-three
would survive the 1878 elections to the Forty-sixth House. The Senate with its six-year terms was slower in reflecting the process of redemption, but the effect was the same. Southern Republican seats
fell from a high of eighteen out of twenty in 1871 to two in 1879.

Whether the Democrats who replaced these Republicans were
backward-looking "Bourbons" or forward-looking "Redeemers" remains a moot point. They were at least of different names if not of
substantial philosophical difference from the generation of the
fifties. Of those prominent in antebellum congresses, only Georgia's
Alexander H. Stephens returned to serve in the 1870s, and as an un-
admiring James G. Blaine remarked, Stephens was "physically a
shattered man" who "now appeared merely as a relic of the past."[2]

2. James G. Blaine, *Twenty Years of Congress: From Lincoln to Garfield* (2 vols.;
Norwich, Conn.: Henry Bill Publishing Co., 1886), II, 547.

Several younger congressmen of the 1850s returned to Washington in the postwar period, but for the most part it was a new bevy of Democrats who restored "home rule" and launched their congressional careers during the seventies.

Although historians have given surprisingly little attention to the southern congressmen, an image of them has emerged that can hardly be considered favorable. The postwar South seemed to scar all who touched it; most of the congressmen left the 1870s with badly blemished reputations. Among the central problems which have haunted them—carpetbaggers, scalawags, blacks, and conservatives alike—are questions of their political legitimacy, their personal character and reputation, and the quality and effectiveness of their representation. In many respects the southern congressmen and their colleagues at the state level have served as the scapegoats for the failure of reconstruction. I believe their image and record merit close examination. With the aid of the techniques of collective biography and roll call analysis and a broad range of primary and secondary sources, I have attempted to come to some understanding of them in the pages that follow.

My initial concern is their personal and political backgrounds, their perceptions of what was going on around them, and the atmosphere from which they emerged as spokesmen for the postwar South. Although I was first interested in the Republicans since they stand at the center of the historiographical controversies of the period, as I progressed the Redeemers became equally fascinating. Most, Republicans and Democrats alike, bear little resemblance to the images and stereotypes first shaped in the 1870s. It is hardly news, for example, that the Dunningite caricatures of the Republicans are at best misleading and in most cases totally inaccurate. But until now no one has relieved those not deserving this stigma, and that alone casts new light on their legislative behavior. The diversity of the men is striking. In terms of their personal and political backgrounds and aspirations, and their perceptions of the South, reconstruction, and the future, the congressmen are so disparate that they defy the creation of a "composite type" or even a meaningful collective profile. The fundamental division, of course, was political, and choice of party hinged upon a number of factors, the most basic being attitudes toward the freedmen and the thrust of reconstruction. As a group, the Democrats were little troubled by internal strife, but Republican unity was frequently more superficial than real. The very heterogeneity of those who initially gathered under the Republican banner doomed the party to a destructive factionalism which often cut across the traditional categories based on race and nativity. The internal discord, coupled with intersectional rifts in the national party, contributed significantly to the failure of southern Republicanism.

The personal and political backgrounds of the congressmen and the milieu from which they emerged provide a context for analyzing their activity and voting behavior in Congress. In this area I am less interested in their generally partisan response to reconstruction issues than I am in their reaction to economic questions. Reconstruction remained a pivotal concern, especially in those unredeemed sections of the South, but as a national issue it was clearly on the wane soon after readmission. In addition, historians have already given considerable attention to the politics and course of reconstruction at the national level during the 1870s.[3] I briefly examine the Southerners' reaction to such measures as the Fifteenth Amendment and the enforcement, amnesty, and civil rights acts primarily for what those struggles reveal about intersectional and intraparty divisions among Republicans.

I have chosen instead to focus on the Southerners' response to the more differentiated economic questions—a set of issues without the politically charged content of reconstruction legislation and one of at least equal, if not greater importance to postwar America. Congress spent an unusual amount of time coping with serious economic problems stemming from the Civil War and, after 1873, from a troubled national economy. In addition to providing appropriations for the normal functions of government, the legislators wrestled with a host of substantive economic issues beginning with the first debates over the sanctity of the public credit and refunding the national debt in the late 1860s and ending with the resumption of spe-

3. In particular: William Gillette, *Retreat from Reconstruction, 1869–1879* (Baton Rouge: Louisiana State University Press, 1979); and Michael Les Benedict, *Let Us Have Peace: Republicans and Reconstruction, 1869–1880* (New York: W. W. Norton, forthcoming).

cie payments in 1879. Along the way central economic concerns included controversies over revenue policy, financial and monetary problems, and appropriations and subsidies for internal improvements. Northeastern and midwestern interests in these matters, especially in the pivotal financial questions, have been ably and amply detailed in the work of Robert Sharkey, Irwin Unger, and others, but the politics of reconstruction have so monopolized scholarly attention that historians have virtually ignored southern interests in the kaleidoscopic economic concerns of the 1870s.[4]

Economic issues were obviously important to the war-torn South and an examination of regional interests, a reading of the extensive congressional debates, and a roll call analysis indicate that Southerners were an active force in the determination of national economic policy. While their reaction to other matters was frequently partisan, sectional and local interests and, more rarely, personal beliefs governed their response to economic issues. National party unity disappeared on such questions, and the commonly accepted notion that southern Republicans defied constituent interests and voted as their northeastern party colleagues instructed is easily dispelled. Southern Republicans were fully as responsive as their Democratic colleagues, if not more so, to what they perceived to be their section's and their constituents' economic interests. On economic questions a surprisingly solid South emerged at readmission.

Finally, and perhaps most important, the congressmen are an ideal vehicle for considering the larger questions of intersectional political and economic relationships in Congress and the interaction between Northerners and Southerners in the two political parties. These are among the neglected areas of Reconstruction historiography, yet I believe understanding them is requisite to understanding the course of the postwar South and the failure of reconstruction. It is apparent that the returning southern Democrats were seldom at ease with their northern brethren. The antebellum party divisions and unpleasant memories of the Charleston convention split of 1860

4.   Robert P. Sharkey, *Money, Class, and Party: An Economic Study of Civil War and Reconstruction* (Baltimore: Johns Hopkins Press, 1959); Irwin Unger, *The Greenback Era: A Social and Political History of American Finance, 1865–1879* (Princeton: Princeton University Press, 1964).

and the war years still haunted the party during the 1870s, and antagonistic sectional economic interests sometimes overshadowed Democratic unity on reconstruction issues. To northern Democrats, the Southerners remained suspect, and the Southerners, particularly the ex-Whigs, continued to be sensitive to long-standing political differences.

The far more portentous sectional split which emerged in the Republican party is one of my principal interests. Southern Republicans should have felt at home in a decade of Republican administrations and congresses; they were, after all, largely the creations of their northern counterparts. Political aims and ideals, the things shared, might have provided a firm bond among party members in both sections. Most certainly, the establishment of a viable party in the ex-Confederate states necessitated a close and harmonious working relationship and mutual respect between the northern and southern wings. The sources of party unity, however, were too few and too frail to counterbalance the forces of sectional discord. The congressional debates and other sources indicate that a serious rift developed between northern and southern Republicans; misunderstanding, distrust, and even open enmity marred their relationship. For much of the decade, Northerners continued to give lip service to southern Republicanism, but additional reconstruction legislation and rhetorical endorsement soon proved insufficient for maintaining the party's southern wing. Southern Republicans never had the full support of Northerners, and their uneasiness, evident as early as 1869, was amply reciprocated. Most Northerners uncritically accepted the negative image of southern Republicans with distressing quickness, and by the early seventies they tended to view Southerners as the ugly stepsisters of the party.

As William Gillette has observed, the goal of northern Republicans during Reconstruction "remained constant—to lodge national political power permanently in the North within the national Republican party and to republicanize the South."[5] In good measure they achieved the first part of their goal, but for a variety of reasons, many of their own making, their effort to establish a lasting Repub-

5. Gillette, *Retreat from Reconstruction,* xiii.

lican party in the South met with disaster. At base, the failure lay in the Northerners' ingrained distrust of all things southern. They simply could not accept Southerners, even those who tried to be Republicans, on an equal basis with themselves. As the experience of the southern Republican congressmen makes clear, the intersectional difficulties stemmed from many factors including disputes over campaign aid, congressional committee assignments, patronage, and reconstruction policy, the precipitous decline of northern Radicalism after 1868, the epidemic factionalism and other problems in the southern wing, and the hard core of racism in both sections. To these sources of discord, I have added and stressed two neglected factors—differing sectional economic interests and the simple failure of Northerners to understand the political and economic needs of their southern colleagues. With such stimuli, the initial party rift grew into a serious and ultimately insurmountable gulf which figured heavily in the collapse of reconstruction.

Several matters of terminology, dimensions, and methodology deserve clarification here. First, there is a tendency in recent revisionist studies to avoid using the terms *carpetbagger* and *scalawag* because of their pejorative connotations. The terms most often substituted are *outside white Republican* and *native white Republican*. I have chosen to continue to use *carpetbagger* and *scalawag* to designate the white factions in the Republican party for the sake of brevity and convenience and without any implied assumption about the character of those so designated. Secondly, the state of Tennessee approved the Fourteenth Amendment in July, 1866, and was readmitted to representation in the same month. While Tennessee's wartime situation and postwar politics varied considerably from the other ten ex-Confederate states, its delegations are excluded from consideration primarily because it was not required to submit to the final plan of congressional reconstruction. I have also chosen to include the Forty-fifth Congress (1877–1879) rather than to terminate with the inauguration of Rutherford B. Hayes in March, 1877. This allows consideration of four additional southern Republicans, a broader range of Democrats, and the implications of Hayes's southern policy. The year 1879 is also a more logical economic terminal point since congressional support for federal subsidies declined sharply toward the end of the decade, the first round of the silver controversy came to a head with the passage of the Bland-Allison Act in 1878, and specie payments were resumed in January, 1879. Finally, this study would have been difficult without the quantitative techniques of collective biography and roll call analysis. The primacy of party and region in determining legislative behavior disappointed my original hopes of explaining voting behavior in terms of personal and constituency characteristics. Still, the computer made possible my management and manipulation of large bodies of biographical, constituency, and roll call data which would have been otherwise impossible to handle. The quantitative methods used in this study are briefly discussed in the Bibliographical Essay.

I The Southerners
A Personal Profile

From June, 1868, when the first states were admitted to the Fortieth Congress, to the conclusion of the Forty-fifth Congress in March, 1879, the ten ex-Confederate states undergoing military reconstruction sent 251 men to Washington. They are as diverse a group as one could desire for a study of a collective political elite; their hopes, successes, problems, follies, and failures reflect the Reconstruction experience in microcosm. The troublesome stereotypes—carpetbaggers, scalawags, blacks, Redeemers, and Bourbons—are all represented, but on close examination these neat categories quickly break down, revealing a complex set of individuals from divergent personal backgrounds arrayed across the political spectrum. Republicans and Democrats alike ranged from a few who achieved a measure of national recognition to transient figures who appeared suddenly, served briefly, and then disappeared. Not surprisingly, the range of surviving biographical data is significantly greater for native conservatives than for Republicans, and within Republican ranks it is more abundant for natives than for outsiders and blacks. In many cases, such background information as religion or former political affiliations has not survived. And with the exception of those few leaving substantial collections of private papers, only rarely can one grasp a man's disposition and thought at a given point in time. In particular, many Republicans remain elusive, evanescent figures who left little evidence of their presence other than a residue of hatred among southern whites.

The congressmen were split almost evenly along party lines into 122 Democrats and 129 Republicans.[1] Proportionally, Texas, Virginia,

---

1. The opportunistic carpetbagger William Wilshire of Arkansas, who was elected as a Republican to the 43rd House and as a Conservative to the 44th, is considered a

and Georgia, all among the last to be readmitted and the first to be redeemed, sent the fewest Republicans to Congress. At the other extreme, South Carolina, with a large and active black electorate, sent solidly Republican delegations until the turmoil surrounding the 1876 elections enabled three Democrats to secure seats in the Forty-fifth Congress. With the exception of North Carolina, where an established contingent of native unionists gave that state, for a time, some semblance of a balanced party system, Republicans dominated most other delegations until redemption (see Table 1).

To their southern contemporaries, the first noticeable variation between Democratic and Republican congressmen lay in their regional origins and their length of residency in the South. Almost 90 percent of the 122 Democrats were born in the slave states, and all but four were antebellum residents of the states they would represent during Reconstruction. Fifty-two percent of the Republicans were free-state natives and over a third claimed the Northeast as their place of birth. Conservative Southerners preferred to identify the carpetbaggers as "alien" Northeasterners, and the closer a Republican could be tied to the locus of New England abolitionism (particularly Massachusetts), the more damned he became in conservative eyes. But by 1860 well over half of the Republicans who ventured south during and after the war were residents of the Midwest.

Place of residency as of April, 1861, is the commonly accepted basis for delineating the carpetbagger and scalawag factions in the Republican party. Richard N. Current's definition of carpetbaggers as "white Northerners who went south after the beginning of the Civil War and, sooner or later, became active in politics as Republicans" splits the white Republican congressmen into factions of sixty carpetbaggers and fifty-three scalawags.[2] The distinction between outsiders and natives is somewhat artificial in that they shared many elements of the Republican ideology, but more often than not they varied in their response to reconstruction issues. They frequently came to represent antagonistic factions at the state level,

Republican in all calculations involving the total membership in each party and as a Democrat in the analysis of the 44th Congress. For the sources and methods employed in collective biography, see the Bibliographical Essay.

2. Richard N. Current, "Carpetbaggers Reconsidered," in David H. Pinkney and Theodore Ropp (eds.), *A Festschrift for Frederick B. Artz* (Durham: Duke University Press, 1964), 144.

Table 1. SOUTHERN CONGRESSMEN, 40TH–45TH CONGRESSES (1868–1879):
POLITICAL PARTY BY CONGRESS, CHAMBER, AND STATE

State	40th Congress (1868–1869) Senate Dem Rep		House Dem Rep		41st Congress (1869–1871) Senate Dem Rep		House Dem Rep		42nd Congress (1871–1873) Senate Dem Rep		House Dem Rep	
Alabama	—	2	—	6	—	2	2	4	1	1	3	3
Arkansas	—	2	—	4	—	2	1	2	—	2	1	3
Florida	—	2	—	1	—	2	—	1	—	2	1	1
Georgia	—	—	2	4	1	1	4	3	1	1	5	3
Louisiana	—	2	1	4	—	2	—	5	—	2	—	6
Mississippi	—	—	—	—	—	2	—	5	—	2	—	5
North Carolina	—	2	—	7	—	2	2	7	1	1	5	2
South Carolina	—	2	—	4	—	2	—	5	—	2	—	4
Texas	—	—	—	—	—	2	1	3	—	2	4	1
Virginia	—	—	—	—	1	1	5	4	1	1	5	3
Total	—	12	3	30	2	18	15	39	4	16	24	31
Combined Total	12		33		20		54		20		55	

Note: Totals include all individuals seated by the Senate and House of Representatives.

State	43rd Congress (1873–1875) Senate Dem	Rep	House Dem	Rep	44th Congress (1875–1877) Senate Dem	Rep	House Dem	Rep	45th Congress (1877–1879) Senate Dem	Rep	House Dem	Rep
Alabama	1	1	3	5	1	1	6	2	1	1	8	—
Arkansas	—	2	1	4	—	2	4	—	1	1	4	—
Florida	—	2	—	2	1	1	1	2	1	1	2	1
Georgia	2	—	7	3	2	—	9	—	2	—	10	—
Louisiana	—	1ᵃ	1	6	—	1ᵃ	4	3	1	1	6	2
Mississippi	—	3	1	5	—	2	4	2	1	1	6	—
North Carolina	2	—	5	3	2	—	7	1	2	—	7	1
South Carolina	—	2	—	6	—	2	—	6	1	1	2	3
Texas	—	2	6	—	1	1	6	—	2	—	6	—
Virginia	1	1	5	5	2	—	8	1	2	—	9	1
Total	6	14	29	39	9	10	49	17	14	6	60	8
Combined Total	20		68		19		66		20		68	

ᵃDue to contests, one Louisiana Senate seat remained vacant for the 43rd and 44th Congresses.

and contemporaries were quick to point out the differences between them. Each state sent at least one carpetbagger to Washington, but outsiders were proportionally most numerous in the delegations of Florida and Louisiana, while natives dominated those of Georgia, North Carolina, and Texas. Blacks were more unevenly distributed; South Carolina, Alabama, and Mississippi contributed twelve of the sixteen black congressmen. Although six of the blacks were carpetbaggers, race was far more important than length of residency and contemporaries lumped the blacks into a category of their own (see Table 2).

Similarly, the four Democrats who arrived after the beginning of the war do not merit separate treatment as their choice of party overshadowed their length of residency in the South. Few objections, for example, could be raised to the wealthy Pennsylvanian William Milnes, Jr., who moved to Virginia in 1865 and purchased the Shenandoah Iron Works. The heavily white sixth district in the valley selected him as a "safe" representative when Virginia was readmitted in January, 1870. Milnes served the year that remained in his term, allowed a native Democrat to take his seat in the following Congress, and returned to his business. Of the four outsiders, only Milnes won the lasting approval of his new southern neighbors. He would prosper, die, and be buried in the Shenandoah Valley.[3]

The southern careers of the other three Yankee Democrats exemplify the power of party labels and conservative hypocrisy regarding the definition of carpetbaggery. The conservative Richmond *Whig*, for example, characterized Gilbert C. Walker, a New York and then Chicago lawyer who located in Norfolk during the war, as a "settler—not a carpetbagger." When Walker ran for governor in 1869 as a candidate of the "True Republicans" (a coalition of moderate to conservative Republicans and Conservatives opposing the Regular Republicans), the *Whig* declared, "We will beat them with a Northern man who is not a carpetbagger." As one Regular Republican explained, the conservatives had cleverly "abandoned their old rebel candidate for Governor, and nominated a man from New York of

---

3. Benjamin P. Poore (comp.), *Congressional Directory for the Third Session of the Forty-first Congress* (2nd ed.; Washington, D.C.: Government Printing Office, 1871), 51; William H. Barnes, *History of Congress: The Forty-first Congress of the United States, 1869–1871* (New York: W. H. Barnes, 1872).

Table 2. SOUTHERN CONGRESSMEN, 40TH–45TH CONGRESSES (1868–1879):
POLITICAL PARTY AND FACTION BY STATE

| | Democrats (n=122) | | Republicans (n=129) | | | | | |
| | | | Scalawags (n=53) | | Carpetbaggers (n=60) | | Blacks (n=16) | |
State	Senate (n=17)	House (n=107)	Senate (n=8)	House (n=45)	Senate (n=17)	House (n=43)	Senate (n=2)	House (n=14)
Alabama	2	15	—	7	2	6	—	3
Arkansas	1	6	—	4	4	5	—	—
Florida	1	3	—	—	4	3	—	1
Georgia	4[a]	20[a]	1	8	—	2	—	1
Louisiana	1	10	—	3	3	9	—	1
Mississippi	1[b]	7[b]	1	3	2	5	2	1
North Carolina	2	13	1	9	1	3	—	1
South Carolina	1	2	2	5	1	4	—	1
Texas	2	11	2	2	—	1	—	—
Virginia	2	20	1	4	—	5	—	—

[a]Total includes Benjamin H. Hill, who served in both chambers.
[b]Total includes L. Q. C. Lamar, who served in both chambers.

doubtful politics, and set him up as a 'Republican.'" Some Virginians
even rationalized that Walker's appearance was that of a native; "he
was not a *Yanky*," declared one supporter, because "he don't look
like one." As governor, Walker ironically promised to rid the state of
the "horde of greedy cormorants and unprincipled carpet-baggers
who came to sap her very vitals" while he led the ill-fated and personally profitable movement to fund the Old Dominion's enormous
debt. After his term, Walker, "the cleverest of all the carpetbaggers
who ever came South" in the opinion of one Virginia historian,
served as a Conservative Democrat in the Forty-fourth and Forty-
fifth Congresses before returning to a lucrative law practice in New
York in 1879—the same year, not coincidentally, that the debt Readjusters began to emerge as a serious force in Virginia politics.[4]

The power of party is even more evident in the cases of the other
outsiders. Had James Mann been a Republican, conservatives would
have ranked him among the most despicable of carpetbaggers. Mann,
a Union army officer and resident of Maine, held a Republican appointment as a treasury agent for Louisiana at the time of his election by a predominantly white New Orleans constituency. He had
no property and could not have been considered a "settler" because
he never moved his family to the South; in fact, he left Louisiana in
1867 to move his family from Maine to Massachusetts. His Republican opponent immediately charged that Mann's legal residence was
not in Louisiana, but the House nevertheless seated him when the
state was readmitted. Any reservations New Orleans conservatives
might have had were relieved when he succumbed to "acute brain
fever" in August, 1868, after having served only nine days at the end
of the second session of the Fortieth Congress.[5]

4. Richmond *Whig*, January 22, May 4, 1869; Alfred Morton to Henry L. Dawes,
July 21, 1869, in Henry L. Dawes Papers, Library of Congress (hereinafter cited as LC);
James W. Walker to William Mahone, April 11, 1869, quoted in Jack P. Maddex, Jr.,
The Virginia Conservatives, 1867–1879: A Study in Reconstruction Politics (Chapel
Hill: University of North Carolina Press, 1970), 75; David Donald, *Charles Sumner
and the Rights of Man* (New York: Alfred A. Knopf, 1970), 424; James Tice Moore,
Two Paths to the New South: The Virginia Debt Controversy, 1870–1883 (Lexington:
University Press of Kentucky, 1974), 16, 25; Hamilton J. Eckenrode, "History of Vir-
ginia Since 1865," 78, quoted in Maddex, *Virginia Conservatives*, 105.
5. *Biographical Directory of the American Congress, 1774–1971* (Washington,
D.C.: Government Printing Office, 1971), 1333; New Orleans *Daily Picayune*, August 27, 28, 1868; *House Miscellaneous Documents*, 40th Cong., 3rd Sess., No. 13,
pp. 29–30; *Congressional Globe*, 40th Cong., 3rd Sess., 240–41.

The final Yankee Democrat, Union army veteran John Conner of Texas, had waged an unsuccessful campaign in 1866 as a National Union candidate for the Indiana house of representatives. After his defeat, Conner rejoined the army as a captain of black troops in Texas, secured an appointment as clerk of Grayson County, and ran successfully for the Forty-first and Forty-second Houses. Texas Republicans had a field day taunting conservatives about their new congressman. "The little political monstrosity," sneered the radical Houston *Union*, was nothing more than a "Yankee adventurer, Federal soldier, nigger Captain, states rights, secession, rebel, anti-reconstruction, southern chivalry candidate for Congress." Although he received support from the future senator Samuel Bell Maxey and other prominent conservatives, some clearly disliked him. Democrat John Hancock, a former unionist who served with him in the House, concluded that Conner "is merely used, or more properly speaking acts in unison with an insidious wanton" with the "once leaders of secession." Former governor and future congressman James Throckmorton privately referred to him as "a carpetbagger of the veriest stripe—and an ass" and the "most abominable liar ever known." Conner's failing health prohibited him from seeking reelection in 1872, and, probably to the relief of Throckmorton and friends, he died the following fall at only thirty-one—the youngest age of death of the 251. In a brief reference to Conner's death, the editor of the Austin *Democratic Statesman* reflected the general reaction of southern conservatives to the Yankee Democrats. "We did not indulge in a fulsome eulogy," the editor admitted, "for we did not feel at all inclined that way." More might have been said about Conner, he added, "but it would not have been in exaltation of the departed. To be candid, we did not much admire the character of the man, but we would let the dead rest in peace."[6]

While party affiliation was more important to Southerners, the most striking variation among the political factions was their age. Over

6. Walter Prescott Webb and H. Bailey Carroll (eds.), *The Handbook of Texas* (2 vols.; Austin: Texas State Historical Association, 1952), I, 393; Francis B. Heitman (comp.), *Historical Register and Directory of the United States Army . . .* (2 vols.; Washington, D.C.: Government Printing Office, 1903), I, 321; Houston *Union*, quoted in Claude Elliott, *Leathercoat: The Life History of a Texas Patriot* (San An-

half of the Democrats and scalawags were forty-five or older when they first entered the House or Senate—a median age comparable to earlier southern leaders in antebellum state legislatures, the secession conventions, and the Confederate congresses. In sharp contrast were the carpetbaggers and blacks, with median ages of thirty-five and thirty-four, respectively. The age disparity is better revealed by the percentages of those entering Congress under forty years of age. For the House during the 1870s, 33 percent of all entering representatives (including the Southerners) were under forty; for southern Democrats and scalawags, the figure was 26 percent. By comparison, 77 percent of the carpetbaggers and blacks had not reached their fortieth birthday when they began their first term.[7]

The youth of the Republicans is striking. The youngest, John Amber Smith of Virginia, was only six months over the minimum age of twenty-five when seated by the Forty-third Congress in 1873. The same House admitted twenty-five-year-old John Roy Lynch, the ex-slave from Mississippi. Carpetbaggers Stephen Dorsey of Arkansas and George Spencer of Alabama, both thirty-one when they began their terms, represent the youngest of the southern senators during the period. One obvious consequence of the carpetbaggers' youth was that they had less opportunity for political experience in the antebellum period. Some 80 percent of the carpetbagger representatives came of age after 1850, 65 percent were not yet twenty-one

---

tonio: Standard Printing, 1938), 205–206; John Hancock to Benjamin H. Epperson, March 11, 1872, James W. Throckmorton to Epperson, April 1, 1872, in Benjamin Holland Epperson Papers, Barker Texas History Center, University of Texas, Austin; Throckmorton to Epperson, October 22, 1869, February 1, 6, June 7, August 2, 1871, in James Webb Throckmorton Papers, Barker Texas History Center, University of Texas, Austin; Austin *Democratic Statesman*, August 1, 24, 1871, December 16, 18, 1873.

7.   See the summary statistics on age in Ralph A. Wooster, *The People in Power: Courthouse and Statehouse in the Lower South, 1850–1860* (Knoxville: University of Tennessee Press, 1969), 29; Wooster, *The Secession Conventions of the South* (Princeton: Princeton University Press, 1962), 16, 30–31, 53, 69, 85, 105, 125, 142, 158, 195–96; Richard E. Beringer, "A Profile of the Members of the Confederate Congress," *Journal of Southern History*, XXXIII (1967), 537–38; Allen G. Bogue, *et al.*, "Members of the House of Representatives and the Processes of Modernization, 1789–1960," *Journal of American History*, LXIII (1976), Table 6, p. 291; and the time series on median age for the House in Stuart A. Rice, *Quantitative Methods in Politics* (New York: Alfred A. Knopf, 1928), 297. The age statistics for this study were compiled from the *Biographical Directory of the American Congress*.

when John C. Fremont carried the Republican standard in 1856, and over 30 percent could not vote four years later. But just how those who came of age during the crises of the 1850s and early 1860s differed in political temperament, ideology, and perspective from those who had participated in the politics of the 1830s and 1840s remains a matter of speculation. Nor can one measure the way these young southern Republicans were perceived by their older northern party colleagues in Congress, but the disparity in age may well have contributed to the friction which developed between the two during the 1870s. The age differential was sharp. In the Forty-first House (1869–1871), the first in which the South achieved full representation, the median age of the twenty-two carpetbaggers and two blacks was only thirty-two. Their scalawag and southern Democratic colleagues were a full decade older. Representatives from the northern states (nearly 70 percent of the House and almost all of its leadership) had a median age of forty-seven and slightly less than 20 percent were under age forty. The same disparity of about fifteen years existed between the Senate carpetbaggers and that body's leadership.

The Democrats generally outranked Republicans in terms of formal education with the sharpest contrast existing at the college or university level. Nearly three-quarters of the Democrats had attended college and slightly more than half had taken at least one degree. By comparison, half of the Republicans gave evidence of college training and only 31 percent had received a degree. As anticipated, college attendance was sharply sectional. Only nine of the sixty-six Democrats received degrees from colleges outside the slave states, while twelve (all scalawags except one) of forty Republicans graduated from southern institutions. Home state training was remarkably strong among North Carolinians; over a third of the state's thirty congressmen were graduates of the state university. That university had thirteen graduates among the congressmen, followed by the University of Virginia with twelve. Harvard contributed seven and the University of Georgia and South Carolina College five each. The others were spread across a total of ninety-seven different institutions.

Among the Republicans, the carpetbaggers rivaled the Democrats in level of education, but nearly three-fifths of the scalawags had no more than elementary training. Only two Democrats and nine Republicans had no formal schooling, but most of the latter were native blacks, who had few educational opportunities until after the war. Five of the blacks had managed to pick up some college-level training outside the South. Blanche K. Bruce of Mississippi had attended Oberlin, Richard Cain of South Carolina spent a year at Wilberforce, James Rapier of Alabama had attended schools in Tennessee and Canada, Hiram Revels of Mississippi was a graduate of Knox College in Illinois, and Robert Brown Elliott of South Carolina claimed to be an 1859 graduate of Eton in England. The remaining blacks, most of them ex-slaves, had scrambled to learn to read and write during the war and immediate postwar years. Robert De Large of South Carolina attended a normal school in North Carolina, Charles Nash spent some time in the New Orleans public schools after the war, and John Roy Lynch went to a night school in Natchez for four months in 1864. Jeremiah Haralson of Alabama, illiterate at the war's end, "learned to handle the language," fellow Alabamian Benjamin S. Turner became literate through "clandestine study," and a local storekeeper tutored North Carolina's John Hyman during the war. By the time the blacks took their places in Congress, all were literate and, if their speeches and comments are reliable indicators, most demonstrated a command of the language equal to that of their white peers.[8]

The educational experience of some natives reflected the upbring-

8. *Biographical Directory of the American Congress*, 689, 1587, 845, 1835; Blanche K. Bruce, Subject File, Mississippi Department of Archives and History, Jackson; Thomas Holt, *Black over White: Negro Political Leadership in South Carolina During Reconstruction* (Urbana: University of Illinois Press, 1977), 230–31, 54; Loren Schweninger, *James T. Rapier and Reconstruction* (Chicago: University of Chicago Press, 1978), 18, 30, 32–36; Hiram R. Revels, Subject File, Mississippi Department of Archives and History, Jackson; Alcee Fortier (ed.), *Louisiana: Comprising Sketches* . . . (3 vols.; Madison, Wis.: Century Historical Association, 1914), II, 191; *Mississippi State Leader* quoted in the Washington *New National Era*, January 18, 1872; Washington *New National Era and Citizen*, January 22, 1874; Elizabeth Balanoff, "Negro Legislators in the North Carolina General Assembly, July, 1868–February, 1872," *North Carolina Historical Review*, LXIX (1972), 26. Elliott's background before 1867 remains largely unknown; Peggy Lamson attempts to separate fact from fabrication in *The Glorious Failure: Black Congressman Robert Brown Elliott and the Reconstruction in South Carolina* (New York: W. W. Norton, 1973), ch. 1.

ing valued by the antebellum elite. Joseph Hayes Acklen, for example, the son of the second largest slaveholder in Louisiana, had received private tutoring at his parents' summer home in Nashville. A mere ten-year-old when the war began, Acklen attended a New Jersey military college during the war, went abroad and received degrees from the Ecole de Neuilly in Paris and Swiss University in Vevay, and then took a law degree from Lebanon Law School in Tennessee in 1871. He subsequently engaged in sugar planting. Another Louisianian, Randall Gibson, the son of a wealthy Terrebonne Parish sugar planter, received his initial education from private tutors in Louisiana and at his mother's home in Kentucky. He attended a Yale preparatory school, was graduated at the head of the Yale class of 1853, took a law degree from the University of Louisiana (now Tulane) in 1855, and spent the next three years traveling in Europe before settling down to sugar planting. For sheer variety, few could match the educational experience of Beverly Browne Douglas of Virginia. After being graduated from a private academy, Douglas attended William and Mary, Yale, and the University of Edinburgh before returning home to study law under the renowned Beverly Tucker. He took a law degree from William and Mary in 1843.[9]

The Republicans had no one comparable in educational experience, and few had more than one degree. Of those, the experience of Charles W. Buckley of Alabama best reveals the restless movement characteristic of many carpetbaggers. Buckley began his public schooling at his birthplace in Unadilla, New York, and completed it in Freeport, Illinois, where his parents had purchased a farm. In 1860 he was graduated from Beloit College in Wisconsin, returned to his native state, and earned a degree from Union Theological Seminary in New York City in 1863. He entered the army as a chaplain and served with the Louisiana Colored Infantry before joining the Freedmen's Bureau in Alabama. Carpetbagger John E. Leonard of Louisiana was probably the best trained of the Republicans. A graduate of the exclusive Phillips Exeter Academy in New Hampshire, Leonard

9. Fortier (ed.), *Louisiana*, I, 21; *National Cyclopaedia of American Biography*, XXX, 192–93 (hereinafter cited as *NCAB*); Donald Eugene Dixon, "Randall Lee Gibson of Louisiana, 1832–1892" (M.A. thesis, Louisiana State University, 1971), 6–22; Lynn Gardiner Tyler (ed.), *Encyclopedia of Virginia Biography* (5 vols.; New York: Lewis Historical Publishing Co., 1915), III, 114–15.

received a law degree from Harvard in 1867 and studied abroad at the Universities of Innsbruck, Heidelberg, and Paris. After taking degrees from the latter two institutions, he purchased a plantation and opened a law practice in northern Louisiana where he successfully cultivated the support of Republicans and Democrats alike.[10]

As a group, the educational level of the Southerners was far above that of their constituents and compared favorably with congressmen from other sections. A recent study of all entering representatives during the 1870s found that 57 percent had some college experience.[11] Over 60 percent of the Southerners entering from 1868 to 1879 had attended college and 42 percent had received at least one degree. Formal education, however, seems of only minor importance. Those possessing no more than an elementary education often had read law privately and had been admitted to the bar before the war. In terms of education, admission to the bar served as the great equalizer; an individual's ability at the practice of law overshadowed his attainments of formal education.

Nearly 60 percent of the 251 Southerners considered the practice of law their primary vocation while only 20 percent claimed to be farmers or planters. A search of the tax records and census schedules revealed another 20 percent with an identifiable secondary interest in agriculture, but it is almost certain that more were at least tangentially engaged in agriculture given the real estate valuations for some who claimed to have been otherwise occupied. Two Georgians illustrate the problems of occupational classification. Archibald T. MacIntyre is listed in the censuses of 1860 and 1870 and other sources as a lawyer. On the eve of the war, however, he held 84 slaves and a decade later he lived in a rural area and owned 6,400 acres of land. MacIntyre is therefore considered a planter with law as

10. Joel Campbell Dubose (ed.), *Notable Men of Alabama, Personal and Genealogical with Portraits* (2 vols.; Atlanta: Southern Historical Association, 1904), I, 25–28; *Biographical Directory of the American Congress*, 662, 1283; Fortier (ed.), *Louisiana*, II, 55; *NCAB*, V, 387–88; John E. Leonard to Henry Clay Warmoth, April 14, 1873, in Henry Clay Warmoth Papers, Southern Historical Collection, University of North Carolina, Chapel Hill (hereinafter cited as SHC); *Congressional Record*, 45th Cong., 2nd Sess., 2647ff.

11. Bogue, *et al.*, "Members of the House of Representatives and the Processes of Modernization," Table 1, p. 282.

a secondary vocation. Similarly, all sources list Dudley M. Du Bose as a lawyer and the 1870 census taker found him living in the town of Washington, but he valued his real estate at $50,000. Du Bose is classified as a lawyer with agricultural interests, even though his landholdings indicate that law might well have been a secondary economic interest.[12]

Well over half of the congressmen had two or more occupations with the carpetbaggers and scalawags tending to be engaged in a greater variety of pursuits than others. Charles Buckley, for example, while trained as a minister, invested in a Montgomery bank and a fire insurance company and purchased a plantation during his service as state superintendent of education for the Freedmen's Bureau. The latter endeavor apparently led to his release from bureau service. He would later help fellow carpetbaggers organize the Tecumseh Iron Company. Gilbert Walker, the Yankee "settler," practiced law and was the organizer and president of a Norfolk bank. He also had investments in the iron industry and railroads and owned real estate valued at $18,000. While 30 percent of the congressmen had no identifiable economic pursuits other than law, less than 9 percent had interests that were exclusively agricultural.[13]

Rare, too, were those in semiskilled or laboring occupations. Exslave Charles E. Nash, probably the most obscure of the 251, apparently continued to consider himself a bricklayer in the postwar period although he occupied minor patronage positions in Louisiana before serving in the Forty-fourth House. Alonzo J. Ransier of South Carolina had been a shipping clerk before the war, but little is

12. Joseph Karl Menn, "The Large Slaveholders of the Deep South, 1860" (Ph.D. dissertation, University of Texas, 1964), 857–58; United States, Department of the Interior, Bureau of the Census, Ninth Census, 1870, Manuscript Population and Agricultural Schedules, Georgia, Thomas County (hereinafter cited as U.S. MS Census . . .); Archibald T. MacIntyre to Andrew Johnson, July 25, 1865, in Amnesty Papers, Georgia, Office of the Adjutant General, Record Group 94, National Archives; Biographical Directory of the American Congress, 883; U.S. MS Census, 1870, Population Schedules, Georgia, Wilkes County.

13. Dubose (ed.), Notable Men of Alabama, I, 25–28; U.S. MS Census, 1870, Population Schedules, Alabama, Montgomery County; William S. McFeely, Yankee Stepfather: General O. O. Howard and the Freedmen (New Haven: Yale University Press, 1968), 5–6; Dictionary of American Biography, XIX, 244–45; U.S. MS Census, 1870, Population Schedules, Virginia, Norfolk County; Maddex, Virginia Conservatives, 74–75, 91.

known about his postwar economic pursuits other than that he was constantly involved in politics before beginning congressional service in 1873. The remaining blacks had acquired land or otherwise established themselves economically. John Roy Lynch, for example, still considered himself a photographer in 1870, a trade he had picked up as an apprentice at the end of the war, but by the time he served in the House he had purchased several pieces of property. Similarly, ex-slave Benjamin S. Turner had quickly turned his Selma livery stable into a $10,000 operation by 1870. Among the whites, only South Carolina scalawag Manuel Simeon Corley pursued a traditional trade, but he also owned nearly 500 acres of woodland. Corley, however, preferred to be known as a tailor, even though as he wrote congressional biographer Charles Lanman in 1868, "since Andrew Johnson is one, that is not saying much."[14]

Occupational breakdown according to political affiliation indicates several variations between the parties. Nearly 95 percent of the Democrats were primarily involved in either law or agriculture or both. The Republicans displayed more diversity with well over a third having primary occupations other than law and agriculture. The vocational profile for the scalawags might have been expected to be similar to that of the native Democrats, but a breakdown by party faction indicates that the profiles for scalawags and carpetbaggers are almost identical. Overall, lawyers, rather than planters, farmers, and businessmen, dominated the congressional delegations from the South. Including those who had prepared for law but were not actively practicing, 68 percent of the congressmen (85 percent of the Democrats, 52 percent of the Republicans) were qualified to practice law. While the figures for agricultural interests must be con-

14. *Biographical Directory of the American Congress*, 1460–61, 1958; Fortier (ed.), *Louisiana*, II, 191; U.S. MS Census, 1870, Population Schedules, Louisiana, Saint Landry Parish; Holt, *Black over White*, 230; Washington *New National Era*, November 28, May 9, 1872; John R. Lynch, *Reminiscences of an Active Life: The Autobiography of John Roy Lynch*, ed. John Hope Franklin (Chicago: University of Chicago Press, 1970), introduction; U.S. MS Census, 1870, Population Schedules, Alabama, Dallas County; U.S. MS Census, 1870, Population Schedules, South Carolina, Lexington County; South Carolina, Lexington County, Assessment Book, December, 1866, and Auditor's Tax Duplicate Book, 1870, in South Carolina Department of Archives and History, Columbia; Manuel Simeon Corley to Charles Lanman, July 28, 1868, in Manuel Simeon Corley Papers, South Caroliniana Library, University of South Carolina, Columbia.

Table 3. OCCUPATION BY PARTY

Occupation	Democrat (n = 122)	Republican (n = 129)	Total (n = 251)
Law:			
Primary	94 (77%)	53 (41%)	147 (59%)
Primary and Secondary	101 (83%)	54 (42%)	155 (62%)
Agriculture:			
Primary	21 (17%)	28 (22%)	49 (20%)
Primary and Secondary	61 (50%)	37 (29%)	98 (39%)
Professional:[a]			
Primary	3 (2%)	29 (22%)	32 (13%)
Primary and Secondary	16 (13%)	43 (33%)	59 (24%)
Business:			
Primary	4 (3%)	19 (15%)	23 (9%)
Primary and Secondary	11 (9%)	30 (23%)	41 (16%)

Note: Occupations were cross-checked through a variety of sources including the *Biographical Directory of the American Congress,* the population schedules of the manuscript censuses, and the *Congressional Globe.* Individuals were classified according to their vocations (other than politics) at the beginning of their service in Congress.
[a]Totals include one Democrat and two Republicans whose only identifiable occupation was public official. All three held appointive federal positions at the time of their election.

sidered minimal, only 39 percent (50 percent of the Democrats, 29 percent of the Republicans) had some identifiable involvement in agriculture. Professional and business interests rivaled those of agriculture. Thirty-nine percent of the congressmen (21 percent of the Democrats, 55 percent of the Republicans) had some interest in professional or mercantile pursuits or such economic concerns as railroads, banking, shipping, manufacturing, and extractive industries (see Table 3).

Judged by the standards of the time, the Southerners were generally well-to-do men of property. A fairly reliable indication of the size of estate for 75 percent of them is revealed in the population and agricultural census schedules for 1870 and a variety of other sources. Of the 202 congressmen found in the voluminous schedules, 17 did not admit to having any real or personal property. Three of the remaining individuals were dead by the time the census takers began their enumerations in June, 1870, 3 were abroad, and the others were either unlisted or remained undiscovered. Democrat William Spencer of Louisiana, for example, owned 29 slaves in 1860 with an estate valued at $160,000, but he was not listed in the 1870 census schedules. More frustrating is the absence of any listing for some such as Texas scalawag Morgan C. Hamilton who were known to be wealthy. Hamilton supposedly retired from his business pursuits in 1852, but at the time he served in the Senate, his contemporaries claimed he owned 80,000 acres of the best land in the state and had accumulated a large fortune.[15]

Others who were listed declined to give any estimation of their real and personal wealth although other sources indicate they were property owners. Democrat John Hancock of Texas, worth $85,000 with 21 slaves in 1860, declared no estate to the census taker who visited his farm just north of Austin in 1870. Similarly, the census taker found Louisiana carpetbagger John S. Harris living in a Vidalia hotel. He claimed no property, yet he had declared an estate value of $72,000 in 1860 while he was still living in Milwaukee, Wisconsin, and he had purchased a large cotton plantation in Louisiana during the war. His plantation was probably listed under an agent's name in the 1870 census. In some cases, such as that of scalawag Alexander S. Wallace of South Carolina, property values can be checked in other ways. Wallace did not indicate any estate to the census taker,

15. U.S. MS Census, 1860, Population, Slave Schedules, Louisiana, Catahoula Parish; Frank Brown, "Annals of Travis County" (Typescript in Frank Brown Papers, Barker Texas History Center, University of Texas, Austin); Republican Party, Texas, *Proceedings of the Congressional Nominating Convention . . . 1871* (Houston: Houston *Union*, 1871), 9. In addition to the 1870 population and agricultural census schedules, the 1860 agricultural and free and slave population schedules, the 1880 agricultural schedules, and the centrally collected county or parish tax records (such as those in South Carolina, Louisiana, and Mississippi) were also searched for figures on wealth. The petitions for pardon in the Amnesty Papers (particularly those coming under the Thirteenth Exception) also contain data on wealth, but these must be used carefully because many applicants either underestimated their wealth in 1865 or simply lied to Andrew Johnson about the size of their 1860 estates. These alternate sources have not been used, however, to project a congressman's wealth in 1870.

yet the agricultural schedules list a farm valued at $375 and South Carolina assessment records show that he paid taxes on an estate of over $12,000 in the same year.[16]

The amount of real and personal estate reported by individual congressmen is subject to dispute on several accounts. Some may have exaggerated the value of their estates to make themselves appear more prosperous than they actually were. Others may have underestimated their value out of personal modesty or for tax purposes. Still others such as scalawag Oliver Dockery of North Carolina had investments which are impossible to trace through existing records. Dockery admitted to a sizable estate of $77,500 of which $75,000 was in real property. He styled himself as simply a large planter, but he had earlier revealed to Benjamin Butler that he also had $40,000 invested in the Charleston brokerage house of Kindall and Dockery. Overall, the wealth figures are probably biased in favor of well established individuals (primarily Democrats) with medium to large estates. Despite the incomplete figures and misgivings about the reliability of the census, the information in Table 4 indicates general variations in wealth in relation to political affiliation.[17]

Although several of the congressmen might have been considered poor by contemporary standards, only two, Alabama Democrat William A. Handley and Alonzo Ransier, a black from South Carolina, admitted to an estate of less than $1,000. Handley recouped his Civil

16. U.S. MS Census, 1860, Population, Slave Schedules, 1870, Population Schedules, Texas, Travis County; U.S. MS Census, 1860, Population Schedules, Wisconsin, Milwaukee County; 1870, Population Schedules, Louisiana, Concordia Parish; Howard W. Jones, "Biographical Sketches of Members of the 1868 Louisiana State Senate," *Louisiana History,* XIX (1978), 80–82; U.S. MS Census, 1870, Population, Agricultural Schedules, 1880, Agricultural Schedules, South Carolina, York County; South Carolina, York County, Assessment Book, 1867, and Auditor's Tax Duplicate Book, 1870, 1875, 1880, in South Carolina Department of Archives and History, Columbia.

17. U.S. MS Census, 1870, Population Schedules, North Carolina, Richmond County; Oliver H. Dockery to Benjamin F. Butler, July 27, 1868, Joseph C. Abbott to Butler, July 29, 1868, A. D. Estill to Butler, August 14, 1868, in Benjamin F. Butler Papers, LC. The census figures on wealth are defective in other ways. As Richard Beringer has noted, the estimations give no indication of the extent to which the estates were mortgaged. But he adds that "the fact of a mortgage would not necessarily detract from the status the owner held in his community. . . . Debt, after all, may indicate wealth as well as poverty." Beringer, "A Profile of the Members of the Confederate Congress," 530n.

Table 4. PERSONAL AND REAL ESTATE EVALUATIONS (1870)
       BY PARTY FACTION

Estate Evaluation	Democrats n=122	Scalawags n=53	Carpet-baggers n=60	Blacks n=16
		Republicans		
Unknown	12	7	26	3
Undeclared	7	1	7	1
Known Evaluations	n=103	n=45	n=27	n=12
Under $1,000	1 (1%)	—	—	1 (8%)
$1,000–4,900	20 (19%)	9 (20%)	5 (19%)	4 (33%)
$5,000–9,900	11 (11%)	10 (22%)	3 (11%)	5 (42%)
$10,000–14,900	18 (17%)	6 (13%)	9 (33%)	1 (8%)
$15,000–19,900	14 (14%)	5 (11%)	3 (11%)	1 (8%)
$20,000–49,900	28 (27%)	6 (13%)	4 (15%)	—
$50,000–99,000	6 (6%)	6 (13%)	1 (4%)	—
$100,000 and Over	5 (5%)	3 (7%)	2 (7%)	—
Median Evaluation	$15,000	$13,700	$11,000	$5,825

War losses and at his death in 1909 he was among the wealthiest men in eastern Alabama. Ransier was not so fortunate. By 1879, the former lieutenant governor and representative in Congress was reduced to working as a night watchman at the customhouse in Charleston for $1.50 per day. The 1880 census taker found him in a crowded boardinghouse on the west side of King Street with a pregnant second wife; poverty-stricken, he died of malaria two years later.[18]

At the other end of the spectrum, 5 Democrats, 3 scalawags, and 2

18. U.S. MS Census, 1870, Population Schedules, Alabama, Randolph County; William Anderson Handley, Subject File, Alabama Department of Archives and History, Montgomery; Holt, *Black over White*, 218–19, 219n, 238; U.S. MS Census, 1880, Population Schedules, South Carolina, Charleston County; South Carolina, Charleston, Death Records, vol. 44 (1882), No. 1268, South Carolina Department of Archives and History, Columbia.

carpetbaggers claimed a valuation exceeding $100,000. The 3 scalawags topped the list. Little is known about North Carolina banker Israel Lash other than the fact that by 1870 he had an estate of $450,000—a sizable increase over the $295,000 he claimed a decade earlier. An inherited estate had launched South Carolinian Thomas J. Robertson on his way to wealth. In 1860, he owned 84 slaves and a large acreage; ten years later, he estimated his worth at $320,000. Considerably more is known about James Lusk Alcorn of Mississippi. From a modest estate of $16,625 and 17 slaves in 1850, Alcorn had accumulated $250,000 and 93 slaves on the eve of secession. By dodging adroitly both Federal and Confederate troops, he engaged in the risky but lucrative cotton smuggling business during the war, survived emancipation, and claimed an estate of $300,000 by 1870. The following year a costly fire caused damages worth over $100,000 to the stored cotton and improvements on his Friar's Point plantation a few days after his fire insurance policy had expired. This might have ruined most men, but Alcorn took it in stride and surprised Scottish journalist Robert Somers with his coolness in accepting a personal loss of "not less than $70,000."[19]

The two carpetbaggers worth over $100,000 present a study in contrasts. In 1865, when fifty-nine-year-old Abijah Gilbert retired for reasons of health to Saint Augustine, Florida, he brought with him a fortune of $150,000 accumulated in over forty years of business activity in New York. Gilbert would be elected senator in 1868 amidst rumors that his campaign contributions to certain legislators had helped secure his election. Less is known about how the young

19. U.S. MS Census, 1860, Population, Slave Schedules, 1870, Population Schedules, North Carolina, Forsyth County; U.S. MS Census, 1860, Population, Slave Schedules, 1870, Population Schedules, South Carolina, Richland County; South Carolina, Richland County, Assessment Book, December, 1866, and Tax Returns, 1865, 1867, Records of the Comptroller General, in South Carolina Department of Archives and History, Columbia; Frederick Sawyer to Charles Lanman, December 12, 1868, in Thomas J. Robertson Papers, South Caroliniana Library, University of South Carolina, Columbia; Lillian A. Pereyra, *James Lusk Alcorn: Persistent Whig* (Baton Rouge: Louisiana State University Press, 1966), 38; U.S. MS Census, 1870, Population Schedules, Mississippi, Adams County; James L. Roark, *Masters Without Slaves: Southern Planters in the Civil War and Reconstruction* (New York: W. W. Norton, 1977), 42–44; Robert Somers, *The Southern States Since the War*, with introduction and index by Malcolm C. McMillan (University, Ala.: University of Alabama Press, 1965), 249–59.

Alexander McDonald managed to parlay a modest estate of $7,000 into $141,000 during the 1860s. A native of Pennsylvania, McDonald had moved to Kansas in 1857 and made a "considerable fortune" in "general business" before relocating in Arkansas during the war. There he quickly became involved in several banking ventures as well as railroad promotion.[20]

Benjamin H. Hill of Georgia led the Democrats with an evaluation of $220,000—all but $20,000 of which was listed as real estate. The war years apparently caused Hill relatively few economic problems; he lost 57 slaves and still more than doubled his 1860 estate. Texan William Smith Herndon had accumulated real estate valued at $122,000 and a personal estate of $55,000 by the time he was thirty-two. The census taker listed Herndon as a lawyer, but he was also involved in railroad construction and later served as vice-president of the Kansas and Gulf Shortline Company. Effingham Lawrence of Louisiana was probably worth considerably more than the $154,000 he claimed in 1870. The agricultural schedules list his Plaquemines Parish holdings at 2,680 acres; the value of an average acre of land in the swampy sugar-producing parish has been estimated at $28 in 1870. Lawrence may have had some useless swamp property, but he also owned some fine sugar and orchard land. His total productions for 1869–1870 were valued at $120,000, and he owned livestock worth $20,000 and equipment including a sugar mill worth $23,000. Georgians ranked fourth and fifth in wealth. Archibald MacIntyre's sugar lands along the Ochlockonee River in southern Georgia were worth only $50,000, but he claimed an additional $60,000 in personal property. Nelson Tift, who styled himself a "merchant and farmer" had $107,500 wrapped up in a number of

20.   Benjamin P. Poore (comp.), *Congressional Directory for the Second Session of the Forty-first Congress* (2nd ed.; Washington, D.C.: Government Printing Office, 1870), 10; U.S. MS Census, 1870, Population Schedules, Florida, Saint Johns County; Testimony of C. B. Wilder, November 14, 1871, in U.S. Congress, *Report of the Joint Select Committee to Inquire into the Condition of Affairs in the Late Insurrectionary States* (13 vols.; Washington, D.C.: Government Printing Office, 1872), XIII, 244, 254; *NCAB*, IV, 173, XII, 336; Janice C. Hood, "Brotherly Hate: A Quantitative Study of Southern Reconstruction Congressmen, 1867–1877" (Ph.D. dissertation, Washington State University, 1974), 233; U.S. MS Census, 1870, Population Schedules, Arkansas, Pulaski County.

ventures including railroads, a packing plant, and lumber, flour, and cornmeal mills.[21]

A comparison of estate values for 1860 and 1870 indicates that the war either had little impact on the personal finances of most natives or that they had quickly regained their losses. To be sure, some individuals lost ground and others were land-poor. Scalawag James Flanagan of Texas claimed only $17,000 of an estate valued at $188,000 ten years earlier; Charles Hays of Alabama was more fortunate to have $56,000 left from his 1860 estate of $211,000. Scalawag Alexander White's antebellum estate of $105,000 had dwindled to $20,000 and all but a thousand of that was in his wife's name. The war had also depleted Democrat William Handley's $25,000 estate; he supposedly sold his Alabama farm and other assets to settle some $10,000 in debts to northern merchants. Others had little to lose. Scalawag Thomas Jefferson Speer of Georgia complained in 1865 that "not a foot of land or any other species of property do I possess in this vast wilderness," but his estate before the war was listed as only $4,500, consisting mostly of 9 slaves inherited from his father.[22]

21. Ralph Wooster, "The Georgia Secession Convention," *Georgia Historical Quarterly*, XL (1956), 51; U.S. MS Census, 1870, Population Schedules, Georgia, Clark County; Benjamin H. Hill, Jr., *Senator Benjamin H. Hill of Georgia: His Life, Speeches, and Writings* (Atlanta: T. H. P. Bloodworth, 1893), 85–86; U.S. MS Census, 1870, Population Schedules, Texas, Smith County; Webb and Carroll (eds.), *Handbook of Texas*, I, 802; U.S. MS Census, 1870, Population, Agricultural Schedules, Louisiana, Plaquemines Parish; Thomas J. Pressly and William H. Scofield, *Farm Real Estate Values in the United States by Counties, 1850–1959* (Seattle: University of Washington Press, 1965), 57; Joseph Karl Menn, *The Large Slaveholders of Louisiana—1860* (New Orleans: Pelican Publishing Co., 1964), 308, 310–11; Somers, *The Southern States Since the War*, 224–25; U.S. MS Census, 1870, Population, Agricultural Schedules, Georgia, Thomas County, Dougherty County; Archibald T. MacIntyre to Andrew Johnson, July 25, 1865, Nelson Tift to Johnson, June 27, 1865, in Amnesty Papers, Georgia.

22. U.S. MS Census, 1860, Population, Slave Schedules, 1870, Population Schedules, Texas, Rusk County; U.S. MS Census, 1860, Population, Slave Schedules, 1870, Population Schedules, Alabama, Green County; Maclyn Philip Burg, "The Careers of 109 Southern Whig Congressional Leaders in the Years Following Their Party's Collapse" (Ph.D. dissertation, University of Washington, 1971), 520; U.S. MS Census, 1870, Population Schedules, Alabama, Dallas County; U.S. MS Census, 1860, Population, Slave Schedules, 1870, Population Schedules, Alabama, Randolph County; Handley, Subject File; Thomas J. Speer to Andrew Johnson, October 10, 1865, in Amnesty Papers, Georgia; U.S. MS Census, 1860, Population Schedules, Georgia, Pike County.

Most of the natives were not as poverty-stricken as they led others to believe. Future Alabama senator George Goldthwaite felt so pressed in 1867 that he requested a position for his son from former provisional governor Lewis E. Parsons: "Were I a half, or a quarter, or a tenth part, as well off, as I was in byegone times, I would not ask any position, but situations of any kind are now very difficult to obtain, and my children must work for themselves." While Goldthwaite had suffered sharp wartime losses, his 1860 estate of $411,500 had only dwindled to $68,000 in 1870, and he still managed to keep 3 black servants as part of his household. "I live more economically than formerly," scalawag Joshua Hill informed Elihu Washburne in 1868, "and am obliged to labor." And yet during the 1860s, despite the loss of 59 slaves, Hill had increased his estate from $72,500 to $75,000.[23]

Some ex-Confederates cultivated an image of being financially broken by the war. Former major general Matthew C. Butler supposedly returned to South Carolina in 1865 "with one dollar and seventy-five cents in his pocket" and a debt of $15,000. He admitted in 1871 that he had lost some land to creditors and that he had not yet paid for all of the remainder, but he still owned 2,192 acres assessed at $5 an acre in addition to his Edgefield residence. In his petition for presidential pardon, Matt Ransom of North Carolina, another Confederate general, doubted that his taxable value would reach $20,000 in 1865 as his land was "encumbered with a debt [that] exceeds its present value." His property before the war had been assessed at "about $40,000" (not including 82 slaves), and by 1870 he declared a personal worth of $78,000. And some even induced friends to plead their poverty. Julian Hartridge persuaded U.S. Supreme Court Justice James M. Wayne, a fellow Georgian, to inform President Andrew Johnson in 1867 that Hartridge was "without property of any kind" and lived solely by his profession as a lawyer, yet half of his $20,000

23. George Goldthwaite to Lewis E. Parsons, August 24, 1867, in Lewis Eliphalet Parsons Papers, Alabama Department of Archives and History, Montgomery; U.S. MS Census, 1860, Population, Slave Schedules, 1870, Population Schedules, Alabama, Montgomery County; Joshua Hill to Elihu B. Washburne, June 11, 1868, in Elihu B. Washburne Papers, LC; U.S. MS Census, 1860, Population, Slave Schedules, 1870, Population Schedules, Georgia, Morgan County.

valuation in 1870 was real estate. That represented an increase over his worth of $17,500 a decade earlier—despite the loss of 4 slaves.[24]

At least two-thirds of the Democrats and slightly less than half of the scalawags had sacrificed some slave property. Democrat Otho R. Singleton of Mississippi was apparently the largest slaveholder. The slave schedules of 1860 listed him as having only 16 slaves, yet in his petition for amnesty he admitted that he held "upwards of 170 slaves" and that his wife had an interest in more than 90 additional ones in her father's estate. Only two others held over 100. Effingham Lawrence employed 184 on his sugar plantation in 1860 and had partial ownership of 46 more, and scalawag James Flanagan and his wife owned 104. Sixteen others had from 50 to 100 slaves, but the majority held less than 10.[25]

The natives who lost slaves and other property during the war proved to be a resilient group. Most, if not adding to their estates by 1870, at least held their own, and almost all remained substantially better off financially than their constituents. For those whose wealth is known, nearly 70 percent of the Democrats were worth more than $10,000 with a healthy 44 percent worth more than $20,000. The median property valuation for Democrats was $15,000 (mean $24,928). In contrast, the property of 60 percent of the Republicans was valued at less than $10,000 with only 20 percent worth more than $20,000. Within the party, the median property valuation was $13,700 (mean $41,888) for scalawags, $11,000 (mean $23,768)

24. *Confederate Veteran* (March, 1900), clipping in Butler Family Scrapbook, South Caroliniana Library, University of South Carolina, Columbia; *DAB*, III, 363–64; South Carolina, Edgefield County, Tax Returns, Records of the Comptroller General, 1865–1867, and Assessment Book, 1867, in South Carolina Department of Archives and History, Columbia; Testimony of Matthew C. Butler, July 21, 1871, in *Condition of Affairs in the Late Insurrectionary States*, IV, 1211; Matthew C. Butler to Attorney General James Speed, August 5, 1865, in Amnesty Papers, South Carolina; Matt W. Ransom to Andrew Johnson, August 15, 1865, in Amnesty Papers, North Carolina; James M. Wayne to Andrew Johnson, January 14, 1867, in Amnesty Papers, Georgia; Thomas B. Alexander and Richard E. Beringer, *The Anatomy of the Confederate Congress: A Study of the Influences of Member Characteristics on Legislative Voting Behavior, 1861–1865* (Nashville: Vanderbilt University Press, 1972), 368–69; U.S. MS Census, 1870, Population Schedules, Georgia, Chatham County.
25. Alexander and Beringer, *The Anatomy of the Confederate Congress*, 384–85; Otho R. Singleton to Andrew Johnson, n.d., Amnesty Papers, Georgia; Menn, *The Large Slaveholders of Louisiana*, 308n, 310–11; U.S. MS Census, 1860, Slave Schedules, Texas, Rusk County.

for carpetbaggers, and $5,825 (mean $5,940) for blacks. The Republicans obviously had less real and personal wealth, but they were hardly without an investment in southern society—a fact amply reflected in their voting behavior on economic issues.

Other purely personal background factors are of less importance. Religious leanings, for example, varied from the three men whose primary occupation at the time of their election was ministry of the gospel, to scalawag Thomas Boles of Arkansas, who considered himself a "liberal" and belonged to no church, to Georgia scalawag Joshua Hill, who made no secret of his atheism.[26] Episcopalians dominated those whose religious preference was identified; Presbyterians, Methodists, and Baptists ran a distant second. The others ranged across the spectrum from a handful of declared Catholics to one Unitarian. Almost all were married, several more than once, and most had fathered at least four or five children. While data on their fathers' occupations and socioeconomic status are fragmentary, most of the congressmen reflected an upward mobility.

Several of the natives were of prominent families. The grandfather, father, and an uncle of Matthew Butler had all served in the House; another uncle had served as governor, and still another had spent eleven years in the antebellum Senate. A few had taken an upward step by marrying into prominent political families. Butler again serves as a prime example; the future senator added to his political capital in 1858 by marrying Maria Calhoun Pickens, the daughter of former Nullifier congressman and secessionist governor Francis W. Pickens. Virginian John Randolph Tucker's family was no less distinguished but of a more scholarly bent. Tucker's political ancestors included a great-uncle who had served in the Continental Congress and the first two Houses and as Treasurer of the United States. His father and uncle also had been representatives in Congress and the eccentric John Randolph of Roanoke was a half uncle. But the Tuckers specialized in law, and over the course of four generations, they became one of the most distinguished families of legalists in the United States. John Randolph Tucker's grandfather taught

26. William S. Speer (ed.), *The Encyclopedia of the New West* . . . (Marshall, Tex.: U.S. Biographical Publishing Co., 1881), 258–61; *DAB*, IX, 42–43.

law at William and Mary, his father headed a noted private law school and was later professor of law at the University of Virginia, and his uncle gained a national reputation in the same position at William and Mary. John Randolph Tucker taught law at Washington and Lee before and after his service in the House and his son, also a congressman, would teach at Washington and Lee and George Washington University. Both would serve as president of the American Bar Association.[27]

Thomas Samuel Ashe of North Carolina best represented the stereotypical gentleman lawyer-planter-politician of an old-line, aristocratic family. Born on his maternal grandparents' plantation the Hawfields in the Piedmont, Ashe grew up on his parents' plantation the Neck on the Cape Fear River. The Ashe family had been prominent in the South since the early eighteenth century and included among their number several revolutionary war heroes and congressmen. After matriculating at the famous Bingham's Academy in Hillsboro, Ashe attended the University of North Carolina, graduated third in the class of 1832, studied law under the celebrated North Carolina chief justice Thomas Ruffin, and commenced practice in 1836. Following his marriage to the daughter of a prominent Cape Fear planter, he bought a small plantation, became an Episcopal vestryman, and dabbled in Whig politics.[28] It is clear, however, that those with such a distinguished lineage were the exceptions among the 251. The values and politics held dear by the antebellum elite certainly found adherents among the natives serving during the 1870s, but if nostalgia for the Old South occasionally echoed through the House and Senate chambers, the perpetrators were essentially new men—men not of aristocratic family lines or prominent social and political status in the antebellum period.

To describe the "typical" Democrat or Republican in terms of the personal characteristics considered thus far is difficult and probably misleading. As a group, the blacks were younger, poorer, and less ed-

27. *DAB*, III, 363, XIX, 34–35; *Biographical Directory of the American Congress*, 680, 682, 683–84, 1541–42, 1833–34; Jon L. Wakelyn (ed.), *Biographical Directory of the Confederacy* (Westport, Conn.: Greenwood Press, 1977), 119–20; Tucker Family Genealogy, Introductory Folder, Tucker Family Papers, SHC.

28. *DAB*, I, 387; Wakelyn (ed.), *Biographical Directory of the Confederacy*, 80.

ucated, but they were set apart automatically by the simple fact of race and all that color symbolized to northern as well as southern whites. The carpetbaggers were nearly as young as the blacks, but wealthier and better educated; the principal difference between the carpetbaggers and others lay in their northern background. The scalawags were similar in background to the native Democrats with the exception of a few variations in level of education and occupational profile. The Democrats were the oldest, best educated, wealthiest, and the most established of the 251. Yet the personal variations among the political factions are not numerous. Those that do exist are seldom surprising and overall they are of little significance in influencing legislative behavior. What emerges as consequential in setting the men and factions apart lies in the areas of political heritage and ideology.

II Choosing Sides
Political Background and Ideology

"In the Southern States, few men, if any, have taken their side in the present politics from any opinions concerning currency, taxation, expenditures, civil service, foreign policy or Indian policy," Georgia Republican Amos Akerman explained to a northern friend in 1875. "Such matters are secondary here. Men are Republican or Democratic according as they are or are not attached to the last three amendments of the Constitution. . . . Southern men allied themselves with political parties at the onset of reconstruction in 1867, and the impetus then received still remains in force."[1] The emotional issues of political reconstruction were undoubtedly primary in splitting Southerners into quarreling factions, but historians have seldom probed beneath the surface duality to examine the complex interplay of personal background, political heritage, expediency and opportunism, constituency and peer pressures, and general political chaos that brought each of the 251 congressmen to his political home during the 1860s. Their political background and beliefs made matters of party allegiance easy and natural for some, but for others the choice and maintenance of political alignments came with considerable difficulty.

The political antecedents of many of the 251 remain obscure. Of the 60 carpetbaggers, for example, only 13 were positively identified as having been prewar Republicans; 5 had been Democrats, and 4 claimed origins in the Whig party. While it is likely that many of the 38 unknowns came into, or at least sympathized with, the Re-

1. Amos T. Akerman to George H. Freidley, August 22, 1875, in Amos Tappan Akerman Letterbooks, 1871–1876, Alderman Library, University of Virginia, Charlottesville. Akerman served briefly as Grant's attorney general in the early 1870s.

publican party prior to 1860, only 18 are known to have voted for
Abraham Lincoln. Ascertaining the carpetbaggers' prewar politics is
complicated by their youth; they had little antebellum political experience in terms of office seeking or holding. Most, in fact, did not
reach voting age until the late 1850s, and over a quarter came of age
after Lincoln's election.

Data on the political backgrounds of the Democrats and scalawags
are somewhat fuller. Of the 50 natives identified as Democrats during the 1850s, only 6 would join the Republicans after the war. The
distribution of the 55 former Whigs between the parties is more significant. Although only 6 supported secession, it is quite clear that
they did not naturally gravitate into the Republican party—35 became Democrats before the advent of congressional reconstruction.
Of the 20 future scalawags, 7 supported Constitutional Unionist
John Bell and another 7 favored northern Democrat Stephen A.
Douglas in 1860. Not one was found to be a secessionist although
the position of 18 remains unknown. The Democrats were more
sharply divided. While the reaction of 45 is unknown, the others
were split into 34 secessionists and 39 who considered themselves
unionists to some degree. Twenty-four actively supported southern
Democrat John C. Breckinridge, 10 favored Bell, and 7 endorsed
Douglas (see Table 5).[2]

For some Democrats, the decision to leave the Union came relatively easily—they believed in the cause. L. Q. C. Lamar, for example, probably drafted Mississippi's ordinance of secession, and he
later admitted to Andrew Johnson that he had "earnestly and con-
scientiously supported" the movement for independence. For North
Carolina's Matt Ransom, the motivation was "a sense of patriotism"; for Florida's Jesse J. Finley it was "honest convictions of
duty." Roger Q. Mills left his wife's sickbed to attend the Texas secession convention, but he assured her that his presence in Austin
had aided the cause: "Texas will secede beyond a doubt and thank
God for it." Others such as North Carolina unionist Robert Vance
became caught up in the movement. Viewing it as his "duty to join

2. Data on the position of the future congressmen in the election of 1860 are too
fragmentary to support conclusions. Even after the blacks and those too young to vote
in the election are eliminated, the position of 45 percent of the men is unknown.

Table 5. NATIVES' POSITION ON SECESSION AND CIVIL WAR SERVICE

	Democrats (n=118)	Scalawags (n=53)
Position on Secession		
Secessionist	34	—
Unionist[a]	39	35
Unknown	45	18
Civil War Service		
Confederate Military	96	15
Confederate Civil Only	11	5
Union Military	—	3
Nonparticipant	9	23
Unknown	4	7

[a]Totals include individuals who were unionist or cooperationist until their state passed an ordinance of secession, as well as unconditional unionists.

heartily in the rebellion," Vance candidly confessed to Johnson "that his heart and mind had become greatly set upon the independence of the Southern States."[3]

Like Vance, a good many of the more conditional unionists acquiesced when their home state seceded. Reflecting the attitude of many in deploring "the madness and folly of secession," former Whig Hiram Bell, a Constitutional Unionist in 1860, opposed it in the Georgia secession convention yet "reluctantly went along" after the ordinance passed. Thomas M. Gunter, another Constitutional Unionist, maintained an antisecessionist stance in the Arkansas convention until the cause was lost, and then like many other condi-

3. James B. Murphy, *L. Q. C. Lamar: Pragmatic Patriot* (Baton Rouge: Louisiana State University Press, 1973), 58–59; L. Q. C. Lamar to Andrew Johnson, July 19, 1865, in Amnesty Papers, Mississippi, Office of the Adjutant General, Record Group 94, National Archives; Matt Ransom to Andrew Johnson, August 15, 1865, in Amnesty Papers, North Carolina; Jesse J. Finley to Andrew Johnson, January 24, 1867, in Andrew Johnson Papers, Library of Congress (hereinafter cited as LC); Roger Quarles Mills to his wife, January 22, 1861, in Roger Quarles Mills Papers, Barker Texas History Center, University of Texas, Austin; Robert B. Vance to Andrew Johnson, July 8, 1865, in Amnesty Papers, North Carolina.

tional unionists he signed the ordinance. After resigning his seat in the Texas legislature because his district favored secession, former Whig David B. Culberson capitulated when Texas seceded in February, 1861. The unionism of Emory Speer of Georgia, who "always regarded secession as a panacea for any imaginary wrong that we were enduring," was somewhat stronger. Speer eventually yielded, but he proudly claimed that he "never shouldered a gun an hour."[4]

Once their home state was out of the Union, 90 percent of the Democrats rallied to the cause, but nearly half of those who became scalawags declined to participate and many of the future congressmen, Democrats and scalawags alike, were reluctant servants. Unionist John Manning, Jr., a North Carolina Democrat, later reviewed the options for those who were of draft age—they could either submit to conscription or abandon their homes or "resort to some shift to keep out of the army." Manning took the third option and became a receiver for the district court. Several other Democrats followed suit. Fellow Tarheels John Dixon and James Harper became Confederate tax assessors—a position which, as Harper explained, was "accepted principally with a view to the exemption it secured against service in the Confederate Army." Railroad builder William Sherrod of Alabama hired a substitute to avoid conscription—a workable ruse until the substitution law was repealed in 1864. Sherrod was then drafted—an action "utterly against his principle, and his will, and . . . wholly unavoidable on his part." Future scalawag James B. Sener of Virginia stayed out of the army by accepting an appointment as a tax collector for Fredericksburg, but he later claimed that "said tax was never collected by him either in whole or in part." Having "firmly made up his mind in the beginning, not to participate in said Rebellion, nor to favor it in any way," North Carolina Whig John Pool sidestepped military service by agreeing to take subscriptions to the "Fifteen Million Loan" in 1861. But he later boasted to Johnson that he "always evaded and postponed tak-

4.   Hiram P. Bell to Andrew Johnson, June 20, 1865, in Amnesty Papers, Georgia; George H. Thompson, Arkansas and Reconstruction: The Influences of Geography, Economics, and Personality (Port Washington, N.Y.: Kennikat Press, 1976), 21; Walter Prescott Webb and H. Bailey Carroll (eds.), The Handbook of Texas (2 vols.; Austin: Texas State Historical Association, 1952), I, 443; Emory Speer to Andrew Johnson, October 16, 1865, in Amnesty Papers, Georgia.

ing said subscriptions" and he believed "that no subscription to said loan was made from his section of the state."[5]

The internal pressures were such that only a few unconditional unionists such as James Freeman of Georgia and John Francis Lewis of Virginia could legitimately claim that they gave the Confederacy absolutely no support. The best that many could do was to attempt to remain neutral or to give aid only in the name of humanity or when compelled to do so. Georgian Joshua Hill, for example, furnished food, clothing, and money for his two sons in the Confederate army, but he later recalled that he had also fed Federal soldiers and had never been a friend of "that corrupt tyranny"—the "pretended government of the Confederate States." Unionists Jason Niles of Mississippi and Nathaniel Boyden of North Carolina, both beyond conscription age, were among the few able to sit out the war relatively undisturbed.[6]

Those bold enough to resist were often subjected to Rebel harassment. Confederate authorities court-martialed and imprisoned Texas scalawag Edward Degener, a German immigrant, for his continuing "devotion to the Union cause," and his future Democratic opponent John Hancock was expelled from the legislature for refusing to take the Confederate loyalty oath. After the Alabama legislature ousted Charles C. Sheats, he was arrested, charged with treason, and held for the duration of the war. Democrat Anthony A. C. Rogers and scalawags Asa Hodges and Thomas Boles of Arkansas also suffered imprisonment for disloyal activities, and Alexander H.

5.   John Manning, Jr. to Andrew Johnson, June 7, 1865, James C. Harper to Johnson, July 18, 1865, John Dixon to Johnson, July 24, 1865, in Amnesty Papers, North Carolina; William Sherrod to Andrew Johnson, November 23, 1865, in Amnesty Papers, Alabama; James B. Sener to Andrew Johnson, July 11, 1865, in Amnesty Papers, Virginia; John Pool to Andrew Johnson, June 19, 1865, in Amnesty Papers, North Carolina. In their petitions for pardon, Southerners often referred to themselves in the third person.

6.   James Freeman to Andrew Johnson, July 16, 1865, in Amnesty Papers, Georgia; Testimony of John Francis Lewis, February 7, 1866, in U.S. Congress, *Report of the Joint Committee on Reconstruction, at the First Session, Thirty-ninth Congress* (Washington, D.C.: Government Printing Office, 1866), Pt. II, 71; J. B. Cochran to John Francis Lewis, May 5, 1865, in Lunsford Lomax Lewis Papers, Huntington Library, San Marino, California; Joshua Hill to Andrew Johnson, July 19, 1865, in Amnesty Papers, Georgia; Jason Niles, Subject File, Mississippi Department of Archives and History, Jackson; Nathaniel Boyden to Andrew Johnson, August 9, 1865, in Amnesty Papers, North Carolina.

Jones of North Carolina, one of three scalawags to serve with Federal forces, spent time in four prisoner of war camps. Few, however, recalled their resistance in as dramatic a fashion as did scalawag Manuel Simeon Corley of South Carolina, who claimed he "could fill a volume with details of my persecutions, trials, dangers, sufferings, and losses, on account of my opposition to slavery and Secession." A self-styled, outspoken Greeleyite, prohibitionist, vegetarian, and abolitionist, Corley summed up his wartime experience in an autobiographical sketch after his election to the Fortieth Congress: "At the peril of life [he] opposed the secession swindle in 1860, Preached at—sneered at, hated and despised—and still refusing to yield, he was nevertheless compelled to go into the rebel army an [sic] become a martyr to the Union cause. He concluded that a 'live dog was better than a dead lion,' and risked the perils of the battle-field, rather than defy rebel authority. Having always *aimed high* it is presumed that he did not depart from the general rule even as a rebel soldier."[7]

While many of the future congressmen were reluctant patriots, 81 percent of the Democrats and 28 percent of the scalawags joined or were drafted into the Confederate army. Five reached the grade of major general and 13 served as brigadier generals while another 71 ranged in rank from colonel down to captain. Most of the 62 who fought on the side of the Union were carpetbaggers, but the Union veterans also included 5 blacks, 3 scalawags, and 3 of the 4 carpetbag Democrats. Unlike the Southerners, most Union veterans served in lower-ranking positions. Eleven, all carpetbaggers, achieved the rank of brigadier general, but 6 of those were brevetted following the war.

Military service was more than a subtle force in reconstruction politics. Union veterans, several of whom became associated with the Freedmen's Bureau, found that their war record ingratiated them with black voters. Confederate veterans, of course, discovered that their service to the Lost Cause had great appeal among conservative

7. *Biographical Directory of the American Congress, 1774–1971* (Washington, D.C.: Government Printing Office, 1971), 843, 1062, 1685, 1626, 609, 1087, 1202; Simeon Corley to Charles Sumner, December 6, 1866, in Charles Sumner Papers, Houghton Library, Harvard University, Cambridge; Manuel Simeon Corley, "A Short Sketch of the Life of Simeon Corley" (MS in Manuel S. Corley Papers, South Caroliniana Library, University of South Carolina, Columbia).

white voters. Still, a large majority of the 171 native whites in this sample were something less than fully devoted to the idea of southern independence. But despite the professions of unionism and misgivings about the Confederate effort expressed in their petitions for amnesty, conservatives would carefully maintain and cultivate their identification with the Confederacy. And as Rebel service was almost a prerequisite for office in the redeemed South (over 80 percent of the Democrats in the Forty-fifth Congress were veterans), several Confederate careers were enhanced in the postwar years. No one, in an appeal to conservative white voters, wanted to be known as a slacker when it came to the Lost Cause.

For natives, the period from April, 1865, to the implementation of the final plan of reconstruction in 1867 was particularly critical. They had to adjust to defeat and emancipation, to death and humiliation, to physical destruction in town and countryside, to the specters of bankruptcy and poverty, and to confusion and indecision regarding the requirements of reunion and their political future. A recent historian has characterized the South after Appomattox as "a giant kaleidoscope of emotions," and yet the natives in this sample remained very much in control of themselves. They adjusted their lives to certain obvious consequences of the war, but they were hardly ready to relinquish control over their future to the victorious North.[8]

The natives among the future congressmen had little difficulty accepting the reality of defeat, and those who were slaveholders resigned themselves, if somewhat ungracefully, to emancipation. The largest body of surviving evidence regarding their attitudes is contained in their petitions for amnesty and other correspondence with Andrew Johnson, and many no doubt expressed their sentiments in a manner most likely to expedite their pardons. Still, most of the applicants appeared both honest and straightforward about their wartime activities; notably absent was any "hat-in-hand" obsequiousness or apologetic tone. Some, including Mississippian James R.

8. James L. Roark, *Masters Without Slaves: Southern Planters in the Civil War and Reconstruction* (New York: W. W. Norton, 1977), 132.

Chalmers, a secessionist Democrat, were noticeably curt. His only reason for requesting a pardon was his service as a brigadier general, Chalmers wrote, and "having been fairly defeated," he asked for amnesty. After making clear his dedication to the Confederate cause, former postmaster general John H. Reagan indicated his acceptance of the "result of the war as the will of God" and then proceeded to offer Johnson page after page of advice on reconstruction policy. Another incarcerated ex-Confederate, Benjamin Hill, also offered extensive advice, but Hill, reflecting a weariness evident in other applications, simply wanted to go home, help his family adjust, and start to reclaim his "devastated estate." Even Alexander H. Stephens, the feisty former Confederate vice-president, conceded the "practical settlement" of the states' rights issue: "The sword was appealed to to decide the question, and by the decision of the sword I am willing to abide."[9]

Of the future congressmen, only Joshua Hill, writing in May, 1865, expressed a "need to know" about the status of slavery; most echoed the sentiments of William Garth of Alabama, who simply indicated his willingness "to accept the new order of things." That "new order" came to include allowing Freedmen's Bureau agents to participate in the making of contracts between planters and the freedmen, and several of the larger slaveholders reassured Johnson that they were treating their ex-slaves fairly. Understanding the full impact of emancipation still came with difficulty. As Stephens explained to his brother: "It seems to be a hard matter for our people to realize that old things have passed away and that all things are new upon this subject." Some of the planters, faced with destruction and waste on their plantations and convinced that the freedmen would not work without coercion, temporarily abandoned their operations. After toying with the idea of emigrating to Brazil, Randall Gibson left his flood-ravaged sugar lands in the hands of his father and opened a law office in New Orleans. Like Gibson, several planters

9. James R. Chalmers to Andrew Johnson, August 4, 1865, in Amnesty Papers, Mississippi; John H. Reagan to Andrew Johnson, July 18, May 28, 1865, in Amnesty Papers, Texas; Benjamin H. Hill to Andrew Johnson, June 15, July 4, 1865, in Johnson Papers; Testimony of Alexander H. Stephens, April 11, 12, 1866, in *Report of the Joint Committee on Reconstruction*, Pt. III, 166.

for whom the practice of law was already a primary or secondary vocation turned more fully to law or to the booming insurance business, which Matthew Butler termed "the common refuge" for ex-
Confederates. But most planters among the congressmen worked to
reclaim their property and reluctantly accepted the new reality of
free black labor. While some cooperated with federal agents to establish what they hoped would become annually binding contracts with
a semifree labor force, others welcomed the creation of the more
stringent black codes.[10]

The Southerners' tolerance of "the new order of things" did
not include sequacious submission to whatever terms of reconstruction the North might choose to dictate. Characterizing the post-
Appomattox mood of the South as one of "defiant optimism," Michael Perman has ably argued that the North's initial failure to
coerce the South and the voluntary nature of the wartime and Johnsonian reconstruction proposals quickly established the legitimacy
of southern resistance. Their particular predicament of being "mili-
tarily defeated, economically ruined and politically vulnerable"
made southern leadership less obsequious, not more, and what little
evidence of submission did exist in April, 1865, was less heartfelt
than it was tactical and conditional.[11] It is apparent, in this sample of
leadership at least, that the natives intended to play an active role in
their own reconstruction and that they sought minimal requirements. They based their anticipation of leniency on the Lincoln pre-

10.   Joshua Hill to Andrew Johnson, May 10, 1865, in Johnson Papers; William W.
Garth to Andrew Johnson, undated, in Amnesty Papers, Alabama; John W. Johnston
to Andrew Johnson, August 9, 1865, in Amnesty Papers, Virginia; Benjamin H. Hill to
Andrew Johnson, July 4, 1865; Augustus Hill Garland to Johnson, October 24, 1865;
Jesse J. Finley to Johnson, November 15, 1865, in Johnson Papers; Otho R. Singleton
to Andrew Johnson, undated, in Amnesty Papers, Georgia; Charles Hays to Andrew
Johnson, August 1, 1865, George Goldthwaite to Johnson, August 12, 1865, in Am-
nesty Papers, Alabama; Alexander H. Stephens to Linton Stephens, November 19,
1865, quoted in George C. Rable, "But There Was No Peace: Violence and Reconstruc-
tion Politics" (Ph.D. dissertation, Louisiana State University, 1978), 75–76; Donald
Eugene Dixon, "Randall Lee Gibson of Louisiana, 1832–1892" (M.A. thesis, Louisiana State University, 1971), 75–81; Testimony of Matthew C. Butler, July 21, 1871, in
U.S. Congress, *Report of the Joint Select Committee to Inquire into the Condition of
Affairs in the Late Insurrectionary States* (13 vols.; Washington, D.C.: Government
Printing Office, 1872), IV, 1211; Roark, *Masters Without Slaves*, 111–55.
11.   Michael Perman, *Reunion Without Compromise: The South and Reconstruc-
tion, 1865–1868* (Cambridge: Cambridge University Press, 1973), 11–12, ch. 1.

cedent, and when Andrew Johnson revealed his true colors, those who fell into one or more of the fourteen excepted classes appealed for pardon and found the Tennessean receptive. Awareness of the potential Radical Republican alternative may have forced some who were inclined to resist even Johnson's modest conditions for restoration into his camp. Besides, it was the only alternative they had during the summer and fall of 1865. Johnson appeared to be in control of the process of reunion, he required few significant adjustments, and Southerners found him flexible. Not surprisingly, they cast their lot with the president.

Unionists and former secessionists, pardoned and unpardoned alike, participated in the Johnsonian restoration. The unionists were particularly quick to flock to Johnson's banner. John Manning rejoiced that the Union had been maintained "by the energy, wisdom, and forcefulness of our late lamented President and his able advisors." The possibility of punishing the secessionists motivated Oliver Dockery, who expressed "a heartfelt desire to crush the power of the old Rebel leaders & restore North Carolina to her proper place in the old union." Thomas Ashe indicated that he had already "helped and used influence to get my people to take the oath." Still others foresaw the future and promised the president "a cordial & hearty support against the 'Radicals.'"[12] Twenty-six of the future congressmen (12 Democrats, 14 scalawags) participated in the constitutional conventions called by Johnson's provisional governors in 1865. Over a third of the 171 natives served either in the restored legislatures or in some other public position and 7 were chosen for the Thirty-ninth Congress to begin in December, 1865.

"The whole South looks to your Excellency for a just and paternal administration of government," Jesse Finley of Florida informed Johnson in November, 1865, and he expressed disbelief in southern apprehensions "that the Radical majority in the two houses of Congress will object to the admission of the Southern members." The refusal of the House and Senate to seat those returned from the

12. John Manning, Jr. to Andrew Johnson, June 7, 1865, Oliver H. Dockery to Johnson, July 29, 1865, Thomas Ashe to Johnson, undated, in Amnesty Papers, North Carolina; Thomas J. Speer to Andrew Johnson, October 16, 1865, in Amnesty Papers, Georgia.

Johnsonian governments a month later caused some ex-Whigs and unionists to rethink their having sided with Johnson, but a good many let the new questions of black political and civil rights shove them over into the Democratic party. Former Whig Benjamin Hill, for example, viewed the early part of Reconstruction as a failure to allow "the old Whigs and the Union men" to take control of the South. If the Republicans had been "magnanimous to the old Whigs after the war in extending us privileges," he later testified, they "might have built up a republican party in the South, and given us control of this country." Instead, in his rendition of the postwar situation, the Republicans had "lumped the old Union democrats and whigs together with the secessionists, and said that they would punish us all alike; would put us all alike under the negro." As late as 1871, Hill lamented the course of events that had driven many of his fellow Whigs "where they did not want to go, into temporary affiliation with the Democratic party."[13]

Like the majority of Whigs who became Democrats, Hill, despite his misgivings, actually had few problems adjusting to his new, and permanent, political home. Still, these new Democrats often expressed nostalgia for the old party of Henry Clay, and some were clearly uncomfortable with the party into which the pivotal racial issue had forced them. The young E. John Ellis of Louisiana, for example, came from a Whig background and had been a Constitutional Unionist in 1860. After reluctantly joining the Confederate army, he expressed his hatred of the secessionist party to his father: "I am in, am willing to enlist and fight till the foul monster Democracy shall cease to exist. If the sanctity of home and friends were left out of this quarrel, like the immortal Cass I would break my sword over a stump and retire to Private life. To me abolitionism is not more odious than Democracy." Twenty years later, while serving as a Democratic representative in Congress, Ellis assured his brother, "Only let me say that I am not a devout believer in the infallibility of the Democratic Party either National or State."[14]

13. Jesse J. Finley to Andrew Johnson, November 18, 1865, in Johnson Papers; Testimony of Benjamin H. Hill, October 30, 1871, in *Condition of Affairs in the Late Insurrectionary States*, VII, 760–62.

14. E. John Ellis to Ezekiel Park Ellis, January 9, 1862, E. John Ellis to Thomas C. W. Ellis, August 9, 1882, in Ellis Family Papers, Middleton Library, Louisiana State

But as the dispute between Johnson and Congress began to unfold in 1866 the Democracy was the only vehicle available to those who could not swallow black suffrage, and most white Southerners, faced with the Radical alternative, clung to the president. Words of encouragement flowed North; typical were those of a Louisianian who offered Johnson congratulations for his "success in resisting the radical crew in Congress." Others such as Georgians John Brown Gordon and Benjamin Hill and Texans John Hancock and James Throckmorton participated in Johnson's resurrection of the National Union party as a conservative coalition against the Radicals. When that effort proved disastrous in the northern congressional elections of 1866, some of the as yet unpardoned, seeing the handwriting on the wall, scrambled to win Johnson's favor before Congress reconvened in December. But most simply sat back, continued to support Johnson by rejecting the proposed Fourteenth Amendment, and anxiously watched as Northerners began to debate the final plan of reconstruction in the lame-duck session of the Thirty-ninth Congress.[15]

Even after the passage of the reconstruction acts, the conservatives were reluctant to abandon Johnson. Hill expressed their sentiments to the president in May, 1867, when he denounced northern Radicals as "the bane of all banes to the peace and stability of the Republic." While some, including several who were on their way into the Republican party, advocated cooperation with the idea of controlling the direction of reconstruction, Hill counseled active opposition to the acts. Others transferred their hopes to the Supreme Court, the last resort at the national level. "We thought," Wade Hampton later commented, "that the Supreme Court would pronounce all reconstruction acts unconstitutional." But, initially at least, many held that inactivity was the only course and agreed with Stephens that "nothing that we of the South can do or not do can save the country."[16]

University, Baton Rouge; Robert Cinnamond Tucker, "The Life and Public Services of E. John Ellis" (M.A. thesis, Louisiana State University, 1941), 55–65.

15.   L. R. Marshall to Andrew Johnson, August 24, 1866, in Amnesty Papers, Louisiana; Perman, *Reunion Without Compromise*, ch. 7.

16.   Benjamin Hill to Andrew Johnson, May 3, 1867, in Amnesty Papers, Georgia; Testimony of Wade Hampton, July 27, 1871, in *Condition of Affairs in the Late Insurrectionary States*, IV, 1224; Alexander H. Stephens to Hershel V. Johnson, July 17, 1867, quoted in Perman, *Reunion Without Compromise*, 326.

Once it became evident that Johnson had been reduced to a political cipher, few Southerners maintained their connection with him and several expressed bitterness and a sense of betrayal. "I thought he knew what he was talking about," Matthew Butler testified in 1871, when Johnson had urged Southerners "by every consideration of honor and self-respect, not to concede to the reconstruction measures of Congress." South Carolina had followed Johnson's plan in good faith, with the result, Butler complained, that "we have simply been ground between the upper and the nether mill-stone—Congress on one side and the Executive on the other." When Johnson and the Supreme Court failed, Southerners faced the reality of congressional reconstruction—an experience which would engender a greater sectional bitterness and a more powerful mythology than the war itself. "The burning of Atlanta and all the devastation through Georgia," John Brown Gordon declared in 1871, "never created a tithe of the animosity that has been created by this sort of treatment of our people." Although he clearly exaggerated the reality of reconstruction, Gordon nevertheless accurately represented conservative perceptions of what was occurring.[17]

But despite the conservatives' frequent public expressions of helplessness, there was never any real question of their self-confidence or their ability to prevail. "We men who fought the North and tried to establish a southern confederacy are the only class in the South who are worth a quote in any movement or enterprise," the former editor of the Atlanta *Confederacy* warned Horace Greeley in 1866. "That class have always controlled the South and always will regardless of all legislation."[18] The natural inclination to resist, evident since the end of the war, quickly replaced the vacillation between cooperation and "masterly inactivity" in 1867, once the conservatives saw exactly what they were going to confront in terms of reconstruction. They needed no schooling in political strategy and tactics to manipulate "their people" or to control the blacks. They did

17. Testimony of Matthew C. Butler, July 21, 1871, in *Condition of Affairs in the Late Insurrectionary States*, IV, 1188–89; Columbia *South Carolina Republican*, June 25, 1870; Testimony of John Brown Gordon, July 27, 1871, in *Condition of Affairs in the Late Insurrectionary States*, VI, 316; Rable, "But There Was No Peace," ch. 6.
18. James P. Hambleton to Horace Greeley, August 27, 1866, in Horace Greeley Papers, LC.

not wait for the inevitable waning of Radical sentiment in Congress, but began again, as they had in April, 1865, to reassert their control.

Southern Republicanism began to emerge while Johnson, Congress, and southern conservatives clashed over the control and direction of reconstruction. The attractions of the party of emancipation for the freedmen were obvious, but the questions of what lured southern whites to the Republican party and what prompted Yankees to settle and become politically involved in the postwar South have long been bones of contention among historians. Such questions are difficult to answer with assurance because of a paucity of hard evidence, but they are nevertheless critical in understanding southern Republicanism. The surviving manifestations of motivation and intent—activity, occasional public statements, and, more rarely, revealing glimpses offered in private correspondence—indicate that the fifty-three scalawags and sixty carpetbaggers who served in Congress displayed a broader and less iniquitous range of motivation than that usually accorded their respective stereotypes.

The most common elements found among those natives who became Republicans were a unionist background, a lingering attachment to Whiggery, and a closely related attraction to the economic philosophy of the Republican party. Initially at least, the strongest factors were memories of past political battles with Democrats and attitudes toward slavery, states' rights, secession, and the Confederacy ranging from a cool tolerance to outright opposition. Some unionists and former Whigs simply would not consider joining the Democracy under any circumstances. Benjamin Hill's fellow Georgian Joshua Hill had followed an almost identical course from Whiggery to Know-Nothingism to Constitutional Unionism and opposition to secession, and yet he was, in Benjamin Hill's view, one of "a few gentlemen in the South so utterly anti-democratic that they would have gone anywhere on earth before they would have affiliated with the democratic party on any terms." Others such as John Pool of North Carolina and James Alcorn of Mississippi never really abandoned the Whig party. Although Pool became a Republican, he frequently referred to himself as a Whig during the postbellum years. Alcorn also joined the Republicans, and even though he became disenchanted with reconstruction, he refused to go over to the Democrats, his lifelong political enemies. "I was a Whig," he proudly proclaimed a few years before his death in 1894, "and I glory in the fact that I am not a Democrat."[19]

These partisan grievances resurfaced in the immediate postwar period when some of the more unconditional unionists and die-hard Whigs expressed misgivings at seeing so many of their opposite number returned to power. Pool, working in Washington to get the North Carolina delegation seated in February, 1866, concluded that the "efforts of the secessionists to work themselves into power, & other foolish talk & newspaper articles are made the basis of a course of policy that will keep us out for some time to come." Southern resistance, Pool feared, "will compel us to submit to conditions that would never have been thought of, if a more prudent & wise course would have been adopted." Even Alexander Stephens was heard to remark that "Johnson confided too much in the Secessionists of the South."[20]

That the former Confederate vice-president himself merited selection over Joshua Hill as one of Georgia's U.S. senators in 1866 obviously raised eyebrows in Congress. Hill's case is instructive in the ways opposition to the Confederacy hurt unionists under the Johnson governments and forced some of them into the Republican party. Many Georgians saw Hill as Johnson's probable choice for provisional governor, but he was not selected, although he fully approved of fellow unionist James Johnson taking the position. To outsiders he seemed to be a natural choice for the Senate, but the

19. *Dictionary of American Biography,* IX, 25–27, 42–43, XV, 64–65; Testimony of Benjamin H. Hill, October 30, 1871, in *Condition of Affairs in the Late Insurrectionary States,* VII, 765; Memphis *Daily Commercial Appeal,* January 5, 1890, quoted in Charles J. Swift, "James Lusk Alcorn," 40 (Typescript in James L. Alcorn and Family Papers, Mississippi Department of Archives and History, Jackson). For a fine summary of the voluminous revisionist literature which has emphasized the scalawags' unionist and Whig backgrounds, see Carl N. Degler, *The Other South: Southern Dissenters in the Nineteenth Century* (New York: Harper & Row, 1974), ch. 7.

20. Lillian A. Pereyra, *James Lusk Alcorn: Persistent Whig* (Baton Rouge: Louisiana State University Press, 1966), 84–93; John Pool to Thomas Settle, Jr., February 4, 1866, in Thomas Settle Papers, Southern Historical Collection, University of North Carolina, Chapel Hill (hereinafter cited as SHC); Alfred Dockery to R. J. Powell, November 13, 1865, quoted in Perman, *Reunion Without Compromise,* 124.

Johnsonian legislature thought otherwise. A former Georgia congressman summed up the conservative view of Hill in a letter to Stephens: "Nor will Josh Hill do, although not so radical yet he is heart and soul against the friends of the South and would do all in his power to bring odium upon those who have earnestly desired our separate nationality . . . he hates the Democratic party with such intensity." Another budding Bourbon argued that Hill's selection might lead congressional Radicals to believe that such men were numerous in Georgia when in fact "there is not a corporal's guard" of them. Hill thought himself "too much of a unionist to suit the majority in the legislature," and when Stephens won the seat by an overwhelming margin, Hill's displeasure was evident. "I am without political ambition," he wrote Johnson in February, 1866, "yet I want these people to know that I am regarded by those in authority at Washington, with respect and favor." He was convinced that he could "not hope ever again to be regarded cordially by the people of Georgia."[21]

The general drift of Johnsonian reconstruction and Hill's numerous political disappointments, along with his well-known hatred of the Democracy, would push him, along with others, into the Republican party. He received some retribution in the 1868 legislative battle to select a senator when conservatives had to abandon Stephens, their first choice, and ally with moderate Republicans to select Hill over Joseph E. Brown, whom the conservatives viewed as a greater evil at the moment. Hill's emergence as a compromise candidate, however, hardly made him the darling of the Democrats. "Hill is a poor devil," Robert Toombs confided to Stephens. "His forlorn condition, powerless under the present circumstances is conclusive evidence of his weakness, his inability to help himself or hurt us. I did my utmost to elect him, and ask of him no other favour than not to join us or speak to me."[22]

21.   Martin J. Crawford to Alexander H. Stephens, January 10, 1866, and Atlanta *Intelligencer*, February 10, 1866, both quoted in Perman, *Reunion Without Compromise*, 163–64; Joshua Hill to William H. Seward, December 20, 1865, Hill to Andrew Johnson, May 10, 1865, February 5, March 19, 1866, in Johnson Papers; Joshua Hill, *Letter of Hon. Joshua Hill, of Georgia, on the Election of U.S. Senators . . .* (Madison, Ga.: n.p., 1866).

22.   Elizabeth Studley Nathans, *Losing the Peace: Georgia Republicans and Reconstruction, 1865–1871* (Baton Rouge: Louisiana State University Press, 1968),

While unionist backgrounds and partisan considerations appear to have been primary in making Republicans out of some natives, a good many others, including a handful of Democrats, were attracted to what they perceived to be the economic principles of the national Republican party—a progressive philosophy at the heart of which lay the advocacy of active state and federal participation in the economy. The more moderate Southerners generally welcomed Yankee settlers who eschewed politics but brought northern capital and economic ideas. North Carolina Conservative James M. Leach reflected the opinion of many natives when he informed House leader William Pitt Fessenden in early 1866 "that every intelligent anti-secessionist desires to see the State built up & again made prosperous by capital and men from the North settling amongst us." Future scalawag representatives Lewis McKenzie and Alexander White were of a similar mind. McKenzie offered the hope that "honest, industrious northern settlers" might in fact replace the secessionists in his area of Virginia. "We need capital and we need labor," White wrote in 1868, and he counseled Alabamians not to resist Yankees bringing wealth into the state.[23]

But the years of sectional discord had ingrained a distrust of all things northern. Louisiana carpetbagger Lionel A. Sheldon characterized Southerners as generally receptive to northern capital and government aid, but he sensed "a disposition not to be placed under any obligation." "Our people have been taught by their reckless & disunionist leaders to dislike Boston, to dislike Massachusetts, to dislike the whole North," Virginia Conservative Robert Ridgeway wrote Massachusetts industrialist Amos A. Lawrence in 1866, "and many of them seriously believe that no good thing can possibly come out of *your* Nazareth." In an address early in the following year, North Carolina scalawag Thomas Settle appealed for a change of attitudes: "There is another thing that must be reformed at once.

109–15; Robert Toombs to Alexander H. Stephens, August 9, 1868, in Ulrich Bonnell Phillips (ed.), *The Correspondence of Robert Toombs, Alexander H. Stephens, and Howell Cobb* (Washington, D.C.: Government Printing Office, 1913), 703.

23.   James M. Leach to William Pitt Fessenden, January 19, 1866, in Settle Papers; Testimony of Lewis McKenzie, January 31, 1866, in *Report of the Joint Committee on Reconstruction*, Pt. II, 12; Sarah Van V. Woolfolk, "Alabama Attitudes Toward the Republican Party in 1868 and 1964," *Alabama Review,* XX (1967), 28–29.

It has been very fashionable to denounce Yankees and ridicule Yankee notions. I tell you Yankees and Yankee notions are just what we want in this country. We want their capital to build factories, and work shops, and railroads, and develop our magnificent water powers. . . . We want their intelligence, their energy and enterprise to operate these factories, and to teach us how to do it. . . . We want some of those same Yankee tricks played down here that have covered the North with rail roads and canals."[24]

Even Mississippian Albert Gallatin Brown, a hardened old veteran of thirty years of southern politics, admitted in 1867, "We want Yankee capital, Yankee ingenuity, Yankee enterprise, and to get all of this, we must agree to accept Yankee politicians." While Brown rightly saw Republican politics as a part of the economic package, he reasoned that "after the Yankee comes, his politics won't be much in his way. When he sees the dollar, he will throw [meta]physics to the dogs." Other Southerners quickly recognized the relationship between economics and politics in the Republican ideology. For Alcorn, the differences between southern Democrats and northern Republicans in this respect had been apparent well before the war. "The one group of thinkers gave their section doctrines on the theory of government," he declared in his inaugural address as governor of Mississippi in 1870, "while the other group gave their section fishing-bounties, coasting-laws, harbor-improvements, steam-ship-subsidies, naval yards, rifle manufactories, railway-grants, and all those other gifts of practical wisdom." The former Whig advised his fellow Southerners to "abandon their political theorizing for the wiser statesmanship which devotes itself, in the first place, to the fosterage of material interests." The Republican Congress, a Tennessean explained, "has brought into successful play Henry Clay's American System—a system that we have advocated *as a Whig* for thirty-five years."[25]

24. Lionel A. Sheldon to Henry Clay Warmoth, November 26, 1865, in Henry Clay Warmoth Papers, SHC; Robert Ridgeway to Amos A. Lawrence, June 27, 1866, in Amos A. Lawrence Papers, Massachusetts Historical Society, Boston; "Notes of a Speech Delivered by Thomas Settle, Sr. . . . in March 1867" (Typescript in Settle Papers).
25. Brown quoted in William C. Harris, *Presidential Reconstruction in Mississippi* (Baton Rouge: Louisiana State University Press, 1967), 167–68; *Inaugural*

As their rhetoric and activity in Congress on economic measures demonstrated, an overwhelming majority of the scalawags in this sample would have wholeheartedly endorsed Alcorn's declaration that the South held "moral claims for large subsidies from the treasury of the United States."[26] In fact, the Republicans' progressive reputation as the party of reform and change in economic areas and its record of liberal expenditures for internal improvements may well have been the primary attraction for the scalawags in this sample. It mattered little what was under congressional consideration— tax and tariff adjustments, an increase in the monetary circulation, aid for education and social institutions, unionist war claims, or appropriations and subsidies for southern projects—the scalawags, with but few exceptions, could be found in the vanguard pushing for passage.

If Republican economics proved attractive to the future scalawag congressmen, most of them found another critical element of the postwar Republican creed troubling. With the exception of a few idealists and a couple of opportunists, the scalawags were noticeably cool toward Radical notions regarding the status and role of the freedmen in southern society. They did, of course, endorse black suffrage, many openly courted the black vote, and most believed that the better educated blacks had a right to hold office. But it is apparent from their congressional record on such matters as enforcement and civil rights legislation that most of the scalawags simply could not lay aside their heritage and embrace the black cause. In this, they may not have differed much from most carpetbaggers, but they were less able to camouflage their ingrained view of the black. "I am not what they term a negro equalitist, or a negro worshipper," Louisianian W. Jasper Blackburn testified in early 1867. "I do [believe] in their political rights; but sir, I am a southern man; I have never been in the north yet, and I will say that there are some equalities that I do not believe in." Blackburn, a Douglas Democrat in 1860, exempli-

---

Address, of Gov. J. L. Alcorn . . . 1870, to the Legislature of Mississippi (Jackson: Fisher and Kimball, 1870); John Vollmer Mering, "Persistent Whiggery in the Confederate South: A Reconsideration," *South Atlantic Quarterly,* LXIX (1970), 139–40.

26. Pereyra, *James Lusk Alcorn*, 98.

fied the uneasiness felt by those who had converted to Republicanism from a unionist basis with the apparent direction of northern Republican views on the future of the black: "My Unionism consists simply in a single-hearted devotion to the Union government, and not in any particular theories about negro suffrage." Racial questions, in fact, often forced former Whigs who held "unionism" as the center of their credo (rather than Henry Clay economics) into association with the Democracy.[27]

Even those who were attracted to the Republicans for the stronger reasons of economics often found full political equality difficult to swallow and evidenced little more than a paternalistic concern for the blacks. In a letter to Elihu B. Washburne in mid-1868, Alcorn introduced himself as "no scalawag, or carpetbagger[;] I had over a hundred slaves set free by the war, am now perhaps the largest planter in the state, a southerner by blood and education but a friend of humanity, a friend to the poor, docile negro race." The following year, he again reflected his perception of the freedman as he touched on a central problem of reconstruction: "The negro is a poor ignorant, landless, homeless creature who does, and will do, when isolated, precisely as his employer tells him to do." Nine times out of ten, Alcorn added, the employers were Democratic—a simple fact which boded ill for southern Republicanism based on a black electorate.[28]

Caught between the native conservatives and the more radical carpetbaggers and blacks, the scalawags suffered from both sides. Their conservatism on race became painfully evident when they were pitted against the carpetbagger element in southern politics. Racial problems, usually in conjunction with disputes over control of federal and state patronage, were instrumental in creating the scalawag-carpetbagger split in Congress as well as at the state level. But at the same time, of course, the scalawags were not spared any of the conservatives' vilification for courting black support. In their attraction to the Republicans' economic record, they clearly underestimated

27.   Degler, *The Other South,* ch. 8; Testimony of W. Jasper Blackburn, January 1, 1867, in U.S. Congress, House of Representatives, *Report of the Select Committee on the New Orleans Riot* (Washington, D.C.: Government Printing Office, 1867), 422–23.

28.   James L. Alcorn to Elihu B. Washburne, June 29, 1868, January 18, 1869, in Elihu B. Washburne Papers, LC; Pereyra, *James Lusk Alcorn,* 90–92, 106.

the power of race as a political issue. Ironically, their new party would disappoint them on economics as well; in Congress it quickly became evident that northern Republicans had little interest in economic measures designed to benefit the postwar South.

It was the carpetbaggers who played the pivotal role in creating a southern wing of the Republican party. In 1870, Arkansas Democrat Anthony A. C. Rogers rendered a representative conservative opinion on the coming of the Yankees: "Under this state of affairs [the launching of congressional reconstruction in 1867] a horde of hungry adventurers . . . suddenly appeared among us, and looking as eagerly as those of old who went down to spy out the 'land of milk and honey.'" They did not come "to till the soil, to obtain homes, to ply their trades or engage in honorable professions," Rogers declared, "but they come with an insatiate desire and greed for office." As historian E. Merton Coulter put it eighty years later: "They had come out of a shady or obscure life in the North, bringing all their earthly belongings in a carpetbag. . . . to play politics and secure offices" and, he might have added, to peculate and plunder.[29] While revisionists have granted the elusive carpetbaggers less attention than blacks and scalawags, what work has been done has sharply modified the stereotype.

The viability of political motivation suffers first from the fact that the carpetbaggers did not suddenly swoop down on the South in 1867. A full 80 percent of the future carpetbag congressmen had established residence in their adopted states before the advent of congressional reconstruction. Two-thirds were residents by late 1865; most had either stayed after being mustered out of the Union army or returned after a brief interlude in the North. They saw the South as something of "a new frontier, another and a better west" with almost limitless economic opportunities. In Wisconsin carpetbagger Albert T. Morgan's often quoted phrase, the new cry had become one of "Go South, young man." And they came south for all the reasons Americans had moved to the frontier before and after Reconstruc-

29. *Congressional Globe*, 41st Cong., 2nd Sess., Appendix, 105; E. Merton Coulter, *The South During Reconstruction, 1865–1877* (Baton Rouge: Louisiana State University Press, 1947), 126.

tion, including a chance for a fresh start in new surroundings and opportunities for speculation and economic exploitation, as well as to establish the roots of home and family. Southern weather was pleasant, the climate healthy, land cheap, soil rich, capital needed, and labor abundant.[30]

Almost to the man, these Yankees had displayed a restlessness characteristic of many Americans; most had moved west at least once, many several times. Typical was the movement of John S. Harris, who left his native New York to settle first in Illinois and then in Wisconsin. John T. Deweese had spent his twenty-five years before the war in Arkansas, Colorado, Kentucky, and Indiana. Frank Morey, born in Massachusetts, settled in Illinois and then headed west to speculate in Kansas and Nebraska lands. Prior to 1860, Kentucky native John Edwards moved to Indiana, to California, back to Indiana, and then to Iowa. John Callis, thirty-three years of age when he joined the Union army, had already wandered from North Carolina to Tennessee, to Wisconsin, to Minnesota, to California, and into Central America before returning to Wisconsin. Fifty-two of the sixty were Union veterans, they had seen promising land for settlement, and most returned to areas in which they had served at some time during the war. With few exceptions, they brought their families south, purchased homes, and invested in property. Over a quarter purchased land, made some form of arrangements with the freedmen, and tried their hand at planting. Another 60 percent began practicing their professions or went into banking, general business, education, railroad construction, or the extractive industries.[31]

Meriting special consideration are the nine carpetbaggers who went directly from federal patronage positions or the army into Congress. Two of the nine quickly found more lucrative positions elsewhere. Francis W. Kellogg, a representative from Michigan until

30.   Richard N. Current, "Carpetbaggers Reconsidered," in David H. Pinkney and Theodore Ropp (eds.), *A Festschrift for Frederick B. Artz* (Durham: Duke University Press, 1964), 148; David H. Overy, Jr., *Wisconsin Carpetbaggers in Dixie* (Madison: State Historical Society of Wisconsin, 1961), 10–13.

31.   *Biographical Directory of the American Congress*, 1074, 854, 1436, 901–902, 694; Overy, *Wisconsin Carpetbaggers*, 37–39, 46; Benjamin P. Poore (comp.), *Congressional Directory for the Third Session of the Forty-first Congress* (2nd ed.; Washington, D.C.: Government Printing Office, 1871), 20.

March, 1865, resigned his job as an internal revenue agent for Alabama when he was admitted to the Fortieth House in 1868. By early the next year he was in New York on his way to settle in Ohio. Similarly, John R. French, a Lincoln appointee to the direct tax commission of North Carolina, served in the Fortieth House until it disbanded in March, 1869, and then began a decade of service (representing his native New Hampshire) as sergeant at arms in the U.S. Senate. Two others, William Pitt Kellogg and David Heaton, also resigned federal positions to serve in Congress. Kellogg left the collectorship of the Port of New Orleans in the same month he took his seat in the Senate, and the widely traveled Heaton gave up his job as a treasury agent in North Carolina when elected to the Fortieth House. Of these four federal servants, only Heaton had established a vocation outside politics—he had used his northern connections to secure a charter for a national bank in New Bern.[32]

Of the remaining five, four were Freedmen's Bureau agents and all were mustered out just before or soon after their election to Congress. Three, Charles W. Pierce of Alabama, Charles M. Hamilton of Florida, and James McCleery of Louisiana, had established their professions and purchased property before leaving bureau service; the fourth, John Callis of Alabama, had not done so. Of the four, Hamilton and Callis quite clearly used their bureau positions to political ends, and the footloose Callis perhaps came the closest of any of the carpetbag congressmen to being the stereotypical "political adventurer." Described as handsome, dashing, flamboyant, and arrogant, Callis, after a serious wound at Gettysburg ended his military career, joined the Freedmen's Bureau, ambitiously took up the cause of Alabama blacks, and allegedly fought several duels with former slaveholders. In appreciation, the freedmen presented him with "a watch engraved with a picture of him restraining a whip-wielding slaveholder" and sent him to Congress. At the end of his short term in 1869, Callis, still suffering from his war wounds, ended forty years of wanderlust by returning to Wisconsin.[33]

32. *Biographical Directory of the American Congress*, 1218–19, 972, 1098; *DAB*, X, 305–306.
33. Thomas McAdory Owen, *History of Alabama and Dictionary of Alabama Biography* (4 vols.; Chicago: S. J. Clarke Publishing, 1921), IV, 1364–65; United

The final army man, Adelbert Ames, resigned his commission only two days before he was sworn in as senator from Mississippi in early 1870. In a statement to the Senate credentials committee, Ames admitted that he owned no property in the state, but that he had "made arrangements, almost final and permanent, with a person to manage property I intended to buy." He had done nothing to establish residency except to declare publicly before his election that he had decided to make Mississippi his permanent home. The committee concluded that Ames was not a citizen of Mississippi within the meaning of the Constitution, but the Senate, following the lead of Radical Charles Sumner, decided that he was entitled to his seat.[34]

The residency of the other eight is also subject to question as is the propriety of running for office while in the army or a federal patronage position. Nor was it perhaps proper that several had established their personal vocations while holding full-time government jobs. But most were in Congress only briefly. McCleery became ill shortly after his election and died the following fall without serving a day in Washington. Although they were seated late in the second session of the Fortieth Congress, French, Pierce, Callis, and Francis Kellogg effectively participated only in the third session (December, 1868—March, 1869), and all had declined to stand for reelection. Both Hamilton and Heaton were reelected to the Forty-first House, but Heaton died in June, 1870, so his total service amounted to about one full term. Ames and William Pitt Kellogg enjoyed longer tenures. Ames held his Senate seat until 1874 when he began an ill-fated stint as governor, and Kellogg endured to serve in the Senate, as governor, in the Senate again, and in the House before he left Louisiana in 1885. To return to the initial question, motivation for these Yankees remains moot. But as these men and their colleagues quickly discovered, conservative Southerners did not particularly

States, Department of the Interior, Bureau of the Census, Ninth Census, 1870, Manuscript Population Schedules, Alabama, Mobile County (hereinafter cited as U.S. MS Census . . .); *Biographical Directory of the American Congress*, 1057, 1360; New Orleans *Republican*, November 7, 1871; U.S. MS Census, 1870, Population Schedules, Louisiana, Caddo Parish; Testimony of Joseph John Williams, November 13, 1871, Testimony of Charles M. Hamilton, November 4, 1871, Testimony of William M. Lowe, October 13, 1871, in *Condition of Affairs in the Late Insurrectionary States*, XIII, 232, 281—91, IX, 882; Overy, *Wisconsin Carpetbaggers*, 46.

34. *Senate Miscellaneous Documents*, 49th Cong., 1st Sess., No. 47, pp. 317—19.

care when or why a Yankee came South. If he engaged in politics as a Republican, then his real reason for coming was to court and array the blacks against the whites, and thereby secure the benefits of office for himself.

The willingness of Yankee settlers to move into a comparative vacuum and take the initiative with the freedmen which Congress desired became the key to northern involvement in southern politics. Reflecting back, Hamilton explained that "army men" simply took hold of reconstruction in order to lead "a new element here that had been enfranchised who were without leaders." Told to implement the congressional plan, they found a void into which few native whites had ventured. Others such as Heaton had northern political connections and worked into the process from that end. As early as January, 1865, Heaton wrote John Sherman that his position could be of benefit to the party: "If permitted to remain here, I feel persuaded that among other things, I can materially aid in bringing North Carolina back into the Union as a free State." Heaton maintained his position, kept pace with the mood of Congress on the suffrage question, and found himself drawn into southern politics.[35]

Kellogg, the future bête noire of Louisiana conservatives, testified at the end of 1866 that he got along quite well with natives in New Orleans because he avoided participation in personal politics. He even expressed a disdain for certain "political adventurers" who, "unlike the Radical men of the North," appeared to be using the freedmen "for personal aggrandizement." But half of the thirty-two clerks in Kellogg's office had been Union army officers, and most of them owed their position to congressional Republicans. Accordingly, the customhouse quickly became a hotbed of Republicanism in Louisiana. Despite his attempt to steer clear of politics, Kellogg, a founding member of the Illinois Republican party and a Lincoln elector in 1860, took advantage of the situation when Congress outlined its reconstruction plan in 1867 and renewed his political career in Louisiana's "Black and Tan" convention.[36]

35. Hamilton Testimony, *Condition of Affairs in the Late Insurrectionary States,* XIII, 289; David Heaton to John Sherman, January 19, 1865, December 17, 1866, in John Sherman Papers, LC.

36. Testimony of William Pitt Kellogg, December 29, 1866, in *Report on the New Orleans Riot,* 301–302; *National Cyclopaedia of American Biography,* X, 82.

Involvement came more quickly for two other new Louisianians, Lionel A. Sheldon and Jacob Hale Sypher, both former Union generals. Sheldon, a free-soil Democrat who moved into the Republican party in 1856, had established a law practice in New Orleans in March, 1865. Bothered by the conservative bias of the local press and the fact that "secession-politicians" seemed to be the beneficiaries of Johnsonian reconstruction, Sheldon became active in the establishment of a newspaper and a party "to act in harmony with the union organization of the north." The more doctrinaire Sypher sank his money into a delta plantation and began "working for the *same cause for which I fought*," with the declaration that "it don't make a *'damn bit'* of difference to me whether I get any credit for it or not." Credit came to both in the form of office. Sheldon spent three relatively peaceful terms in the House while Sypher fought his way through contests to four terms—three of them partial and all of them stormy.[37]

Union veteran George E. Spencer represented yet another type. "I am strongly of the opinion that I should settle somewhere South," he explained to his benefactor Grenville Dodge in May, 1865. "I think the chances of making a fortune there [are] the best." He thought about applying for the collectorship of Mobile but instead began purchasing cotton in Alabama and found it so lucrative that he invited Dodge to "come South and operate." In the interim he lobbied with Johnson for the appointment of northern Alabama friends to political positions, but he soon became disillusioned with the conservative thrust of presidential reconstruction, and by August he was advocating black suffrage. After selling his cotton in New York at a great profit to himself and his partner, Senator William Sprague of Rhode Island, he decided that Alabama was not the place to settle until the political situation changed, so he headed for California to scout speculative possibilities. With the advent of congressional reconstruction in early 1867, Alabama suddenly became more promising. He returned to Decatur in April, wrangled a personally profit-

37.   Sheldon to Warmoth, November 26, 1865, Jacob H. Sypher to Warmoth, September 9, 1867, October 18, 1867, in Warmoth Papers; Testimony of Lionel A. Sheldon, December 29, 1866, in *Report on the New Orleans Riot*, 280–82; *Biographical Directory of the American Congress*, 1686, 1784.

able appointment as register in bankruptcy, immersed himself in politics, and emerged as a United States senator.[38]

For most northern settlers political involvement was less calculated. Benjamin Norris, for example, came to Alabama as a paymaster in the Freedmen's Bureau, resigned in August, 1865, and purchased a large plantation in Elmore County. He later recalled that he "had no purpose to take part in politics," but an antislavery background extending back to the Free Soilers convention of 1848 led him rather naturally into the Alabama Republican party at its organization. Lawyer Joseph P. Newsham, a Louisiana resident since disabilities forced his resignation from the Union army in 1864, found himself drawn into politics by his willingness to take freedmen as clients. He soon discovered, as he wrote Henry Clay Warmoth early in 1866, that he was the only lawyer in Donaldsonville who would represent them in court. There he was invariably "met by 3 or 4 good rebels of the same ilk, before courts of Rebel Judges, with the whole force of public opinion against me." After threats on his life compelled him "to save my bacon" and leave his new home, he reopened his practice in the Felicianas. When the blacks were enfranchised, they rewarded his attentiveness by sending him to Washington.[39]

The case of Willard Warner best illustrates the turnabout in conservative attitudes toward northern settlers when the Yankees made known their Republican politics. Warner had purchased an Alabama plantation in 1866, divided his time between Ohio (where he was completing a term in the state senate) and Alabama for the next year, and settled permanently in late 1867. He informed his friend Senator John Sherman in 1866 that "a Northern man who is not a fool, or foolish fanatic may live pleasantly in Alabama without abating one jot of his self-respect, or independence." His initial reception was cordial, and he developed a circle of friends that included prominent conservatives. "When we talk about carpetbaggers we want you

38.   George E. Spencer to Grenville M. Dodge, April 16, May 1, 25, August 1, October 14, 1865, January 11, 28, October 4, 1866, June 1, 1867, in Grenville M. Dodge Papers, Iowa State Historical Department, Des Moines.

39.   Testimony of Benjamin W. Norris, June 6, 1871, in *Condition of Affairs in the Late Insurrectionary States*, VIII, 64–65, 69; *Biographical Directory of the American Congress*, 1476, 1469; Joseph P. Newsham to Henry Clay Warmoth, April 5, 1866, March 19, 1867, in Warmoth Papers.

to understand that we don't mean you," one of his ex-Confederate friends assured him shortly after his arrival. "You have come here and invested what means you have in property here, and you have the same interest here that we have." With northern encouragement, however, Warner became involved in Republican politics, and in 1868 the Alabama legislature elected him to the Senate. His "designs" (in the conservatives' lexicon) had finally surfaced. The same conservative who had been so reassuring in 1866 later declared, "Before his seat in Ohio got cold, he was running the negro machine among us to put himself in office."[40]

When a choice had to be made, there was little doubt as to which political party most northern settlers would favor. As a general rule, the natives who converted to Republicanism were hesitant to take the lead in the initial stage of the congressional plan, and since black leadership had not yet emerged as a contending force in most states, the movement of northern men into southern politics and offices was a natural one. And they saw it as their duty to participate. "If I had only been there eight months, instead of eight years," George McKee of Mississippi later declared, "my right would be the same." Another Mississippian, Henry W. Barry, defined others like himself as simply "American citizens, natives of other States, who, under the protection of the Federal Constitution, have transferred their citizenship to the South." Not one to overlook the larger picture, Barry thought carpetbaggers belonged to that class of Americans who had "rescued the North American continent from the disjointed civilization of Europe and . . . secured the reign of free democratic brotherhood of humanity." "For my own part," added Warner, "I glory in that progressive spirit which made me a carpetbagger."[41]

Warner's comment suggests the curious mixture of economics, politics, and idealism in Republican thought. At one time or another, most of the carpetbaggers demonstrated their conviction that

---

40. Current, "Carpetbaggers Reconsidered," 141–42; Testimony of Willard Warner, June 3, 1871, Testimony of James H. Clayton, July 8, 1871, in *Condition of Affairs in the Late Insurrectionary States*, VIII, 33–34, 233; John Burkett Ryan, Jr., "Willard Warner: Soldier, Senator, and Southern Entrepreneur" (M.A. thesis, Auburn University, 1971), 49–56.

41. *Congressional Globe*, 42nd Cong., 1st Sess., 427, Appendix, 265, 40th Cong., 3rd Sess., 86.

southern society should be restructured along northern (Republican) lines; thus a strain of mission often accompanied the more practical economic and political motives. As Missouri Republican Carl Schurz argued in 1865, "The whole organism of southern society . . . must be . . . constructed anew, so as to bring it in harmony with the rest of American society." Two centuries of slavery, Republicans believed, had created a South badly out of step with the North. They seemed little concerned with the institution's impact on the black, but they frequently echoed the ingrained notion that slavery so detracted from the free labor value system that southern whites had degenerated into slothfulness and their society had become stagnant and backward-looking. Two years as a New Orleans lawyer had given Lionel Sheldon the impression that southern whites "are not, as a people, inclined to be industrious." George Spencer testified early in 1866 that during his travels in Alabama, he had become "strongly of the opinion" that there was "more disposition exhibited by the negroes to work than among the white people." Slavery, John Edwards had declared before the war, "is a foul political curse on the institutions of our country . . . and worse than that it is a curse upon the poor, free laboring white man." "Slavery has been a barrier to civilization, and has tended to the degeneration of the people who have lived under its baleful influence for almost three generations," Charles Hamilton concluded, "and the result is that, to a great extent, the southern people counsel with, and are moved, actuated, and controlled by the impulses of passion, prejudice, and sentiment, rather than reason or cool judgement."[42]

Whatever the impact of such conceptions of southern society, so well learned in prewar Republican politics, on the carpetbaggers' actual experience in the section, the Yankees did manifest a certain crusading spirit to reeducate, reform, and elevate the South. Such a spirit probably induced James McCleery, planter, lawyer, and Freedmen's Bureau agent, to tell the census taker in 1870 that he was in

42. *Senate Executive Documents*, 39th Cong., 1st Sess., No. 2, pp. 38, 40–41; Sheldon Testimony, *Report on the New Orleans Riot*, 282; Testimony of George E. Spencer, January 26, 1866, *Report of the Joint Committee on Reconstruction*, Pt. III, 9; F. I. Herriott, "Iowa and the First Nomination of Lincoln," *Annals of Iowa*, 2nd ser., VIII (1907), 198; Hamilton Testimony, *Condition of Affairs in the Late Insurrectionary States*, XIII, 288.

fact a missionary. But Ames best expressed the ultimate objective in a letter to Massachusetts Governor William Claflin just before Mississippi's elections in 1869. He thanked the New Englander for his financial support of Mississippi Republicans and ventured the opinion that they would prevail: "I hope and believe that the state will be raised to a purer atmosphere to move with other states in the road of progress and enlightenment." The Republicans carried the state, and two months later Alcorn, the scalawag governor-elect, requested Claflin to explain how his state's government was organized. As one might have anticipated, the ex-Whig expressed a special interest in the structure and function of the Massachusetts departments of finance, public instruction, and public works.[43]

The racial sensibilities of those who, as Radical Benjamin Butler put it, "have gone from the north to aid in the regeneration of the South," are difficult to assess. In a letter to William Lloyd Garrison, L. Cass Carpenter of South Carolina declared that his "first Republican inspirations had been drawn from the 'Liberator.'" Texan William T. Clark asserted that he had learned to detest slavery on his mother's knee, and Francis Kellogg claimed to have been among "that band of men known as original abolitionists."[44] Rumors that one had been associated with the antislavery crusade were, of course, politically useful, but few of the carpetbagger congressmen could legitimately claim such connections. Obviously, some used the black electorate as a means to political and personal ends. Others displayed a considerable disparity between public rhetoric and private practice and occasionally, as in South Carolina and Louisiana, carpetbaggers and blacks became antagonistic rivals.

Still, white endorsement of the black cause, if occasionally misdirected and tactlessly handled, was often maintained under ex-

43. U.S. MS Census, 1870, Population Schedules, Louisiana, Caddo Parish; Adelbert Ames to William Claflin, November 8, 1869, James L. Alcorn to Claflin, January 24, 1870, in William and Mary B. Claflin Papers, Rutherford B. Hayes Presidential Center, Fremont, Ohio.
44. Undated draft of Benjamin F. Butler to Thomas J. Mackey, written on Mackey to Butler, June 3, 1868, in Benjamin F. Butler Papers, LC; L. Cass Carpenter to William Lloyd Garrison, June 28, 1878, in Lewis Cass Carpenter Papers, South Caroliniana Library, University of South Carolina, Columbia; Janice C. Hood, "Brotherly Hate: A Quantitative Study of Southern Reconstruction Congressmen, 1867–1877" (Ph.D. dissertation, Washington State University, 1974), 37–38.

tremely trying circumstances. And several such as Ames showed a sincerely held, idealistic conviction to aid the freedmen. "That I should have taken a political office seems almost inexplicable," he wrote historian James W. Garner in 1900. "My explanation may seem ludicrous now, but then it seemed to me that I had a mission, with a large M." As he explained in earlier testimony: "I believed that I could render [the freedmen] great service. . . . and I unhesitatingly consented to represent them and unite my fortune with theirs."[45] The blacks who served in Congress must have been distressed as they watched their erstwhile supporters fall away as reconstruction wore on, but for what it was worth, and for whatever reasons, their last white allies would include Ames and most of his fellow carpetbaggers.

The snarl of economics, politics, and mission which often crossed the line into opportunism can scarcely be shaped into a coherent ideology adequately descriptive of southern Republicanism. The war years, the practicalities of power, and the arrival of political maturity had further shaped the Republicans' prewar ideology, and the northern party exhibited at least surface solidarity on certain basic tenets in the immediate postwar years.[46] In the South, however, the carpetbaggers, scalawags, and blacks held differing perceptions of the ideology and how it was to be translated into practice. Southern Republicanism has seldom been recognized for what it was—a variously interpreted and confused tangle of northern ideas and attitudes about economics, politics, and race, modified by certain southern realities, the whole of which was hastily and incompletely grafted onto the postwar remnants of antebellum society. The resulting confusion as to the nature and direction of the South would mark Reconstruction politics.

Whatever the motives of Yankees and natives for becoming Republicans and participating in reconstruction, theirs would prove a

45. James W. Garner, *Reconstruction in Mississippi* (New York: Columbia University Press, 1901), 290n, 277n.

46. See Eric Foner, *Free Soil, Free Labor, Free Men: The Ideology of the Republican Party Before the Civil War* (New York: Oxford University Press, 1970); and W. R. Brock, *An American Crisis: Congress and Reconstruction, 1865–1867* (New York: St. Martin's Press, 1963), especially ch. 6.

difficult task. Sectional feeling remained overpowering through the 1870s and beyond. Given the limitations of the final plan of reconstruction and the hard core of racism in both North and South which lay at the base of postwar problems, the task was perhaps doomed from the beginning. Southerners had simply dominated the black too long to grant him the political and civil rights desired by an ever-dwindling number of northern Radicals. Northerners had inadequately planned the process of "regeneration" and underestimated southern resistance to change. The job of doing whatever it was that Northerners believed should be done was left to southern Republicans, who quickly found themselves ill-supported by their northern creators and undermanned, outclassed, and outgunned in a struggle for survival with southern conservatives.

III The Travail of Election Politics Southern Style

Southerners, regardless of political conviction, tended to reduce the surrealistic snarl of divergent background characteristics, motives, and value systems of their politicians to a simple dualism. One was either a Democrat or a Republican, the labels symbolized good or evil depending on one's perspective, and politics in the postwar South became a world with little middle ground. In many respects, as Richard N. Current has observed, the antagonists simply continued to pursue their respective war aims. Conservatives fought for "home rule and white supremacy," while Republicans sought reunification on northern terms and economic and political freedom for the black.[1] Going into the congressional campaigns, the conservatives enjoyed advantages of experience, wealth, economic leverage, and home ground, but hindsight suggests that the key element may well have been their realization that the nation was not ready to face the responsibilities of emancipation. For their part, southern Republicans entered the fray with a good bit of missionary zeal and the backing of the dominant northern party and the newly enfranchised freedmen—a potentially large and dependable electorate. They had some disadvantage in terms of prior political experience, but they quickly encountered a number of more serious political handicaps. The ostracism and intimidation they faced, of course, came from outside the party, and the debilitating image of corruption which followed them was partially earned and partially manufactured by their political opponents. But some of the primary problems came from within the party. Chief among these were a

1. Richard N. Current, "Carpetbaggers Reconsidered," in David H. Pinkney and Theodore Ropp (eds.), *A Festschrift for Frederick B. Artz* (Durham: Duke University Press, 1964), 155–56.

rampant and crippling factionalism throughout the southern wing and the inexplicable failure of northern Republicans to provide campaign aid for their southern allies. In contrast, southern Democrats had few internal problems, and, unlike their Republican counterparts, they had no real need for material support from party colleagues in other regions of the country. The chaotic political milieu from which the 251 congressmen emerged merits consideration, for it further shaped them and increased the burdens which they carried to Washington.

The congressmen brought varying levels of political expertise to the struggle. Native Democrats had the edge over their Republican opponents in terms of prior political experience, but the Republicans were hardly novices. Only fourteen Democrats and eight Republicans had not held public office prior to the beginning of their first term in Congress, and several of those had campaigned unsuccessfully for political position. In fact, Southerners of both parties had a greater amount of officeholding experience at all levels than others entering the House of Representatives during the two decades after 1860. Only slightly over 60 percent of all entering representatives, for example, had any service at the state level; the comparable figure for Southerners was 83 percent (see Table 6).[2]

Officeholding background varied widely. Some had extensive experience at the local level. Prior to his service in the Fortieth House, Louisiana carpetbagger Joseph Newsham had served as parish judge, parish attorney, district attorney, judicial clerk, and on the police jury in West Feliciana Parish. Others such as Democrat George Goldthwaite had compiled a long record of service in a particular branch at the state level. Before his disqualification in 1867, Goldthwaite had spent nearly twenty-five years in the Alabama judicial system. In terms of total experience, Alexander H. Stephens had no match. In a political career that began in the Georgia legislature in 1836, Stephens served sixteen years in the U.S. House and then in

2. Allen G. Bogue, et al., "Members of the House of Representatives and the Processes of Modernization, 1789–1960," *Journal of American History,* LXIII (1976), Table 5, p. 289. Within the Republican party 92 percent of the scalawags, 81 percent of the blacks, and 75 percent of the carpetbaggers had served in some capacity at the state level.

Table 6. PRIOR POLITICAL EXPERIENCE

	Democrat (n=122)	Republican (n=129)
Federal		
Congress	9	5
Appointive[a]	2	33
Confederate		
Congress	11	—
Appointive	5	2
State		
Governor	4	4
Executive[b]	6	9
Legislative	75	53
Judicial	30	14
Secession Convention	18	5
Constitutional Convention		
1865–1866	12	14
1867–1869	1	52
Other	7	26
Total[c]	102 (84%)	107 (83%)
Local[d]	27	38
Party[e]	36	28
No Officeholding Experience[f]	14	8

[a]Includes positions of U.S. district attorney, internal revenue collector, postmaster, treasury agent, and eight ranking Freedmen's Bureau officials. Twenty-five of the 33 Republicans appointed to federal positions were carpetbaggers.
[b]Includes elective executive branch positions.
[c]Total number and percentage of southern congressmen of each party having at least one position at the state level.
[d]The figures for local political experience are undoubtedly too low. The sources often fail to detail the range of experience at the local level.
[e]Includes service as presidential elector, delegate to national party conventions, etc.
[f]Several in this category had waged unsuccessful campaigns for political position.

the secession convention and the Confederate provisional congress prior to his selection as the Rebel vice-president.[3]

Other, more obscure Democrats were big men in their own bailiwicks. Otho R. Singleton, a wealthy planter-lawyer, served in the Mississippi house and senate and as a representative in Congress for three terms before withdrawing when the state seceded in early 1861. His constituents promptly sent him to the Confederate house of representatives for the duration of the war. The political background of Charles E. Hooker is more typical of the general level of officeholding experience among Democrats. Hooker, a lawyer of modest means, spent one term in the Mississippi house prior to the Civil War. After a tour in the Confederate army, he served as state attorney general until removed by military authorities in 1868. Most of the Democrats had acquired their political experience in their native states, but a few such as Jesse J. Finley of Florida had held office in several states. A native of Tennessee, Finley was successively a member of the Tennessee senate, a member of the Arkansas senate, mayor of Memphis, a Florida senator, and a federal and then a Confederate judge prior to his joining the Confederate army as a private in 1862.[4]

In terms of major officeholding, no Republican had compiled a record comparable to the most prominent Democrats, but some, such as scalawag Robert S. Heflin, had attempted to make politics a career. The Georgia native had served in the state house of representatives and senate before moving to Alabama in 1849, where he was elected as a Democrat to that state's house and senate. The younger carpetbaggers had less total experience than the scalawags, but many had held office in several different states—a reflection of the adventurous, restless character often associated with the Yankees who came South. David Heaton, for example, had spent time in the

3. Alcee Fortier (ed.), *Louisiana: Comprising Sketches* . . . (3 vols.; Madison, Wis.: Century Historical Association, 1914), II, 249–50; *Dictionary of American Biography*, IV, 368–69; Thomas E. Schott, "Alexander H. Stephens: Antebellum Statesman" (Ph.D. dissertation, Louisiana State University, 1978).

4. Jon L. Wakelyn (ed.), *Biographical Directory of the Confederacy* (Westport, Conn.: Greenwood Press, 1977), 386–87, 186–87; Otho R. Singleton to Andrew Johnson, n.d., in Amnesty Papers, Georgia, Office of the Adjutant General, Record Group 94, National Archives; Otho Robards Singleton, Subject File, Charles Edward Hooker, Subject File, Mississippi Department of Archives and History, Jackson.

Ohio and Minnesota senates and had cultivated a useful relationship with prominent northern politicians which led to his appointment in 1863 as a treasury agent for North Carolina. The well-traveled John Edwards, a Kentucky native, had served in the Indiana house, as a California alcalde, in the Indiana senate, the Iowa constitutional convention, and the Iowa house—all within the span of fifteen years prior to the war. After being brevetted brigadier general and mustered out of the Union army in January, 1866, he settled in Fort Smith, Arkansas, and President Johnson rewarded him with an appointment as assessor of internal revenue. Nearly half the carpetbaggers had held federal patronage positions in the South, and the so-called "Black and Tan" constitutional conventions of 1867 and 1868 provided an important forum for twenty-two scalawags, twenty carpetbaggers, nine blacks, and a solitary Democrat.[5]

Although previous officeholding experience was not an essential prerequisite either to election or success in Congress, those who had it frequently seemed to wield more influence than did political newcomers. Experienced politicians, such as John H. Reagan and James W. Throckmorton of Texas, received better committee assignments, they were more active, and they had more impact during their first term in the Forty-fourth House than did, for example, their fellow freshmen, Charles Nash of Louisiana and Jeremiah Williams of Alabama, neither of whom had ever held public office. There were obviously other factors involved, such as personality and political context, but it is no less apparent that an individual's quickness of adaptation to the House or Senate, his activity and influence, and even his constituents' expectations were to some degree correlated with his level of prior political experience. More important, in campaigns against the Republicans, particularly against the carpetbaggers and blacks, the more seasoned conservatives, some of whom had been successful politicians for thirty years, clearly had the upper hand.

    5.   Benjamin P. Poore (comp.), *Congressional Directory for the Second Session of the Forty-first Congress* (2nd ed.; Washington, D.C.: Government Printing Office, 1870), 6; *Biographical Directory of the American Congress, 1774–1971* (Washington, D.C.: Government Printing Office, 1971), 1098, 901–902; Richard L. Hume, "The 'Black and Tan' Constitutional Conventions of 1867–1869 in Ten Former Confederate States: A Study of Their Membership" (Ph.D. dissertation, University of Washington, 1969).

Those who lacked political experience gained it quickly in the steamy caldron of southern politics. The selection of U.S. senators was often a closed proceeding and a matter of maneuver and political trading, but senatorial incumbents and aspirants usually campaigned for their party, and candidates for the House were subjected to a rigorous stump canvass. Wherever the Republican party remained a competitive organization and the black electorate large, the contests were invariably bitter and occasionally dangerous affairs. The Republicans' use of federal troops or state militia, the Democrats' paramilitary organizations, economic and political intimidation, fraud, and violence muddied the electoral process. If all else failed, then control of the ballot boxes and returning boards could swing an election one way or another.

As far as Republican candidates for Congress were concerned, the most obvious political abuse was the intimidation which began as soon as they initiated political activity among the freedmen. The vilification, launched in the conservative press, quickly turned into concerted anti-Republican activity. In early 1868, for example, the editor of an Alabama journal called for driving the "office-seeking, nigger-loving, hypocritical-canting, whining and selfish Carpet-Baggers howling back to their northern homes." At the same time, Ryland Randolph, the vituperative proprietor of the Tuskaloosa *Independent Monitor*, advised conservatives to create a Ku Klux Klan in every community for the "condign cleansing of neighborhoods of all human impurities" and began printing crude but effective woodcuts depicting the despised carpetbaggers and scalawags in various stages of persecution at the hands of the Klan.[6]

Such invective surprised and baffled some Republicans. "I never knew such things in Maine," Representative Benjamin F. Norris of Alabama declared. "Republicans and Democrats were tolerated

6. Wilcox *Vindicator* quoted in Charles C. Colton to Benjamin Butler, April 10, 1868, in Benjamin F. Butler Papers, Library of Congress (hereinafter cited as LC); Randolph quoted in Allen W. Trelease, *White Terror: The Ku Klux Klan Conspiracy and Southern Reconstruction* (New York: Harper & Row, 1971), 85; Sarah Van V. Woolfolk, "The Political Cartoons of the Tuskaloosa *Independent Monitor* and Tuskaloosa *Blade*, 1867–1873," *Alabama Historical Quarterly*, XXVII (1965), 140–66. Randolph's tirades against the Republicans shocked even some of his fellow conservatives. See H. M. Summerville to Robert McKee, October 3, 1868, in Robert McKee Papers, Alabama Department of Archives and History, Montgomery.

there." Others expressed despair at continuing to advocate the Republican cause. A Mississippi Republican applauded carpetbagger George McKee's successful fight to win election to the House, but lamented to Benjamin Butler, "We are too few and scattered, and the Freedmen and Southern white loyalists too timid to compete on equal terms with almost the entire body of rampant, half-horse, half-alligator, walking arsenals" in the Democratic party. Alabama carpetbagger Charles Buckley, a newly elected representative, lamented in May, 1868, that the blacks were depressed and that the Republicans were already "overworked, poor and dispirited, with no hope of results" in the presidential election of 1868 "so favorable as in the last election."[7]

Like their party colleagues at the state and local levels, the Republican congressmen faced constant abuse ranging from mild rebukes in the conservative press to assassination. Some of the racial moderates such as Lionel A. Sheldon, who represented the "more civilized" New Orleans district, or Senator Willard Warner of Alabama encountered but little serious trouble. Warner claimed that he was respected by many conservatives, seldom interrupted while speaking at political rallies, and "treated more kindly than any other Republican" in the state. Others, particularly those in the more isolated areas of the South, caught the brunt of intimidation. Republican candidates frequently complained about campaigning before audiences of unarmed blacks and armed whites, being driven off the stump and from their homes, and having their lives threatened. In many districts the most overt intimidation occurred in the redemption elections, such as those of 1875 in Mississippi and 1876 in South Carolina. In other areas, violence broke out during every campaign over a period of several years.[8]

The Republicans' ultimate fear was assassination. Sometimes their anxiety stemmed from empty warnings or simple paranoia

---

7. Testimony of Benjamin W. Norris, June 6, 1871, in U.S. Congress, *Report of the Joint Select Committee to Inquire into the Condition of Affairs in the Late Insurrectionary States* (13 vols.; Washington, D.C.: Government Printing Office, 1872), VIII, 69; J. Tarbell to Benjamin F. Butler, July 13, 1868, in Butler Papers; Charles W. Buckley to Elihu B. Washburne, May 1, June 15, 1868, in Elihu B. Washburne Papers, LC.

8. Lionel A. Sheldon to Henry L. Dawes, November 30, December 18, 1868, in Henry L. Dawes Papers, LC; Testimony of Willard Warner, June 3, 1871, in *Condition*

from being involved in violent campaigns and witnessing threats and attempts on the lives of others. But at least a dozen, and some more than once, were the targets of assassins. Another five were wounded. Louisiana scalawag W. Jasper Blackburn was shot while stumping in 1872, scalawag C. C. Bowen of South Carolina was wounded in the leg while running from a riot, black Robert De Large took a bullet in his hand, "hooded nightriders" critically wounded Florida carpetbagger William J. Purman, and carpetbagger Henry W. Barry of Mississippi lost the use of his right arm when shot during a "political disturbance." Two of the congressmen were murdered. A disgruntled Democrat ambushed and killed Arkansas carpetbagger James Hinds during the campaign of 1868 and the following year Alabama scalawag Thomas Haughey was assassinated by a supporter of his carpetbagger opponent while making a stump speech.[9]

The Republicans responded in various ways. Some initially tried peace offerings to their opposition. Alabama Senator George E. Spencer, for example, promised to send government documents to Robert McKee, the conservative editor of the Selma *Southern Argus*, and offered the hope that the two could get along like "gentlemen." McKee was apparently too much of a gentleman to respond, but when Spencer made a similar gesture and sent a copy of his speech on the tax and tariff bill of 1870 to Ryland Randolph, the editor indignantly dismissed it. "We did not even look to see what side of the question the Senatorial adventurer took," he assured his readers. "We will not thank the toad-resembling 'Senator' for his remembrance of the MONITOR." At the other extreme, South Carolina black Richard

---

of Affairs in the Late Insurrectionary States, VIII, 25, 33–34; Janice C. Hood, "Brotherly Hate: A Quantitative Study of Southern Reconstruction Congressmen, 1867–1877" (Ph.D. dissertation, Washington State University, 1974), 150–52, 162–73, 358–62; George C. Rable, "But There Was No Peace: Violence and Reconstruction Politics" (Ph.D. dissertation, Louisiana State University, 1978), chs. 6–10.

9. Hood, "Southern Reconstruction Congressmen," 167–68, 358–62; Charleston *Republican*, October 10, 1876; New Orleans *Weekly Louisianian*, September 28, 1872; Little Rock *Arkansas Gazette*, October 24, 27, 28, 31, 1868; Benjamin F. Rice to William Claflin, October 27, 1868, in William and Mary B. Claflin Papers, Rutherford B. Hayes Presidential Center, Fremont, Ohio; *Congressional Globe*, 40th Cong., 3rd Sess., 436–37, 552–53; Sarah Woolfolk Wiggins, *The Scalawag in Alabama Politics, 1865–1881* (University, Ala.: University of Alabama Press, 1977), 55–57; Testimony of Governor Robert B. Lindsay, June 16, 1871, in *Condition of Affairs in the Late Insurrectionary States*, VIII, 173.

Cain and carpetbagger Benjamin F. Whittemore urged violent retaliation against Wade Hampton's Red Shirts as they watched Republican majorities disappear in district after district.[10]

Although the Republicans initially had the upper hand in most
states, one of the keys to postwar southern politics was the Democrats' ability to keep campaigns focused on race, reconstruction, and
the Republican record in office. When Republicans, particularly the
scalawags, attempted to soft-pedal the race question and emphasize
economic issues, Democrats countered with charges of corruption,
blasted reconstruction, and raised the specter of race. The congressional campaigns often became intensively personal. Men of both
political persuasions dug into their opponents' backgrounds for ammunition to be used for character assassination. Republicans reminded their black audiences that many Democrats had defended
slavery; Democrats alleged that certain scalawags had been unusually cruel masters. Past political affiliations frequently came
back to haunt the congressmen. In 1871, for example, Texas scalawag Edward Degener, a German immigrant, circulated with good
effect a Know-Nothing campaign document which his opponent
John Hancock had authored in 1856. Hancock's supporters countered with the charge that Degener was a "good for nothing. . . . in-
finitesimally small quantity, less than zero," who knew "as much
about the proper duties of a Congressman as the devil knows about
holy water." Besides that, he was an atheist, an advocate of "freelov-
ism and woman's suffrage," and had stolen cotton from the Confederacy, while Hancock, a unionist Democrat, had held a commission in the Union army. It might have pained conservatives to defend Hancock's war record, but it paid off as Degener went down to
defeat.[11]

Part of the Republicans' problem in this war of invective was the
lack of an established party press to articulate party positions and to
respond to attacks on their integrity. As early as 1865, carpetbagger
Lionel Sheldon, distressed because "the people now only hear one

10. George E. Spencer to Robert McKee, December 21, 1870, in McKee Papers;
Tuskaloosa *Independent Monitor,* July 19, 1870; Hood, "Southern Reconstruction
Congressmen," 171.
11. Austin *Democratic Statesman,* September 9, 16, 21, 1871.

side," called for the founding in Louisiana of an "organ of some strength to support the Republican party." Scalawags Lewis McKenzie and John Francis Lewis testified in 1866 that disloyal and "secessionist" newspapers and "copperhead" sheets from the North had a powerful influence in determining public opinion in Virginia. Early in the same year, a Louisiana Republican claimed that future scalawag representative W. Jasper Blackburn, editor of the Homer *Iliad*, was "the only white man south of Pennsylvania" who published a newspaper acceptable to Republicans.[12]

Republican newspapers were established in many southern towns and cities, but they faced a constant struggle for support, and occasionally, as was twice the case with Blackburn's *Iliad*, they were physically destroyed. Southern Republicans, with much justification, complained constantly about the need for party newspapers, the factional leanings of what papers they had, their treatment in the Democratic press, and even the lack of support by established northern Republican journals. They frequently attributed their negative image in the North to the conservative bias of the southern associated press reporters who fed northern newspapers. Louisiana Republicans protested the prejudiced dispatches of the associated press correspondent working out of the *Picayune* office in New Orleans, scalawag Charles Hays alleged that every agent of the associated press in Alabama and the South generally was a Rebel and a Democrat, and the southern Republican convention of 1874 denounced the news-gathering organization, but little could be done to eliminate the problem. Early in the period, some northern Republican journals warned their readers of the probable exaggeration of telegraphic news reports from the South, but soon they too accepted the associated press version of southern events—or so it seemed to southern Republicans. The actual role of the associated press in forming the opprobrious northern image of southern Republicanism

12.   Lionel A. Sheldon to Henry Clay Warmoth, October 26, 1865, in Henry Clay Warmoth Papers, Southern Historical Collection, University of North Carolina, Chapel Hill (hereinafter cited as SHC); Testimonies of Lewis McKenzie, January 31, 1866, and John Francis Lewis, February 7, 1866, in U.S. Congress, *Report of the Joint Committee on Reconstruction, at the First Session, Thirty-ninth Congress* (Washington, D.C.: Government Printing Office, 1866), Pt. II, 11, 69, 73; Thomas J. Durant to Warmoth, February 12, 1866, in Warmoth Papers.

remains a matter of conjecture. But once it was established, the southern wing had no real means of overcoming it.[13]

The origins of the imagery lay, of course, with southern conservatives. All it really took was the participation of former slaves in politics to trigger a torrent of malediction on anyone associated with them. The negative caricatures of Republicans emerged full-blown during the registration of black voters and the 1867 campaigns to select delegates to the constitutional conventions—before Republicans had a chance to perform in office at any level. Conservatives were particularly hard on those who had been active as Freedmen's Bureau agents or in such party auxiliaries as the Union League or Lincoln Brotherhood in promoting black political activity. Florida Democrats, for example, happily perpetuated rumors that bureau agents Charles Hamilton and William Purman had "agitated" among the freedmen and "charged them $1 or $1.50" each for renegotiating their contracts with planters. An Alabama conservative testified to rumors that Benjamin Norris had been "distracting the negroes with false ideas" by selling them a "little striped stick for four or five dollars" and telling each "that he had nothing to do but go and stick that down somewhere in the forty acres he wanted and that would be *bona fide* title to the land." In these and similar cases, the conservatives were clearly less concerned about the blacks' being deluded than they were about the Republicans' success in securing black votes for convention seats. On the whole, Republicans did reputable work in the conventions, but their occasional miscues and their sometimes radical articulation of party goals provided further ammunition for the conservatives.[14]

13. *Nation*, November 26, 1868, p. 429, November 12, 1868, p. 381; Simeon Corley to Charles Sumner, September 28, 1869, in Charles Sumner Papers, Houghton Library, Harvard University, Cambridge; Lionel A. Sheldon to Henry Clay Warmoth, December 12, 1869, in Warmoth Papers; George E. Spencer to National Republican Committee [1872], Lewis E. Parsons to William E. Chandler, January 29, 1873, in William E. Chandler Papers, LC; William Pitt Kellogg to Oliver P. Morton, November 12, 1873, in Oliver Perry Morton Papers, Indiana State Library, Indianapolis; New York *Times*, September 16, 1874; Washington *New National Era*, October 22, 1874.

14. Testimonies of Jos. John Williams, November 13, 1871, T. T. Long, November 13, 1871, Charles Hamilton, November 14, 1871, William Purman, November 11, 1871, and Daniel Taylor, October 20, 1871, in *Condition of Affairs in the Late Insurrectionary States*, XIII, 231–32, 205, 215, 281–91, 144–56, IX, 1130–34; Hume, "'Black and Tan' Conventions," *passim*.

After the conventions and once the Republicans entered political offices across the South, charges of Republican fraud and corruption became the central feature of their opponents' campaigns. The most common allegations were abuse of the electoral process through bribery, trickery, and occasionally intimidation, misuse of the patronage power, and involvement in various and sundry "rings" and "deals" to influence legislation for personal gain. All of the Republican wrongdoing at the state level, alleged and otherwise, was part of the burden Republican congressmen carried to Washington, but some had made their own contributions to the disreputable party image. Charges of buying a senatorship were perhaps best documented against carpetbagger John J. Patterson, who earned the sobriquet "Honest John" after handing out sizable sums to members of the South Carolina legislature to insure his election in 1872. Patterson, reared under the political tutelage of Simon Cameron in Pennsylvania, had already established a reputation in his new state as a manipulator of railroad lands and bonds. In the opinion of a former Republican associate, Abijah Gilbert of Florida was "a nice man" with money who "likes office," and his detractors rumored that his liberal contributions to the campaigns of Republican legislators in 1868 had helped secure his Senate seat. Similar charges, somewhat less substantiated, plagued carpetbaggers George E. Spencer of Alabama and Powell Clayton of Arkansas and were freely extended by conservatives to others. The *Arkansas Gazette*, for example, periodically reinforced the "generally believed fact" that carpetbagger Stephen Dorsey "bought his way to the United States Senate," but the charges were never documented. Like the others, Dorsey was hardly reproachless, but his more questionable political activity occurred after Reconstruction and in areas other than Arkansas.[15]

Another handful incurred public censure. Two, carpetbaggers John T. Deweese of North Carolina and Benjamin F. Whittemore of

15. Hood, "Southern Reconstruction Congressmen," 150–63, 352–56; South Carolina General Assembly, *Report of the Joint Investigating Committee on Public Frauds and the Election of Hon. John J. Patterson to the United States Senate* (Columbia, S.C.: Calvo & Patton, 1878); Francis Butler Simkins and Robert H. Woody, *South Carolina During Reconstruction* (Chapel Hill: University of North Carolina Press, 1932), 119–20, 136–37; Charleston *Daily News*, January 1, 1873; Columbia *Daily Union*, November 13, 1872; Testimony of C. B. Wilder, November 14, 1871, in *Condition of Affairs in the Late Insurrectionary States*, XIII, 244, 254; Sarah Van V.

South Carolina, resigned from the House in 1870 shortly before they were to be expelled for selling cadetships to the military and naval academies. Of the two, the well-traveled Deweese appears to have been the less reputable. He stayed in the army until August, 1867, when, as he informed Elihu B. Washburne, "I strayed down here and was appointed Register in Bankruptcy by Judge Chase and to use one of our Western *Phrases* am making it *pay.*" He quickly became active in the Republican cause and was elected to the Fortieth and Forty-first Houses. He admitted having accepted an unsolicited five hundred dollars for a naval academy appointment, but he denied knowing at the time that he "was violating any of the privileges or rules of the House." He returned the money and resigned before the House unanimously passed a resolution of censure. Whittemore, an agent of the Freedmen's Bureau and the American Missionary Association and founder of the *New Era* at Darlington, freely acknowledged that he had set a price for appointments and used the money "for the relief and benefit of the people of my district" and for political purposes. He denied having done anything wrong and retained Benjamin Butler as his legal counsel. Butler promptly charged that the Methodist Episcopal minister was being made a "scapegoat for the sins of the rest of Congress," but Whittemore resigned when it became apparent that the House would expel him. He later secured reelection with over 80 percent of the vote, but the House refused to seat him.[16]

Of the scalawag congressmen, South Carolinian Christopher Columbus Bowen best resembled the stereotype. A native of Rhode Island, Bowen moved to Georgia in 1850 where he reportedly made a living as a faro dealer and gambler. He joined the Confederate army

---

Woolfolk, "George E. Spencer: A Carpetbagger in Alabama," *Alabama Review*, XIX (January, 1966), 41–52; *Senate Miscellaneous Documents*, 49th Cong., 1st Sess., No. 47, pp. 386–422, 556–78; Little Rock *Daily Arkansas Gazette*, October 21, 1874; Thomas Allen to Henry L. Dawes, January 6, 1875, in Dawes Papers; Allan Peskin, *Garfield* (Kent, Ohio: Kent State University Press, 1978), 485–88, 503–505, 579–80.

16.   John T. Deweese to Elihu B. Washburne, October 30, 1867, in Washburne Papers; *Congressional Globe*, 41st Cong., 2nd Sess., 1597, 1616–17, 1469–72, 1522–30, 1544–47; Simkins and Woody, *South Carolina During Reconstruction*, 117–18; Benjamin F. Whittemore to Charles Lanman, July 18, 20, 1868, Whittemore to Benjamin Perley Poore, December 10, 1868, in Benjamin Franklin Whittemore Papers, South Caroliniana Library, University of South Carolina, Columbia; Columbia *South Carolina Republican*, June 25, 1870.

and was later implicated in the murder of an officer, court-martialed, and jailed in Charleston. After being freed when Union forces occupied the city, he was imprisoned in 1868 for allegedly embezzling funds belonging to freedmen, acquitted in 1872 on a bigamy charge, convicted on another charge, sentenced to two years, and pardoned by President Grant. In the interim, he became embroiled in Republican infighting in Charleston and served two terms in the House. Deweese, Whittemore, and Bowen remained key figures in the politics of their states after their respective disgraces and continued to contribute to their personal notoriety and that of the Republican party.[17]

Notwithstanding evidence of wrongdoing, the southern Republican congressmen were actually little involved in major political corruption, and several were prominent in movements to clean up their party. Furthermore, their nefarious activities paled in comparison to the wholesale excesses of the Grant administration and the involvement of northern Republican congressmen in such episodes as the Credit Mobilier scandal. Even the southern conservatives participated in shady schemes both before and after redemption. With much justification, Republicans claimed that the real "corruption" in southern society was Democratic intimidation and violence. "There are evils directly traceable and chargeable to the republican party," carpetbag Senator J. Rodman West admitted in 1875. "But when I am defending my house against the assaults of my mortal enemies on the outside, I have no time to reform the abuses existing within my doors. . . . By revolt, by violence, by murder, the democrats of Louisiana propose to get their wrongs redressed. I propose to do them fair and equal justice, to condemn wrong-doing, whether outside of or within the republican party; but if there is a party of thieves, which I deny, I will uphold the party of thieves against the party of murderers." Nevertheless, the brutal reality of southern political life and the "horror stories" which floated North mattered little. The mere act of joining the Republican party was sufficient to

17. Simkins and Woody, *South Carolina During Reconstruction*, 118; A. G. Mackey and T. J. Mackey, *The Political Record of Senator F. A. Sawyer and Congressman C. C. Bowen of South Carolina* (Charleston: n.p., 1869); Testimony of James Chestnut, June 15, 1871, in *Condition of Affairs in the Late Insurrectionary States*, III, 468; New Orleans *Louisianian*, March 16, 1871.

bring down the full force of conservative ostracism, intimidation, and violence. The party label became a stigma in the South; upon assuming it, one acquired a disreputable image.[18]

Adding to the imagery and perhaps the most serious problem Republicans faced in their campaigns was one largely of their own creation—a bitter factionalism which ranged from the pettiest of personal dislikes to irreconcilable hatreds. The petty was best represented by Jacob Hale Sypher's revulsion at the personal manners of fellow carpetbagger Joseph Newsham. "Newsham is the same damn fool here that he was in LA," Sypher wrote Governor Henry Clay Warmoth from Washington. "He gets drunk, talks loud, and lies like a Turk. . . . His general deportment is bad enough, but his *stable manners* are so *damnable* that I'm ashamed to be seen in the dining hall where he is—(we board at Willards)—He talks loud enough, and in his *boastful* style, to be heard over the entire hall, he eats sliced tomatoes and even meats with his fingers, *blows his nose* on his napkin, and does other equally indecent and outrageous things at the table." Sypher had "spoken to him several times about his conduct, and I have determined if I cant keep him with in the bounds of decency, to say nothing about *propriety, to black both his eyes*, so as to keep him in his room until after the adjournment."[19]

Northerners boarding at Willard's may have been similarly offended by Newsham, but such personal distastes were not going to destroy the party. Serious policy, power, patronage, and racial divisions, however, plagued the party at various times in all of the states. The most visible split occurred between the scalawags and carpetbaggers with the blacks usually siding with the latter, but sometimes blacks opposed whites, and frequently factions emerged which took no notice of the groupings based on nativity or race. Because the congressmen were largely responsible for dispensing federal patronage, they were often the central participants in and occasionally the casualties of intraparty factionalism.

---

18. *Congressional Record*, 43rd Cong., 2nd Sess., 877. For the dimensions and causes of postwar political corruption see Morton Keller, *Affairs of State: Public Life in Late Nineteenth Century America* (Cambridge: Belknap Press of Harvard University Press, 1977), especially ch. 7.

19. Jacob H. Sypher to Henry Clay Warmoth, July 19, 1868, in Warmoth Papers.

"The real vice of the present system is the patronage of members of congress," former attorney general Amos Akerman declared in 1871. "Many of them think that their business here is not to make laws but to make appointments. They have friends to reward and enemies to punish in this way and often abuse their power." The Georgia scalawag might have had any one of a number of southern congressmen in mind, but the situation in Alabama serves as a splendid example. There a dispute over political appointments between Senators George E. Spencer and Willard Warner, both carpetbaggers, broke out into the open in 1870. As the battle lines were drawn, Spencer undertook a power play and secretly supported the Democratic candidate for governor while Warner stumped for the scalawag nominee. Spencer hoped to secure a Democratic legislature which would bypass Warner, who was up for reelection, and put a Democrat in Warner's Senate seat. The plan worked. With Warner out of the way, Spencer, as the only Republican senator, had the patronage power to wipe out Warner's supporters, and he even persuaded Grant to withdraw his nomination of Warner as collector of the Port of Mobile—a lucrative consolation prize. Warner was incensed at Spencer's "treachery" and Grant's acquiescence, but he could do nothing other than denounce Spencer to influential northern friends such as John Sherman and Rutherford B. Hayes. He actively supported Greeley against Grant in 1872 and then turned to his iron business in central Alabama. In the interim, the crafty Spencer secured reelection in 1872 and served out the decade as the chief patronage dispenser for Alabama. He made enemies right and left, particularly among the more moderate scalawags, but he was untouchable until his term ran out in 1879. While the Republicans fought among themselves, the Democrats redeemed the state in 1874.[20]

In Mississippi it was the idealistic carpetbagger Adelbert Ames who clashed with the moderate scalawag James Lusk Alcorn in a

20. Amos T. Akerman to Hon. T. A. Tucker (?), July 18, 1871, in Amos Tappan Akerman Letterbooks, 1871–1876, Alderman Library, University of Virginia, Charlottesville; Willard Warner to John Sherman, August 23, 1870, February 29, 1872, January 10, 1876, in John Sherman Papers, LC; Willard Warner to Rutherford B. Hayes, July 7, 1876, December 25, 1880, Warner to John Sherman, May 5, 1877, in Rutherford B. Hayes Papers, Rutherford B. Hayes Presidential Center, Fremont, Ohio; John Bur-

split that was more a matter of party policy toward the blacks than it was of patronage. The showdown came in 1873 when Ames and Alcorn, both senators at the time, vied for the Republican nomination for governor. Ames won and Alcorn bolted to run on a separate ticket supported by moderate Republicans and many Democrats. Ames was more successful in securing the black vote, and Alcorn, embittered at his defeat, returned to the Senate. As governor, Ames quickly encountered difficulties including continuing disputes between his supporters and those still loyal to Alcorn. To Ames, Alcorn became "a scheming tricky demagogue who has betrayed the party and has been repudiated by it." In Alcorn's opinion, "Ames has pretty well wound up the republican party in this State. . . . I am a republican now as in the past, have done all I could to save Mississippi from democratic rule, have spent six years of my life in the cause. All my labor is lost." In the interim, the Democrats conducted the "Revolution of 1875" and drove Ames from the state.[21]

In other states, motivation and factional lines frequently differed, but the destructive influence was similar. In the labyrinthine confusion which marked Louisiana politics throughout the period, carpetbaggers J. Rodman West, John S. Harris, William Pitt Kellogg, all of whom served in the Senate, Governor Henry Clay Warmoth, and several of the representatives chose sides in a series of shifting alignments. The primary split emerged between West, Warmoth, and Congressmen Jacob H. Sypher and Lionel Sheldon on the one hand and Kellogg and the customhouse faction on the other. Caught in between and exploited by both sides were the blacks, led in part by P. B. S. Pinchback. In North Carolina the splits were partially scal-

kett Ryan, Jr., "Willard Warner: Soldier, Senator, and Southern Entrepreneur" (M.A. thesis, Auburn University, 1971), 66–98; John A. Steele to Charles W. Dustan, September 25, 1876, George E. Spencer to Dustan, September 28, 1876, in Charles William Dustan Papers, Alabama Department of Archives and History, Montgomery; Wiggins, *The Scalawag in Alabama Politics*, especially 63–71, 85–86, 110–14, 119–21.

21.   William C. Harris, *The Day of the Carpetbagger: Republican Reconstruction in Mississippi* (Baton Rouge: Louisiana State University Press, 1979), 459–80; Lillian A. Pereyra, *James Lusk Alcorn: Persistent Whig* (Baton Rouge: Louisiana State University Press, 1966), 148–63, 171–77; Adelbert Ames to F. C. Harris, August 4, 1874, in Governor Adelbert Ames Letterbook D, Mississippi Department of Archives and History, Jackson; James L. Alcorn to P. B. S. Pinchback, October 29, 1875, in Hayes Papers.

awag/carpetbagger, sometimes east/west, and generally cliquish, with the radical "Wilmington ring" being the best example of the latter. Carpetbag Senator Joseph Abbott, scalawag Senator John Pool, and Representatives Oliver Dockery and Clinton Cobb played prominent roles, with scalawag Thomas Settle serving as the arbitrator who attempted to soothe the feelings of those who were "out" at any given moment.[22]

Republican factionalism in Arkansas, following familiar carpetbagger/scalawag-radical/moderate lines, culminated in the Brooks-Baxter War of 1874 between rival Republican claimants for the governorship, with the intimate involvement of carpetbag Senators Powell Clayton and Stephen Dorsey and several of the state's representatives. In Florida, the shifting split between radicals and moderates which emerged in the "Black and Tan" convention endured until redemption. In South Carolina, where black leadership emerged as a powerful force, a particularly rampant factionalism continuously racked the party with divisions both among the blacks and occasionally along racial lines. In Texas, Governor Edmund J. Davis and fellow radicals such as carpetbag Representative William T. Clark opposed Republican moderates while cantankerous scalawag Senator Morgan Calvin Hamilton alienated everyone at one time or another, including his own brother, former provisional governor Andrew Jackson Hamilton.[23]

Given the disparate interests in the Republican coalition and the explosive question of race, which Democrats wisely kept at the cen-

22. Joe Gray Taylor, *Louisiana Reconstructed, 1863–1877* (Baton Rouge: Louisiana State University Press, 1974), chs. 5–7; W. McKee Evans, *Ballots and Fence Rails: Reconstruction on the Lower Cape Fear* (Chapel Hill: University of North Carolina Press, 1966), 106–109, 154–65; Catherine Silverman, "'Of Wealth, Virtue, and Intelligence': The Redeemers and Their Triumph in Virginia and North Carolina" (Ph.D. dissertation, City University of New York, 1971), ch. 6.

23. Martha Ann Ellenburg, "Reconstruction in Arkansas" (Ph.D. dissertation, University of Missouri, 1967), ch. 8; George H. Thompson, *Arkansas and Reconstruction: The Influence of Geography, Economics, and Personality* (Port Washington, N.Y.: Kennikat Press, 1976), chs. 9–10; Jerrell H. Shofner, *Nor Is It Over Yet: Florida in the Era of Reconstruction, 1863–1877* (Gainesville: University Presses of Florida, 1974), chs. 10–19; Thomas Holt, *Black over White: Negro Political Leadership in South Carolina During Reconstruction* (Urbana: University of Illinois Press, 1977), chs. 2, 5–7, 8–9; Carl H. Moneyhon, *Republicanism in Reconstruction Texas* (Austin: University of Texas Press, 1979), chs. 5–10.

ter of politics, some Republican factionalism was inevitable, but the Southerners showed little ability to compromise and control it. Patronage, race, personality, and policy disputes strained party unity; economic questions at the state level—revenue and spending policy, debt and land management, relations with railroads and industry— only irritated the divisions. Furthermore, alignments among the congressmen and their colleagues never stabilized along radical-moderate-conservative lines, but rather constantly shifted—depending upon who had the upper hand at a given moment and what was at stake. All too often, bypassed or defeated candidates for patronage positions or elective offices simply bolted the party. Intraparty factionalism imparted a special confusion and rancor to the politics of Reconstruction and contributed significantly to the Republicans' demise. More than superficial party unity was needed to contest the Democrats at the polls.

In addition to their political problems at home, southern Republicans encountered serious difficulties from an unexpected source— their party colleagues in other parts of the nation. The relationship between northern and southern Republicans is one of the intriguing and neglected problems of Reconstruction. Given the rhetoric of northern Republicans regarding the political necessity of establishing a southern wing, their neglect of it from its inception is surprising. In their congressional campaigns, Southerners needed aid other than troops and coercive legislation, yet they seldom received the types of positive support they believed they deserved from the national party. In particular, their frequent pleas for campaign funds were either only partially fulfilled or simply ignored, and prominent northern Republicans invariably declined invitations to come South to assist and speak in behalf of party candidates.

Northern financial backing was especially critical if the party was to establish a foothold in the South. The southern Republicans' predominantly black clientele could provide votes but little in terms of contributions to party coffers. "It is really a poor party and needs outside aid," Adelbert Ames explained to an already knowing William E. Chandler in 1873. "Anything you can do for us as the representatives of the national republican party will be gratefully re-ceived."[24] The Republican congressmen themselves were among the more affluent men in the party, but their means were generally less than those of Democrats who could tap the resources of wealthy conservatives. Funds were needed to maintain a party press, print campaign literature, cover travel expenses, and throw barbecues and demonstrations. While they could do little to combat the Demo-crats' use of economic intimidation, they needed at least to attempt to counter their opponents' efforts to persuade, purchase, or other-wise secure votes. They appealed constantly to northern Republi-cans and the national campaign committees for financial assistance, but they never received as much as they considered their rightful share, and the amount dwindled as the period wore on.

The Louisianians' efforts to secure political funds early in the pe-riod are representative. Scalawag W. Jasper Blackburn went to Wash-ington early in 1867, as he told Charles Sumner, "to raise a little money" for the party. He secured promises of aid from Republican Senators James W. Grimes of Iowa, Henry Wilson of Massachusetts, and George H. Williams of Oregon, who advised him to "get some old Senators." Blackburn's success is unknown, but later that year, Henry Clay Warmoth and several of the state's future congressmen began to press northern Republicans and national party organiza-tions for support. In August, Thomas L. Tullock of the Union Re-publican Congressional Executive Committee promised to send "funds from time to time as means are furnished" to help Warmoth's forces carry the upcoming election of delegates to the constitutional convention.[25]

Meanwhile, Warmoth dispatched carpetbagger Jacob H. Sypher north on a fund-raising mission. When he arrived in Washington he found that Tullock's committee had recently received two thousand dollars. Sypher believed he could "count on half of that for LA," but Tullock had gone on to New York after sending only three hundred dollars to Warmoth. Chief Justice Salmon P. Chase, whom Sypher

24. Adelbert Ames to William E. Chandler, September 2, 1873, in Chandler Papers.
25. W. Jasper Blackburn to Charles Sumner, March 4, 1867, in Sumner Papers; Thomas L. Tullock to Henry Clay Warmoth, August 24, 1867, in Warmoth Papers.

had marked as another potential source, had also left town. Other party kingpins offered encouragement but no material aid. Senator George F. Edmunds of Vermont thought Louisiana Republicans should establish a Union League as a support group, and John Russell Young of the New York *Tribune* could only advise him that "you young fellows must control things down there." Somewhat subdued, Sypher secured letters of introduction to Sumner and informed Wilson that he was coming to Boston. Before he left Washington, he met with fellow Louisianian Thomas J. Durant, who was functioning as a lobbyist for the state. Durant recognized the necessity of Sypher's mission, but he reminded Warmoth "that the administration of party affairs and the machinery of the republican party are not in the hands of men who are radicals from conviction, or even in name, and consequently they do not see as clearly as we do the necessity of a strong effort to put the organization of the party in Louisiana and elsewhere on the basis of extreme radical principles."[26]

On his way north, Sypher visited Thaddeus Stevens and "smaller guns of the party" including William D. Kelley in Pennsylvania. By the time he arrived in New York, he had raised no more than Tullock's three hundred dollars. Horace Greeley of the *Tribune* greeted his request with the statement that "*La. don't need any assistance.*" "The truth of the matter," Sypher informed Warmoth, "is the old '*Cus*' don't know anything about affairs in the South." Sypher did secure a promise of five thousand dollars from New York Senator Edwin D. Morgan, but he found that other "prominent politicians and *heavy men* are either in Europe or at watering places spending the summer." Although Wilson recognized the "urgency and importance of the cause," he regretfully declined to extend aid. In his travels, Sypher figured that he had "influenced about $1,500. into the hands of the Congressional committee, and Louisiana should have received it." Tullock, however, sent another two hundred dollars and claimed that the fund was exhausted, and there is no evidence that Morgan's five thousand dollars ever reached Louisiana. By mid-October, after two months of work, Sypher had little to show

26. Jacob H. Sypher to Henry Clay Warmoth, August 24, 1867, Thomas J. Durant to Warmoth, September 9, 1867, in Warmoth Papers.

for his labors. He was forced to draw on Warmoth for two hundred dollars to meet his expenses and, although he had already spent more, he promised to keep his total expenses "inside $500." Disillusioned, the former Union brigadier general and future congressman returned to his plantation near New Orleans.[27]

Others duplicated the Louisianians' search for funds. Individual northern politicians undoubtedly wearied of being pressed for contributions, but even the national party committees were reluctant to share their resources or to canvass the North for funds in behalf of the South. The Southerners were clearly in a bind. Within the span of a year, they had to wage a campaign for delegates to the constitutional conventions, draft constitutions, enter into another campaign to ratify the documents, elect state officials and U.S. representatives, set up state governments, and then attempt to carry their states for Grant in November, 1868—all in the face of increasing conservative opposition. In most states the conservatives had quickly replaced their tactic of "masterly inactivity" with one which brought the forces at their command—money, economic intimidation, and physical violence—to destroy the emerging Republican party. As an observer for the national Republican committee in South Carolina put it, "Rich rebels coax with one breath and threaten with the next."[28]

Late in the summer of 1868, the national committee allowed five thousand dollars to each of six southern states and lesser amounts to the other four. With this aid and the heavy use of personal funds, Republicans prevailed in some states, but in others, they failed at some stage of the process. In Mississippi, for example, the new constitution was defeated. "The situation here seems not to be understood, or not expressed neither by the Press of the North, nor by members of Congress," a Mississippian complained to Benjamin Butler. The military had been of little help, but the central problem was "no money to spend in the election and none to be had of the National Executive Committee." In his opinion, five thou-

27. Jacob H. Sypher to Henry Clay Warmoth, September 5, 1867, Henry Wilson to Warmoth, September 20, 1867, Thomas L. Tullock to Warmoth, September 25, 1867, Tullock to Jacob H. Sypher, September 28, 1867, Sypher to Warmoth, September 30, October 9, 11, 18, 1867, Henry Wilson to Warmoth, March 17, 1868, all in Warmoth Papers.
28. John M. Morris to William Claflin, September 14, 1868, in Claflin Papers.

sand to ten thousand dollars would have given the election to the Republicans.[29]

At least some northern financial support continued through 1868—primarily, it seems, to insure the election of Grant. Outside money then dried up, leaving those states not yet readmitted in a precarious position as they still faced important elections to state and congressional offices. A typical situation existed in Texas where carpetbagger William T. Clark, a candidate for the House in 1869, sought financial support from George W. Curtis, editor of *Harper's Weekly*, and several other old New England friends. He traveled north to gain the endorsement of the National Union League of America and pressured party chairman William Claflin of Massachusetts for funds. "The duty of the National Executive Committee is now made plain," Clark declared on the eve of the election. "If the Republican Party of the North would save Texas from the impending fate of Democratic rule men and means must be sent them to meet the gigantic efforts" made by conservatives, who "have at their command all the wealth of their Rebel friends." "There is not time to be wasted," he informed Claflin. "While it is true that the colored votes rarely can be bribed, it is hard to overcome the effect of the popular demonstrations inaugurated and carried out by rebel money. If we fail, it will be because of our poverty." Clark apparently received some funds from the national party. He also used a considerable amount of his own money in the campaign, and Texas fell into Republican hands—at least for a short period.[30]

In response to requests from Adelbert Ames and John Roy Lynch, Claflin also allowed some funds for the regular Republican organization in Mississippi in 1869 which were politely acknowledged, but as even token northern financial support declined, southern pleas for assistance became more strident. Although some campaign money went south in 1872, again primarily in Grant's behalf, it was clear that Southerners could not count on significant aid from the national party. "Evidently there is a suspicion prevailing that we are

29. Leon Burr Richardson, *William Eaton Chandler, Republican* (New York: Dodd, Mead, 1940), 113–15; Harris, *Day of the Carpetbagger*, 183–98; J. Tarbell to Benjamin F. Butler, July 13, 1868, in Butler Papers.

30. William T. Clark to William Claflin, July 29, October 4, 1869, in Claflin Papers.

floating in a sea of money," an irate William Pitt Kellogg wrote Chandler in late 1873. "I assure you I look around me in vain and see no ocean of greenbacks." "All we need is more money," George E. Spencer pleaded the following year. "Help me to carry Ala & you may have a mortgage on the State." Both Kellogg and Spencer were able to touch Grenville M. Dodge and Thomas A. Scott of the Texas & Pacific Railroad for campaign funds, but others did not have such well endowed friends. Their pleas for financial aid continued to flow north, but in vain, particularly after the defeats of 1874. In the campaign of 1876, North Carolina Republicans managed to pry ten thousand dollars out of Zach Chandler, the national party chairman, but the other southern states were written off as lost causes and did not share in the eighty thousand dollars doled out to "critical" northern states. Nor apparently did they benefit from the estimated two hundred thousand dollars the national committee spent on speakers, documents, party newspapers, and other expenses.[31]

In lieu of national support, the congressmen and their colleagues resorted to other means to aid the party. While most of these were legitimate in that they were frequently used by both parties in the North as well as the South, they were also easily abused. It became common practice, for example, to assess federal and state officeholders for contributions to party coffers. "Officeholders *must* support Grant," Kellogg informed Warmoth in 1868, and as the party in Louisiana disintegrated into warring factions, it is not surprising

31.   Adelbert Ames to William Claflin, January 24, November 8, 1869, John Roy Lynch to Claflin, August 10, 1869, in Claflin Papers; Jack B. Scroggs, "Southern Reconstruction: A Radical View," *Journal of Southern History*, XXIV (1958), 423–27; George E. Spencer to Thomas Settle, October 24, 1872, in Thomas Settle Papers, SHC; William Pitt Kellogg to William E. Chandler, December 17, 1873, Chandler to Kellogg (draft), December 26, 1873, George E. Spencer to Chandler, October 15, September 17, July 21, August 23, September 7, 1874, in Chandler Papers; George E. Spencer to Grenville M. Dodge, October 23, 30, 1871, in Grenville M. Dodge Papers, Iowa State Historical Department, Des Moines; R. C. McCormick to William E. Chandler, August 27, 1876, undated note on "Expenditures for Political Purposes During Presidential Campaign of 1872 by Gen. G. M. Dodge," "Hayes-Tilden Canvass in 1876" (Typescript), W. H. H. Stowell to Chandler, October 3, 1874, Pinkney Rollins to Chandler, March 22, 1875, George E. Spencer to Chandler, July 15, 1876, all in Chandler Papers; Richardson, *William Eaton Chandler, Republican*, 152, 158–60, 182; James A. Rawley, *Edwin D. Morgan, 1811–1883: Merchant in Politics* (New York: Columbia University Press, 1956), 239–44; Keith Ian Polakoff, *The Politics of Inertia: The Election of 1876 and the End of Reconstruction* (Baton Rouge: Louisiana State University Press, 1973), 139–42.

that the contenders fought for control of the New Orleans custom-house. While customhouse employees in the semicircle of port cities were a particularly good financial source, others contributed as well, but the practice created problems in a strife-ridden party. A west Texas postal clerk, for example, chafed when Clark asked him if he "had paid a sort of black mail assessment of 5% on a years salary which had been levied by the State Central Committee." Failure to pay, he supposed, "would be cause of removal." The less scrupulous also utilized their congressional franking privilege to distribute campaign literature. Kellogg notified Warmoth in 1869 that he was sending a packet of "flyers for colored voters . . . in envelopes & *franked* for distribution." Deweese was indicted in the same year for distributing Union League materials under his congressional frank. Since the privilege was a free means of distributing literature to constituents, most southern congressmen were understandably reluctant to give it up, and several sought to have it fully reinstituted after Congress limited it in the early 1870s.[32]

Republican editors, ill-supported by subscriptions and advertising, also turned to the party for subsidies. Although the national committees often aided party newspapers in the North during campaigns, they did their best to ignore numerous pleas from "impecunious organs, especially in the South." The competition to secure state printing contracts under Republican regimes was intense, those not favored often folded, and printing interests and claims became a source of corruption in some states. The only two congressmen to suffer imprisonment for corruption, L. Cass Carpenter and Robert Smalls of South Carolina, were convicted of misusing public funds in what was clearly a politically motivated search for scapegoats after redemption—the former for making fraudulent printing claims on the state, the latter for accepting a bribe to favor a printing claim. But without some sort of external support, the party press

32.   William Pitt Kellogg to Henry Clay Warmoth, July 30, 31, 1868, in Warmoth Papers; Taylor, *Louisiana Reconstructed,* 156–240; Holt, *Black over White,* 115; Isaac H. Caldwell to Benjamin H. Bristow, September 14, 1871, in Benjamin Helm Bristow Papers, LC; Hood, "Southern Reconstruction Congressmen," 353. Regarding the franking privilege, see the comments and votes in *Congressional Globe,* 41st Cong., 2nd Sess., 4634, 4654, Appendix, 453–54; and *Congressional Record,* 43rd Cong., 1st Sess., 5091, 43rd Cong., 2nd Sess., 4654.

faced great difficulties, and its survival was critical to southern Republicanism.[33]

Many of the congressmen pumped personal funds into their campaigns and hoped that victory might bring the means to recoup their expenditures. In his statement to the congressional committee investigating the sale of cadetships, Deweese bluntly noted that he had contributed twelve thousand dollars "to control the presidential election in my state" in 1868. Whittemore spent two thousand dollars of his own money in the same campaign. He later recalled a conversation regarding the cadetships in which he was offered a five-hundred-dollar contribution to his political fund after he had explained that "the national committee has not helped us very much, or any other committee; we have had to hoe our own row and to paddle our own canoe." It is not surprising that when the party did attract men of means such as John J. Patterson or Abijah Gilbert, the common reward was political positions including nominations for House seats and consideration for the Senate. The connections between money and office became close in the Reconstruction South because Republicans never developed the capacity for generating needed funds. They were forced to rely either on a few individuals or on methods that were conducive to misuse. The image of corruption which clouded southern Republicanism was certainly due in part to their efforts to secure funds for legitimate party activities. Fuller northern financial support might have alleviated many of these difficulties.[34]

The steadfast refusal of northern Republicans to venture into the South and campaign for party candidates was also detrimental to the southern wing of the party. The national party committees com-

33. Richardson, *William Eaton Chandler, Republican*, 104; Simkins and Woody, *South Carolina During Reconstruction*, 542–43; L. Cass Carpenter to William E. Chandler, November 22, 1877, in Chandler Papers; L. Cass Carpenter to William Lloyd Garrison, June 28, 1878, in Lewis Cass Carpenter Papers, South Caroliniana Library, University of South Carolina, Columbia; New York *Tribune*, December 3, 1877; Okon Edet Uya, *From Slavery to Public Service: Robert Smalls, 1839–1915* (New York: Oxford University Press, 1971), 82–87.
34. *Congressional Globe*, 41st Cong., 2nd Sess., 1617, 1472; Benjamin F. Whittemore to William Claflin, September 7, 1868, in Claflin Papers; Benjamin F. Whittemore to William E. Chandler, September 16, 1868, in Chandler Papers.

monly asked prominent congressmen to speak in northern states, and they set up schedules and covered travel expenses for popular party speakers such as Robert Ingersoll. As their correspondence makes clear, Northerners frequently honored requests to campaign for colleagues from other states who were caught in tight races. The divisions among northern Republicans were largely forgotten during campaigns; even Benjamin Butler, whose financial doctrines alienated most of the party's leadership, asked for and received help and reciprocated when asked to aid someone else. But northern Republicans almost never honored similar requests from their southern colleagues.

In 1867, before readmission, a few prominent Northerners ventured South. Senator Oliver Morton of Indiana went to his favorite bathing place in Arkansas, Senator Henry Wilson spoke in several southern cities, and Horace Greeley proceeded as far as Richmond. They faced a few hecklers but generally created no disturbances other than among several northern Radicals who promptly blasted Wilson and Greeley for being too conciliatory to southern conservatives. The more radical William "Pig Iron" Kelley traveled to Mobile in May, 1867, and made a speech in defense of the Republicans' right to organize and campaign. He was promptly treated to a display southern Republicans would witness countless times in the next decade. His audience was largely black, but a few whites on the fringes began heckling. Kelley responded in fine stump fashion, a scuffle ensued when the chief of police attempted to arrest a heckler, shots rang out, and the crowd scurried for cover. Kelley found that he had created a small riot in which two were killed. He was quickly spirited back to the hotel and placed under military protection until he left the city.[35]

Perhaps Kelley's experience cooled any desire others had to stump the South in behalf of their party. The invitations, often in the form of pleas, were numerous. Some went to the party's executive com-

---

35. Richard H. Abbott, *Cobbler in Congress: The Life of Henry Wilson, 1812– 1875* (Lexington: University Press of Kentucky, 1972), 186–92; Michael Les Benedict, *A Compromise of Principle: Congressional Republicans and Reconstruction, 1863– 1869* (New York: W. W. Norton, 1974), 259–62; Sarah W. Wiggins, "The 'Pig Iron' Kelley Riot in Mobile, May 14, 1867," *Alabama Review,* XXIII (1970), 45–55.

mittee or the congressional campaign committees to send anyone available; others went to individual northern Republicans with
promises to cover all expenses. Some wanted only one speaker. Michael Hahn, for example, invited Elihu Washburne to New Orleans
in 1868; Lewis McKenzie tried unsuccessfully to lure President
Grant across the Potomac River to Alexandria the following year.
Others tried the tactic of inviting a group in the hope somebody
would appear. Virginia Representative Charles Porter attempted to
cover his bets by inviting Sumner, Morton, Butler, Kelley, and John
Logan to address Richmond Republicans in 1870. None appeared.
Northerners simply showed no interest in coming south. Some apparently thought that little could be accomplished from such en-
deavors. One of Butler's northern correspondents was "rather glad"
that Butler had decided against a southern trip in 1868 since he was
"satisfied from the reports from that Section, that it would do little
or no good." The potential danger also had to be considered. Grant's
announcement in early 1873 that he planned a swing through the ex-
Confederate states pleased southern Republicans, but "threatening
letters from a few cranks" apparently dissuaded him, and he never
entered the section while he was president. One Georgia Republican
warned Butler and George S. Boutwell not to come to the Georgia
State Agricultural Fair in 1869 because the "Rebel Democracy . . .
would contribute liberally to any party who would take your life."[36]

Other southern Republicans scoffed at the danger. "The Southern
Democracy dare not imperil their cause by any act of hostility to-
wards Northern political Speakers at this time, however much inclined to do so," a Georgia Republican declared in 1876. "This Section thus far since the War has been held sacred from the intrusion
of Repn Speakers from the North. . . . No Republican voices of encouragement from the North, have been heard at the South, during a
political canvass." At least one Northerner agreed that well-known
speakers "backed by the full force of the Republican Party" should

36. Michael Hahn et al., to Elihu B. Washburne, June 22, 1868, in Washburne Pa-
pers; Horace Porter to Lewis McKenzie (telegram), May 11, 1869, in Ulysses S. Grant
Papers, LC; Charles H. Porter to Charles Sumner, May 18, 1870, in Sumner Papers;
Allan Nevins, Hamilton Fish: The Inner History of the Grant Administration (New
York: Dodd, Mead, 1937), 743n.; A. W. Latham to Benjamin F. Butler, August 19, 1868,
James Fitzpatrick to Butler, September 17, 1869, in Butler Papers.

be sent south. "Of course there is some danger of assassination," he cautioned, "but with the eyes of the North upon them the danger would be lessened; and I think suitable persons could be found who would be willing to go." The Georgian advised the Republican national committee to "take this matter in hand, and come themselves, or send Speakers of National repute. . . . your best orators to discuss political questions freely, openly and boldly to the Southern people." It would be "exciting and amusing" for squads of northern speakers to make "Democratic leaders wince" and give southern Republicans "instructions in their political rights and duties of free Citizens, and encouragement to stand up like men for their rights." Only in that way, he concluded, could Republicans "be aroused to use the necessary force to remove obstructions in the way of their voting."[37]

Perhaps more than anything else, the carpetbaggers, scalawags, and blacks wanted their northern colleagues to experience southern politics firsthand. After a particularly bitter 1876 campaign swing in South Carolina with Republicans Daniel Chamberlain and Solomon Hoge and Democrats W. Gilmore Simms and George Tillman, carpetbagger L. Cass Carpenter vented his frustration in a long letter to Chandler. During one meeting in Barnwell County, a Republican stronghold, Carpenter detailed how six hundred mounted and armed conservatives joined the predominantly Republican gathering. The Rebels threatened the Republican speakers with their pistols, cursed Chamberlain as a "G-d D--n Son of a b-tch," and issued Rebel yells as Simms engaged in "a violent and abusive tirade against 'Carpet Baggers'" and Tillman "boldly and openly advocated" assassinating the Republicans on the spot. "Must we be subjected to these continued insults, this abuse and degradation in order that our republican friends of the north may be able to hold us up to scorn and [dereliction?]?" he asked. "The republicans of this state, I care not what is said of them outside, do not compare unfavorably in character, ability, integrity, and honesty with the republicans of Ohio, of N.Y. of

37. V. Spalding to William E. Chandler, June 26, 1876, in Chandler Papers; Jasper W. Johnson to James M. Comly, June 30, 1876, in James M. Comly Papers, Rutherford B. Hayes Presidential Center, Fremont, Ohio (original in Ohio State Historical Society Library, Columbus).

New Hampshire, or any other northern state." "We cannot continue," he concluded, "unless the republican party of the north will stand by us, and in such a way as will be of some avail to us. . . . Why can't [the] Nat'l committee send down speakers from the north to accompany our speakers & see for themselves?"[38]

"Can any one answer the political conundrum why it is that republican speakers will eloquently vibrate from Maine to Indiana and from New Hampshire to Maryland, and yet never put a foot across the Potomac River to help us in the Southern States fight the same great battles for principle and country?" Florida carpetbagger William Purman asked a packed House during the electoral crisis of 1877. "Can any one explain to the satisfaction of a southern republican why money was collected from office-holders in the South and then not one dollar was contributed by any of our national committees for campaign purposes in Florida?" Even popular northern speakers avoided the South. Former vice-president Schuyler Colfax, for example, lectured throughout the North on such topics as "Abraham Lincoln" and "Across the Continent," but he did not venture into the South. "Naturally, it would not be much desired in the South," he explained in 1876. "They don't patronize lectures of any kind in that region as we do North." Other than a few such as Morton and James G. Blaine, who periodically ventured into "wilds of Arkansas" to indulge in the hot springs, or Kelley, who boldly regaled Atlantans with good effect on financial questions in 1875, northern congressmen went south only as members of committees to collect testimony on reconstruction "problems" as in the Klan investigations of 1870 and the Louisiana dispute of 1874, or, as was the case after the campaign of 1876, to "save" the election of a Republican president. These were hardly favorable circumstances for establishing a working relationship with Republicans in the South.[39]

The situation did not change with the inauguration of Rutherford

38.   L. Cass Carpenter to William E. Chandler, August 26, 1876, in Chandler Papers.
39.   *Congressional Record*, 44th Cong., 2nd Sess., 1535–36; Schuyler Colfax to Elbridge G. Spaulding, July 17, 1876, in Schuyler Colfax Papers, Indiana State Library, Indianapolis; Oliver Morton to Henry Wilson, August 23, 1874, in Morton Papers; James G. Blaine to his wife, December 30, 1877, in James G. Blaine Papers, LC; H. V. M. Miller to Thomas F. Bayard, October 26, 1875, in Thomas F. Bayard Papers, LC.

B. Hayes and the advent of different strategies to maintain a southern branch of the party. When Hayes toured the section in the fall of 1877, he shared the platform not with southern Republicans, but rather with Democratic Governor Wade Hampton of South Carolina, and no effort was made to assist the fragments of the southern wing in the interim elections of 1878. Shortly after James Garfield's election in 1880, his longtime friend and advisor Burke Hinsdale again suggested that surviving southern Republicans must be helped with money and speakers. "On these points there has been surprising indifference on the part of Northern Republicans. Not a speech was made in a Southern State in the late canvass by the immediate direction of the National Committee, so far as I have ever learned. The fact is, multitudes of Republicans, including many leaders are well content to have the South 'Solid,' since it gives them a chance to scare (or try to scare) the people North about 'another war' or some other impossible thing."[40]

The Northerners' "surprising indifference" toward their southern colleagues which Hinsdale discovered in 1880 had been present since readmission. Northern and southern Republicans simply had little intercourse with each other outside Congress. Northerners seemed oblivious to the necessity for funds to launch and maintain a party in the ex-Confederate states, and they never recognized the benefits that both branches of the party might have derived from their participation in southern campaigns. Indeed, they had an obligation to extend aid if they sincerely expected to establish a viable southern wing.

By comparison, southern Democrats faced few external or internal problems in their campaigns for Congress. Although they periodically complained about the failure of the national Democratic organizations to send campaign funds and speakers, they were largely self-sufficient and had no real need for outside aid. When the national Democratic party endorsed Horace Greeley in 1872, conserva-

---

40. Vincent P. De Santis, *Republicans Face the Southern Question: The New Departure Years, 1877–1897* (Baltimore: Johns Hopkins Press, 1959), 86–87; Burke A. Hinsdale to James A. Garfield, December 21, 1880, Garfield to Hinsdale, December 30, 1880, Albion Tourgee to Garfield, December 14, 1880, in James A. Garfield Papers, LC.

tives faced the alternative of either supporting and campaigning on the Liberal Republican ticket or staying home on election day. Most of the Democratic congressmen supported the ticket as the lesser of two evils, but their response was half-hearted, and some simply could not swallow Greeley.[41] The 1872 division healed quickly, however, and the stigma attached to the few who enthusiastically supported Greeley was not lasting. The split temporarily set back the tide of redemption, but in the long run the Grant-Greeley schism hurt the Republicans more by widening the breach between the carpetbagger and scalawag factions. Many of the southern Republicans, primarily native, who joined conservatives to support the Greeley ticket found that the experience eased their way into the Democratic party.

Most rifts in the party were relatively minor. Former Whigs such as Benjamin Hill and E. John Ellis occasionally belittled their new political home, and some of the dedicated ex-Confederates distrusted the ex-Whigs and unionists and "new departure" advocates. But these misgivings seldom surfaced into public view. Attitudes toward states' rights and issues involving greater federal participation in the economy caused some division of opinion, but it never took a serious form. Similarly, specie-minded conservatives tolerated such soft-money advocates as John Brown Gordon as long as they walked the straight and narrow line on Democratic and white solidarity.

More bothersome to dyed-in-the-wool Democrats were party colleagues who had willingly accepted Republican support at some time during Reconstruction. The most notable casualty of this transgression was North Carolina Senator Augustus S. Merrimon, who in 1872 had accepted seventy-two Republican and fifteen Conservative votes in the legislature to defeat the prominent Zebulon Vance, who was backed by eighty Conservatives. The blacks in the

41. Polakoff, *Politics of Inertia,* 177; George C. Rable, "Southern Interests and the Election of 1876: A Reappraisal," *Civil War History,* XXVI (1980), 354; Alexander H. Stephens to Edward Alexander Porter, July 13, 1872, in Edward Alexander Porter Papers, SHC; Wade Hampton to Jno. Mullaby, May 19, 1872, in Wade Hampton III Papers, South Caroliniana Library, University of South Carolina, Columbia; John Brown Gordon to Samuel L. M. Barlow, August 22, 1872, in Samuel L. M. Barlow Papers, Huntington Library, San Marino, California; William Gillette, *Retreat from Reconstruction, 1869–1879* (Baton Rouge: Louisiana State University Press, 1979), 58–72.

legislature expressed their approval of Merrimon, and Republicans hoped to win him over. One party regular figured it was only a matter of time before Merrimon "will be in full accord with the Republican Party. He can never ignore the solid vote of the party which placed him in his present position." Merrimon remained a Democrat, and over the course of his six-year term, he won bipartisan plaudits in both North and South. But Vance and his supporters did not forget that Merrimon "stole the senatorship" with Republican support. They acknowledged that he was "very generally regarded as a man of labor and ability," but "there was no escape from the consequences of his action in accepting an election at the hands of the Republican party." Democratic Representative Alfred Scales advised Merrimon to "settle down" and give up his position "as a matter of sheer justice" to Vance. The stigma of Republican support was decisive, and in 1878 the Democratic legislature put Vance in Merrimon's Senate seat.[42]

Of greater concern was "Independentism," which first reared its head in the person of William H. Felton of Georgia. Felton, a former Whig, had favored secession and joined the Democrats, but during the 1870s he became something of an agrarian insurgent. With Republican help, he won election to the Forty-fourth House by defeating the regular Democratic candidate. Felton actually posed little threat. He continued to consider himself a Democrat, as he made clear to an inquiring Rutherford B. Hayes in 1877, and he usually voted with the Democrats, who did not challenge his reelection in 1876. They did challenge him, unsuccessfully, in 1878 when the movement appeared threatening to the Democratic establishment. John Brown Gordon, for example, implored L. Q. C. Lamar of Mississippi to come and "help us kill Independentism which is uniting with the worst elements of the Rad. party & threatening us with the loss of our state." Gordon's panic was largely unfounded. Only Felton and one other Independent Democrat won elections, and in

42. *DAB*, XII, 569–70; Hampton *Southern Workman*, January, 1873; A. S. Merrimon to W. S. Tate, undated, W. S. Tate to Thomas Settle, July 22, 1873, in Settle Papers; John B. Hufer (?) to Zebulon B. Vance, May 17, 1878, Walter L. Steele to Vance, May 21, 1878, in Zebulon Baird Vance Papers, North Carolina State Archives, Raleigh; Augustus S. Merrimon to Samuel A. Ashe, April 6, 23, 25, 27, 29, May 29, June 3, 1878, in Samuel A'Court Ashe Papers, North Carolina State Archives, Raleigh.

1880, Felton wrote John Sherman that his "bitter foes," including Gordon, Alfred H. Colquitt, and Joseph E. Brown, had defeated his bid for reelection "by the usual Southern method. Fraud, intimidation, bribery—State money—convict rings—ku-klux politicians— were all used with good effect."[43]

With the exception of some concern with the Greenbacker challenges in Alabama, Texas, and certain areas of other states, and the far more serious threat posed by the Virginia Readjusters late in the decade, the Democrats were seldom troubled by intraparty divisions. While they differed on methods of redemption and in their attitudes toward black participation in politics, the common bond against carpetbaggers, scalawags, and "Negro domination" was more than sufficient to assure party unity and guarantee success. They shrewdly kept their campaigns focused on the racial issue and Republican misdeeds, avoided potentially divisive issues, and waited for the inevitable waning of northern support for the great experiment. They needed only to rationalize that the evils of reconstruction justified the extreme means they used to overthrow it. At this too, they proved quite skillful.

Over the course of the six congresses, Democrats and Republicans faced one another in 51 elections to the Senate and in 344 elections to the House. Although most aspirants for the twenty Senate seats campaigned statewide, their primary battleground was the state legislature, where they had to secure a majority in both houses. Candidates for the House, of course, had to win a plurality in their congressional district. Under the apportionment of 1860, valid through the Forty-second Congress, the South was allotted 50 seats in a House of 243 members; the reapportionment based on the 1870 census increased southern seats to 63 and the total number of representatives to 293.

The addition of the Republican freedmen to the electorate made

43. *DAB*, VI, 319; Felton to Andrew Johnson, July 25, 1865, in Amnesty Papers, Georgia; John E. Talmadge, *Rebecca Latimer Felton: Nine Stormy Decades* (Athens: University of Georgia Press, 1960), 32–45, chs. 7–8; William H. Felton to Rutherford B. Hayes, April 2, 1877, in Hayes Papers; John Brown Gordon to L. Q. C. Lamar, October 7, 1878, in L. Q. C. Lamar and Edward Mayes Papers, Mississippi Department of Archives and History, Jackson; William H. Felton to John Sherman, November 4, 1880, in Hayes Papers.

racial composition the key consideration for those charged with shaping congressional districts, and both parties showed an adeptness at gerrymandering. Mississippi serves as a splendid example of the process. As Speaker of the state house of representatives, ex-slave John Roy Lynch drafted the bill to reapportion the state from five to six districts in 1872. According to Lynch, there were two options: "One plan was so to apportion the State as to make all the districts Republican; but in doing so the majority in at least two of the districts would be quite small. The other was so to apportion the State as to make five districts safely and reliably Republican and the remaining one Democratic." After careful consideration, Lynch chose the latter plan and an examination of the black-white ratio in each district before and after his reapportionment indicates that he did his job well. But Lynch's creative restructuring did not last long. In 1876, the legislature, then in Democratic hands by virtue of the so-called "Mississippi Plan" of redemption, reapportioned the state into five safely white districts and one black district—the famous sixth "shoestring district"—which ran for nearly the full length of the state in the heavily black delta country along the Mississippi River.[44] Such gerrymandering yielded but few southern districts with an equal balance between the races. The values for percent white in each district ranged from a low of 19.8 in Mississippi's shoestring to a high of 97.2 in the northwestern fourth district of Arkansas at the 1870 apportionment (see Map 1).[45]

Not surprisingly, 92 percent of the blacks were elected from pre-

44. John R. Lynch, *The Facts of Reconstruction* (New York: Neale Publishing, 1913), 67–68; James E. Baxter, "Congressional Redistricting in Mississippi from 1817–1939" (M.A. thesis, Duke University, 1939), 81–144. The percent white in each district at each restructuring was as follows:

		Percent White				
Districts:	1	2	3	4	5	6
Before 1872	54%	53%	45%	37%	46%	—
Lynch Apportionment (1872)	71%	39%	41%	43%	44%	42%
Democratic Restructuring (1876)	54%	50%	52%	47%	50%	20%

45. Map 1 is based on U.S. Department of Agriculture, Division of Publications, Outline Maps of the United States by Counties, for June 1, 1860, June 1, 1870, and June 1, 1880; the ward maps in E. Robinson and R. H. Pidgeon (comps.), *Atlas of the City of New Orleans, Louisiana* (New York: E. Robinson, 1883), facilitated tracing the division of the only city split by congressional district lines; the sources for counties

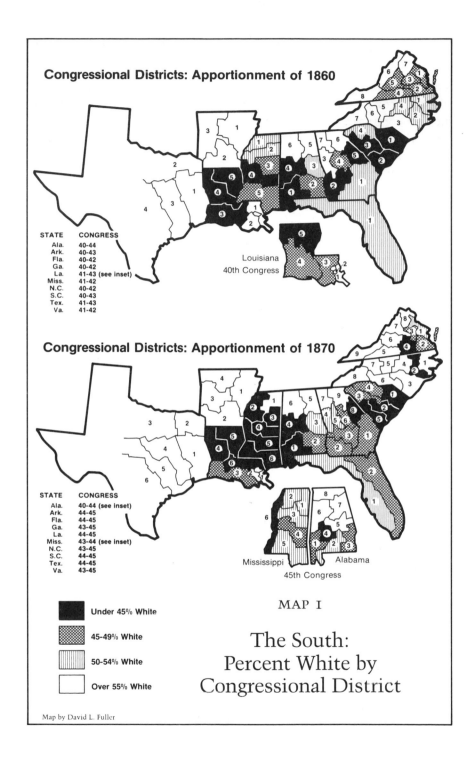

Congressional Districts: Apportionment of 1860

STATE	CONGRESS
Ala.	40-44
Ark.	40-43
Fla.	40-42
Ga.	40-42
La.	41-43 (see inset)
Miss.	41-42
N.C.	40-42
S.C.	40-43
Tex.	41-43
Va.	41-42

Louisiana
40th Congress

Congressional Districts: Apportionment of 1870

STATE	CONGRESS
Ala.	40-44 (see inset)
Ark.	44-45
Fla.	44-45
Ga.	43-45
La.	44-45
Miss.	43-44 (see inset)
N.C.	43-45
S.C.	44-45
Tex.	44-45
Va.	43-45

Mississippi   Alabama
45th Congress

Under 45% White

45-49% White

50-54% White

Over 55% White

MAP I

The South:
Percent White by
Congressional District

Map by David L. Fuller

dominantly black districts. The same type of district favored carpetbaggers (or vice versa), but the Yankee settlers also did well in urban
districts, two-thirds of which were marginally white. Interestingly,
most scalawags represented districts from 45 to 55 percent white but
particularly those that were only marginally white. The correlation
between the racial composition of a district and the political affiliation of its representative, of course, depended upon the peculiar circumstances of the contest. In the elections to the Fortieth Congress
in 1868, for example, many Republicans had only token opposition
from conservative candidates because of white apathy or a conservative boycott. Thereafter, Republican hegemony varied in duration
from district to district; seldom were all the districts of a particular
state redeemed at the same time. With the exception of the coastal
districts of South Carolina, where black leadership remained aggressive, Democrats rarely conceded a district to Republicans, and after
state redemption they seldom encountered difficulty in carrying the
heavily black districts. The Lynch reapportionment, for example,
worked as he had planned in the elections to the Forty-third House
in 1872. Two years later, however, three of the five districts so carefully designed to be "safely and reliably Republican" elected Democrats—thanks to an all-out effort to intimidate Republican voters. In
1876 the Democrats swept all the districts including the newly created and 80 percent black shoestring.

Although economic and political intimidation and general abuse
of the system limits the value of southern election returns during
the period, statistics on margin of victory do suggest some variations
between the Democrats and the factions in the Republican party. In
335 elections to the House, the distributions of margin of victory for
Democrats and carpetbaggers were about equal. But the scalawags
and, to a lesser degree, the blacks were much more likely to be involved in close contests, and the scalawags fell considerably behind
other factions in the over 20 percent and unopposed categories (see

---

in each district at each apportionment were the various editions of Benjamin Perley
Poore (comp.), *Congressional Directory;* population figures for each congressional
district were compiled from county-level statistics in Francis A. Walker (comp.), *The
Statistics of the Population of the United States . . . 1870* (Washington, D.C.: Government Printing Office, 1872).

Table 7). In elections, as in other areas, the scalawags found themselves in an uneasy position between the carpetbaggers and the Democrats. Their more frequent involvement in tight campaigns, a phenomenon applicable to scalawag losers as well as winners, resulted primarily from the fact that they tended to be nominated in closely contested districts often only marginally black or white.[46]

An abnormally large number of contested elections, vacancies, and partial terms reflected the political chaos in the South. Of the 344 elections to the House, 48 were contested—15 successfully. Most of the contests came from states where the party struggle was particularly intense, of long duration, and marred by fraud. Floridian Josiah Walls, a black, twice lost his seat by contests; Democrat Jesse Finley of the same state twice unseated his opponent. Louisiana carpetbagger Chester B. Darrall was contested three times, and four Republicans each faced two serious challenges from their Democratic opponents. Nor was it always a matter of Democrat versus Republican. Arkansas scalawag Thomas Boles, running as a Regular Republican, unseated carpetbagger John Edwards, a Liberal Republican, in the Forty-second Congress. In the same Congress, South Carolina scalawag Christopher C. Bowen contested black Robert De Large and succeeded in getting the seat declared vacant for the remainder of the Congress. In another South Carolina dispute, carpetbagger Charles W. Buttz contested scalawag E. W. M. Mackey, the Forty-fourth House declared the seat vacant, and Buttz was subsequently elected to the vacancy. And odd turnabouts occurred. After Arkansas Democrat Thomas Gunter unseated carpetbagger William Wilshire in the Forty-third House, the wily Yankee took advantage of a reapportionment that removed Gunter from his district, changed parties, and ran successfully (under the banner "Vote for Wilshire & Home Rule"!) for the following House. He thereby became the only Southerner to represent both parties in Washington during Reconstruction.[47]

46. Margin of victory was calculated from county-level election returns on machine-readable tape from the Inter-University Consortium for Political and Social Research at the University of Michigan. These are incomplete and must be supplemented with returns in newspapers and in three compilations of contested elections in *House Miscellaneous Documents*, 41st Cong., 2nd Sess., No. 152, 45th Cong., 2nd Sess., No. 52, 47th Cong., 1st Sess., No. 57.

47. Little Rock *Daily Arkansas Gazette*, November 3, 1874. The data on contests and partial terms were compiled from *Biographical Directory of the American Con-*

Table 7. Representatives' Margins of Victory, Term Lengths, and Contests by Party Faction

	Democrat (n=180)		Republican (n=164)		
			Scalawag (n=64)	Carpetbagger (n=76)	Black (n=24)
Margins of Victory:[a]					
Unknown	4		1	3	1
1–2%	16	(9%)	16 (25%)	9 (12%)	5 (21%)
3–5%	18		9	10	4
6–10%	28		10	6	2
11–20%	29		12	14	2
Over 20%	72 }	(47%)	16 }(25%)	29 }(45%)	8 }(42%)
Unopposed	12 }		— }	5 }	2 }
Lengths of Terms:					
Full Terms	139		32	30	18
Partial Terms	41	(23%)	32 (50%)	46 (61%)	6 (25%)
Average Length of Term (Months)	20.7		16.7	15.6	21.5
Contested Elections:					
Challenged Opponent's Election	13		9	15[b]	3
Seated by Contest	8		5	2	—
Had Seat Challenged	17		7	12	6
Unseated by Contest	2		1	7	3

Note: For each party or faction, n equals the number of successful elections or terms.
[a]Margin of victory is defined as the difference between the percentages of total vote won by the top two candidates in each contest.
[b]Three additional carpetbaggers were involved in contests; each succeeded in getting the seat declared vacant, and each was subsequently elected to the vacancy.

Regardless of which party controlled the House, the Democrats and scalawags generally fared better in contests than did the carpetbaggers and blacks. The Democrats won eight of thirteen challenges, the carpetbaggers only two of fifteen. Democrats were unseated in only two of seventeen challenges, the carpetbaggers lost their seats in seven of twelve challenges (see Table 7). But the hour of glory for some successful contestants was brief. Silas Niblack of Florida served but thirty-three days after unseating Josiah Walls in 1873; his fellow Democrat Jesse Finley had only eleven days to serve after successfully contesting carpetbagger Horatio Bisbee, Jr., in 1879. On the final day of the Forty-third Congress, former Union general George A. Sheridan won his celebrated contest with P. B. S. Pinchback and received, as one editor put it, "15 hours honor and several thousand dollars backpay." Not to be accused of partisanship, the Republican House minutes later declared that Democrat Effingham Lawrence, also of Louisiana, had unseated carpetbagger Jacob Sypher.[48]

The press commonly speculated that the prospects of financial gain figured in many contests. In his commentary on one such dispute, the editor of the Atlanta *Constitution* denounced the Republican contestant, charging that the "Radical congress will pay him for his trouble, and that is all he is working for." But it was not only "unscrupulous" Republicans who took advantage of the situation. After South Carolina Democrat John S. Richardson tried to unseat Joseph Rainey in the Forty-fifth Congress, Richardson's attorney in the contest informed him that "as Uncle Sam has a very plethoric pocket, I have taken the liberty of changing my account to what I think the services were really worth." "Of course," Livingston added, "if you should have to pay it, I will request only the original amount charged."[49]

---

gress; *House Miscellaneous Documents*, 41st Cong., 2nd Sess., No. 152, 45th Cong., 2nd Sess., No. 52, 47th Cong., 1st Sess., No. 57; and the original *House Reports* and *Documents* on the individual cases.

48. New Orleans *Republican*, March 5, 1875.

49. Atlanta *Constitution*, January 7, 12, 1873; Richmond *Whig*, November 16, 1870, December 21, 1871; Knox Livingston to John Smyth Richardson, December 14, 1881, J. H. Innis to Richardson, December 13, 1878, Contest Receipts, June 10, July 12, 1878, Richardson to Chas. A. Buckheit, September 9, 1882, in John Smyth Richardson Papers, South Caroliniana Library, University of South Carolina, Columbia.

Deaths, resignations, and the staggered readmission of the states also contributed to the unusually high number of Southerners who served only partial terms. Ten Southerners died while in office, the House forced two to resign, and two others left to reenter state politics. Representatives from seven states, including Georgia, were sworn in over the course of a two-month period in mid-1868 and thus effectively served only in the lame-duck session of the Fortieth Congress. Georgia, denied admission to the first session of the following Congress, was not readmitted until the third session after Virginia, Mississippi, and Texas had rejoined the Union midway in the second session. In addition, late elections forced the Alabama delegation to miss the first session of the Forty-first Congress and the Texas delegation the first session of the next one.

Southern representation in the Senate suffered from the same problems. While the House seated six of Georgia's seven representatives in the Fortieth Congress, the Senate declined to seat the state's senators for over two years. Georgia Senator Dr. H. V. M. Miller served but eight days—one of the shortest Senate terms on record. Readmission problems delayed the seating of senators from Mississippi, Texas, and Virginia until midway in the Forty-first Congress, and three Southerners missed the first session of the following Congress because of contests. Scalawag James Alcorn missed the same session because he preferred to remain governor of Mississippi. Carpetbagger William Pitt Kellogg resigned in November, 1872, and the ensuing series of contests would leave that Louisiana seat vacant until Democrat James Eustis successfully claimed it five years later. Resignations and delayed seatings created additional vacancies in the Senate ranks.

Southern strength during the six Houses averaged slightly less than 80 percent—not counting vacancies because of absences and several cases of extended sickness that bordered on total incapacity. Thirty-six percent of the 344 terms were partial terms averaging only 9.9 months (of the full 24 months) in duration. Fully half the terms served by scalawags and over 60 percent of those served by carpetbaggers were partials (see Table 7). Only one of the 251, carpetbag Senator George E. Spencer of Alabama, served for the entire period from July, 1868, to March, 1879. His closest rival was Conservative John Warfield Johnston, a senator from Virginia's readmission in early 1870 until he fell victim to the Readjuster movement in 1883. Among the representatives, carpetbagger Chester B. Darrall of Louisiana and black Joseph H. Rainey of South Carolina served parts of five terms. Several others served parts of three or four terms, but the average length of service was only slightly over one full term.

With such a turnover rate, the Southerners obviously ranked near the bottom of the seniority scale. The situation was particularly disconcerting to natives who were well aware that the habit of returning men to Congress in the antebellum period had, as Representative Alfred M. Waddell put it in 1872, "contributed as much to the supremacy of the South in Govt in past years as any other cause." One thing, Waddell continued, "is very certain, viz that if the Southern people want to remain forever powerless here, just let them adopt the policy of sending new men to every Congress or two." "The fact is, the North has learned wisdom from the South," declared another Democratic representative. "Formerly, we controlled the legislation of the Country by Keeping our members in Congress for such a time of years. . . . This always gave the South the advantage in the discussion and management of the great issues between the sections." "But now," he lamented, "the thing is reversed. They retain their men, and we are constantly changing."[50] To Southerners in the 1870s, seniority and congressional leadership positions belonged to the past and a more stable future.

A wide assortment of personal and political baggage accompanied the 251 Southerners when the first of them went to Washington in 1868. They ranged across a series of spectrums in terms of personal background and motivation, political heritage and experience, and in their perceptions of the political and economic future of the South. And yet in the political arena a vehement interparty struggle submerged the diversity. Democrats experienced few problems in their campaigns, but Republicans entered the fray with a number of

---

50. Alfred Moore Waddell to Samuel A'Court Ashe, March 13, 1872, in Ashe Papers; William P. Burwell to Edmund Wilcox Hubard, August 10, 1874, in Edmund Wilcox Hubard Papers, SHC; John H. Caldwell to Robert McKee, May 15, 1874, in McKee Papers.

serious handicaps. Those who emerged from the chaotic political milieu as national representatives had no real political security and little outside support. Furthermore, they represented an intimidated, impecunious, faction-ridden party saddled with a negative image which Northerners accepted with distressing quickness. Partisan divisions continued in Washington, but there sectionalism remained an equally, if not more powerful force. Northern congressmen, especially the Republicans, tended to view their colleagues from the ex-Confederate states as Southerners first and only secondarily as fellow party members. Once in Washington, southern Republicans soon discovered that the reluctance of their northern counterparts to provide campaign aid was only a foreshadowing of further sectional difficulties in their party.

IV   In Congress: Sectionalism and the Politics of Reconstruction

The return of the South to national councils after being unrepresented for nearly a decade created a unique and difficult situation for Southerners and Northerners alike. The established northern leadership in each party suddenly had to integrate seventy new senators and representatives back into the congressional structure and deal with them as party colleagues on a day-to-day basis. Northerners now had to confront the Southerners' special legislative interests, they had to think about sharing the federal largess which had grown dramatically in recent congresses, and they had to consider the impact of these new men on the whole complex of legislation approved since the beginning of the war. The newcomers, particularly the Republicans who dominated the early delegations, naïvely assumed that Northerners would allow them a proportional share of power and give their legislative needs due consideration. They were sorely disappointed. The sectional stress of the past decade, the ongoing turmoil of reconstruction, and North-South disputes in Congress sharply limited reconciliation and the full integration of the South back into the Union.

Like the Southerners who returned in 1868, the Reconstruction congresses themselves bore little resemblance to those of the late antebellum period. The legislative branch was now Republican-dominated; the party of Lincoln controlled the House until the Forty-fourth Congress convened in late 1875 and the Senate into 1879, but the northern party underwent a transformation in the 1870s. Radicalism had started its decline by the time Southerners reappeared in Washington. Death or defeat soon removed such stout members of the Radical vanguard as Thaddeus Stevens, John Covode, George H. Williams, George W. Julian, James Ashley, and Benjamin Wade, but the change in the party was more ideological than generational.

In the transition group were some leaders with impeccable Radical credentials such as James G. Blaine of Maine, who presided over the House while it remained in Republican hands. Behind Blaine in the Republican hierarchy were the durable and influential delegations from Massachusetts led by Henry L. Dawes, Benjamin F. Butler, George F. Hoar, William B. Washburn, and the lingering Charles Sumner. At the western end of the Republican axis, Ohio added John Sherman, James Garfield, and Robert C. Schenck. Others of authority included Oliver P. Morton of Indiana, Zachariah Chandler of Michigan, William B. Allison of Iowa, William D. Kelley of Pennsylvania, and Roscoe Conkling of New York. Most of the Republican leaders had emerged during the war years, and all had participated in the formulation of reconstruction policy, but by the 1870s much of their enthusiasm for reconstruction had disappeared. As one old antislavery warrior aptly explained in 1871: "The Republican party, whose issues . . . fired men's blood, has lost the manly mettle of its early youth. Its soul is languid. Ceasing to battle for ideas, it now sits down to count figures. It does not sow new seed—it is only garnering its former harvest."[1] While some northern Republicans remained adept at waving the bloody shirt at election time, most reflected an increasing preoccupation with the new issues of the 1870s.

The northern Democracy also had a new set of leaders. The key figures included Samuel J. Randall of Pennsylvania, Michael C. Kerr and William S. Holman of Indiana, James Beck of Kentucky, Thomas F. Bayard of Delaware, Allen G. Thurman of Ohio, and Samuel S. Cox and Fernando Wood of New York. A much troubled party during the war and immediate postwar years, the Democrats had problems shaking the copperhead image which made them the target of every bloody-shirt-waving Republican. They made a surprisingly respectable showing against Grant in 1868, but failed miserably with their endorsement of Liberal Republican Horace Greeley four years later.

1. Theodore Tilton in *Golden Age*, September 9, 1871, quoted in Hans L. Trefousse, *The Radical Republicans: Lincoln's Vanguard for Racial Justice* (New York: Alfred A. Knopf, 1968), 442.

In the congressional elections of 1874, however, in the midst of Republican scandals and an economic depression, they jumped from being an obstructionist minority of under 30 percent in the House to a somewhat confused majority of over 60 percent. After having played the minority role since before the Civil War, they were more than a little unsure how to handle their sudden status as a majority party, but they maintained control of the House for the remainder of the decade with Kerr and then Randall as Speakers. They also steadily gained Senate seats and finally achieved a majority in 1879—thanks to a nearly solid Democratic South.

Historians have given but scant attention to the relationships which developed between Northerners and Southerners in the postwar congresses. The chaotic political conditions in the South and a high turnover rate, of course, limited the Southerners' chances to gain the seniority and respect necessary to attain leadership positions. But it was equally apparent that Northerners, particularly the Republicans, were not about to let senators and representatives from the ex-Confederate states crack the power structure. A perceptive North Carolina Republican struck close to the truth when he concluded in 1871 that "the great body of Northern Republicans, controlled by the Grant Army, hate the Southern Democrats and distrust the Southern Republicans."[2] That Northerners, even the Democrats, would be leery of the largely ex-Confederate southern Democrats is not particularly surprising, but the Republicans in the southern delegations did not anticipate similar treatment from their northern party colleagues.

Committee assignments and patronage policy, two important matters anterior to substantive legislative business, offer revealing indications of the repute in which Northerners held their southern counterparts. In December, 1869, the Southerners admitted to the Fortieth House were placed at the tail end of minor committees with the exception of carpetbagger Francis Kellogg of Alabama, formerly a representative from Michigan, who gained a seat on the important Commerce Committee. Only three months remained in the Con-

2. William W. Holden to Joseph W. Holden, August 16, 1871, in William Woods Holden Papers, Perkins Library, Duke University, Durham, N.C.

gress and most southern Republicans, including Kellogg, were already lame ducks. Committee assignments thus mattered little although the northern Republican leadership might have placed some of their returning southern colleagues on major committees so that they could advance as they accumulated seniority.[3]

The late readmission of Texas, Mississippi, Virginia, and Georgia and the delayed seating of most of the Louisiana and South Carolina delegations complicated committee assignments in the Forty-first House. Southerners were initially denied seats on the powerful standing committees such as Ways and Means, Appropriations, Commerce, Judiciary, Foreign Affairs, and even Agriculture. Scalawag Israel G. Lash, the wealthy North Carolina national banker, managed a seat on Banking and Currency, probably through the good graces of committee head James Garfield, who favored the national banking system. Another southern Republican secured a place on the Committee on the Pacific Railroad and two partial termers were added later to both the Pacific Railroad and Commerce. The other seats were minor and Southerners headed only three committees. Coinage, Weights, and Measures went to North Carolina carpetbagger David Heaton, a former treasury agent whose political friends included Senator John Sherman and Chief Justice Salmon P. Chase, and Revolutionary Pensions, a dumping ground for lesser lights in the party, went to John Deweese, another North Carolina carpetbagger. Neither Heaton nor Deweese would last out the Congress, since the former died in 1870 and the House forced the latter to resign early in the same year. The third committee, Freedmen's Affairs, went to still another North Carolinian, scalawag Oliver H. Dockery. Northern Republicans apparently considered Freedmen's Affairs the special bailiwick of Southerners. Six, including two Democrats, served on it during the Forty-first House, and they would dominate it until it was discontinued in 1875.

In the next two Houses, the South, now at full strength, might have expected more, but they received little. Speaker Blaine excluded them from Ways and Means, Appropriations, Judiciary, and Foreign Affairs in the Forty-second House. Carpetbagger Lionel A.

---

3. The following discussion of committee appointments is based on the lists in the *Congressional Globe* and *Congressional Record* at the beginning of each Congress and the numerous changes and additions made during each session.

Sheldon of Louisiana managed a seat on Commerce and the chairmanship of Militia—undoubtedly with the help of Garfield, his comrade from the Forty-second Ohio Regiment. Southerners had only one seat on Banking and Currency (that went to a hard-money Democrat from Alabama) and two on the Pacific Railroad. They chaired seven committees—all minor with the exception of the medium-level Committee on Education and Labor, which was headed by Mississippi carpetbagger Legrand W. Perce, a veteran of the educational section of the Freedmen's Bureau. The new committee on the Mississippi Levees, which almost had to be chaired by a Southerner, went to carpetbagger Frank Morey of Louisiana. The Forty-third House, the last of the decade to be organized by the Republicans and the last in which a substantial number of southern Republicans served, brought more disappointment. Sheldon received a seat on Ways and Means, and Southerners again headed several second-level committees. North Carolina scalawag Clinton L. Cobb continued to chair Freedmen's Affairs, Alabama scalawag Charles Hays headed Agriculture, and Mississippi carpetbagger George McKee chaired Territories. The others were minor. Southerners managed only one seat on the Pacific Railroad and one on Banking and Currency, and they placed two Democrats on Commerce and one on Appropriations.

In short, southern Republicans never cracked any of the powerful House committees and had reason to complain of shabby treatment. They could not have expected to dominate Ways and Means, Appropriations, Commerce, Banking and Currency, or the Pacific Railroad (all important for economic legislation), or Judiciary or Foreign Affairs, but some of the more promising Southerners at least might have been placed on them and given the chance to advance. Sheldon, who through Garfield's influence served both on Ways and Means and on Commerce, was the only southern Republican ever seated on either of these committees. Otherwise, Southerners usually managed one seat on Banking and Currency and one on the Pacific Railroad, but they were excluded from the other major committees.

Southern Democrats, many of them freshmen, received far better treatment when their party organized the Forty-fourth and Forty-fifth Houses. They complained constantly about how Speakers Kerr and Randall handled committee assignments, but they headed ten committees under Kerr and fourteen under Randall, and many were major committees. Over the course of those two congresses, southern Democrats chaired Commerce, the Pacific Railroad, Mississippi Levees, Railways and Canals, Agriculture, Education and Labor, Indian Affairs, and Coinage, Weights, and Measures, as well as a number of lower-ranking committees. In addition, they placed three of their number on Ways and Means under Kerr and four under Randall.

Southern Republicans fared somewhat better on committee assignments in the Senate. Although they were totally excluded from Foreign Affairs and only briefly represented on the Judiciary Committee, they did secure a proportional share of the seats on several important economic committees. Beginning with the Forty-first Senate in 1869, they maintained at least two seats on Appropriations, Commerce, and Railroads. Louisiana carpetbagger Joseph Rodman West chaired the latter in the Forty-fourth Senate, but otherwise Southerners headed none of the major committees. Alabama carpetbagger George E. Spencer should have moved into the chairmanship of Commerce in 1875 when the Michigan legislature declined to return Zachariah Chandler, but Roscoe Conkling of New York moved ahead of Spencer and headed Commerce for the last half of the decade. Spencer had always ranked Conkling on the committee so the switch was unusual since he was given nothing of comparable stature. The exact reasons for denying him the position are unknown, but the implication is that the Republican leadership simply did not want a carpetbagger heading the committee which framed the important rivers and harbors appropriations bills. Willard Warner, another Alabama carpetbagger and an old friend of committee head John Sherman, represented the South on the prestigious Finance Committee early in the decade. When Warner was not re-elected, thanks to the manipulations of Spencer, the seat went to carpetbagger Adelbert Ames of Mississippi, but Ames resigned in 1874, and the South did not have a seat on the committee for the remainder of the 1870s.

Most of the Senate committees Southerners chaired were lower level. As was the case in the House, someone from Louisiana or Mississippi almost had to head the new Select Committee on the Levees of the Mississippi River established at the insistence of the southern Republicans. During the five congresses, it was chaired consecutively by William Pitt Kellogg, James L. Alcorn, and Blanche K. Bruce—the latter being the only black to head a congressional committee during Reconstruction. For some reason, Southerners were also allowed to chair and dominate the medium-level committee on Education and Labor. And for what little it was worth, they controlled such minor committees as those on the District of Columbia and Revolutionary Claims—pallid duty to be sure. In the Forty-third Senate, for example, John Francis Lewis of Virginia chaired and Southerners were given five of the six seats on the District of Columbia and four of five on Revolutionary Claims. The relative importance of the latter committee was made evident when the Republican majority allowed Conservative John Warfield Johnston of Virginia to head it in the Forty-fifth Senate.

In contrast, when the Democrats organized the Forty-sixth Senate in 1879, Southerners headed twelve committees including Commerce, Agriculture, Railroads, Territories, and the newly constituted Committee on the Improvement of the Mississippi River and Its Tributaries. They also secured the second positions on Commerce, Appropriations, Railroads, Foreign Relations, Territories, and Privileges and Elections, and a third seat on Commerce, Foreign Relations, and Privileges and Elections. Thus in one Congress southern Democrats received more power on the major committees than their opponents had in the previous six senates combined.

The southern Republicans' failure to secure a proportional share of power in the congressional committee structure was only partially a function of tenure and numbers. The seniority problem hurt them to a greater extent in the House, and the Democratic takeover in 1875 curtailed their opportunities to chair committees. But even those who served three or more consecutive terms never received the recognition they deserved. Openings on the powerful committees invariably went to Northerners or Westerners—many of whom were either freshmen or had less seniority than Southerners. Their treatment at the hands of their northern leadership becomes particularly damning when compared to the way northern Democrats favored their southern counterparts. That the carpetbaggers, scalawags, and blacks were allowed to populate and occasionally chair low-ranking committees was little solace.

Patronage disputes further irritated the already uneasy relationship between northern and southern Republicans on Capitol Hill. Before readmission, federal patronage positions in the South were at the disposal of northern congressmen and the president. Several of the carpetbaggers and scalawags who later served in Congress, in fact, were indebted to northern politicians for appointments as treasury agents, tax commissioners, internal revenue assessors, judges, customhouse employees, and the like. After readmission southern congressmen slowly gained control of most federal appointments in their section from outsiders who surrendered that power only reluctantly. Although the unseemly scramble for positions led to backbiting, intraparty free-for-alls which became the bane of Republicanism in several states, federal patronage positions were particularly critical to the impecunious southern wing.

Still, southern Republicans never shared fully in the immense patronage at the disposal of Grant, the attorney general, the postmaster general, and the secretaries of the treasury, state, and interior. When Southerners argued that the executive patronage ought to be divided equally among the states, their northern colleagues responded that the best men, regardless of geographical location, should be sought for such positions. To Southerners, this was nothing more than a convenient rationale to deny their section a fair share and one certainly not followed in other regions. Another excuse, understandably not widely circulated, was that southern congressmen should not expect to share fully in executive branch patronage because they did not represent a large number of white voters. To the embarrassment and denials of northern Republicans, scalawag Frederick Sawyer raised this point in the Senate in 1870. The administration and Congress, the South Carolinian maintained, had told southern Republicans that "the charges the late rebels make against you are true; you represent nobody; you must be expected to be ignored in the disposal of the executive." Within the last twenty-four hours, "someone in high position" had reminded Sawyer "that the white [Republican] vote of the South was a very small affair." Sawyer, a moderate and one of the most diligent the South sent to Congress during the decade, wondered just how the administration weighed the respective values of white and black votes, and he charged that such rabidly antireconstruction Democrats as Garrett Davis and Thomas McCreery of Kentucky had more executive patronage than southern Republicans.[4]

At the highest levels of patronage, Southerners could see no reason why they should not be considered for Supreme Court and cabinet positions. When two seats were added to the Court in 1869, they believed at least one should have gone to a southern native.[5] Several were promoted for the appointments including Mississippi scalawag James L. Alcorn, who modestly suggested himself as a candidate to Illinois Representative Elihu Washburne. Southerners went along with Grant's nomination of former secretary of war Edwin M. Stanton of Pennsylvania to the first seat, but they united to stop the nomination of Ebenezer Rockwood Hoar of Massachusetts to the second. As the current attorney general, Hoar had incurred the wrath of southern Republicans for what seemed to be decisions favorable to conservatives on the test oath and other reconstruction-related matters. "Congress must repudiate the weak, impotent, and contradictory opinions of Judge Hoar which Shelters rebels, and keeps loyalists Shivering in the cold," Representative-elect Charles H. Porter fumed in 1869. "The recent opinion of Attorney General Hoar, turns over the loyal people of Virginia, and ultimately of the whole South, to the tender mercies of blood-thirsty rebels, unless Congress repudiates it." Thanks to the fact that Hoar also had enemies among northern Republicans, Southerners were able to kill his nomination.[6]

4. *Congressional Globe*, 41st Cong., 3rd Sess., 575. One national journal estimated that there were 46,000 federal patronage positions. *Nation*, April 29, 1869, p. 325.
5. In 1866, Congress reduced the number of justices from ten to nine (there was currently one vacancy) and provided for a further reduction to seven with the next two vacancies. In part, the move was an attempt to reduce southern influence on the Court. After Grant was inaugurated, Congress raised the number of justices to nine. In the interim, one justice had died and another planned retirement, so Grant was initially given two appointments. See Stanley I. Kutler, "Reconstruction and the Supreme Court: The Numbers Game Reconsidered," *Journal of Southern History*, XXXII (1966), 42–58.
6. James L. Alcorn to Elihu B. Washburne, January 5, 18, 1869, in Elihu B. Washburne Papers, Library of Congress (hereinafter cited as LC); Charles H. Porter to Charles Sumner, September 7, 25, 1869, in Charles Sumner Papers, Houghton Library,

In the interim, they put forth several candidates of their own and attempted to secure a bill requiring the appointee to be a resident of the southern circuit which had been vacant since the death of Justice James Wayne of Georgia in 1867. Lyman Trumbull's Judiciary Committee, however, sat on their bill, and in early 1870 Grant nominated Joseph P. Bradley, a prominent New Jersey railroad lawyer, for the position. "We were all disappointed when Bradley['s] name came in," Louisiana Senator John Harris wrote Warmoth. "I shall do all I can to have him rejected. . . . We shall have at least expected the nomination of a man that lives in the [southern] District." Two weeks later, Harris thought Bradley would be rejected and hoped "for a Southern man in his place." In the belief that the carpetbaggers and scalawags had stopped Bradley, the editor of the *South Carolina Republican* called for the nomination of a southern unionist, but he feared the continuing sectional prejudice: "Southern men cannot but feel unpleasantly that there is, even yet a lack of complete confidence in them." The Southerners voted several times to postpone or recommit the nomination to the Judiciary Committee, but northern Republicans overwhelmed them. When the Senate finally confirmed Bradley by a margin of 46–9, only Johnston, the Virginia Conservative, Robertson of South Carolina, and Warner of Alabama voted with the majority, and both Robertson and Warner had opposed him on earlier votes. The other southern Republicans either voted against him or abstained.[7]

Of seven vacancies on the Court during the 1870s, all were filled with Northerners with the exception of Hayes's appointment of John Marshall Harlan of Kentucky in 1877. The ex-Confederate states would not place a native on the Court until L. Q. C. Lamar

---

Harvard University, Cambridge; John S. Harris to Henry Clay Warmoth, January 6, 1869, in Henry Clay Warmoth Papers, Southern Historical Collection, University of North Carolina, Chapel Hill (hereinafter cited as SHC); *Senate Executive Journal*, 41st Cong., 2nd Sess., 322, 330, 357; *Nation*, January 6, 1870, pp. 5–6; Allan Nevins, *Hamilton Fish: The Inner History of the Grant Administration* (New York: Dodd, Mead, 1937), 303–307; William S. McFeely, *Grant: A Biography* (New York: W. W. Norton, 1981), 385–87.

7. John S. Harris to Henry Clay Warmoth, February 23, March 10, 1870, Lionel A. Sheldon to Warmoth, December 19, 1869, January 6, 1870, in Warmoth Papers; Columbia *South Carolina Republican*, February 12, 1870; *Senate Executive Journal*, 41st Cong., 2nd Sess., 376, 382, 401, 402; *Nation*, March 31, 1870, p. 200.

was seated in 1888. Whether a Northerner or Southerner sat on the Supreme Court perhaps mattered little, but it was of symbolic importance to southern Republicans. They justifiably believed the appointment of one of their number would demonstrate that the Republican administration and Congress had confidence in the southern wing of the party.

The Grant and Hayes administrations also bypassed southern Republicans for cabinet positions although they agitated for representation throughout the decade. "I trust we shall have a representative in the Cabinet who lives in the south, who has felt the weight of rebel vengeance and proscription and in whom we can trust," a Chattanooga Republican wrote Washburne before Grant announced his first appointments in early 1869. Southerners pushed several candidates, but the only southern Republican to sit in the cabinet during the 1870s was Amos T. Akerman of Georgia, who served briefly as attorney general from July, 1870, to January, 1872. According to Jacob D. Cox, Grant's secretary of the interior, Akerman won the position only because of a deal between Grant and southern Republicans to secure their votes for the annexation of Santo Domingo. Southerners had been pressing Grant for removal of Attorney General Hoar and they clearly wanted something in return for opposing Senator Charles Sumner, the chief opponent of annexation. Grant supposedly asked for Hoar's resignation and promised the Southerners "an Attorney-General who would give them all the patronage in their states—the Federal attorneyships and marshalships—at his disposal." If indeed a bargain had been struck, it did not include all the southern Republicans. They did support annexation, but only by a margin of 9–6 and the treaty failed, 28–28.[8]

By getting rid of Hoar, Grant not only struck a blow at Sumner, Hoar's friend, but he also forced southern Republicans to make a dif-

8. W. J. Colburn to Elihu B. Washburne, January 7, 1869, in Washburne Papers; John Pool to Thomas Settle, December 12, 1868, in Thomas Settle Papers, SHC; Tod R. Caldwell to John Pool, March 1, 1869, in John Pool Papers, Rutherford B. Hayes Presidential Center, Fremont, Ohio; Jacob Dolson Cox, "How Judge Hoar Ceased to be Attorney-General," *Atlantic Monthly,* LXXVI (1895), 162–73; David Donald, *Charles Sumner and the Rights of Man* (New York: Alfred A. Knopf, 1970), 447; Nevins, *Hamilton Fish,* 365–71; McFeely, *Grant,* 362–66; *Senate Executive Journal,* 41st Cong., 2nd Sess., 502.

ficult choice. In the long run, the Southerners were the losers. They had the unwanted option of alienating either Grant or Sumner, and it was indicative of their position vis-à-vis the administration that they would have to "deal" to gain control of patronage in their states which rightfully belonged to them in the first place. Akerman served for a year and a half, Northerners opposed him almost constantly, and Grant finally replaced him with George H. Williams of Oregon. It would seem logical for Grant and northern Republicans to have allowed their southern colleagues a voice in the cabinet. It was highly doubtful that they would have chosen a carpetbagger or black, but there were certainly a number of well qualified scalawags who might have been appointed. Yet even the natives were disregarded; much perception lies in a North Carolina representative's later observation that he "never liked Grant because he thought all native Southern men unworthy to hold any position under the Government which amounted to anything."[9]

Southern Republicans hoped for more from Hayes and flooded him with names to consider for his cabinet. Former congressman Oliver Dockery of North Carolina suggested that at least two natives, preferably ex-Whigs, ought to have cabinet positions. Thomas Settle of North Carolina and James Alcorn were among the scalawags most prominently mentioned, but some prominent carpetbaggers disliked the idea of a scalawag appointment. "Our Northern Republican friends have not heretofore and never will comprehend our Situation and they cannot help us as we would wish," George Spencer wrote fellow Senator Stephen Dorsey. "The Native Republicans of the South, or rather those who merely affiliate with our party are unfitted, as you well know, for the important work of Southern regeneration. It is a grave mistake to place them in positions of power." To carry on the work of "regeneration" (a term which had long since disappeared from the northern vocabulary), the two car-

9. McFeeley, *Grant*, 366–74; James G. Blaine to Walker Blaine, December 15, 1871, in James G. Blaine Papers, LC; William A. Smith to Thomas Settle, July 19, 1879, in Settle Papers. Settle was the most frequently mentioned candidate for the cabinet. He had been president of the Republican National Convention in 1872, and North Carolinians and others pushed him after Grant's reelection. See R. W. Douglas to Settle, January 24, February 7, 1873, J. G. Hester to Settle, January 31, 1873, Ed. P. Brooks to Settle, February 17, 1873, in Settle Papers.

petbaggers pushed Louisiana Senator J. Rodman West, who had been born in Louisiana but had spent most of his life outside the South. Dorsey noted that "the Republican Party of the South has had little or no representation in the executive departments," yet he cautioned Hayes against appointing native Republicans who had "proven untrue" to the party and were inclined to go "over to the Democracy."[10]

Hayes, of course, would have nothing to do with West or any other carpetbagger, although he apparently considered both Settle and Alcorn. But Southerners could not bring enough pressure to convince him to appoint either native. Hayes apparently thought Alcorn would lend little strength to the party in the South, and he may have agreed with fellow Ohioan Murat Halstead's reinforcement of the rumor that Settle was "believed to be Blaine's man, and that he is *wanted in the cabinet as P. M. General with a view to the manipulation of the next National Republican Convention.*"[11]

When the only Southerner in the Hayes cabinet turned out to be a Democrat, David M. Key of Tennessee, and the general thrust of his patronage policy became clear, most southern Republicans were appalled. "The President cares nothing for the endorsement of Southern Republicans, but has thrown himself bodily into the embraces of the democratic party of the south," Alcorn declared. "I would feel no more humiliated in requesting an appointment at the hands of Jeff Davis, if he were President, than I would at the hands of President Hays [sic]—[and] would have as much reason to hope in one, as in the other case." "The perfidy of the d--d Buckeye fraud!" one of Set-

10. Oliver H. Dockery to Rutherford B. Hayes, February 19, 1877, Thomas B. Keogh to Governor Edward F. Noyes, February 16, 1877, James B. Sener to Rutherford B. Hayes, February 21, 1875, Sam Bard to Ulysses S. Grant (telegram), March 4, 1877, in Rutherford B. Hayes Papers, Rutherford B. Hayes Presidential Center, Fremont, Ohio; Clinton L. Cobb to Thomas Settle, February 15, 1877, William A. Smith to Settle, February 23, 1877, in Settle Papers; Murat Halstead to Rutherford B. Hayes, March 13, 1877, in Murat Halstead Papers, Rutherford B. Hayes Presidential Center, Fremont, Ohio (originals in Cincinnati Historical Society); James Longstreet to L. Q. C. Lamar, January 3, 1877, in L. Q. C. Lamar and Edward Mayes Papers, Mississippi Department of Archives and History, Jackson; William W. Mills to John Hancock, February 26, 1877, in William Wallace Mills Papers, Barker Texas History Center, University of Texas, Austin; George E. Spencer to Stephen W. Dorsey, February 19, 1877, Stephen W. Dorsey to Rutherford B. Hayes, February 17, 1877, in Hayes Papers.

11. T. Harry Williams (ed.), *Hayes: The Diary of a President, 1875–1881* (New York: David McKay, 1964), 69, 78–79; Murat Halstead to Rutherford B. Hayes, February 24, 1877, in Halstead Papers.

tle's friends raged. "Hayes has proven himself to be a traitor to his friends . . . his name should be John=Tyler,=Millard=Filmore=Andrew=Johnson=Benedict=Arnold=Judas=Iscariot." Hayes's policy, carpetbagger Albion Tourgee explained to Garfield, "has been to regard a Republican as unworthy of preferment, unless the Democrats favored him. The result has been that galvanized Democrats have been preferred." "In fact Democrats from the South in Congress has [sic] treated Southern Republicans with more respect," a former North Carolina congressman wrote in 1879. "If we can not get better stuff in the white house & cabinet next time it would be better to take a Hell Hardened Democrat, we might at least be kicked by a gentleman."[12]

Unfortunately, the strained relationship between Southerners and members from other regions was not limited to matters of patronage and committee assignments. As the two chambers considered legislation, sectional splits widened in each party, and North-South relations frequently deteriorated into open enmity. The congressional debates and an analysis of roll call behavior during the 1870s suggest that many Northerners would have preferred the South to remain unrepresented. Still, men from the ten ex-Confederate states comprised over 20 percent of the House and over 25 percent of the Senate, and they were active. Throughout the decade the Southerners' general level of activity including absence/abstention rate, number of bills, resolutions, and petitions introduced, and number of speeches, remarks, and committee reports was comparable to that of members from other regions. In terms of bills introduced, the carpetbaggers, especially those in the Senate, tended to be the most active of any regional party group. The scalawags and Democrats were above average with the blacks submitting fewer than the average in the two chambers. As for participation in the debates, scalawags

12. James L. Alcorn to Kenneth Raynor, February 3, 1878, in Kenneth Raynor Papers, SHC; Ed. P. Brooks to Thomas Settle, March 9, 1877, in Settle Papers; Albion W. Tourgee to James A. Garfield, December 14, 1880, in James A. Garfield Papers, LC; William A. Smith to Settle, July 19, 1879, in Settle Papers. For the patronage policy of Hayes and Key, see Vincent P. De Santis, *Republicans Face the Southern Question: The New Departure Years, 1877–1897* (Baltimore: Johns Hopkins Press, 1959), 73–78.

Frederick Sawyer of South Carolina and John Pool of North Carolina, carpetbaggers Willard Warner of Alabama and Joseph Abbott
of North Carolina, and Democrats Augustus Merrimon of North
Carolina and John Brown Gordon of Georgia were among the most
active of any in the Senate. In the larger House, of course, the northern leadership of each party tended to dominate and control the debates, and Southerners, like lesser-ranking members from other regions, often had to be content with spreading their comments on the
record. Nevertheless, when they were able to achieve unity and ally
with like-minded colleagues from other regions, they constituted a
powerful voting bloc with which Northerners and Westerners had to
reckon.[13]

Two central clusters of issues occupied Congress during the decade
after readmission, and the South had an intimate interest in both.
On the one hand, the legislators continued to wrestle with the
thorny problem of reconstruction; on the other, they spent an increasing amount of time coping with a series of serious and inter-
twined economic problems. The amount of attention given to foreign affairs, civil service reform, territorial and Indian problems, and
other concerns pales by comparison. With a few notable exceptions,
the politics of reconstruction have overshadowed economic issues
in the literature dealing with the national scene in the 1870s. The
overlapping questions of reconstruction, race, and "home rule" were
undeniably important—particularly to those unredeemed sections
of the South. The final pieces of reconstruction legislation, periodic
investigations of the process in the South, contested elections, and
related matters occupied a substantial amount of congressional attention after readmission. But despite a few sharp party encounters
reminiscent of earlier years and the periodic reappearance of the
bloody shirt, reconstruction as a national issue was on the wane

13.   The number of bills, resolutions, petitions, committee reports, speeches, and
remarks were tabulated from the indexes and text of the *Congressional Globe* and
Congressional Record, 1868–1879; and the absence/abstention rates for each congressman were calculated from the House and Senate roll call records, 40th–45th
Congresses, which were collected and made available in machine-readable form by
the Inter-University Consortium for Political and Social Research at the University of
Michigan, Ann Arbor.

after 1868. Reconstruction legislation during the period consisted of the Fifteenth Amendment in 1869, which hardly satisfied surviving and "principled" Radicals; the enforcement acts, which were accompanied by some trenchant political clashes in the early 1870s; and the Civil Rights Act of 1875, a last-gasp, watered-down Republican tribute to the memory of Senator Charles Sumner.[14]

Reconstruction issues generally split the southern congressmen, like their colleagues from other regions, along party lines. The Democrats certainly could be counted on to respond as a bloc against additional reconstruction, enforcement, or civil rights legislation and for conservative claimants in contested southern elections. Early in the period Republican backing for additional reconstruction measures was strong, but there were clear signs, as early as 1869 when Congress debated the Fifteenth Amendment, of serious differences of opinion within Republican ranks and declining northern support.

Northern Republicans clung to the panacea of black suffrage, yet they could tolerate no more than a qualified statement of impartial suffrage which proved less than satisfactory for the maintenance of a southern wing of the party. Although their rhetoric was occasionally more radical than their voting behavior, most of the twenty-four carpetbaggers and eighteen scalawags newly seated in the House and Senate favored a much more positive version of the Fifteenth Amendment than was finally adopted. In the Senate, southern Re-

14.   The congressional debates and divisions on reconstruction issues have received considerable scholarly attention. In addition to the biographies of southern congressmen, particularly the blacks, and the numerous specialized works cited below, of particular importance are the broader recent studies such as William Gillette's fine *Retreat from Reconstruction, 1869–1879* (Baton Rouge: Louisiana State University Press, 1979); John Kent Folmar, "The Depletion of Republican Congressional Support for Enforcement of Reconstruction Measures: A Roll-Call Analysis, 1871–1877" (Ph.D. dissertation, University of Alabama, 1968); Philip J. Avillo, Jr., "Slave State Republicans in Congress, 1861–1877" (Ph.D. dissertation, University of Arizona, 1975); Janice C. Hood, "Brotherly Hate: A Quantitative Study of Southern Reconstruction Congressmen, 1867–1877" (Ph.D. dissertation, Washington State University, 1974); and the final chapters of Michael Les Benedict, *A Compromise of Principle: Congressional Republicans and Reconstruction, 1863–1869* (New York: W. W. Norton, 1974). Benedict's *Let Us Have Peace: Republicans and Reconstruction, 1869–1880* (New York: W. W. Norton, forthcoming) promises to add significantly to this literature. Although I have conducted my own analysis of the southern congressmen's reaction to reconstruction issues, I am much indebted to recent scholarship for my summary of the problem.

publicans overwhelmingly rejected a weak House-passed version prohibiting discrimination "by reason of race, color, or previous condition of servitude," and they strongly endorsed Massachusetts Radical Henry Wilson's sweeping proposition to outlaw racial, literacy, property, and religious suffrage tests. Likewise, nearly half of the southern representatives, 70 percent of whom were lame ducks, backed Ohio Republican Samuel Shellabarger's radical proposal which coupled universal suffrage with disfranchisement of all former Confederates. Assured by Republican leaders that neither plan had a chance for ratification, the House defeated both, yet southern representatives were far more receptive than their northern allies to the idea of universal suffrage, and they were nearly unanimous in seeking an explicit guarantee of officeholding rights.[15]

Southern spokesmen, most notably Senate carpetbaggers Willard Warner of Alabama and Joseph Abbott of North Carolina and scalawags John Pool of North Carolina and Frederick Sawyer of South Carolina, warned that nothing short of a comprehensive statement of universal rights to suffrage and officeholding would suffice. Among the representatives, only scalawag W. Jasper Blackburn of Louisiana expressed some ambivalence about black suffrage; as a trade-off, he sought a declaration of amnesty as part of the suffrage amendment. The rhetoric and voting behavior of the others, with the exception of the two Georgia Democrats, indicates that they would have preferred a positive statement of universal suffrage. Yet with time running out in the session and northern Republicans dominating the proceedings, a moderate conference version with no guarantee of officeholding and barring only racial tests prevailed. Having no alternative, Southerners dutifully lined up behind the proposal with the exception of seven abstentions—at least three of whom favored universal suffrage. In the Senate, Warner exemplified

15.   *Congressional Globe*, 40th Cong., 3rd Sess., 1300, 745, 1029, 1040, 744, 1226, 1563; Philip J. Avillo, Jr., "Principles and Power: Southern Republican Congressmen and the Passage of the Fifteenth Amendment," unpublished paper delivered November 11, 1978, at the Southern Historical Association Convention, Saint Louis; Hood, "Southern Reconstruction Congressmen," 77–80, 271–80; Benedict, *Compromise of Principle*, ch. 17; William Gillette, *The Right to Vote: Politics and the Passage of the Fifteenth Amendment* (Rev. ed.; Baltimore: Johns Hopkins Press, 1969), ch. 2.

the Southerners' reaction to the conference report with his call for a "grand affirmative proposition which shall protect every citizen of this republic in the enjoyment of political power." Although Warner and seven other Southerners acquiesced and voted for passage, Pool resolutely opposed it, and Sawyer and Abbott abstained in protest.[16]

As intimidation and violence against southern Republicans increased, the Fifteenth Amendment's enforcement section became the basis for three acts passed in 1870 and 1871 to protect the black voter. The central provisions of the acts of May, 1870, and February, 1871, outlawed various forms of voter intimidation, prohibited disguised groups intent on intimidation from interfering with the electoral process, and made available election supervisors and enforcement officers. Congressional reaction to these first two acts was rigidly partisan. There was some disagreement among southern Republicans on the preliminary votes, with the carpetbaggers tending to favor harsher measures, but the only solid indication of opposition came from scalawag Senator Joshua Hill of Georgia, who refrained from voting on the second act. The Southerners were not particularly active in the debate although a few contributed so-called "outrage speeches" detailing acts of violence against Republican voters.[17]

The confusing language of the acts, the indecisiveness and inefficiency of federal authorities, the lack of funds, and conservative cries of unconstitutionality hampered implementation from the beginning. In the interim, an extensive debate developed among southern Republicans at the state level over the efficacy of further en-

16. *Congressional Globe*, 40th Cong., 3rd Sess., 862, 980–81, 997–99, 1012, 1199, 1299, 1301, 1563, 1628–29, 1641, Appendix, 241–42, 94–97, 101–102, 125–27, 146–49; Hood, "Southern Reconstruction Congressmen," 271–80; Benedict, *Compromise of Principle*, 370–73, 374–77. Almost all of the Southerners' set speeches in the 40th House dealt with the Fifteenth Amendment, and most were relegated to the appendix of the *Globe*.

17. *Congressional Globe*, 41st Cong., 2nd Sess., 3678–90, 3726, 3809 (H.R. 1293), 1563–64, 1986–88, 2018–20, 2711–13, 2812, 3668, 5342, Appendix, 263–67, 41st Cong., 3rd Sess., 1640, 1643, 1646, 1655 (H.R. 2634), 108–14, 530; Gillette, *Retreat from Reconstruction*, 25–26; Avillo, "Slave State Republicans in Congress," ch. 8; Hood, "Southern Reconstruction Congressmen," 85–90, 295–306; Allen W. Trelease, *White Terror: The Ku Klux Klan Conspiracy and Southern Reconstruction* (New York: Harper & Row, 1971), chs. 24–25.

forcement legislation. In some states, particularly Alabama and Mississippi, Republicans disagreed over the extent of intimidation and terror, with the moderates accusing their more radical colleagues of exaggerating "southern disorders." In Alabama, for example, Warner acknowledged the existence of intimidation but took a moderate stance on the question of federal intervention—a position which his fellow senator George E. Spencer roundly denounced. Spencer catalogued specific "outrages" against Alabama Republicans and decried weak-kneed Republicans who seemed to be surrendering to conservative pressure. Above all, he stressed the absolute necessity for federal protection for southern Republicans.[18]

Like Spencer, the more radical Southerners supported the most rigorous proposals during the framing process. Others questioned the usefulness of additional enforcement legislation, and some would have preferred trying tactics such as aid for economic rehabilitation. Given the framework of reconstruction, however, coercion seemed to be the only course that would draw the support of northern Republicans. Locked into a policy based on force which only stimulated the rabidity of their conservative opposition, most southern Republicans supported enforcement legislation because their political survival depended upon it. When the third and harshest enforcement act, the Ku Klux Klan Act, was debated early in the Forty-second Congress, Hill and scalawag Senator Thomas Robertson of South Carolina openly opposed it while several others failed to vote on some of the framing roll calls. On the final and the conference report votes, a sizable number of scalawags and carpetbaggers in both chambers abstained rather than have their names heralded in the conservative press as being in favor of more coercion.[19]

The enforcement acts offered little more than a brief respite in the

18. Gillette, *Retreat from Reconstruction*, ch. 2; Everette Swinney, "Enforcing the Fifteenth Amendment, 1870–1877," *Journal of Southern History*, XXVIII (1962), 202–18; *Congressional Globe*, 41st Cong., 2nd Sess., 2018–20, 2811–12, 3493, 2668, 41st Cong., 3rd Sess., 573, 1816, 1817, 42nd Cong., 1st Sess., 665–66; Trelease, *White Terror*, chs. 15–16; Sarah Woolfolk Wiggins, *The Scalawag in Alabama Politics, 1865–1881* (University, Ala.: University of Alabama Press, 1977), 56–61, 68–71.

19. *Congressional Globe*, 42nd Cong., 1st Sess., 522, 652, 702–709, 724–25, 806, 808, 728, 779. Southern Republican lines on the Ku Klux Klan Act in the House tended to be harder than those in the Senate. Only carpetbagger John Edwards (Ark.)

conservatives' push to redeem the South. After their disastrous performance in the elections of 1874, the lame-duck Republican majority in the House made a final effort to secure additional enforcement
legislation. At the urging of some southern Republicans, a handful
of die-hard Radicals such as Benjamin Butler of Massachusetts and
John Coburn of Indiana managed to rally enough Northerners to
pass a modest bill in the waning moments of the Forty-third Congress. Southern Republicans voted 28–4 for passage, but all involved
understood that the Senate was not disposed to take action on it. For
most northern Republicans, as William Gillette has noted, the effort
was little more than a symbolic gesture to southern Republicans
amidst the ongoing northern retreat from reconstruction.[20]

Their search for different methods of placating the Democrats led
most southern Republicans to support a general amnesty for ex-
Confederates prohibited from holding political office by the Fourteenth Amendment. A few, however, feared that a blanket pardon
would only add to their party's problems in the South. Some black
representatives and several carpetbaggers such as Spencer and Adelbert Ames of Mississippi, reluctant to surrender their control of the
pardoning process, preferred continuing the selective but cumbersome procedure of reviewing each individual case. Spencer, for example, was convinced that many prominent ex-Confederates did not
deserve amnesty. They should not be forgiven, he thought, because
they had no intention of repenting their past "errors" and amnesty
would only bolster the conservative force to redeem Alabama. Accordingly, when Sumner attempted to replace the amnesty bill with
a civil rights proposal or, at the very least, to couple amnesty with a
guarantee of civil rights, he found ready support among most Senate
carpetbaggers. But the more conservative scalawags, including Hill,

---

consistently opposed it, but carpetbaggers George E. Harris (Miss.) and Lionel Sheldon
(La.) frequently refrained from voting. In the Senate, five carpetbaggers and two scalawags voted for the final conference report, while five scalawags and three carpetbaggers were absent. At least five of the latter were clearly abstaining.

20. *Congressional Record,* 43rd Cong., 2nd Sess., 1929–35, 689–96, 870–77,
1152, 1851–53, 1926–29, 2110–16, Appendix, 106–109; Gillette, *Retreat from Reconstruction,* ch. 12. Twenty of the twenty-eight southern Republicans supporting
the bill were lame ducks. The four who opposed it were all conservative scalawags.

Robertson, John Pool of North Carolina, Frederick Sawyer of South Carolina, John F. Lewis of Virginia, and James L. Alcorn of Mississippi, joined moderate northern Republicans and the Democrats to defeat such efforts.[21]

During the framing of the amnesty act in 1872, the Radicals among the Southerners were noticeably hesitant to restore office-holding privileges to unpardoned ex-Confederates, and several either abstained or openly opposed it. Most southern Republicans, however, agreed with scalawag Representative Oliver Dockery of North Carolina, who declared that "we have had quite enough of the peddling process" of considering individual cases for pardon and thought it time for a blanket amnesty. They somewhat futilely hoped that such an olive branch might cool the political warfare in the South. The bill finally adopted did remove one of the conservatives' grievances, but its primary effect was simply to allow higher-ranking ex-Confederates, who were even more popular with conservative whites, to stand for office against Republicans.[22]

Finally, the southern delegations split along party lines on the numerous attempts during the first half of the 1870s to pass civil rights legislation. In the Senate, Sumner had long pushed for a comprehensive measure guaranteeing equal access to public accommodations. In 1872, during Sumner's absence, the Senate passed a weakened version of his proposal with schools and juries excluded, but the House twice refused to take action on it. In both chambers, southern Republicans offered the strongest support of any regional group. Shortly after Sumner's death in March, 1874, the Senate passed his bill intact, and among the Southerners, only Virginia scalawag John F. Lewis dissented. Once again the House voted not to consider the bill. Southern Republican representatives favored it on several roll calls by a margin of about 5–1, but there were a significant number

21. *Congressional Globe*, 41st Cong., 2nd Sess., 881–82, 41st Cong., 2nd Sess., 2018–20, 3668, 42nd Cong., 1st Sess., 102, 665, 42nd Cong., 2nd Sess., 3268, 3736, 3738.

22. *Ibid.*, 42nd Cong., 2nd Sess., 398–99, 263–83, 912–28, 3258–70, 3736–38, Appendix, 386–88, 600–604, 732; Hood, "Southern Reconstruction Congressmen," 72–76, 258–69; Avillo, "Slave State Republicans in Congress," ch. 8; James A. Rawley, "The General Amnesty Act of 1872: A Note," *Mississippi Valley Historical Review*, XLVII (1960), 480–84.

of abstentions by Southerners who either feared the issue as a campaign burden in the coming elections or simply opposed it but did not want to go on record as defying the interests of their black electorate.[23]

Although most southern Republicans would have preferred to avoid it, the pending civil rights legislation became the central issue in the southern campaigns of 1874. As a result, southern Republicans found their congressional ranks sharply trimmed. When the issue resurfaced in the following lame-duck session, the Republicans, most now removed from political life in the South, lined up to fire a parting shot at southern conservatives. With the exception of a few scalawags already on their way into the Democratic party or out of politics, the section's Republicans supported the drastically weakened proposal finally adopted early in 1875—a position the freedmen obviously approved, but one which an overwhelming majority of southern whites opposed. The act offered some hope to the Republicans' dedicated black electorate, but the national willingness to live up to the pledges of the measure had long since disappeared.[24]

In short, the issues of reconstruction united congressional Democrats but failed to do the same for their Republican counterparts. The primary problem lay with the final plan of reconstruction which, at its base, relied exclusively on black suffrage as the means

23. *Congressional Globe*, 42nd Cong., 2nd Sess., 3728–39, 3932, 4322 (S. 99), 1954–56, 3383 (H.R. 1647); *Congressional Record*, 43rd Cong., 1st Sess., 4162–76, 4242, 4691, 5329 (S. 1). The five southern Republican representatives who joined the Democrats in opposition to the 1874 Senate bill were all scalawags. Present but not voting were three scalawags and two carpetbaggers.

24. *Congressional Record*, 43rd Cong., 2nd Sess., 704, 888–902, 936, 1011, 1867–70; Gillette, *Retreat from Reconstruction*, 190–279; Folmar, "The Depletion of Republican Congressional Support for Enforcement of Reconstruction Measures," chs. 4–5; Bertram Wyatt-Brown, "The Civil Rights Act of 1875," *Western Political Quarterly*, XVIII (1965), 763–75; Hood, "Southern Reconstruction Congressmen," 80–85, 282–93, Alfred H. Kelly, "The Congressional Controversy over School Segregation, 1867–75," *American Historical Review*, LXIV (1959), 537–63; James M. McPherson, "Abolitionists and the Civil Rights Act of 1875," *Journal of American History*, LII (1965), 493–510. In addition to the eight scalawag representatives either abstaining or voting against the measure, scalawag Senators John F. Lewis of Virginia and Morgan C. Hamilton of Texas opposed it, and carpetbagger Abijah Gilbert of Florida missed all the roll calls as he had when the Senate considered its bill in the first session.

for southern "regeneration." To their credit, northern Republicans probably went as far as northern public opinion would allow in their attempt to work the freedmen into an equitable position in American life, but their efforts were not sufficient. As reconstruction encountered difficulties, some northern Republicans immediately pronounced it a failure. Others attempted to buttress the process with bloody-shirt rhetoric, enforcement legislation, and more federal troops. When these failed, they too abandoned it and attempted to save face by shifting the blame for its failure to the Southerners. By the middle of the decade, if not before, northern support for reconstruction and southern Republicans had all but disappeared. The few Republican congressmen who doggedly backed the experiment to its bitter end did so in the face of northern public opinion.[25]

Waning northern support left southern Republicans in a precarious position. As both the creations and implements of the final plan of reconstruction, southern Republicans recognized its shortcomings almost immediately. In Congress, as in their home states, they were pulled apart by disparate forces. Their desires to protect and enhance the political and civil rights of their predominantly black electorate conflicted with their apprehensions of further arousing their conservative opposition. Some wanted additional enforcement legislation and federal protection, others feared this would only invite more trouble. Some wanted a general amnesty in the hope of pacifying southern conservatives, others believed the officeholding restrictions of the Fourteenth Amendment should continue. Some wanted a civil rights act, others knew such legislation would be an additional campaign burden. A few southern Republicans, particularly the scalawags, began to drag their feet by either not voting or openly opposing additional coercive or civil rights leg-

25. See in particular Trefousse, *Radical Republicans*, ch. 13; Folmar, "The Depletion of Republican Congressional Support for Enforcement of Reconstruction Measures," *passim*; Patrick W. Riddleberger, "The Radicals' Abandonment of the Negro During Reconstruction," *Journal of Negro History*, XLV (1960), 88–102; Otto H. Olsen, "Southern Reconstruction and the Question of Self-Determination," in George M. Frederickson (ed.), *A Nation Divided: Problems and Issues of the Civil War and Reconstruction* (Minneapolis: Burgess Publishing Co., 1975), 113–41; Gillette, *Retreat from Reconstruction, passim*; and Chapter VIII below.

islation. And yet they were locked into the shortsighted framework adopted in 1867; Southerners had no real alternative but to go along with whatever actions a declining number of Northerners were willing to support. If properly planned, reconstruction might have brought unity to the Republican party; as it was, it only added to the sources of sectional discord.

V Economic Issues
Debt Management and Revenue Policy

While the issues of political reconstruction considered after read-mission were obviously important to the South and the fate of southern Republicanism, Congress actually spent more time coping with substantive economic problems stemming from the Civil War and, after 1873, from a troubled national economy. In a turbulent economic decade beginning with the first debates over the sanctity of the public credit in the late 1860s and ending with specie resumption in 1879, legislators fought over questions of debt management, internal revenue and tariff rates, monetary problems, appropriations, and subsidies for internal improvements. Historians have focused so intensely on the politics of reconstruction that they have overlooked southern activity and interests in the broad-ranging economic concerns of the 1870s. Even the specialized economic histories of the period—Irwin Unger's prize-winning *Greenback Era* is a prime example—virtually ignore the South. The war-torn section, in fact, had a vital interest in economic legislation, and her congressmen played a significant role in determining national economic policy. Furthermore, the economic debates reveal much about intersectional and intraparty relationships, and the more differentiated set of economic issues is clearly a better vehicle than reconstruction measures for examining the activity of the 251 southern congressmen and judging the quality of their representation.

Two important problems, one historiographical, the other methodological, merit consideration at the outset. First, it is paradoxical, yet fully reflective of the partisan patterns of Reconstruction historiography, that several notions regarding the Southerners' *anticipated* behavior on economic issues have shaped the historical image of their *actual* performance. The Democratic congressmen have actually been little troubled in this area. At worst, they have been characterized as simply brutal, backward-looking Bourbons out of step with the progressive thrusts of the times, or at best, as insignificant and ineffective in the area of economic legislation. But the Republican congressmen have suffered from the charge that they had no real stake in southern society and no sense of sectional economic interests. Because southern Republicans owed their existence to northern Radicals, the Dunningites assumed that they voted as their northeastern party colleagues instructed on economic as well as political measures.[1]

That assumption became a basic ingredient in the most prominent economic interpretation of the origins of reconstruction. Charles and Mary Beard, who interpreted the Civil War as the "Second American Revolution" in which the forces of capitalism finally triumphed over those of agrarianism, concluded that while the planting South was out of the Union, northeastern capitalists, through their faithful Republican agents in Congress, not only secured political power but also reaped long-sought economic benefits which included a protective tariff, high interest rates on war bond issues, a national banking system, and a sound currency. According to Howard K. Beale, who corroborated and extended the Beards' thesis into the Reconstruction period, the Radical Republicans feared that under Johnsonian reconstruction a solidly Democratic South would unite with western agrarian interests in Congress to dismantle the new economic order. For economic considerations, then, the Radicals stymied Johnson and drove a series of harsh military reconstruction measures through Congress with the aim of fastening the

---

1. For a sampling, see William Garrott Brown, "The South in National Politics," *South Atlantic Quarterly,* IX (1910), 104–106; James W. Garner, "Southern Politics Since the Civil War," in *Studies in Southern History and Politics Inscribed to William Archibald Dunning* (New York: Columbia University Press, 1914), 370; Holland Thompson, *The New South: A Chronicle of Social and Industrial Evolution* (New Haven: Yale University Press, 1919), 26, 200; Hugh B. Hammett, *Hilary Abner Herbert: A Southerner Returns to the Union* (Philadelphia: American Philosophical Society, 1976), 84; C. Mildred Thompson, "Carpet-baggers in the United States Senate," in *Studies in Southern History and Politics Inscribed to Dunning,* 161–76; Samuel Denny Smith, *The Negro in Congress, 1870–1901* (Chapel Hill: University of North Carolina Press, 1940); and E. Merton Coulter, *The South During Reconstruction, 1865–1877* (Baton Rouge: Louisiana State University Press, 1947), especially ch. 7.

Republican party on the South. The transformed region would then return Republicans to Congress to offer further support for the party's economic as well as political program. "If Southern economic interests had coincided with those of the rising industrial groups of the North," Beale wrote, "there would have been no Radical reconstruction. The real danger from 'a return of rebels to power' was not overthrow of the Union, but an ousting of the new industrial forces from control in Washington through a renewed union of Southern planters and Western farmers."[2]

As a logical corollary to the Beard-Beale thesis, historians have generally accepted the behavior supposedly *anticipated* of southern Republicans as what actually evolved—that they violated their section's economic interests and voted with their northern party colleagues to consolidate the wartime gains of northern capitalists. On tariff questions, for example, Rembert Patrick asserted that southern Republicans "followed the leadership of protectionists in the House and Senate, disregarding the benefits of a low tariff for their raw material-producing region." In return the congressmen "demanded approval" of their regimes in the South. In his influential work on the Compromise of 1877, which he refers to as the Thermidor of the "Second American Revolution," C. Vann Woodward declared that "the votes of both Carpetbagger and Negro in Congress had proved a prop to the new economic order" during Reconstruction. "So long as Republican rule lasted in the South the region had proved a bulwark to the new economic order . . . the congressmen it sent to Washington had voted solidly with Northern Republicans in support of the more pragmatic aims of economic privilege." Those more pragmatic aims were "centered in the protection of a sectional economy and numerous privileged interests, and were reflected in new statutes regarding taxes, money, tariffs, banks, land, railroads, subsidies, all placed upon the law books while the South was out of the Union."[3]

2.   Charles Beard and Mary Beard, *The Rise of American Civilization* (2 vols.; New York: Macmillan, 1927), II, 54, 105–11; Howard K. Beale, *The Critical Year: A Study of Andrew Johnson and Reconstruction* (New York: Harcourt, Brace, 1930), 225, 297–99, 397–99, 406.

3.   Rembert Patrick, *The Reconstruction of the Nation* (New York: Oxford University Press, 1967), 177; C. Vann Woodward, *Reunion and Reaction: The Compromise of 1877 and the End of Reconstruction* (Boston: Little, Brown, 1951), 45, 12–13.

Woodward's emphasis on the role of economic factors in the Compromise of 1877 dovetails neatly with the Beard-Beale thesis. The compromise serves as the final dramatic episode in the "Second American Revolution."

In work completed in the late 1950s and early 1960s, revisionist historians refuted the simplistic agrarian-versus-capitalist interpretation of the period and destroyed the notion that the northeastern business community and the Republican party were united on economic questions. Not only were the economic interests of various northern industrial and financial groups often conflicting and contradictory, but the Republicans themselves were far from united behind a specific economic program. The party harbored free traders and protectionists, currency expansionists and contractionists, greenbackers and bullionists, and resumptionists and anti-resumptionists in a bewildering array of combinations.[4] But while the revisionists have overturned the basic tenets of the Beard-Beale thesis, its corollary regarding the anticipated behavior of southern Republicans, which should have fallen with the thesis, has escaped systematic investigation. The assumption has been that southern Republicans were under the thumb of their northeastern party colleagues on economic as well as political issues, and the revisionists, lacking a specific study to attack, have overlooked the problem.

Any close analysis of legislative behavior in the nineteenth century encounters several more general problems—most of which stem from a paucity of source material. The most intractable is that of motivation. Charged as each legislator was with representing the attitudes and guarding the welfare of his constituency, one might assume that a measurable relationship exists between his behavior and his constituents' interests—particularly in the area of economics. Constituent concerns, of course, are only one element in the

4.   Irwin Unger, "Businessmen and Specie Resumption," *Political Science Quarterly*, LXXIV (1959), 46–70; Stanley Coben, "Northeastern Business and Radical Reconstruction: A Re-examination," *Mississippi Valley Historical Review*, LXVI (1959), 67–90; Robert Sharkey, *Money, Class, and Party: An Economic Study of Civil War and Reconstruction* (Baltimore: Johns Hopkins Press, 1959); Irwin Unger, *The Greenback Era: A Social and Political History of American Finance, 1865–1879* (Princeton: Princeton University Press, 1964).

configuration of influences on legislative behavior, but, in theory at least, they should be one of the more important factors. The behavior, in the form of roll call responses, bills offered, petitions presented, and general level of activity, is easily determined, and roll call analysis offers a variety of techniques for comparing the behavior of one legislator to another. But a satisfactory, statistical demonstration of an individual's responsiveness to those he represented remains difficult, primarily because exact definition of constituent interests borders on the impossible.

Census statistics, for example, indicate that a large majority of the southern congressmen represented districts which were primarily if not predominantly agricultural in terms of value of productions. The distribution of values ranged from a low of 18 percent agricultural for the district including the Richmond manufacturing complex to a high of 96 percent for the district carved out of the delta land in northeastern Louisiana. But the median values for percent agricultural were 79 (1860 apportionment) and 81 (1870 apportionment); less than 10 percent of the districts created at each apportionment were under half agricultural. The agricultural and similar indexes such as land value per acre and per capita wealth are little more than incondite indicators of economic interests within a particular congressional district or state. Furthermore, with the exception of certain aspects of the tariff issue, they are seldom significantly correlated with voting behavior.[5]

Newspapers and special interest publications offer a more timely indication of the economic attitudes of a particular area or interest group within the South, but spokesmen for southern interests were frequently subjective and contradictory (often for political reasons), and they may or may not have accurately reflected the economic interests of a given area. There were, of course, legitimately differing perceptions of what the economic dimensions of the "New South" should be. Many Republicans and former Whigs of both parties promoted fulfillment of the antebellum dream of a diversified economy.

5. The various statistical indexes are discussed more fully in Terry L. Seip, "Southern Representatives and Economic Measures During Reconstruction: A Quantitative and Analytical Study" (Ph.D. dissertation, Louisiana State University, 1974), 65, 77–81.

Their support for tariffs, for example, often seemed contradictory to the interests of their agrarian constituents, but they argued that protection was necessary for encouragement of manufacturing and industry and essential if the section was ever going to break out of the staple crop mentality. But the notion that the southern way to wealth lay in "King Cotton" and other staple crops not only lingered but flourished. One of the primary factors luring northern settlers was their conviction that with free labor and Yankee management the profits from planting would be even greater than before the war.[6] Despite the efforts of industrial and manufacturing promoters, Republicans and Redeemers alike, the South clung to the agrarian economy.

A conflict of interests, however, existed within the agricultural community. Sugar and rice growers, for example, clamored for tariff protection, but cotton producers had opposite interests. Cotton interests worked against a tariff on cotton bagging materials; hemp growers favored such a levy. Cotton demanded credit; tobacco was more interested in the tax structure. Delta cotton and sugar planters wanted federal aid to rebuild and maintain levees while lumbering and mining interests sought a better transportation network. Tobacco and rice interests often opposed federal subsidies for such internal improvements. Conflict also existed among the producers of each crop. The concerns of leaf tobacco farmers, for example, varied from those who grew plug varieties. The producers of raw sugar and molasses had different tariff interests than those who could offer a more refined product. Those involved with cotton unanimously favored refunding that portion of the federal cotton tax collected after the war, but were sharply split among laborers, planters, and factors as to who should be the beneficiaries of the refund. Southern manufacturers using agricultural commodities—particularly the textile mills and tobacco industries—had still different concerns as did the iron industries in Virginia and Alabama. And to the configuration must be added the special interests of debtors and creditors and the merchants, lawyers, bankers, and northern investors. Furthermore,

6. See Lawrence N. Powell, *New Masters: Northern Planters During the Civil War and Reconstruction* (New Haven: Yale University Press, 1980), chs. 1–2.

the economic values often associated with an agrarian region (*e.g.*, free trade, soft money, free banking, and federally subsidized transportation systems) were functions of time and circumstance. Additional factors included the availability of credit, interest rates, labor supply, weather conditions, domestic and world markets, transportation costs, and state and federal tax policies in any given season.

Most Southerners appeared sensitive to the diverse economic interests of their constituents, and they at least gave lip service to the notion that they should trust and reflect what they believed to be majority opinion at any given moment. Rare was the individual such as Abijah Gilbert, a carpetbag senator from Florida, who flew in the face of constituent interests on nearly every economic issue. Nor is there any substantial evidence that some Republicans, particularly the blacks, took their cues on economic legislation from prominent northern Radicals as some historians have maintained. Occasionally a Southerner voted against the expressed will of his constituency because of some stoutly held personal principle. L. Q. C. Lamar of Mississippi, for example, defied constituent interests and voted against remonetization of silver in 1878—rather than violate his monometallist beliefs. Others held that the congressman's duty was to provide a grading influence and not to react to a "temporary clamor" of the people. Vermont Senator George F. Edmunds perhaps best expressed this rationalization for differing with constituent sentiment. "Public opinion ought to be consulted," he declared during the currency debate of 1874, "but . . . the only public opinion which we have a right to consult is that long and sober public opinion which covers a period of time wider than a temporary excitement . . . [and] which depends upon the intelligence, upon cultivation, upon experience, upon observation of the progress of society for a period of years."[7]

A final factor at work in southern congressman/constituency rela-

7. *Congressional Record*, 45th Cong., 2nd Sess., 1061, 43rd Cong., 1st Sess., 3894. Compare Edmunds' remarks to those of Augustus S. Merrimon (N.C.) and Oliver P. Morton (Ind.) in *Congressional Record*, 43rd Cong., 1st Sess., 3893–94, 2519, 2677. The concepts of representation during the Middle Period have not been thoroughly investigated. For an introduction to the problem in a later period, see Morris P. Fiorina, *Representatives, Roll Calls, and Constituencies* (Lexington, Mass.: D. C. Heath, 1974).

tions was the question of legitimacy, which went beyond the bounds of normal political partisanship. When southern Republicans introduced, supported, and secured economic legislation beneficial to their areas, the dominant Democratic press remained silent. Without a strong newspaper network of their own, it was difficult for Republican congressmen to make known their legislative work. Conservative newspapers, of course, were quick to point out Republican miscues and applaud the most minor Democratic accomplishment. Republicans soon learned that they could do nothing to please white conservatives, a critical portion of the electorate who refused to accept them as legitimate representatives.

In short, isolating and measuring influences on legislative voting behavior in the nineteenth century is problematic. Absences and abstentions are frequently impossible to explain. Nonvoters may have been legitimately or irresponsibly absent, uninterested in the issue at hand, unwilling to cross party lines to register personal or constituent preferences, or abstaining because of serious disagreement with part of the proposal under consideration. Absences and abstentions were not a particular problem for the Southerners, although a few were not terribly conscientious about voting or pairing on every roll call. During the Forty-third Senate, for example, Arkansas carpetbagger Stephen Dorsey missed 59 percent of the roll calls and Florida carpetbagger Abijah Gilbert 52 percent. On the other hand, Texas scalawag James Flanagan voted 81 percent of the time and North Carolina Democrat Augustus Merrimon 94 percent, well above the average of about 70 percent. The most frequent excuse given for absences was sickness. Scalawag John F. Lewis of Virginia missed over half of the roll calls in the Forty-third Senate because of medical problems, Democrats John Warfield Johnston of Virginia and George Goldthwaite of Alabama had similar troubles, and an extended sickness forced venerable conservative Alexander H. Stephens to miss about 90 percent of the roll calls in the Forty-third House. Generally, however, the Southerners' absence/abstention rate was comparable to that of members from other regions.

Greater difficulties arise with efforts to measure the impact of less tangible factors such as party competitiveness, length of service, security of office, and such personal data as level of education, vocation, and religion. On economic issues at least, the racial and economic dimensions of an individual's constituency and the configurations of personal and political background characteristics were seldom significantly correlated with voting behavior. When they appeared to be, some other factor such as party or region more often explained the behavior. The impact of regional and national interest groups, such longstanding congressional practices as logrolling and feeding at the pork barrel, and a host of institutional and peer influences is generally indefinable. As a pioneer in legislative analysis remarked thirty years ago: "Legislative policy-making appears to be the result of a confluence of factors streaming from an almost endless number of tributaries. . . . a kaleidoscopic and largely irresponsible interplay of ideas, interests, institutions, and individuals."[8]

A congressman's reaction to the multifaceted economic issues of the 1870s obviously depended upon his individual interests and expectations and his perceptions of constituent interests as well as the economic circumstances of the moment. Economic opinion freely crossed party lines—a situation which frequently made strange bedfellows. On bank note redistribution, for example, carpetbagger Willard Warner of Alabama found himself in league with the rabidly antireconstructionist Democrat Allen G. Thurman of Ohio. Ex-Confederate John Brown Gordon of Georgia and Radical Republican Oliver P. Morton of Indiana teamed in favor of soft money in 1874. Hard-money principles brought together such divergent types as Radical Charles Sumner of Massachusetts, Democrat Thomas F. Bayard of Delaware, scalawag James W. Flanagan of Texas, and ex-Confederate L. Q. C. Lamar of Mississippi. The most improbable pair was Radical Benjamin Butler of Massachusetts and former Confederate vice-president Alexander H. Stephens of Georgia, who worked side by side for remonetization of silver in 1878.

Individuals became well known for their stance on a particular economic issue. Thus free traders and revenue reformers in the House rallied around Democrat Samuel S. "Sunset" Cox of New York while protectionists gathered behind Radical William D. "Pig

8. Stephen Kemp Bailey, *Congress Makes a Law: The Story Behind the Employment Act of 1946* (New York: Columbia University Press, 1950), 236, 240.

Iron" Kelley of Pennsylvania and a host of New Englanders led by
Henry L. Dawes of Massachusetts. Republican John Sherman of
Ohio, probably the most important figure on financial matters during the decade, directed Senate resumptionists; House hard-money
advocates followed Republican James A. Garfield of Ohio and Democrat Michael S. Kerr of Indiana. At the other end of the monetary
spectrum, soft-money forces clustered around Radical greenbackers Butler, Kelley, and Ebon Ingersoll of Illinois in the House and
Gordon, Morton, Republican John Logan of Illinois, and Democrat
Augustus S. Merrimon of North Carolina in the Senate. Lamar
and Democrat James Throckmorton of Texas joined carpetbaggers
Joseph R. West of Louisiana and Stephen Dorsey of Arkansas to lead
forces requesting additional subsidies for the Texas & Pacific Railroad. Another group of Southerners, this one seeking appropriations
for rebuilding the levees of the Mississippi River and reclaiming the
delta, looked to scalawag Senator James L. Alcorn of Mississippi and
Democratic Representative E. John Ellis of Louisiana for leadership.
The early advocates of railroad regulation followed the lead of Republican George McCrary of Iowa and former Confederate postmaster general John H. Reagan of Texas. And retrenchment-minded William S. Holman of Indiana, nicknamed Objector by subsidy-seekers,
became the focal point of opposition to all subsidies and large
appropriations.

The construction of economic legislation during the 1870s was
something less than an orderly process. The congressional committee system gained power during the early postwar period, but its authority remained primarily negative—an unfriendly committee majority would simply refuse to consider and report bills referred to it.
Much of the legislative action on economic proposals still took
place on the floor in the procedural committee of the whole or after
they were reported to the chamber. Committee chairmen frequently
watched in bewilderment as the full membership either refused to
consider their bills or emasculated them with amendments and substitute proposals. Party caucuses became more important in uniting
their members behind specific measures during the period, but party
discipline on economic issues was virtually impossible to maintain

and rarely attempted. Neither party in either chamber encountered much success in limiting discussion, and, as was the case during the "Inflation Session" of 1874 and the silver agitation of 1877–1878, the debates often became protracted and repetitious. More disconcerting was the habit of allowing major pieces of legislation and appropriation bills to languish in committees until the last few days of a session or Congress. The final hours before adjournment invariably became a confusing rush of limited floor consideration of bills by the score, hastily convened conference committees to resolve differences between the chambers, and last-minute passage of ill-considered measures whose actual content was fully known to few congressmen. Sometimes important economic measures simply became lost in the chaos preceding adjournment.

Despite the disorderly and unpredictable nature of the legislative process, Congress still managed to consider a broad range of significant economic issues during the 1870s. And some order does finally emerge from the confusion; with a few important exceptions, local and sectional interests were the chief determinants of voting behavior on economic measures. The ability of southern Republicans and Democrats to lay aside political differences and unite behind what both perceived to be sectional economic interests was remarkable. Given the conditions and limitations under which they were forced to labor, Southerners served their section well. Southern Republicans were as cognizant of their region's economic needs as their Democratic colleagues and frequently more active in their defense and promotion. But differing economic interests created difficulties in both national parties. Intersectional disagreements among Democrats, while at times serious, were less important than those in the Republican party. There the discord on economics contributed significantly to the failure of southern Republicanism.

"At best the subject is a dry one," Senator John Sherman intoned in his *Recollections*. "Still . . . to provide for the payment of the vast debt created during the war was next in importance to the conduct of armies." As chairman of the Senate Finance Committee and the chief architect of postwar financial policy, Sherman was keenly aware that debt management underlay most economic controversies during the seventies. Certainly one of the foremost legacies of the Civil War was a copious federal debt—an incredible array of certificates of indebtedness, loans, notes, bonds, and securities with differing terms, rates of interest, and maturities. Federal obligations, including legal tenders, peaked at nearly $2.85 billion in August, 1865—approximately forty-four times that owed at the end of the 1860 fiscal year. Thanks to the Fourteenth Amendment, there was never any real threat that the debt would be scaled down or repudiated, but the questions of whether the interest on the bonds could be taxed, in what kind of money the bonds were to be redeemed, and how they might be refunded into lower-interest, longer-term securities generated considerable political controversy in the late 1860s and early 1870s.[9]

The South showed little concern one way or another with the issues of public credit and debt management, but they merit attention because they formed the base of a pyramid of economic matters in which the section did have a vital interest. Since the debt had to be serviced, it influenced revenue policy—the setting of tax and tariff rates. Debt and revenue policy had a direct effect on the funds available for rivers and harbors appropriations and monetary and public land subsidies for building railroads and canals. Equally tied to the public credit issue were the resumption of specie payments, the full range of money questions, and the broader matters of national fiscal stability and the government's credit standing in foreign countries. Perhaps most important, the Southerners' reaction to debt management problems harbingered their independent stance on other economic issues.

Southerners drifted back into Congress as the issue of public credit came to a head in early 1869. During the campaign of the previous fall, the problem had been the focus of a partisan dispute over whether the debt was to be paid in "coin" (generally understood to mean gold), or in nonspecie-backed United States notes which

9. John Sherman, *Recollections of Forty Years in the House, Senate and Cabinet: An Autobiography* (Chicago: Werner Company, 1895), iv; Robert T. Patterson, *Federal Debt-Management Policies, 1865–1879* (Durham: Duke University Press, 1954), 6, 44–45, 50; Joseph B. James, *The Framing of the Fourteenth Amendment* (Urbana: University of Illinois Press, 1956), 24–27, 49, 92–94, 158–61, 164.

had been issued during the war. The "greenbacks," as they were more commonly known, were legal tender for all debts except import duties, but they had quickly depreciated and were worth only seventy-five cents in gold in 1868. The laws establishing certain of the wartime bond issues, most notably the popular series known as "five-twenties," initially allowed the bonds to be purchased with depreciated greenbacks and stipulated that the interest was to be paid in gold, but were silent as to the kind of money in which the principal could be paid. Although Horatio Seymour, the Democratic nominee, opposed the idea, many Democrats, particularly those from the Midwest, and the party platform endorsed the so-called "Ohio Idea" to pay the bonds in the same "lawful money" (greenbacks) with which they had been purchased. To most Republicans, this amounted to nothing less than repudiation of the national debt—a clear violation of the public trust. The Republican platform of 1868 accordingly pledged "the payment of public indebtedness in the utmost good faith . . . not only according to the letter, but the spirit of the laws under which it was contracted." In short, Republicans intended to pay the principal as well as the interest of the bonds in gold—a position naturally applauded by the nation's bondholders and conservative financial interests. Reconstruction issues overshadowed financial questions during the campaign, but Republicans took Grant's victory as an indication that the "repudiators" had been repudiated.[10]

The matter might have rested there had not President Johnson revived it in his last annual message in December, 1868. On the assumption that bondholders had already received a just return on their investment, Johnson advised the government to confiscate the interest and apply it to the principal in order to retire the bonds. Thus challenged, congressional Republicans moved quickly to guar-

10. John Hope Franklin, "Election of 1868," in Arthur M. Schlesinger, Jr. (ed.), *History of Presidential Elections, 1789–1968* (4 vols.; New York: Chelsea House Publishers, 1971), II, 1267, 1270; Martin E. Mantell, *Johnson, Grant, and the Politics of Reconstruction* (New York: Columbia University Press, 1973), 58–62, 107–12, 136–37; Chester M. Destler, *American Radicalism, 1865–1901: Essays and Documents* (New London, Conn.: Connecticut College, 1946), chs. 2–3; Unger, *Greenback Era,* 79–91.

antee the sanctity of the public debt, first by resolution, then by law. The House resolution declared "that all forms and degrees of repudiation of national indebtedness are odious to the American People. . . . Under no circumstances will their Representatives consent to offer the public creditor, as full compensation, a less amount of money than that which the Government contracted to pay him." Reaction was partisan and the southern Republicans seated in the lame-duck third session of the Fortieth Congress (the section was at about half strength) favored it on four roll calls. A host of similar resolutions was introduced in the Senate, including one by Alabama carpetbagger Willard Warner denouncing as "dishonest" Johnson's proposition "to appropriate the interest of the public debt to the payment of the principal." The Senate wasted little time in passing their own resolution condemning Johnson's proposal. Southern senators, carpetbaggers and scalawags all, approved it as the upper chamber split along party lines.[11]

In February, 1869, two weeks before the end of the Congress, the House turned to a bill pledging the faith of the United States to pay in coin all interest-bearing obligations, unless the law authorizing the issue stipulated otherwise. Motions to table or weaken the measure were easily defeated and the House passed it by a partisan margin of 121–60. The Senate approved an amended version three days later. A conference committee resolved the differences and returned the bill to both chambers with an additional clause promising "to make provision at the earliest practicable period" for the resumption of specie payments. Both houses passed the conference report on the last day of the session, but Andrew Johnson dealt the final blow with a pocket veto. The Republican effort to sanctify the public credit, however, was not lost. In his inaugural address on the following day, Grant announced that he favored paying in gold "every dollar of Government indebtedness . . . unless otherwise expressly stipulated in the contract." With Grant's blessing, the Forty-first Congress, meeting immediately in its first session, revived and passed "An Act

11. James D. Richardson (comp.), *A Compilation of the Messages and Papers of the Presidents, 1789–1897* (10 vols.; Washington, D.C.: Government Printing Office, 1897), V, 3876; *Congressional Globe*, 40th Cong., 3rd Sess., 71–73, 67, 128.

to Strengthen the Public Credit of the United States," and on March 18 it became the first act to receive the new president's signature.[12]

Whether the carpetbaggers and scalawags properly represented their section's interests on the issue is a moot and somewhat irrelevant point. With the implication that they somehow sacrificed sectional interests in deference to party, Robert Sharkey dismissed southern supporters as merely demonstrating "subservience to whatever Republican dogma might be fashionable at the time." That unsubstantiated explanation might apply equally well to midwestern Republicans who toed the line and favored the measure by a substantial majority on the several votes in both sessions—despite the strong sentiment for the Ohio Idea in their region. Sharkey also overlooks the fact that a sizable number of Southerners (in the Fortieth Congress, six of twenty-six in the House and seven of ten in the Senate) opposed the measure on one or more votes. Judging from their reaction to related bank note redistribution and greenback issues, the dissenters were undoubtedly soft-money advocates who feared that the bill's promise of specie resumption would mean contraction of the greenback circulation—something few Southerners could have approved given the scarcity of currency in their region. Whatever their motivation, they willingly lined up against such powerful proponents of the "Republican dogma" as Robert Schenck, James A. Garfield, George S. Boutwell, Henry L. Dawes, and Elihu Washburne in the House, and Charles Sumner, John Sherman, Lyman Trumbull, William Pitt Fessenden, and Roscoe Conkling in the Senate.[13]

To be sure, if any specific group benefitted from the promises of the Public Credit Act it was the holders of government securities, and there were few bondholders in the ex-Confederate states. But Southerners, with their attention riveted on reconstruction, scarcely noticed the issue. Southern manuscript collections are silent on the matter; it evoked little comment in southern newspapers and those

12. *Congressional Globe,* 40th Cong., 3rd Sess., 1446, 1534–39, 1679, 1834, 1839, 1883; Sharkey, *Money, Class, and Party,* 123–30; Richardson (comp.), *Messages and Papers of the Presidents,* VII, 7; *Congressional Globe,* 41st Cong., 1st Sess., 60–61, 66, 70, Appendix, 35.

13. Sharkey, *Money, Class, and Party,* 128; Seip, "Southern Representatives and Economic Measures During Reconstruction," 105–11, 133–34.

that did notice it were of a divided mind. The New Orleans *Daily Picayune*, for example, disliked the idea of "legislating bonds into a higher value for the benefit of brokers" and doubted that Johnson was a "repudiator." But the *Picayune* favored specie resumption, and other conservative journals such as the Richmond *Whig* at least disliked perpetuating a paper currency with no specie base. Although the Atlanta *Constitution* doubted that Grant's policy would "meet with popular favor . . . outside of New England and the bonded interest," the *Arkansas Gazette* and the New Orleans *Times*, both Democratic newspapers, went so far as to approve his inaugural promise to maintain the public credit. Few of the extant southern Republican newspapers commented on the public credit issue; those doing so favored the party position.[14]

Despite the shortage of currency and lack of credit facilities in the section, southerners were tired of the unsecured state and local scrip, and the Confederacy's experience with nonspecie-backed currency had left a bitter taste. Most conservatives stoutly maintained hard-money principles and could swallow paying the government's obligations in coin on the assumption that it was a first step toward specie resumption. To a large degree, such values went hand in hand with a belief in the sanctity of the public credit, whether at the national or state level. Although several southern states were forced to scale down or repudiate their debts during the 1870s, the conservatives who did become scalers or repudiators only did so ot desperation, to save their states from bankruptcy, or when evidence of corruption tarnished the bonds issued under Republican regimes. And such actions were often taken over the opposition of other conservatives who refused to abandon their antirepudiation stance.[15]

The bloated New England (and Republican) bondholder was a

14. New Orleans *Daily Picayune*, December 19, 1868, January 21, March 4, 1869; Richmond *Whig*, January 1, 1869; Little Rock *Arkansas Gazette*, March 9, 1869; New Orleans *Times*, March 5, 1869; Atlanta *Constitution*, March 6, 1869; Raleigh *Register*, September 24, 1867, March 4, 1868; Little Rock *Evening Republican*, December 26, 1867; New Orleans *Louisianian*, May 11, 1871.

15. B. U. Ratchford, *American State Debts* (Durham: Duke University Press, 1941), chs. 7–8; James Tice Moore, *Two Paths to the New South: The Virginia Debt Controversy, 1870–1883* (Lexington: University Press of Kentucky, 1974); Robert B. Jones, *Tennessee at the Crossroads: The State Debt Controversy, 1870–1883* (Knoxville: University of Tennessee Press, 1977).

common scapegoat in the section's conservative press, and Southerners might well have applauded a contemporary's description of the five-twenty, seven-thirty, and ten-forty classes of government bonds as meaning "laboring men shall rise at 5.20 in the morning & work until 7.30 in the evening, [so] that the bloated bond holder may rest upon his hd of down until 10.40 in the morning." But however much Southerners might have disliked seeing their tax dollars absorbed in servicing the federal debt, no conservative leader called for its repudiation. "Repudiation is not avowed by any considerable portion of our citizens," a prominent Georgia Democrat wrote Delaware Senator Thomas F. Bayard in 1875, "but the suspicion that we advocate measures for the purposes of making it inevitable would be more fatal to our full recognition by all people as trustworthy citizens of a common country." Another of Bayard's southern correspondents, Robert Alston, the editor of the Atlanta *Herald*, perhaps best expressed conservatives' attitudes toward the federal debt. After lamenting that the Confederate debt had been declared void, Alston still "argued the necessity of keeping bonds backed with gold." "Every reflecting man at the North must realize, that while the Southern people are ready to bear their share of taxation in the discharge of the Federal debt, yet they do not 'hanker after it,'" he continued. "We were compelled to repudiate our debt which was incurred for our defense, & it is only natural that nothing less than a high sense of honor will make us as willing to pay the Northern debt which was incurred for our subjugation." Bayard, a man much admired by southern conservatives, responded with a pamphlet advising Southerners "to crown your pledge of citizenship with a new proof of fealty; put under foot the dangerous methods of assault upon the credit and property of our common country."[16]

The sanctity of the public credit was one of the few economic issues during Reconstruction on which the Republican party was able to maintain its discipline. This, along with the support of a small

16.   Clipping in M. R. Waite to John Sherman, October 5, 1869, in John Sherman Papers, Library of Congress (hereinafter cited as LC); Robert B. Rhett, Jr., *A Farewell to the Subscribers of the Charleston Mercury* (Charleston: Charleston Mercury, 1868); H. V. M. Miller to Thomas F. Bayard, October 26, 1875, Robert Alston to Bayard, October 27, 1875, *Letter of Senator T. F. Bayard, November 5, 1875* (pamphlet), in Thomas F. Bayard Papers, LC.

but powerful group of northeastern resumptionist Democrats and the threat of an inevitable presidential veto, helped repulse the periodic attempts of some soft-money advocates to reverse the declaration of intent. For the next decade, the Republican party, particularly the northeastern wing, cited the Public Credit Act as a solemn pledge of the government's good faith to its creditors and a sacred promise to resume specie payments. Most southern Republicans agreed, if somewhat reluctantly, and southern conservatives would offer little more than occasional rhetorical opposition.

The public credit issue was closely associated with the more important effort during the second session of the Forty-first Congress to refund and consolidate the national debt into lower-interest, longer-term bonds with principal and interest payable in coin. Refunding was a sound fiscal move since the government was then paying relatively high rates of interest on several short-term issues. Of particular consequence were the five-twenties, issued between 1862 and 1868, which accounted for approximately 75 percent of the interest-bearing part of the federal debt. Optionally redeemable at any time five years after their purchase and payable in twenty years, these securities were tax-exempt and returned 6 percent interest in gold. Some $800 million of five-twenties had been issued by the end of the war, but Hugh McCulloch, Johnson's secretary of the treasury, had inflated their amount by allowing the conversion into five-twenties of a number of short-term, higher-interest securities. In 1869, after the conversion had been completed, the amount of five-twenties stood at $1.6 billion. Most were optionally payable by 1870 and all would become redeemable by July 1, 1873.[17]

Both chambers generally agreed that the five-twenties should be refunded, but the exact means of doing so sparked a protracted debate. In early 1870, under John Sherman's astute leadership, the Senate considered and passed a bill (S. 380) which proposed to refund the bonded indebtedness with three new issues of $400 million each, at interest rates varying from 4 to 5 percent and of differing maturities. The new bonds were to be sold at par, principal and interest were

17. Patterson, *Federal Debt-Management Policies*, 61–81; Sherman, *Recollections*, 365–68.

payable in coin and tax exempt, and all three classes were payable in forty years. Additional clauses provided for a sinking fund and the conversion of the five-twenties then held by national banks as security for their circulation into the new lower-interest bonds.[18]

As was often the case on financial legislation during the 1870s, the opposition came from a curious and incompatible collection of Democrats and Republican malcontents. Bayard, for example, objected to the bill because it came before specie payments, and he hinted that the South might not support it because of "congressional injustices." Other Democrats appear to have blindly opposed the measure because it was Republican-sponsored and not because it violated some dearly held hard- or soft-money principles. Virginia's John Warfield Johnston, the solitary southern Democrat, was almost always in the minority and equally receptive to hard-money and soft-money amendments and to pro- and anti-national-bank amendments. Guardians of the greenback interest such as Republican Oliver Morton of Indiana disliked the clauses requiring new national banks to pay for their new bonds with greenbacks—greenbacks which the secretary of the treasury was not allowed to return to circulation. Morton appealed to southern and western senators not to consent to any currency contraction, and on several votes to keep the greenbacks in circulation, Morton regularly carried with him four of the nine southern Republicans. Morton eventually voted for passage as did all southern Republicans with the exception of carpetbagger Alexander McDonald of Arkansas, who opposed the section requiring established national banks to exchange their old securities for the new lower-interest bonds. McDonald was simply looking after his personal interests, which included the presidency of a national bank.[19]

The Senate proposal quickly encountered opposition in the House—especially from national-banking interests. Under the pressure of the approaching end of the session and the arrival of the hot and muggy Washington summer, the House limited debate under the five-minute rule and in less than two days passed its own refund-

18. *Congressional Globe,* 41st Cong., 2nd Sess., 1587–94, 1883–94.
19. Sherman, *Recollections,* 379; *Congressional Globe,* 41st Cong., 2nd Sess., 1657–59, 1787, 1843, 1871, 1880, 1882, 1883, 1884, Appendix, 136–41.

ing bill (H.R. 2167) as a substitute. Convinced that a lower-interest, longer-term bond would be more in the government's interests and still attractive to bondholders, the representatives proposed a single refunding issue of $1 billion, redeemable in thirty years and bearing 4 percent interest. Absent from the bill was any mention of national banks' having to convert their higher-interest bonds into lower-interest bonds in order to continue banking.[20]

The differences between the chambers necessitated two conference committees. The first resurrected the Senate bill and modified it to authorize three issues: $1 billion at 4 percent interest, redeemable after thirty years; $300 million at 4.5 percent, redeemable after fifteen years; and $200 million at 5 percent, redeemable after ten years. The House rejected the first conference report for reasons other than the terms of the proposed refunding issues. In particular, Southerners and Midwesterners disliked section seven, which compelled new national banking associations, most of which would be organized in their areas, to purchase the new lower-interest bonds at par in gold. Established banks, on the other hand, would have a distinct advantage, for they could continue to base their banking on bonds paying 6 percent interest—at least until those bonds would be refunded. As a wartime creation, the national banking system was highly sectional in character; most of the established banks were in the Northeast. On the surface, the distinction seemed minor, but Radical Republican John F. Benjamin of Missouri found ready support among southern members when he declared that section seven was "a gross injustice to the South and to the West." Accordingly, thirteen of seventeen southern Republicans joined a slight majority of midwestern Republicans and a solid Democratic bloc to defeat the report. Northeastern Republicans, carefully protecting their banking interests, favored it 53–5.[21]

The second conference committee eliminated section seven and reported it back to the House. Those who favored payment of the new bond issues in greenbacks and most of the Democrats now stood alone against the refunding measure, and it passed easily. A

20. *Congressional Globe*, 41st Cong., 2nd Sess., 5018–26, 5055–71.
21. *Ibid.*, 5461–67; Seip, "Southern Representatives and Economic Measures During Reconstruction," 137–40.

Table 8. FUNDING SCALOGRAM: FORTY-FIRST HOUSE

Scale Position	Region and Party													
	NE		MA		MW		SS		BS		PS		Total	
	D	R	D	R	D	R	D	R	D	R	D	R	D	R
0	—		10		15		1		10		2		38	
		—		—		1		—		1		—		2
1	—		4		—		1		2		—		7	
2	1		2		—		—		1		1		5	
		—		1		1		1		—		—		3
3	—		—											
		—		1		6		5		—		—		12
4	—		—		—		1		—		—		1	
		1		5		18		6		5		—		35
5	—		—		—		—		—		—		—	
		18		27		21		4		3		2		75
Not Scaling	—		6		3		7		1		—		17	
		6		5		10		11		2		—		34
Total	1		22		18		10		14		3		68	
		25		39		57		27		11		2		161

Coefficient of Reproducibility = .984
Note: Regional codes in this table and all subsequent tables are a modified version of the Inter-University Consortium for Political and Social Research code. NE (New England) includes Connecticut, Maine, Massachusetts, New Hampshire, Rhode Island, and Vermont. MA (Middle Atlantic) includes Delaware, New Jersey, New York, and Pennsylvania. MW (Middle West) includes Illinois, Indiana, Iowa, Kansas, Michigan, Minnesota, Missouri, Nebraska, Ohio, and Wisconsin. SS (Solid South) includes the ten ex-Confederate states considered in this study. BS (Border States) includes Kentucky, Maryland, Tennessee, and West Virginia. PS (Pacific States) includes California, Nevada, Oregon, and Colorado after its admission in 1876. The vote totals in each table include paired and announced votes. For the methods used in scale construction, see the Bibliographical Essay.

Scale Position	SCALOGRAM ITEMS Identification

Scale Position / SCALOGRAM ITEMS
0 / Identification

0
1 To amend H.R. 2167 by striking out the words "coin in the Treasury of the United States" and inserting "United States notes in the Treasury of the United States arising from the sale of bonds authorized to be issued by this act, or other such notes in the Treasury." 42–127; + = Nay. *Congressional Globe,* 41st Cong., 2nd Sess., 5059 (July 1, 1870).
2 To pass H.R. 2167. 128–43; + = Yea. *Ibid.,* 5070 (July 1, 1870). To adopt the second report of the conference committee on S. 380. 139–53; + = Yea. *Ibid.,* 5523 (July 13, 1870).
3 To table the first report of the conference committee on S. 380. 55–123; + = Nay. *Ibid.,* 5467 (July 12, 1870).

  4 To amend H.R. 2167 by providing that "nothing in this act shall authorize the
    Secretary of the Treasury to allow or pay any commission or percentage for the
    sale of the bonds so issued, or any part thereof." 57–103; + = Nay. *Ibid.*, 5026
    (June 20, 1870).
  5 To adopt the first report of the conference committee on S. 380. 88–102; + =
    Yea. *Ibid.*, 5467 (July 12, 1870).
The higher the scale position, the more receptive a representative was to funding
legislation.

scalogram of key votes clearly indicates the partisan nature of the
issue (see Table 8). Seventy-five percent of the Democrats opposed
refunding at every opportunity (scale position 0) while 60 percent of
the Republicans supported it on every vote (scale position 5). Southern Republicans generally followed their party, but they were less
enthusiastic than Republicans from other regions, and when they
perceived that sectional interests would be harmed, as in the case
of section seven, they readily opposed party colleagues from the
Northeast.[22]

The refunding measure ultimately worked, although not as
quickly as Sherman had anticipated. The financial panic of 1873 and
ensuing depression, the silver agitation, and the vicissitudes of the
foreign market periodically slowed the refunding operation. Secretary of the Treasury George S. Boutwell arranged with a syndicate
headed by Jay Cooke & Company to open subscription for the 5 percent bonds, which were finally disposed of by August, 1876. The
treasury then managed to sell some $185 million of the 4.5 percents
before Sherman, now secretary of the treasury in the Hayes administration, decided that the market would accept the 4 percents in
1877. Sherman used the remaining 4.5 percents to stockpile gold in
preparation for resumption of specie payments, and once that was
achieved, sales of the 4 percents soared. By April, 1879, the debt had
been fully refunded.[23]

  22.   Only two Southerners, scalawag Lewis McKenzie (Va.) and Democrat William
Sherrod (Ala.), opposed the bill on the final vote. The other seven southern Democrats
failed to vote as did six of the twenty-eight Republicans. The Senate approved it without a roll call division. For the text of the act and that of an 1871 supplemental act
raising the amount of 5 percent refunding bonds to $500 million, see A. T. Hunt-
ington and Robert J. Mawhinney (comps.), *Laws of the United States Concerning
Money, Banking, and Loans, 1778–1909* (Washington, D.C.: Government Printing
Office, 1910), 203–206.
  23.   Patterson, *Federal Debt-Management Policies*, ch. 6.

The refunding process between 1871 and 1879 reduced the nation's annual interest obligation by approximately $20 million. Using tax and tariff revenues and the sinking fund, the government also retired about $600 million of the debt by 1880. Although the Democrats periodically tried to eliminate it, the sinking fund was never the subject of much dispute, but questions relating to tax and tariff rates and the uses to which revenues were to be put frequently disrupted Congress during the 1870s. Debt reduction and tax and tariff reduction, both desirable, were to a certain degree incompatible, and revenue policy affected appropriations and subsidies—all areas of interest to the postwar South.

Southern Democrats and Republicans usually voted together on measures adjusting rates of taxation with a bloc including most Democrats and a sizable number of midwestern Republicans. Northeasterners, especially the Republicans, were frequently on the opposite side of the question. The Forty-first Congress made the most important general reduction during the period when it eliminated many of the wartime taxes and reduced some tariff duties for an annual revenue reduction of approximately $80 million. The bill found substantial opposition only among Democrats from the mid-Atlantic and border states. The conservative southern press reprinted the act but most editors refrained from comment—an indication of backhanded approval of their Republican-dominated delegations.[24]

One internal levy not completely eliminated was the income tax—another product of the wartime search for revenue. Northeastern Republicans and most northern Democrats conducted a strong campaign to repeal the income tax, but Southerners were more ambivalent. Some conservative newspapers urged repeal; the Atlanta *Constitution*, for example, referred to it as "odious," and the New Orleans *Price Current* found it unconstitutional. Still, the tax affected but few Southerners—they paid only 5 percent of the total income tax collected in 1871, and after 1873 they frequently sought

24. *Congressional Globe*, 41st Cong., 2nd Sess., 5238, 5522, Appendix, 701–707; New Orleans *Daily Picayune*, July 20, 21, 1870; Atlanta *Constitution*, June 9, 1870; Richmond *Whig*, July 12, 19, December 31, 1870; Tuskaloosa *Independent Monitor*, November 1, 1870; *De Bow's Review*, VIII (1870), 686. Only the Richmond *Whig* commented (favorably) on the bill.

to reinstitute it as a just tax on northeastern wealth.[25] In the 1870 debate, most Southerners voted to reduce the tax rate and increase the level of exemption, but few favored complete abolition. After extensive debate in both chambers, the rates were reduced from 5 to 2 percent, the exemption was increased from one thousand to two thousand dollars, and the tax was to be abolished completely in 1872 (see Table 9).[26]

Sectionalism emerged more sharply on the southern Republicans' effort in 1873 to refund the $57 million in taxes collected on raw cotton from 1862 to 1868. Southerners charged that the tax had been an unconstitutional levy upon the products of a section not represented in the national councils—a simple case of "taxation without representation" according to one North Carolina editor. Most Southerners were willing to concede that portion of the tax collected during the war, but they unanimously favored refunding the balance. Carpetbagger Legrand W. Perce of Mississippi, the leader of the refunding movement, argued that the "subject is entirely outside party issues. . . . It is an appeal from one entire section of the country, including all classes, all colors, all parties, to the General Govern-

25. Atlanta *Constitution*, July 12, 1870, February 28, 1871; New Orleans *Price Current*, January 3, 1873; *House Executive Documents*, 42nd Cong., 3rd Sess., No. 4, p. 115; Carl V. Harris, "Right Fork or Left Fork? The Section-Party Alignments of Southern Democrats in Congress, 1873–1897," *Journal of Southern History*, XLII (1976), 489–93; Sidney Ratner, *American Taxation: Its History as a Social Force in Democracy* (New York: W. W. Norton, 1942), 121–28, 130–35. Scalawag Charles Hays (Ala.) and carpetbagger Logan H. Roots (Ark.) best summarized southern arguments for continuing the tax in *Congressional Globe*, 41st Cong., 2nd Sess., 2202–2204, 4308.

26. Southern senators reacted similarly; see the divisions in *Congressional Globe*, 41st Cong., 2nd Sess., 5087–98, 5099, 5102, 5237. It would seem that a legislator's reaction to the income tax issue might be directly related to such factors as personal wealth, but such was not the case. A number of statistical measures of association were used to test the relationships between legislators' voting behavior on economic issues and their personal characteristics such as occupation, level of wealth, political faction, and, for representatives, the social and economic characteristics of their districts. With very few exceptions, the correlation analysis failed to reveal significant relationships because of the sectional (and occasionally political) nature of congressional divisions on economic issues. On the income tax issue, for example, Goodman and Kruskal's gamma, a measurement of association (with values ranging from -1 to $+1$) between ordered categorical variables, was used to test the relationship between a representative's scale position and his personal and constituency characteristics. The highest correlation was a modest gamma = $-.348$ which existed between scale position and the percent agricultural index—that is, members from more heavily agricultural districts tended to favor retaining the income tax.

Table 9. INCOME TAX SCALOGRAM: FORTY-FIRST HOUSE

Scale Position	NE D	NE R	MA D	MA R	MW D	MW R	SS D	SS R	BS D	BS R	PS D	PS R	Total D	Total R
0	—		—		3		1		3		—		7	
		5		2		20		4		5		—		36
1	—		1		1		2		1		—		5	
		2		3		20		7		3		—		35
2	—		1		1		—		1		—		3	
		1		8		5		6		3		—		23
3	—		—		4		1		—		—		5	
		5		8		3		5		—		—		21
4	—		18		5		2		7		3		35	
		10		15		3		1		—		2		31
Not Scaling	1		2		4		3[a]		2		—		12	
		2		3		6		5[b]		—		—		16
Total	1		22		18		9		14		3		67	
		25		39		57		28		11		2		162

Coefficient of Reproducibility = .978

[a] James K. Gibson (Va.), A. A. C. Rogers (Ark.), and Francis E. Shober (N.C.) did not scale because of excessive absences.

[b] Alfred E. Buck (Ala.), Charles W. Buckley (Ala.), Clinton L. Cobb (N.C.), Solomon L. Hoge (S.C.), and Alexander H. Jones (N.C.) did not scale because of excessive absences.

Scale Position	SCALOGRAM ITEMS Identification
0	

1 To amend H.R. 2045, a bill to reduce internal taxes, by increasing the amount of income exempted from $1,500 to $2,000. 138–52; + = Yea. *Congressional Globe*, 41st Cong., 2nd Sess., 4063 (June 3, 1870).

2 To amend H.R. 2045 by reducing the income tax rate from 5% to 3%. 114–76; + = Yea. *Ibid.*

3 To suspend rules and pass a bill to repeal the income tax (H.R. 2994). 91–116; + = Yea. *Ibid.*, 41st Cong., 3rd Sess., 1851 (March 2, 1871).

4 To suspend rules and strike out a section in a Senate amendment to H.R. 2045 relating to the income tax. 67–116; + = Yea. *Ibid.*, 41st Cong., 2nd Sess., 5415 (July 9, 1870).

The higher the scale position, the more receptive a representative was to income tax reduction and repeal.

ment." He might have added that the refund would give a healthy boost to the languishing southern economy.[27]

Although they argued among themselves as to who was to receive the refund, a caucus of southern representatives finally agreed to support a bill (H.R. 3564) making restitution to the party paying the tax. But southern unity was of little value as the House was not disposed to consider, let alone pass, a refund of the cotton tax. Mississippi carpetbagger George McKee's motion to call up the bill in January, 1873, and make it a special order of business "from day to day until the same is disposed of" split the House along sectional lines. Representatives from the southern and border states favored the motion 60–3, but members from the other regions offered a resounding 14–102 negative vote. Northern Republicans opposed it 3–74. Three weeks later, Southerners voted 45–0 in a final attempt to suspend the rules and set a time for consideration, but the movement failed 94–83. Southerners continued to press the issue, but the later efforts of solidly Democratic delegations were no more successful than that led by carpetbaggers, scalawags, and blacks in the Forty-second House.[28]

Taxable commodities viewed as specific southern interests (such as tobacco) also evoked a unified response from the section's delegations. Following the lead of the Virginians, who frequently reminded the country that the Old Dominion paid in more internal revenue than all of New England, the carpetbaggers, scalawags, blacks, and conservatives responded as a bloc to measures aiding tobacco growers and manufacturers. A typical division came early in 1875 when southern representatives voted 41–1 to suspend the rules and pass a bill facilitating the retail sales of leaf tobacco. Democrats

27. Raleigh *Register,* July 5, 1867; *Congressional Globe,* 42nd Cong., 2nd Sess., Appendix, 411–19. For a sampling of the broad base of refund sentiment, see Little Rock *Evening Republican,* December 26, 1867, January 18, 1868; Atlanta *Constitution,* March 8, 1873; New Orleans *Price Current,* January 3, 1873; Vicksburg *Daily Herald,* January 14, 1873; Jackson *Weekly Clarion,* October 31, 1872; New Orleans *Republican,* March 29, 1874; Austin *Democratic Statesman,* December 20, 1874; David Heaton to John Sherman, December 19, 1867, Willard Warner to Sherman, March 5, 1869, in Sherman Papers; *Congressional Globe,* 42nd Cong., 2nd Sess., 540–41, 1300–1301, 42nd Cong., 3rd Sess., Appendix, 48–52. Southern Republicans submitted five of the eight bills presented during the Congress to refund the tax.

28. *Congressional Globe,* 42nd Cong., 3rd Sess., 891, 1430.

from outside the South supported the move, but Republicans from the Northeast and Midwest responded with a 10–99 negative vote to deny rules suspension. A reduction in the tobacco tax was the most prominent feature of the second major internal revenue act of the decade passed in early 1879. Southern Republican senators and representatives, now numbering only a dozen, sided unanimously with the Democrats in both chambers to pass the bill over the nearly united opposition of Republicans from other regions.[29]

Considerably less unanimity existed among Southerners on tariff questions. Outside of a shifting and variously motivated free trade–revenue reform group dominated by the Democrats, voting behavior on tariff issues reflected special and local interests, contradictory opinions of the impact of tariff adjustments, and, in the case of the South, differing perceptions of the region's economic future. With the exception of the sugar and rice interests, the idea of protection won little support in the South. Occasionally an influential newspaper such as the Richmond *Whig* questioned the wisdom of the antiprotectionist stance and wondered if the tariff really deserved the blame it was frequently accorded for southern economic problems. The *Whig*'s editor bravely declared in early 1870 that Virginia's iron industries needed protection and cautiously speculated that the state "may come to the conclusion that her welfare may best be promoted by a high protective tariff." Virginia's congressmen should "ponder this matter very seriously before they determine to settle down in the old rut."[30]

29. *Ibid.*, 41st Cong., 3rd Sess., 747; Richmond *Southern Planter and Farmer*, XXXIV (1874), 166; "Tobacco—Its Future in the South," Richmond *Southern Review*, XXV (1879), 380–94; *Congressional Record*, 43rd Cong., 2nd Sess., 886, 45th Cong., 2nd Sess., 4770, 45th Cong., 3rd Sess., 1527. For similar divisions on the tobacco tax, see *Congressional Globe*, 42nd Cong., 2nd Sess., 4100; *Congressional Record*, 43rd Cong., 2nd Sess., 1976, 45th Cong., 2nd Sess., 3210, 4169, 4203, 45th Cong., 3rd Sess., 1463, 1521, 1552.

30. Richmond *Whig*, January 25, 1870. For similar opinion see Richmond *Daily Dispatch*, January 6, 1872, clipping in Jabez Lamar Monroe Curry Papers, Alabama Department of Archives and History, Montgomery; *To the Old Whigs of Louisiana*, March 1, 1876 (pamphlet), in J. R. G. Pitkin Papers, Middleton Library, Louisiana State University, Baton Rouge; *De Bow's Review*, VIII (1870), 285; and the debate at the end of the decade in the Richmond *Southern Planter and Farmer*, XL (1879), 68–71, 121–25, 239–43, 288–90. In terms of value of productions, Virginia was only 57 percent agricultural—the lowest of any southern state.

But generally the various rationales and intersectional agreements which prompted some northern farmers and laborers to support protection had little appeal in the South, and most conservatives never considered the potential benefits of protection. The Atlanta *Constitution*, for example, continued to crusade for free trade while simultaneously proclaiming that the city's future lay in manufacturing and industry. Even the Louisianians, traditionally protective of sugar, were well aware of strong southern opposition to their position. "It may not suit some of the people of free trade notions in New Orleans," carpetbagger Lionel Sheldon acknowledged in 1870, "but I could not help taking a view in behalf of a tariff for the benefit of agriculture in order to be effective for sugar. . . . So many consume and so few produce sugar that it becomes a hard question." "The pet idea of all Southern statesmen, the main political principle upon which the Southern people of all political shades have ever been a unit," a conservative New Orleans editor asserted, "is that of unrestricted trade." And Henry Adams reflected northeastern opinion when he declared in 1870 that to be for free trade in the South was like "having worn a rebel uniform or having been out with the Ku-Klux klan."[31]

The major divisions on the tariff occurred in 1872 with the passage of a major downward revision of duties, including an across-the-board 10 percent reduction on many protected items, and in early 1875 when that reduction was repealed and the rates further adjusted. Auspicious financial conditions, particularly a redundant revenue, prompted the 1872 reductions. After paying appropriations and the interest on the public debt, the government surplus averaged nearly $100 million in both 1871 and 1872—an amount greatly exceeding sinking fund requirements. The surplus shrank to dangerous levels in the aftermath of the Panic of 1873, and Republicans justified the repeal of the 1872 reduction as necessary to replenish declining revenues.

31. Atlanta *Constitution*, July 8, 1870, January 1, 1871, April 2, 1872, January 23, 1873; Sugar Petitions and Letters File, in Justin S. Morrill Papers, Baker Library, Harvard University, Cambridge; Lionel A. Sheldon to Henry Clay Warmoth, February 2, 1870, in Henry Clay Warmoth Papers, Southern Historical Collection, University of North Carolina, Chapel Hill; New Orleans *Times*, March 4, 1869; Henry B. Adams, "The Session," *North American Review*, XCI (1870), 45.

Southern Republicans and Democrats supported the final version of the 1872 bill, but the numerous preliminary roll calls indicate that Democrats voted, often indiscriminately, for nearly every proposal to reduce or eliminate duties while Republicans were more reluctant to abandon all the protective features of the tariff. They were certainly more protectionist than Democrats on such southern commodities as sugar and rice, but they were also more vocal in efforts to secure reductions on such items as cotton bagging materials—a position which brought them into conflict with some northeastern manufacturers. Moreover, they were not as protectionist as their northeastern party colleagues, particularly those from the mid-Atlantic states, and they often found themselves in conflict with northern Republicans on tea, coffee, salt, spices, and a large number of items which were added to the free list (see Tables 10 and 11).[32]

Southerners disagreed most sharply over duties on coal, pig iron, and a variety of steel products. Typical divisions came on a House resolution to repeal the duty on coal which southern Republicans opposed 4–13 and southern Democrats favored 16–1, and on a motion to pass a resolution "encouraging passage of a bill to reduce the tariff on pig iron" which Republicans opposed 3–14 and Democrats approved 13–0. To conclude from such behavior, however, that southern Republicans "sold out" to protectionists like William "Pig Iron" Kelley of Pennsylvania is to overlook the snarl of interests and perceptions which entered the tariff debate. Both Virginia and Alabama, for example, already had substantial iron and coal interests, and several other southeastern and border states were hopeful of developing such concerns. Republicans from those areas and the few Democrats who joined them can hardly be condemned for support-

32. See the remarks and amendments of southern Republicans on H.R. 2045 in *Congressional Globe*, 41st Cong., 2nd Sess., 2202–2204, 2262–63, 2695–96, 2257, 5419, 4927–28, and on H.R. 2322 in *Congressional Globe*, 42nd Cong., 2nd Sess., 3234–35, 3569, 3403, 3564, 3569, and Francis Peabody to Charles Sumner, May 29, 1872, in Morrill Papers. For a useful comparison of the rates on each item in each piece of legislation passed during the period, see *Senate Reports*, 49th Cong., 1st Sess., No. 12, especially Table III, 162–226, and Table IV, 230–94. Tables 10 and 11 offer only a general indication of attitudes. Tariff measures are the least receptive of any questions to scale analysis because the votes on some items do not scale with those on other items; accordingly the scale distribution on one set of items often varies sharply with that on another set.

Table 10. TARIFF SCALOGRAM: FORTY-SECOND HOUSE

Scale Position	Region and Party												
	NE		MA		MW		SS		BS		PS		Total	
	D	R	D	R	D	R	D	R	D	R	D	R	D	R
0	—		6		1		—		—		—		7	
		3		16		5		—		1		—		25
1	—		1		—		—		—		—		1	
		4		8		8		8		1		—		29
2	—		1		—		2ᵃ		—		—		3	
		2		2		4		5		1		1		15
3	—		1		—		—		—		—		1	
		1		—		3		2		—		—		6
4	1		—		—		1		—		—		2	
		3		2		3		5		—		1		14
5	1		4		—		—		1		—		6	
		7		2		10		2		—		1		22
6	—		1		3		4		1		—		9	
		1		—		7		1		—		—		9
7	2		12		15		11		18		2		60	
		—		—		9		—		—		—		9
Not Scaling	—		4		4		2ᵇ		2		—		12	
		1		1		3		5ᶜ		—		—		10
Total	4		30		23		20		22		2		101	
		22		31		52		28		3		3		139

Coefficient of Reproducibility = .953
ᵃJames C. Harper (N.C.), James M. Leach (N.C.).
ᵇJohn Hancock (Tex.) and Francis E. Shober (N.C.) did not scale because of excessive absences.
ᶜHenry W. Barry (Miss.), Robert DeLarge (S.C.), Charles Hays (Ala.), George C. McKee (Miss.), and Charles H. Porter (Va.), did not scale because of excessive absences. Their scattered votes indicate that DeLarge, Hays, and McKee generally favored and Barry and Porter generally opposed tariff reductions.

Scale Position	SCALOGRAM ITEMS Identification
o	

1 To suspend the rules and pass H.R. 173, a bill repealing the duty on salt. 147–46; + = Yea. *Congressional Globe*, 42nd Cong., 1st Sess., 81 (March 13, 1871).
2 To suspend the rules and pass a resolution suspending the rules and passing H.R. 2322, a bill reducing import duties and internal taxes. 149–61; + = Yea. *Ibid.*, 42nd Cong., 2nd Sess., 3652 (May 20, 1872).
3 To refer H.R. 2322 to the Ways and Means Committee with instruction to report a bill reducing by 10% the duties on most protected items. 117–75; + = Yea. *Ibid.*, 3159b (May 7, 1872).

4 To amend the instructions referring H.R. 2322 to the Ways and Means Committee by requiring a clause in the revised bill reducing by 10% the duties on most protected items. 111–77; + = Yea. *Ibid.,* 3159a (May 7, 1872).
5 To suspend the rules and pass a resolution calling for the placing of salt and coal on the free list of any bill levying import duties. 102–87; + = Yea. *Ibid.,* 1118 (February 19, 1872).
6 To suspend the rules and pass a resolution encouraging the passage of a bill to reduce the tariff on pig iron. 75–99; + = Yea. *Ibid.,* 1217 (February 26, 1872).
7 To amend H.R. 2322 by reducing from 90% to 80% the rate of duties on cotton, wool, iron, and straw. 80–110; + = Yea. *Ibid.,* 3158 (May 7, 1872).

The higher the scale position, the more receptive a representative was to tariff reduction.

ing protection for their established or fledgling industries. It is also evident that a good many Republicans had a personal stake in southern manufacturing and extractive industries. Most believed that an antiprotectionist stance would prove detrimental to these and to their vision of a diversified and balanced economy, a dream shared by some "New South"–minded Democrats and one of those Whiggish notions attracting natives to the Republican party.[33]

The primary weakness of a horizontal tariff reduction is that it can be easily revoked. The Forty-third Congress repealed the 10 percent reduction, increased duties on sugar, and elevated revenue taxes on whiskey and tobacco in a maneuver that was primarily partisan. Arguing that declining revenues necessitated the increases, Republicans labeled the measure "an act to further protect the sinking fund and to provide for the exigencies of government." Democrats recognized the problem but called for the reimposition of duties on tea and coffee as a better means of increasing revenues. Southerners tried unsuccessfully to strike the additional tax on tobacco but did not protest the increase in sugar duties. On the final vote, however, they split along party lines. Southern Republicans appeared to agree with a Tennessee colleague who reasoned that repeal of the 10 per-

33. *Congressional Globe,* 42nd Cong., 1st Sess., 82, 42nd Cong., 2nd Sess., 1217; Francis A. Walker (comp.), *The Statistics of the Wealth and Industry of the United States . . . 1870* (Washington, D.C.: Government Printing Office, 1872), 494, 507, 556, 568, 578, 755–56, 761–65. Overall, 44 percent of the 129 Republicans had some personal economic interest in professional (other than law) or mercantile pursuits or such concerns as railroads, banking, shipping, manufacturing, and extractive industries. Of the 122 Democrats, only 19 percent were identified as having either primary or secondary interests in those areas; nearly 95 percent of the Democrats were primarily involved in either law or agriculture.

Table 11.   TARIFF SCALOGRAM: FORTY-SECOND SENATE

Scale Position	Region and Party													
	NE D	NE R	MA D	MA R	MW D	MW R	SS D	SS R	BS D	BS R	PS D	PS R	Total D	Total R
0	—		—		—		—		—		—		—	
		1		1		1		1		—		—		4
1	—		—		—		—		—		—		—	
		4		2		3		1		1		3		14
2	—		—		—		—		—		—		—	
		1		1		1		1		—		—		4
3	—		—		—		—		—		—		—	
		1		—		1		2		—		—		4
4	—		1		—		—		—		—		1	
		—		—		2		4		—		—		6
5	—		—		—		—		—		—		—	
		—		—		1		1		—		—		2
6	—		—		1		—		—		—		1	
		—		—		1		2		—		—		3
7	—		2		2		4		4		2		14	
		—		—		1		1		—		—		2
Not Scaling	—		—		—		—		2		—		2	
		5		1		6		3ᵃ		1		1		17
Total	—		3		3		4		6		2		18	
		12		5		17		16		2		4		56

Coefficient of Reproducibility = .958
ᵃBenjamin F. Rice (Ark.), George E. Spencer (Ala.), and Joseph R. West (La.) did not scale because of excessive absences.

Scale Position   SCALOGRAM ITEMS
                                        Identification

0

1 To pass H.R. 2322, "an act to reduce duties on imports, and to reduce internal taxes, and for other purposes." 50–3; + = Yea. *Congressional Globe*, 42nd Cong., 2nd Sess., 4088 (May 30, 1872).

2 To amend H.R. 2322 by excepting imports of pig iron and steel rails from the general reduction of tariff rates. 19–35; + = Nay. *Ibid.*, 3906 (May 27, 1872).

3 To amend H.R. 2322 by taxing bulk salt at 9¢ per pound and packaged salt an additional 6¢ per package. 24–33; + = Nay. *Ibid.*, 4051 (May 30, 1872). To amend H.R. 2322 by placing the tariff on sulphate of quinine at 23% *ad valorem*. 19–25; + = Nay. *Ibid.*, 4065 (May 30, 1872).

4 To amend H.R. 2322 by adding a 20% *ad valorem* tariff on all paper and its manufacturers, except books and other printed matter. 20–23; + = Nay. *Ibid.*, 4057 (May 30, 1872).
To amend H.R. 2322 by removing skins from the 10% reduction list. 25–24; + = Nay. *Ibid.*, 3917 (May 27, 1872).

5 To amend H.R. 2322 by striking the tariff on books at 12½ cents per pound.
   25–20; + = Nay. *Ibid.*, 3955 (May 28, 1872).
6 To amend H.R. 2322 by adding earthware to the 10% reduction list. 19–24; + =
   Yea. *Ibid.*, 4061 (May 30, 1872).
7 To concur in an amendment to H.R. 2322 which strikes out a section allowing ⅔
   of import duties to be paid in gold and ⅓ in U.S. legal tender notes. 37–18; + =
   Nay. *Ibid.*, 4076 (May 30, 1872).
The higher the scale position, the more receptive a senator was to tariff reduction.

cent reduction would encourage the exploitation of "the great depository of iron and coal in the country [which] lies south of what is known as Mason and Dixon's line." Louisiana carpetbagger Jacob H. Sypher, obviously pleased that the bill raised duties on molasses and sugar of all kinds by 25 percent, added that the West and South might "find some profit" in following the northeastern example of protection to develop their manufacturing and industrial interests.[34]

In supporting the tax and tariff increase, southern Republicans appear to have flown in the face of regional economic interests. Some of them had opposed the tariff reduction in the first place because manufactures of cotton, iron, and steel were included. Others may well have believed northeastern arguments that the sinking fund, and thereby the nation's credit, was in jeopardy because of the sharp decline in revenues after the Panic of 1873. But the 1875 tariff and tax hike best demonstrates the Southerners' awareness of the connection between revenue levels and appropriations. The Senate debates indicate that southern Republicans favored the bill not because they wished to elevate tobacco taxes, increase tariff rates, or protect the sinking fund, but rather because its passage would guarantee approval of a large rivers and harbors appropriations bill which was particularly generous to southern projects. It was well understood that if the revenue bill failed, all pending appropriations legislation would also go down to defeat. On March 2, 1875, with

34. Edward Stanwood, *American Tariff Controversies in the Nineteenth Century* (2 vols.; New York: Houghton Mifflin, 1903), II, 187–91; *Congressional Record*, 43rd Cong., 2nd Sess., 1180–91, 1208–19, 1385–1416, 1530–39, 1543–60, 1655–67, 1943–84, 2057–65. In the House, southern Democrats opposed the measure 0–23, Republicans supported it 18–5; all six Senate Democrats opposed it, Republicans favored it 9–2.

one day left in the Congress, southern Republicans provided nine votes for the revenue bill, which barely passed 30–29. After a fury of activity on the following day, they secured a rivers and harbors act which, in addition to giving about $1.4 million to southern projects, allowed James B. Eads to begin his controversial but ultimately successful jetty scheme to clear the mud bars from the mouth of the Mississippi River—a project of tremendous importance to southern commerce. The Eads scheme committed the government to an expenditure that would eventually total $8 million. Critics of the southern Republicans have failed to note that the additional burdens placed on the South by the tariff and tax act were relatively insignificant when compared to benefits the section derived from the rivers and harbors act.[35]

Of all the economic issues considered during the 1870s, Southerners were least concerned with debt management. The Republicans among them generally supported refunding and their party's pledges to the nation's creditors in the Public Credit Act. Because the issue took on partisan overtones, southern Democrats, like their party colleagues from other regions, periodically denigrated northeastern bondholders and the decision to pay the debt in coin. But Democrats shared basic bourgeois beliefs in the sanctity of property and the responsibility of government to maintain the public credit. They might disagree over interpretations of the law, but no American politician wished to become tainted with repudiation or charged with violation of the rights of private property.

The closely related revenue questions held more interest for Southerners. Because of their personal economic interests and differing visions of their region's economic future, Republicans frequently

35. *Congressional Record*, 43rd Cong., 2nd Sess., 1943, 1947, 1975–76, 2036, 2161–79. See also Chapter VII below. The tariff issue merits reconsideration. Historians have never fully explained how the protective features of the tariff harmed the South and what kinds of revision would have helped. Fuller understanding of the problem will come only with a close analysis of southern attitudes and interests, the congressional debates on each item, and the interplay between revenue policy and appropriations—as well as some hard statistical measurement of the tariff's impact on the South.

disagreed with their Democratic colleagues on tariff matters, but they were quick to defend what they and the Democrats perceived to be sectional interests on internal revenue questions. Their reaction to the public credit and debt refunding measures offered an early indication that southern Republicans were not going to line up faithfully with their northeastern party colleagues on economic questions. Their independence, fully evident on revenue policy, paralleled their often belligerent stance against the Northeast on the money questions considered during the decade after readmission.

VI The Money Questions
Bank Notes, Greenbacks, and Silver

"The present financial system," an irritated Southerner informed Andrew Johnson in 1867, "is a greater curse to the South than would be a standing army of 200,000 men to be supported by the South."[1] He did not greatly exaggerate the situation; with the exception of racial problems, the most important set of questions facing Congress in the postwar period related to money. Like racial questions, the monetary problems defied simple solutions, but whereas the former often boiled down to a yes-no proposition whose importance waned in congressional eyes, issues involving money provided a broad range of conflicting interests and demanded an increasing amount of congressional attention. Forced off the gold standard in late 1861, the Union had resorted to two nonspecie-backed forms of currency, United States notes (greenbacks) and national bank notes. Irritated by the Panic of 1873 and subsequent economic troubles, the questions of how and when the nation should resume specie payments, and the matters of how much and what kinds of money the country needed excited a decade of controversy over the future of gold, bank notes, greenbacks, and silver in the monetary system. Because participants in the dispute clung to their personal money beliefs as immutable principles, agreement was difficult and the problems were passed along from Congress to Congress.

Southern interests in the money questions were direct and intimate. By all accounts, the rebuilding section needed credit and banking facilities and an adequate circulating medium. The dearth of currency was particularly critical. At the end of the war, Confederate

1. H. H. Day to Andrew Johnson, September 7, 1868, quoted in George LaVerne Anderson, "The National Banking System, 1865–1875: A Sectional Institution" (Ph.D. dissertation, University of Illinois, 1933), 146.

money was worth less than the paper on which it was printed, and state banks surviving the war found themselves facing a prohibitive 10 percent federal tax on their circulation. The establishment of national banks in the section was nearly impossible because most of the authorized national bank note circulation had been taken up by northern national banks. With the occasional exception of New Orleans and certain areas in Texas, suspension of specie payments had driven gold from common circulation, and the silver dollar had similarly disappeared because it commanded a premium even in gold until the mid-1870s. Furthermore, between 1865 and 1868, the secretary of the treasury had contracted the national greenback circulation from $400 million to $356 million.[2] Given these circumstances, the South had little recourse but to turn to various kinds of unauthorized scrip, which in addition to being notoriously unstable was taxed by Congress in 1867. Bank notes and greenbacks were acquired by the slow method of influx in payment for staple products which, while relatively heavy in 1865 and 1866, slowed with poorer crops in the following years.

Throughout the decade after readmission, southern congressmen sought to rectify this situation. Conservatives generally disliked the national banking system established during the war, but they loathed their dependence on northeastern banking facilities, and most supported efforts to redistribute and/or expand the available volume of bank notes so that national banks could be established in the South. And despite their aversion to irredeemable paper, later efforts to contract the greenback circulation in preparation for resumption won little support in the South, and expansion, particularly after the Panic of 1873, found much favor. Resumption of specie payments posed a dilemma. If it entailed a sharp contraction of the currency as most believed, then the South could ill afford the process. But southern leadership had long thrived on hard-money principles, and the Jacksonian notion that specie or specie-backed paper was the only proper circulating medium had been reinforced

2.   Robert T. Patterson, *Federal Debt-Management Policies, 1865–1879* (Durham: Duke University Press, 1954), ch. 10; Robert P. Sharkey, *Money, Class, and Party: An Economic Study of Civil War and Reconstruction* (Baltimore: Johns Hopkins Press, 1959), chs. 2–3, pp. 231–35.

for years by the conviction that the staple crops commanded gold worldwide. Advocates of hard money wavered in the face of a currency shortage and when the agitation for remonetization of silver began in 1876, Southerners found an attractive alternative between irredeemable paper and the harsh fact of gold resumption. By the time the silver debate climaxed two years later, Southerners, with most problems of political reconstruction behind them, openly rallied to silver and the bimetallic standard.

In one form or another the money questions were before Congress almost constantly. The major episodes included efforts to adjust the bank note circulation just after readmission, the push for greenback and bank note expansion in 1874 which ironically ended with the Resumption Act early in the following year, and the debate over remonetization of silver from 1876 to 1878. With few exceptions, sectional rather than political interests governed legislative behavior, and the Southerners, Democrats and Republicans alike, showed a remarkable unity in their perceptions of sectional needs. Whether or not those perceptions accurately reflected economic realities is not at question here. Southerners believed they understood the problem, and their proposed solutions became the basis for section-party alignments in Congress. If overshadowed for much of the decade by the politics of reconstruction, financial questions were nonetheless important to the South, and her congressmen played a far more active role in the national discussions than previous commentators have indicated.

For Southerners the first phase of the money question began shortly after readmission with a modest effort to correct some of the glaring sectional inequities in the national banking system. With the goal of providing more stable banking facilities and a sound and uniform currency during the war, Congress had stipulated that "associations" of at least five persons, with a minimum capital of $50,000 and a deposit of federal bonds with the newly created office of the comptroller of the currency, would be granted charters as national banks. They were then allowed to issue bank notes in specified proportion to their bond deposits and required to maintain a "lawful money" reserve on their circulation and deposits. National bank notes, limited in volume to $300 million and redeemable in green-backs, were receivable for most public debts and government obliga-tions. The number of national banks grew slowly until March, 1865, when a congressionally imposed 10 percent tax on state bank notes accelerated the conversion of state banks to national banks. By early 1866, while the South remained in limbo, new national banks in the North had absorbed most of the allotted $300 million.[3]

The national banking system had a number of shortcomings, but the most evident sectional inequity was the maldistribution of bank notes. Originally, they were to be allotted to each state on the basis of population, existing bank capital, resources, and business inter-ests, but through misadministration and ambiguities in the law, New England, New York, and Pennsylvania ended up with 999 of the 1,647 national banks and $218 million of the $293 million in bank notes that were issued. Comparative statistics on the actual distri-bution show an incredible sectional imbalance. Providence, Rhode Island, had about one and one-half times the combined circulation of the ten ex-Confederate states, the circulation of the tiny burg of Waterville, Maine, equaled that of Alabama, and Florida had no bank note circulation at all. On a per capita basis, Rhode Island had $77.17 while Arkansas had 13¢. When the problem became apparent in the spring of 1866, Northeasterners argued that they needed more cir-culation for trade and manufacturing, but it was equally evident that the South and West lacked an adequate supply of sound currency and the readily available credit instruments and facilities which the Northeast used to conduct business.[4]

The maldistribution was the subject of much debate but little ac-tion until 1868 when the Senate passed a bill (S. 440) to withdraw up

3. A. T. Huntington and Robert J. Mawhinney (comps.), *Laws of the United States Concerning Money, Banking, and Loans, 1778–1909* (Washington, D.C.: Gov-ernment Printing Office, 1910), 330–62; Fritz Redlich, *The Molding of American Banking: Men and Ideas* (2 vols.; New York: Hafner Publishing Company, 1951), II, 99–121; Sharkey, *Money, Class, and Party,* 221–29; John Jay Knox to Justin S. Mor-rill, February 19, 1868, in Justin S. Morrill Papers, Baker Library, Harvard University, Cambridge.

4. Sharkey, *Money, Class, and Party,* 229–37; Anderson, "National Banking Sys-tem," chs. 3–4; John A. James, "Financial Underdevelopment in the Post Bellum South," *Journal of Interdisciplinary History,* XI (1981), 443–54; Richard E. Sylla, *The American Capital Market, 1846–1914: A Study of the Effects of Public Policy on Economic Development* (New York: Arno Press, 1975), 48–70.

to $20 million from states whose bank note circulation exceeded their lawful quota and distribute it to those with less than $5 of such circulation per capita. The House Committee on Banking and Currency did not report the measure until early 1869 after seven southern delegations had been seated. The committee recommended a slightly larger redistribution, but on the floor, currency-hungry Southerners and Midwesterners, under the lead of Indiana Republican John Coburn, amended the bill to provide for a complete redistribution. Half of the original $300 million would be allotted to states according to their representation in Congress, and half according to the official valuation of all real and personal property in each state. The vote on the Coburn amendment and the subsequent votes on S. 440 as amended were bipartisan and sectional. The New England and mid-Atlantic states, guarding their bank note circulation jealously, lined up in opposition while the Southerners, carpetbaggers, scalawags, and conservatives alike, combined with most members from the midwestern and border states to send the measure back to the Senate (see Table 12: A).

The twelve southern senators, all Republicans, got their first look at redistribution when the House returned S. 440, and in a sectional alignment similar to that in the lower chamber, the Senate barely failed to concur in the Coburn amendment (see Table 12: B). With the end of the Congress less than ten days away, the Southerners quickly called for a conference committee to resolve the differences between the chambers. "I am extremely desirous, as I suppose nearly every Senator here who represents a southern State is, to secure additional circulation," carpetbagger Joseph Abbott of North Carolina declared, and he hoped a conference committee might settle on a redistribution of at least $40 million. A committee was appointed, but the Senate conferees opposed any redistribution over the original $20 million and the question died for the moment.[5]

It resurfaced two weeks later in the Forty-first Congress when John Sherman of the Senate Finance Committee reported a measure (S. 43) nearly identical to the Senate bill in the previous Congress. This time the Southerners were better prepared and more vocal, and

5. *Congressional Globe*, 40th Cong., 3rd Sess., 1181–86, 1269–74, 1319–34, 1435, 1446, 1816, 1897–98.

Table 12. SELECTED VOTES ON BANK NOTE REDISTRIBUTION: FORTIETH
HOUSE AND SENATE

A. House vote on the Coburn amendment to S. 440[a]

Region	Yea Dem.	Yea Rep.	Nay Dem.	Nay Rep.
NE	—	1	1	21
MA	2	—	11	36
MW	8	42	2	10
SS	2	22	—	—
BS	5	8	2	1
PS	1	2	1	1
Total	18	75	17	69
Grand Total	93		86	

B. Senate vote to concur in the Coburn amendment[b]

Region	Yea Dem.	Yea Rep.	Nay Dem.	Nay Rep.
NE	—	—	—	10
MA	—	—	1	5
MW	2	10	—	4
SS	—	9	—	—
BS	3	2	2	—
PS	—	—	—	5
Total	5	21	3	24
Grand Total	26		27	

[a] *Congressional Globe*, 40th Cong., 3rd Sess., 1325 (February 17, 1869).
[b] *Ibid.*, 1435 (February 22, 1869).

almost immediately several new elements entered the debate. Arguing that withdrawal of circulation would "disturb" his state, Massachusetts Republican Henry Wilson proposed that instead of redistribution, the bank note currency should be expanded by $50 million, but he stipulated that as the new bank notes were issued, the greenback circulation would be contracted by an equal amount to avoid any expansion of the combined circulation. Speaking for the Southerners, Abbott immediately called for the defeat of Wilson's amendment because the greenbacks were the chief national circulation in the South; to exchange one type of money for another would be of no value to the section.

Believing the measure to be the first of "practical importance" for the South since readmission, South Carolina scalawag Frederick Sawyer intensified the sectional dispute by charging that the Wilson and several other New England–sponsored amendments were designed to embarrass the bill so that it would fail in the House. Sawyer's comments provoked a series of sharp exchanges between several Southerners including Abbott, carpetbaggers William Pitt Kellogg of Louisiana and Willard Warner of Alabama, scalawags John Pool of North Carolina and Thomas Robertson of South Carolina, and New England Republicans including Wilson, Charles Sumner of Massachusetts, William Buckingham of Connecticut, and William Pitt Fessenden of Maine. The controversy revolved around Wilson's amendment, the refusal of New Englanders to give up any of their banking circulation, and a certain self-righteousness which the Southerners found particularly irritating. Fessenden best exemplified the latter with his declaration that New England deserved the extra circulation for her patriotic efforts during the war and that the Southerners should not be so aggressive and expect everything to be equalized at once between the sections. The carpetbaggers and scalawags countered with criticism of the New Englanders' selfishness and argued that redistribution and expansion would free their states from dependence on northeastern credit and banking facilities. Sawyer, a resident of Boston until 1859 and an ostracized unionist during the war, chided Northeasterners for bringing the question of their wartime "sacrifices" into the debate, Robertson thought it hardly "fair that Massachusetts and other States should have privileges which we do not enjoy," and Warner, noting that Massachusetts had $35-per-capita circulation while his state had 35¢, reminded New Englanders that the House had already recommended complete redistribution.[6]

The Southerners' perceptions of their local situations varied, but

6. *Ibid.*, 41st Cong., 1st Sess., 129–30, 267, 269, 294, 297, 304, 354, 357, 366–68.

all believed that their states needed additional circulation. According to Sawyer, South Carolina's antebellum banking capital of $14 million had dwindled to $400,000. South Carolinians possessed capital to invest in national bank stock if circulation was available, and he pleaded for a redistribution of at least $30 to $40 million. Particularly bothersome was the fact that the South had to "buy" its circulation from the Northeast. New England's circulation was actually "scattered all over the South," but the catch was that southern states had to "pay tribute" to use it. The "tribute" was expensive. Kellogg noted that the exchange rate in New Orleans varied between ¾ and 1 percent per month, Abbott averred that North Carolinians paid 2½ to 3 percent to secure circulation, and Sawyer said that his state typically bought circulation from New York at 5 to 7 percent. Finding injustice in the fact that Southerners were taxed "to pay off the bonds on which Northern banking is based," Pool admonished northern senators that the southern economy must be "lifted" and stabilized if the nation expected to resume specie payments. To Pool, the committee's proposal of a $20 million redistribution was a "mere shadow . . . to put us off until next Session." The ex-Whig wanted a minimal redistribution of $40 to $50 million, but if all else failed he offered to take $20 million "as a mere pittance, as the best I can get, feeling though as an injustice has been done my section." The Southerners' ultimate concern was that they would have to tell their constituents that they secured nothing, as Sawyer put it, "calculated to relieve the wants of the business communities of the South." Voting as a bloc, they aligned themselves with a bipartisan majority from the midwestern and border states, rejected a rash of New England–sponsored amendments, raised the amount to be redistributed from $20 to $30 million, and approved the bill over the stolid opposition of northeastern Republicans.[7]

With few exceptions, the sectional alignment set during the Senate deliberations in March, 1869, emerged in both chambers whenever Congress considered questions relating to money for the remainder of the decade. As additional Southerners of both parties were admitted they joined the southern-midwestern coalition against a nearly

7.   *Ibid.*, 269, 274, 304–305, 357, 370.

solid New England, most congressmen from the mid-Atlantic states, and the hard-money-minded west coast congressmen. The only New Englanders consistently supportive of the Southerners were Senator William Sprague of Rhode Island, a wealthy industrialist and arch foe of resumption, and greenbacker Representative Benjamin Butler of Massachusetts. Among the most prominent midwestern Republicans, Southerners found Senator Oliver Morton the most reliable and, more often than not, they lined up in opposition to John Sherman, chairman of the Senate Finance Committee, and James Garfield, who headed the House Committee on Banking and Currency during the Forty-first Congress. Both opposed paper currency expansion of any kind, and both became obsessed with achieving resumption. On the question of redistribution, the carpetbaggers and scalawags found themselves in the uneasy company of such vehemently antireconstruction Democrats as Senators Garrett Davis of Kentucky and Allen Thurman of Ohio, who were obviously delighted with the Republican split. That the southern Republicans would ally with Democrats who hated all they stood for, and against northeastern Republicans who were largely responsible for their existence, indicates the strength of their identification with the South. It also gives credence to Michael Les Benedict's recent suggestion that the Southerners' differing economic interests "help explain why orthodox, hard-money Republicans so quickly agreed to the 'carpetbagger' and 'scalawag' labels Democrats fastened on them."[8]

When Garfield's committee failed to report S. 43 to the House, the Senate turned to another currency bill as the second session opened in December, 1869. As initially reported by Sherman, the new measure (S. 378) acceded to the wishes of New Englanders and ignored redistribution altogether. Instead, Sherman recommended an additional issue of $45 million in bank notes to banking associations in states or territories having less than their share. As compensation for this expansion, the bill proposed cancellation of the $45 million in 3 percent temporary loan certificates—most of which were circulating with the remainder being held in northeastern national

8. Michael Les Benedict, *A Compromise of Principle: Congressional Republicans and Reconstruction, 1863–1869* (New York: W. W. Norton, 1974), 51–56, 263–64.

banks as a portion of their reserve requirement. As the new bank notes were issued, the certificates would be retired at the same rate, and those serving as bank reserves would have to be replaced with greenbacks then in circulation.[9]

With their numbers now augmented by two newly seated Virginians, Republican John Francis Lewis and Conservative John Warfield Johnston, the same coalition of Southerners and Midwesterners evident in the earlier debates immediately began to work on the bill. Republican Timothy Howe of Wisconsin set the tone by arguing that the bill "proposes to silence our complaints of you by flinging us a pittance of $45,000,000 to growl over among our selves." Sawyer and Warner served as the primary spokesmen for the South. Sawyer reiterated that the South was tired of paying tribute to the money power centered in the Northeast and argued that bank note expansion was essential "for the resuscitation and regeneration of the industrial interests of the South." In a set speech, Warner referred to the pending measure as "tardy and incomplete justice" and then called for a comprehensive program for the economic rehabilitation of the South: "Dig out her harbors; give her the share of bank circulation which belongs to her; aid to build her railroads, and in every way by your practical legislation aid to upbuild her material interests, and to give encouragement to her national enterprises, and you will not simply have benefited your common country, but you will have done a wise work in the matter of the reconstruction of these States." In a series of sharply sectional roll calls, the coalition added several important clauses, including a redistribution of $20 million after the newly authorized $45 million was taken up, and sent the proposal to the lower chamber (see Table 13).[10]

The disposition of the House in favor of complete redistribution had been evident in the previous Congress and in February, 1870, it passed a resolution instructing Garfield's Committee on Banking and

9. *Congressional Globe*, 41st Cong., 2nd Sess., 700, 733. The secretary of the treasury issued the temporary loan certificates as a stopgap measure in 1867 and 1868 to meet government obligations to pay a large amount of maturing compound interest notes being presented by banks for payment. Congress had made the low-interest certificates more attractive by allowing banks to hold them as part of their required "lawful money" reserve in place of greenbacks.

10. *Ibid.*, 706, 812–13, 819–21, 788–89, 907, 970.

Table 13. BANK NOTE SCALOGRAM: FORTY-FIRST SENATE

Scale Position	NE D	NE R	MA D	MA R	MW D	MW R	SS D	SS R	BS D	BS R	PS D	PS R	Total D	Total R
0	—	9	—	2	—	—	—	—	—	—	—	—	—	11
1	—	1	—	—	—	1	—	—	—	—	—	1	—	3
2	—	—	1	1	—	—	—	—	—	—	—	—	1	1
3	—	—	—	1	1	—	—	—	—	—	—	3	1	4
4	—	—	—	—	—	1	—	—	2	1	1	1	3	3
5	—	1	—	—	—	6	1[a]	1	—	1	—	—	1	9
6	—	—	2	—	2	8	—	11	2	2	—	—	6	21
Not Scaling	—	1	—	1	—	1	—	1[b]	—	—	—	—	—	4
Total	—	12	3	5	3	17	1	13	4	4	1	5	12	56

Coefficient of Reproducibility = .940

[a] John Warfield Johnston (Va.) was not seated when the vote on S. 43 (scale position 6) was taken.

[b] John Francis Lewis (Va.) did not scale due to excessive absences because of an extended illness. His solitary vote indicates that he favored both bank note expansion and redistribution.

SCALOGRAM ITEMS

Scale Position	Identification

0

1 To amend S. 378 to increase the redistribution from $13 million to $20 million and to reduce bank note expansion from $52 million to $45 million. 43–15; + = Yea. *Congressional Globe*, 41st Cong., 2nd Sess., 969 (February 2, 1870).

2 To amend S. 378 by striking the clause providing for a new apportionment based upon the 1870 census to determine each state's share of bank note circulation to be issued or redistributed. 16–44; + = Nay. *Ibid.*, 944 (February 1, 1870).

3 To concur in an amendment to S. 378 allowing banks in a state having more than its proportion of circulation to relocate in a state having less than its proportion, provided the circulation of said banks shall not be deducted from the amount of new circulation provided for in this act. 43–20; + = Yea. *Ibid.*, 968 (February 2, 1870).

4 To amend S. 378 to increase the expansion of bank notes from $45 million to $52 million. 39–21; + = Yea. *Ibid.*, 943 (February 1, 1870).

5 To amend S. 378 by providing that the circulation of banks removing from one state to another shall not be deducted from the expansion of circulation provided for in this act, but shall be accounted for as between states from which and to which these banks move. 21–36; + = Nay. *Ibid.*, 969 (February 2, 1870).

6 To amend S. 43 to increase the amount to be redistributed from $20 million to $30 million. 32–30; + = Yea. *Ibid.*, 41st Cong., 1st Sess., 363 (March 30, 1869).

The higher the scale position, the more receptive a senator was to measures redistributing and expanding the national bank currency.

Currency to report "at as early a day as practicable, a bill to increase the currency to the amount of at least $50,000,000." Northeasterners opposed it by a margin of 9–57, while a potent bipartisan coalition of Southerners and Midwesterners favored it 84–10. When Garfield did finally report a bill in June, it was not S. 378, which had been in his committee since early February, but rather a conservative proposal to issue an additional $95 million in bank notes to states having less than their share, to retire the $45.5 million in 3 percent certificates, and to cut the greenback circulation by $39.5 million leaving a net addition to the currency of only $10 million. Among the other features of the bill was a provision for the redistribution of $25 million after the $95 million in new bank notes had been taken up.[11]

The bill appeared doomed from the moment Garfield closed his introductory remarks. Most Northeasterners would have preferred a measure looking toward the resumption of specie payments, and in addition, they disliked the redistribution section. But it was the Midwesterners who raised the greatest howl. Unlike the Senate, the House had a vocal greenbacker minority who hated the "monopolistic" national banking system and its currency. Not only did Garfield's bill fail to fulfill the request for an expansion of $50 million, but it proposed to retire a sizable portion of the greenback circulation. Furthermore, greenbackers calculated it would actually contract the volume of currency in circulation by up to $28 million rather than to increase it by about $13 million as Garfield predicted.[12]

The southern representatives were relatively quiet during the debate with only Texas carpetbagger William T. Clark making a major

11. *Ibid.*, 1460, 4179–82.

12. The net expansion or contraction of the actual circulation could be (and was) argued in both ways and depended in large part on how the national banks handled their reserve requirements. See the exchanges in *ibid.*, 4180–94, 4225–30.

speech. Having established one of the first national banks in Texas after the war, the Connecticut native knew the South's financial problems well, and he demanded redistribution while offering a special plea for his new home—"despised, maligned, and a by-word as she is and has been in the mouths of men in high position." But while the Southerners watched, midwestern expansionists and greenbackers proposed nearly thirty amendments and substitutes. Finally, on June 8, Garfield demanded the previous question on the bill, and amid general confusion over a ruling on the status of the amendments, an unlikely combination of resumptionist northeastern Republicans, indignant greenbackers, and antibank Democrats voted to adjourn over the opposition of southern and midwestern Republicans—a move which virtually killed the measure by placing it at the bottom of all bills on the Speaker's table. Garfield, obviously not overly disturbed, likened the scene to a monstrous "smash-up" between trains carrying greenbackers, inflationists, national bankers, and resumptionists. "No one can predict the outcome except that any bill offered under these circumstances is likely to be defeated," he added.[13]

Southern and western Republicans, "convinced that they had been sacrificed by the East with the aid of the Democracy," nevertheless appealed to Garfield the following morning to offer another measure. He obliged by reviving the previously unconsidered S. 378 with a committee amendment in the form of a substitute nearly identical to the defeated bill. Again a host of amendments, mostly from the greenbackers, greeted the bill, but only one, eliminating the retirement of $39.5 million in greenbacks, was adopted. With their feelings somewhat soothed, the Southerners and Midwesterners, aided this time by a substantial number of mid-Atlantic Republicans, passed the measure over the opposition of northern Democrats and northeastern Republicans. A conference committee to resolve the differences between the chambers agreed to the redistribution of $25 million but reduced the bank note expansion to $45 million as stipulated in the original Senate bill. The House rejected the conference report and called for a new committee. The

13. *Ibid.*, 4240–44; Theodore Clarke Smith, *The Life and Letters of James Abram Garfield* (2 vols.; New Haven: Yale University Press, 1925), I, 452.

second set of House conferees increased the new bank note issue to $54 million, but otherwise the bill remained unchanged. With the end of the session only a week away, Southerners and Midwesterners voted to take what they could get, and the modest measure became law.[14]

Throughout the year and a half of consideration of the various measures for bank note redistribution and expansion, Southerners endeavored to augment their section's monetary circulation. They expressed individual preferences for bank notes or greenbacks, but they were considerably less principled than their colleagues from other regions in their devotion to one type of currency over another. Southern Democrats seem to have preferred greenbacks to bank notes, but only three of the nine consistently opposed bank note expansion. Although several took the easy but scarcely responsible route out by not voting, the others supported S. 378 over the opposition of most of their party. The section's Republican representatives, twenty-eight in number, were nearly unanimous in support of bank note redistribution and expansion. They also opposed greenback contraction, and when the possibility of greenback expansion surfaced, much to the antipathy of the northeastern wing of the party, they joined the Democrats to favor it by much greater margins than did Republicans from other regions. Louisiana carpetbagger Lionel A. Sheldon best stated their position when he indicated his willingness to vote for an expansion of $300 million in either bank notes or greenbacks, yet advised fellow Southerners to vote for the conference report, not because "this is all we want or ought to have," but rather because it was all Northeasterners were about to offer. For his own part he declared that he was "not willing to deny to Louisiana the advantage of seven or eight millions more of banking capital because we cannot get all that I think we ought to have."[15]

Despite the conservatives' proclivity for hard money and misgiv-

14. Smith, *Life and Letters of Garfield*, I, 453; *Congressional Globe*, 41st Cong., 2nd Sess., 4472–73, 4477–78, 4948–50, 4961–64, 4966–70, 5302–5303; Huntington and Mawhinney (comps.), *Laws of the U.S. Concerning Money, Banking, and Loans*, 369–72; Richard H. Timberlake, *The Origins of Central Banking in the United States* (Cambridge: Harvard University Press, 1978), 94–97.

15. *Congressional Globe*, 41st Cong., 2nd Sess., 4478, 4950.

ings about the national banking system, there was broad support for redistribution and currency expansion in the South. Most conservatives desired the resumption of specie payments, but the prevailing notion was that resumption would involve currency contraction, and the South, already faced with a paucity of currency and agricultural production problems which hindered the influx of northern currency, simply could not afford further contraction. Only a few journals, the New Orleans *Price Current* chief among them, were consistent in their plea for resumption. Most editors supported redistribution and at least moderate expansion of the circulation. Northeasterners were roundly criticized for their reluctance to redistribute and for "their hostility," as *De Bow's Review* put it, "to an expansion of the currency for the benefit of the West and South." The editor of the Richmond *Whig* echoed other southern newspapers in observing that "increased banking capital is the peculiar want of the Southern States," and he endorsed a movement in the North Carolina legislature to instruct that state's congressmen to procure additional banking facilities. Regarding redistribution, he wondered, "How long will it take the country to understand that, if all the vital fluid is confined to one part of the body, the other parts must wither and waste away?"[16]

The *Whig* favored currency expansion in any form and cautioned against immediate resumption of specie payments. Other conservative newspapers were often contradictory, partially because of their ingrained hard-money philosophy, but, more important, because the question frequently took on political overtones. Political affiliation meant so much to some conservatives that they might endorse a greenback or inflationist proposal if offered by a northern Democrat and then turn about and disapprove of a similar measure sponsored by Republicans. In reaction to one of Radical Benjamin Butler's periodic greenback proposals in 1869, the editor of the New Orleans

16. New Orleans *Price Current, Commercial Intelligencer and Merchants' Transcript*, October 30, December 1, 11, 1869; "Apportionment of the National Currency," *De Bow's Review*, VIII (1870), 249–51; Richmond *Whig*, February 24, December 14, 17, 1869, March 15, 1870; Montgomery *Advertiser* as quoted in *De Bow's Review*, VIII (1870), 686; New Orleans *Republican*, November 23, 1870; Raleigh *Weekly North Carolina Standard*, April 4, 1869; Columbia *South Carolina Republican*, February 5, 1870; Austin *Democratic Statesman*, August 15, 1871, November 7, 1872.

Daily Picayune, for example, belittled inflationists "who live in terror of the contracting process through which we can return to a sound currency." Still, he approved of S. 378 (without giving credit to southern Republicans for helping pass it) and noted, "That the South needs more currency is apparent to all engaged in business." Always suspicious of Republican motives, he thought the act might be a calculated maneuver to gain additional southern recruits for the Republican party, and he speculated that the currency expansion might be "more apparent than real." Still, he concluded, "Whatever the motives, we must be thankful for favors, even if small." Ironically, Lionel Sheldon, the carpetbagger representing the *Picayune*'s home district, had expressed similar sentiments earlier in the week. A few days later, this time in response to a Republican soft-money proposal, the editor reversed positions again and proclaimed, "We have paper money, too much to count, and irredeemable at that."[17]

Such chameleonic behavior, dictated by partisanship, was characteristic of the southern press throughout Reconstruction. That, coupled with the understandable refusal of the dominant conservative papers to recognize the creditable performance of southern Republican congressmen on economic measures (the common tactic was to ignore Republican-sponsored measures benefiting the South), indicates the degree to which the section was politicized, but it also makes the southern press something less than reliable as an objective source of economic opinion. As a significant case in point, one of the most frequently expressed desires of the conservative press and leadership during the decade was to effect a "natural alliance" between the South and West against the Northeast on economic issues. But the fact that the bipartisan coalition of Southerners and Midwesterners emerged in the Fortieth and Forty-first Congresses when Republicans dominated the southern delegations and not after redemption was virtually ignored by the section's conservative press—as it has been by subsequent commentators.[18]

17. New Orleans *Daily Picayune*, January 21, 1869, July 10, 14, 16, 1870.
18. For a sample of conservative arguments for an alliance between South and West, see Richmond *Whig*, August 13, 1869, January 28, 1870; Atlanta *Constitution*, July 15, 1870, March 3, 1874; Charleston *Chronicle*, May 4, 1874; Little Rock *Daily Arkansas Gazette*, April 4, 1869; *De Bow's Review*, VII (1869), 837–38; M. M. Cooke to Robert McKee, June 21, 1868, in Robert McKee Papers, Alabama Department of

The importance of the neglected redistribution/expansion controversy lies in its reflection of the early sectional divisions in the Republican party. After a unified party response in the highly partisan atmosphere from which the Fifteenth Amendment and two enforcement acts emerged in 1869 and 1870, the Republicans found their ranks badly divided on the monetary questions. Hints that some southern Republicans were of a different mind had been apparent during consideration of the Public Credit Act, and they were less enthusiastic than their party colleagues from other regions when it came to refunding the national debt. But on currency the split with the Northeast was complete. The Southerners, particularly the "alien" carpetbaggers, many of whom had personal ties with northern Republicans, quickly discerned and supported their section's monetary interests and immediately encountered unyielding northeastern opposition. The notion that southern Republicans would be the subservient tools of their northeastern party colleagues on economic questions was quickly laid to rest.

The funding and currency legislation passed in July, 1870, quieted the monetary unrest for the next three years—a period encompassing the last session of the Forty-first Congress and all of the Forty-second.[19] The currency act had quieted the demands of the South and West, and those areas sat back to see if the measure would resolve their monetary problems. More important, the times were relatively prosperous. Southern crops were good in comparison to earlier years and the nation experienced something of an economic boom. But the banking panic in September, 1873, shattered the

Archives and History, Montgomery; E. John Ellis to Thomas C. Ellis, October 28, 1877, in Ellis Family Papers, Middleton Library, Louisiana State University, Baton Rouge; Speech of Alfred Moore Waddell, May 17, 1877, in Alfred Moore Waddell Scrapbook, Southern Historical Collection, University of North Carolina, Chapel Hill (hereinafter cited as SHC); Beverly Tucker to Edmund Wilcox Hubard, April 18, 1878, in Edmund Wilcox Hubard Papers, SHC; John T. Morgan, "The Political Alliance of the South with the West," *North American Review,* CXXVI (1878), 357−78.

19. The 42nd Congress was the least productive of those during the 1870s in terms of significant economic legislation. Only 3 of 803 roll calls in the 42nd Senate, for example, related to currency matters. The sectional alignments previously established continued on the few monetary votes. See *Congressional Globe,* 42nd Cong., 2nd Sess., 1585, 42nd Cong., 3rd Sess., 1425, 627−31, 1042−52, 1065−76, 1199−1207.

financial calm, and the Forty-third Congress convened in the early months of one of the longest depressions in American history.[20]

The impact of the depression on the South and the Southerners' role in the lengthy monetary debates of 1874 has received surprisingly little attention. Thanks to the Liberal Republican/Democratic debacle of 1872, Republicans still dominated the delegations to the Forty-third Congress, but there was evidence that the tide was changing. The Democrats picked up two seats in the Senate, one for Confederate war hero and soft-money advocate John Brown Gordon of Georgia and another for Augustus S. Merrimon of North Carolina, a key figure in the monetary debates. Republicans held their own in the House in terms of numbers, but even there the character of the Democrats had changed; the number of former slaveholders, secessionists, and Confederate veterans had increased sharply—largely because of the general amnesty passed in 1872. Texas, for example, prided itself for being the first southern state to return a solidly Democratic delegation to the House; four of the six Texans had held slaves and five had served in the Confederate army.[21]

Returned too were some prominent figures including Alexander H. Stephens of Georgia, a frail symbol of the past whose election the Atlanta *Constitution* heralded as "the return of Southern statesmanship to national activity." But even the *Constitution*, a citadel of conservatism, reminded Stephens "that the times have changed—sadly changed, perhaps—but irrevocably changed" and advised him to be "practically progressive while adhering to the grand old principles of constitutionalism." The "progressive" element among the newly elected Democrats was better exemplified by L. Q. C. Lamar of Mississippi, a veteran of the antebellum House, prominent seces-

20. Rendigs Fels, *American Business Cycles, 1865–1897* (Chapel Hill: University of North Carolina Press, 1959), 98–112; William S. McFeely, *Grant: A Biography* (New York: W. W. Norton, 1981), 392–95; Irwin Unger, *The Greenback Era: A Social and Political History of American Finance, 1865–1879* (Princeton: Princeton University Press, 1964), 213–33; Samuel Rezneck, "Distress, Relief, and Discontent in the United States During the Depression of 1873–78," *Journal of Political Economy*, LVIII (1950), 494–513.

21. *Dictionary of American Biography*, VII, 424–25, XII, 569–70; Austin *Democratic Statesman*, August 8, 1872. Over the course of the two sessions, the House seated thirty-nine Republicans and twenty-nine Democrats from the ten ex-Confederate states.

sionist, and Confederate diplomat whose return in 1873 launched a new political career which would culminate with his appointment to the Supreme Court.[22] Changes in the political composition of the delegations, however, had little effect on the Southerners' reaction to monetary questions. With few exceptions, they continued to vote as a bloc for currency expansion and were a significant and overlooked element of the soft-money forces in the Forty-third Congress.

In a debate that was easily the most extensive of any focusing on monetary problems during the 1870s, Congress spent most of the so-called "Inflation Session" from December, 1873, to June, 1874, considering currency expansion of one type or another to relieve the economic distress. Among the several score of proposals, two that were heavily debated early in 1874 set the alignment which would mark the later and more comprehensive measures. In the Senate, Sherman offered a simple measure to begin immediately the redistribution of $25 million in bank notes promised in the 1870 act. Much to the distress of the South and West, the comptroller of the currency had refused to start the redistribution until every last dollar of the additional $54 million in bank notes had been literally "taken up"—a nearly impossible demand. Indiana Republican Oliver Morton quickly characterized Sherman's bill as "a mere tub thrown to a whale" and claimed that the South and West now needed $50 to $60 million above that provided in the 1870 act. Newly seated Augustus Merrimon of North Carolina countered with a substitute to increase the total bank note circulation by $46 million to $400 million. To justify this increase, Merrimon asserted that the South, with "a scarcity of money that is hardly endurable," was now borrowing money at rates of 1 to 2 percent per month—the same arguments Frederick Sawyer and other Republicans had used in the 1870 debates.[23]

22. Atlanta *Constitution*, November 30, March 8, 1873; James B. Murphy, *L. Q. C. Lamar: Pragmatic Patriot* (Baton Rouge: Louisiana State University Press, 1973).

23. U.S. Treasury Department, *Annual Report of the Secretary of the Treasury . . . 1875* (Washington, D.C.: Government Printing Office, 1875), 215; *Congressional Record*, 43rd Cong., 1st Sess., 1141, 1175–76, 1382–83, 1439, 1432–33, 1472, 1668–71, 1761–65.

Over the periodic protests of Sherman, Merrimon's substitute launched the Senate on a three-month-long dogfight between expansionists and their opponents. Sherman, intent on achieving specie payments, and Northeasterners, Far Westerners, and a sprinkling of hard-money Democrats from other regions squared off against the expansionist coalition of Southerners whose primary spokesmen were Democrats Merrimon and John Brown Gordon, and midwestern Republicans led by Morton and John Logan of Illinois. The only Southerners avoiding the soft-money camp were Florida carpetbagger Abijah Gilbert and Texas scalawags Morgan C. Hamilton and James W. Flanagan. Gilbert, a wealthy New York merchant who had retired to Florida in 1865, resolutely refused to cave in to the obvious expansionist sentiment in his state and was frequently absent when key votes were taken.[24] The Texans' position was more understandable. Their state seemed immune to the currency shortage plaguing other southern states, specie circulated in Texas, and the state's leadership, Democratic and Republican alike, clung to the hard-money philosophy. Flanagan, the more active of the two, frequently reminded the Senate that his state wanted no more "depreciated currency" and was ready to resume. With these exceptions the South regularly delivered six Democratic and ten Republican votes for currency expansion in either greenbacks or bank notes. The ten ex-Confederate states in fact frequently provided more votes for expansion than did the midwestern states because the Southerners were less particular about the type of currency to be expanded; the question of greenback or bank note expansion often split the Midwesterners.[25]

In the interim, the monetary alignment in the House became clear in a dispute over the legal volume of greenbacks. The wartime acts

24. Gilbert's performance in the Senate from 1869 to 1875 was easily the least distinguished of any Southerner. He never spoke, except to give committee reports, and he typically sided against fellow Southerners on economic issues. Given his constituency, his hard-money views baffled his Senate colleagues. See the remarks of Simon Cameron in *Congressional Record*, 43rd Cong., 1st Sess., 1678.

25. *Ibid.*, 1417–20, 1534; Anderson, "National Banking System," 145; Austin *Democratic Statesman*, April 26, 1874. The greater willingness of the South to consider radical expansion was best shown in John Brown Gordon's proposal to establish free banking and create an interconvertible bond which would provide elasticity to the greenbacks by allowing their conversion into low-interest bonds which could be

had authorized a circulation of $400 million, but by early 1868, the secretary of the treasury had contracted that to $356 million. The circulation generally remained at that level until October, 1873, when Secretary of the Treasury William A. Richardson began to re-issue the retired greenbacks to help ease the effects of the panic. By early the next year, Richardson, without congressional approval, had released $26 million to bring the greenback circulation to $382 million. Kentucky Democrat James B. Beck brought the question to the House floor with a bill setting the legal circulation at $400 million—thus sanctioning Richardson's issue and providing for the release of an additional $18 million. When the measure came up for final consideration in March, expansionists handily defeated amendments to reduce the authorized circulation and passed it—much to the chagrin of most Northeasterners and hard-money advocates. New England voted 1–22 against the bill and the middle Atlantic states split 29–28, but the Midwest and South favored it by lopsided majorities of 75–11 and 40–7. "We might as well address the patients in the lunatic asylum on finance," Garfield lamented, "as to hope to change the tone of the House at present."[26]

Two days after passing Beck's proposal, the House took up the more comprehensive H.R. 1572 to establish free banking by permitting national banks to increase their capital and circulation as much as they wished. A second section proposed a gradual method of returning to specie payments, and a third relieved national banks from keeping a greenback reserve on their circulation. Debate on the bill opened in late March and continued almost unabated until the first votes were taken on pending amendments on April 10. Southerners and Midwesterners quickly eliminated the resumption clause and

converted back into greenbacks at the option of the holder. The proposal split midwestern Republicans 8–6, but southern Democrats favored it 4–1 and southern Republicans 7–2. Southerners also offered the strongest support (35–13) of any regional group to a similar proposal in the House where it was promoted by Radical Republican greenbackers William D. Kelley and Benjamin Butler. *Congressional Record*, 43rd Cong., 1st Sess., 1635, 3007. For the origins of the idea, see Unger, *Greenback Era*, 99–119.

26. Unger, *Greenback Era*, 213–15; *Congressional Record*, 43rd Cong., 1st Sess., 839, 2376; Garfield to Burke Aaron Hinsdale, March 26, 1874, in Mary L. Hinsdale (ed.), *Garfield-Hinsdale Letters: Correspondence Between James Abram Garfield and Burke Aaron Hinsdale* (Ann Arbor: University of Michigan Press, 1949), 280.

killed a host of antiexpansion amendments. In its final form, H.R. 1572 was essentially a free banking bill, although it released most of the greenback reserves and set the maximum greenback circulation at $400 million. Opposition was pronounced among New England Republicans and national-bank-hating northern Democrats, yet nearly half the southern Democrats abandoned their party and sided with southern and midwestern Republicans and a sizable Republican bloc from the mid-Atlantic states to pass the bill on April 14.[27]

While the House shaped H.R. 1572, Senate expansionists spent six weeks riddling Sherman's redistribution proposal before turning on a substitute which he moved in late March. Conceding little to the expansionists, the new bill (S. 617) limited greenback circulation to $382 million, provided free banking for states having less per capita bank note circulation than New York, and called for specie resumption in coin or bonds on the first day of 1876. To facilitate the latter, the secretary of the treasury was to retire an amount of greenbacks equal to 70 percent of the new bank notes issued until the greenback circulation was reduced to approximately $300 million. The alignment on the thirty-odd roll calls on S. 617 was rigid, and the exchanges indicate that monetary beliefs were held with religious conviction. But with fifteen of the nineteen southern votes and sixteen of the twenty midwestern votes, the expansionists had the upper hand.[28]

After three weeks of rancorous debate, the expansionists replaced the committee's bill with a simple substitute offered by Merrimon which set the greenback circulation at $400 million and added $46 million in bank notes to go to states having less than their quota. On final passage, Southerners favored the measure 15–2 and Midwesterners 15–5. Of the seventeen Northeasterners, only Republicans William Sprague of Rhode Island and Simon Cameron of Pennsylvania voted for it; west coast senators opposed it 1–5 as did those

27. *Congressional Record*, 43rd Cong., 1st Sess., 1007, 2508, 2739–42, 3871–74, 3055, 3002, 3005, 3022, 3072, Appendix, 180–82.
28. *Ibid.*, 2385–93; Unger, *Greenback Era*, 217–18. The South should have had twenty votes, but one Louisiana seat stood vacant for the entire 43rd Congress because of a contest. In addition, scalawag James L. Alcorn was inexplicably absent for all the roll calls on S. 617. He apparently favored hard money and simply abstained rather than to defy Mississippi expansionists.

from the border states 3–4. The irony of the fact that midwestern and southern Republicans had abandoned their president, their secretary of the treasury, and their Senate Finance Committee and accepted Merrimon's substitute was not lost on hard-money Democrat Allen G. Thurman of Ohio, who marveled that "it was reserved for the pine woods of North Carolina to shape the financial destiny of this country." He advised the badly split Republican party to disband, but he noted that the divisive debate had fragmented the Democracy as well. Thurman's observation applied equally well to the House, where the alignment was similar to that on H.R. 1572 with the exception that a greater number of southern and midwestern Democrats now joined Republicans from the same sections to send S. 617 to the White House.[29]

The "Inflation Bill," as its opponents dubbed it, quickly became the focus of public controversy. Soft-money advocates were confident that Grant, who seemed aware of the powerful expansionist sentiment in his party and in the country, would sign it. But Grant was also under intense pressure from businessmen, bankers, reformers, and resumptionists opposed to the bill, and he surprised everyone with a veto on April 22. In his message, Grant recalled the Public Credit Act's promise of an early return to specie payments and declared that the $44 million in greenbacks should be held as a reserve. When the additional bank note circulation created by the act of 1870 was taken up and the redistribution completed, "or when specie payments are fully restored or are in rapid process of restoration, [then] will be the time to consider the question of 'more currency.'" Senate antiexpansionists attempted to delay the vote to override the veto in the hope that they might muster a majority to

29. *Congressional Record*, 43rd Cong., 1st Sess., 2519, 2393–96, 2443, 2484–89, 2513, 2617, 2677–79, 2894–95, 2489–90, 2719, 2818–21, 2829–35, 2075–78. Unger refers to S. 617 as "a product of the same coalition of western and Pennsylvania Republicans which had dominated currency legislation since the War's end." Most of the Pennsylvanians were expansionists, but their 13–6 vote (including one paired no; three not voting) was hardly as important as the southern Republicans' 27–5 vote or the thirty-nine votes (including Democrats) Southerners provided for passage. In the Senate (the bill, of course, was a "product" of the Senate, the House did not debate it), the Pennsylvania Republicans split, with Simon Cameron favoring the bill and John Scott opposing it. See Unger, *Greenback Era*, 235. For a definition of *paired no*, see the Bibliographical Essay.

sustain Grant. The question of party loyalty, including the revival of unpleasant Republican memories of what had happened to Charles Sumner when he had opposed Grant over the treaty to annex Santo Domingo, entered into the debate, but the southern and midwestern Republicans refused to budge. They failed 36–32 (including two pairs) to override, but they prevented Grant from securing his majority.[30]

The final chance at passing currency legislation during the first session lay in H.R. 1572, the free banking proposal. The Senate expansionists initially held their ground, but with the threat of another veto hanging over their heads, they were forced to compromise. The resulting bill, after consideration by two conference committees, set the greenback volume at $382 million, released those greenbacks held as a reserve for bank note circulation, and promised the South and West an immediate redistribution of $55 million in national bank currency. Hard-money advocates bemoaned the failure to set a date for resumption; expansionists believed it did nothing to alter the currency volume significantly. The Southerners were particularly disappointed that their session-long efforts had yielded so little. They had obviously played a critical role in securing passage of S. 617 and the initial version of H.R. 1572 (see Tables 14 and 15). Grant's veto, however, had stopped what they considered to be needed currency for their section and added to the southern Republicans' burdens. But it was now late June, Congress had spent the greater part of six months on the question, and the expansionists, apprehensive that they would have nothing at all to show for their efforts, fell into line. Despite the opposition of diehard resumptionists and Northeasterners disturbed by redistribution, passage came easily. Southern senators favored the measure 14–2, the section's representatives, 50–4.[31]

---

30. James D. Richardson (comp.), *A Compilation of the Messages and Papers of the Presidents, 1789–1897* (10 vols.; Washington, D.C.: Government Printing Office, 1897), VII, 268–71; McFeely, *Grant,* 395–97; Unger, *Greenback Era,* 220–33, 235–45, 249–50; *Congressional Record,* 43rd Cong., 1st Sess., 3425–36. One of the pairs, that between Democrat Matt Ransom (N.C.) and Republican Carl Schurz (Mo.), was not announced. For a definition of *pair,* see the Bibliographical Essay.

31. *Congressional Record,* 43rd Cong., 1st Sess., 3834–45, 3876–96, 4347–49, 4852–70, 4901–13, 4958–61, 5179–83, 5189, 5310–16.

Table 14. CURRENCY SCALOGRAM: FORTY-THIRD SENATE

Scale Position	NE D	NE R	MA D	MA R	MW D	MW R	SS D	SS R	BS D	BS R	PS D	PS R	Total D	Total R
0	—	1	2	2	—	1	—	1[a]	1	—	2	2	5	7
1	—	6	1	1	—	1	—	1[b]	—	—	—	1	1	10
2	—	2	—	—	—	—	—	—	2	—	—	—	2	2
3	—	—	—	—	1	—	—	—	1	—	—	—	2	—
4	—	—	—	1	—	1	—	—	—	—	—	—	—	2
5	—	—	—	—	—	—	—	2	—	—	—	—	—	2
6	—	—	—	—	—	1	3	—	1	1	—	—	4	2
7	—	1[c]	—	1[d]	2	12	3	6	1	—	—	1	6	21
Not Scaling	—	2	—	—	—	1	—	3[e]	—	1	—	—	—	7
Total	—	12	3	5	3	17	6	13	6	2	2	4	20	53

Coefficient of Reproducibility = .990

[a]Morgan C. Hamilton (Tex.). [b]James W. Flanagan (Tex.). [c]William Sprague (R.I.). [d]Simon Cameron (Penn.). [e]James L. Alcorn (Miss.), Abijah Gilbert (Fla.), and John F. Lewis (Va.) did not scale because of excessive absences.

SCALOGRAM ITEMS

Scale Position	Identification
0	
1	To amend S. 1048 (specie resumption bill) to require the secretary of the treasury to cancel and destroy $2 million in U.S. notes each month. 6–44; + = Nay. *Congressional Record*, 43rd Cong., 2nd Sess., 206 (December 22, 1874).
2	To amend S. 617 ("Inflation Bill") to reduce U.S. note volume from $382 million to $356 million. 18–40; + = Nay. *Ibid.*, 43rd Cong., 1st Sess., 2484 (March 26, 1874).
3	To amend S. 617 to expand national bank note circulation by $46 million. 33–19; + = Yea. *Ibid.*, 2723 (April 2, 1874).
4	To agree to the first conference report on H.R. 1572 to set U.S. note volume at $382 million and to redistribute $55 million in bank notes. 32–23; + = Yea. *Ibid.*, 4913 (June 12, 1874).
5	To amend S. 617 to fix maximum amount of U.S. notes at $400 million. 31–26; + = Yea. *Ibid.*, 2488 (March 26, 1874).

196   The South Returns to Congress

To amend S. 617 by striking the section providing for specie resumption on January 1, 1876. 28–23; + = Yea. *Ibid.*, 2610 (March 30, 1874).

To pass S. 617 over presidential veto. 34–30; + = Yea. *Ibid.*, 3436 (April 28, 1874).

6 To amend the instructions recommitting S. 432 (bank note redistribution bill) to request Finance Committee to provide for redemption of bank notes in specie or bonds. 28–30; + = Nay. *Ibid.*, 1595 (February 18, 1874).

7 To amend S. 432 to remove limits on national bank note circulation. 26–32; + = Yea. *Ibid.*, 1635 (February 19, 1874).

The higher the scale position, the more receptive a senator was to measures expanding the volume of U.S. notes (greenbacks) and national bank notes.

Given the behavior of her congressmen in the first session, one might conclude that the South was blatantly expansionist, but southern opinion, although somewhat less well defined and articulated than that in the North, was strung along a similar spectrum from the advocacy of immediate resumption to open support for expansion of any kind. Out of simple need, most preferred at least a modest expansion in either bank notes or greenbacks, with the conservatives leaning toward the latter. Still, the traditional hardmoney leanings of the section remained powerful; few Southerners favored an expansion of irredeemable paper to the extent that it would jeopardize the ultimate goal of resumption.

The Panic of 1873 accentuated the South's currency problems in that it hit when a ready supply of cash was needed for crop movement. In addition, northern banks were forced to call in their obligations, and many southern bankers had no alternative but to pay up in currency. In some areas of the South, federal currencies seemed to disappear. Shortly after the panic, Senator John Warfield Johnston of Virginia noted, "Money is scarce here as it seems to be everywhere in the country now." An Alabama Republican leader remarked that "money is the scarcest thing in this country—The cane brake section of Alabama heretofore the richest in the state is now the poorest." A poor cotton crop compounded the problem. "What we will do God only knows," he continued. "I am very much afraid that a large number of our citizens will go to Mississippi to live and everyone that leaves is a republican." At the height of the panic, even the hard-money New Orleans *Price Current* observed that its city had been "*victimized* for the benefit of the North and the West, especially of New York, and while our banks were never in sounder

Table 15. CURRENCY SCALOGRAM: FORTY-THIRD HOUSE

Scale Position	NE D	NE R	MA D	MA R	MW D	MW R	SS D	SS R	BS D	BS R	PS D	PS R	Total D	Total R
0	2		7		1		1[a]		2		3		16	
		12		11		—		1[b]		—		1		25
1	—		4		1		1[c]		1		—		7	
		8		5		6		3[d]		2		1		25
2	—		1		—		—		1		—		2	
		1		3		3		—		—		—		7
3	—		—		—		—		—		—		—	
		—		4		2		—		—		—		6
4	—		2		3		2		1		—		8	
		—		2		—		3		—		—		5
5	—		1		—		1		3		—		5	
		—		5		4		—		1		—		10
6	—		—		7		3		2		—		12	
		—		7		25		7		2		—		41
7	—		—		10		13		8		1		32	
		1[e]		14		27		16		5		5		68
Not	—		—		5		4		1		—		10	
Scaling		3		2		—		7		—		—		12
Total	2		15		27		25		19		4		92	
		25		53		67		37		10		7		199

Coefficient of Reproducibility = .966
[a]William S. Herndon (Tex.). [b]Frederick G. Bromberg (Ala.). [c]John Hancock (Tex.).
  [d]Robert B. Elliott (S.C.), Jason Niles (Miss.), James H. Platt, Jr. (Va.). [e]Benjamin F. Butler (Mass.).

Scale Position	SCALOGRAM ITEMS Identification

o

1 To agree to the second conference report on H.R. 1572, to set U.S. note volume at $382 million and to redistribute $55 million in bank notes. 221–40; + = Yea. *Congressional Record*, 43rd Cong., 1st Sess., 5316 (July 20, 1874).

2 To amend H.R. 1398 (a bill setting the U.S. note circulation at $400 million) by reducing the amount of U.S. notes in circulation to $356 million. 70–171; + = Nay. *Ibid.*, 2376 (March 23, 1874).
  To amend H.R. 1398 by limiting U.S. note circulation to $382 million. 74–173; + = Nay. *Ibid.*, 2376 (March 23, 1874).

3 To pass H.R. 1398, a bill fixing the amount of U.S. notes at $400 million. 169–77; + = Yea. *Ibid.*, 2377 (March 23, 1874).

4 To amend H.R. 1572 by providing that as additional national bank notes are issued, U.S. notes shall be canceled until those outstanding are reduced to $300 million. 79–160; + = Nay. *Ibid.*, 3002 (April 10, 1874).

   5 To suspend the rules and consider a resolution instructing the Banking and Currency Committee to report a bill increasing the circulating medium of the country. 135–98; + = Yea. *Ibid.*, 767 (January 19, 1874).
   6 To pass S. 617, a bill fixing the amount of U.S. notes at $400 million and increasing the amount of national bank notes by $44 million. 140–102; + = Yea. *Ibid.*, 3078 (April 14, 1874).
   7 To amend H.R. 1572 by providing for a limit of $400 million in U.S. notes and making the U.S. notes interconvertible with 3.65 percent bonds. 120–122; + = Yea. *Ibid.*, 3007 (April 10, 1874).
The higher the scale position, the more receptive a representative was to measures expanding the volume of U.S. notes (greenbacks) and national bank notes.

condition . . . they were compelled to discontinue payments in currency and resort instead to certified checks." The editor warned northeastern bankers and financiers not to place any "obstacle in the way of our obtaining our legitimate supply of currency," but he regretted "that a determined effort will be made in Congress to inflate the currency." Resumption was still highly desirable, and the sooner the better: *"We pay all the rest of the world in gold, or its equivalent. Why can't we settle accounts among ourselves on the same basis?"*[32]

   The hard-money conservative newspapers were caught in a bind. The Austin *Democratic Statesman* lamented the "absence of money and consequent dullness of trade," but like most other Texas papers, the *Statesman* favored resumption and cautiously speculated that Grant had probably acted wisely in stopping the undesired inflation. The conflict between his personal hard-money principles and the general expansionist sentiment around him bothered Robert McKee of the Selma *Southern Argus*: "Of course the debt burdened people of this section would like to discharge their obligations in depreciated money, and inflation is just what they want. But we cannot see how any statesman capable of rising above the wants and wishes of a local constituency can reconcile it with his conscience or obligations to advocate inflation now." Although he periodically blasted "the contractionist and national bank monopolists" and "eastern

   32. John Warfield Johnston to John F. McMullen, October 13, 1873, in McMullen Family Papers, Perkins Library, Duke University, Durham, N.C.; George M. Duskin to Thomas Settle, November 2, 23, 1873, in Thomas Settle Papers, SHC; New Orleans *Price Current*, September 27, October 4, 18, December 8, 1873, January 8, 23, February 1, 1874.

capitalists" who opposed the South and West, he could never bring his paper to endorse the expansionist movement. He obviously favored Grant's veto, but like several other specie-minded editors he refrained from editorial comment.[33]

Other southern newspapers ranged from the position typified by the *Price Current* across the spectrum to advocacy of more soft money. Within the confines of New Orleans alone, the newspapers offered a wide range of opinion. The effects of the panic had cooled the *Picayune*'s resumptionist ardor and by April, 1874, it declared that Congress had wisely postponed specie payments. The conservative editor was somewhat amused that the carpetbag congressmen had opposed specie resumption, and thus "the East, which built up the carpet-bag Governments . . . now find their instruments returning to plague the inventors." He still claimed, however, that "the people want no more irredeemable paper currency," and in a rare display of impartiality he rejoiced that the inflation bill had been killed: "We respect and applaud President Grant for giving it its *coup de grace.*" The New Orleans *Republican* and the city's *Bee* were more receptive to currency expansion, and the two frequently skirmished on the issue with the *Picayune*. Claiming it was "well known that our planters, laborers, merchants, and bankers deplore the insufficiency of circulating capital," the *Republican* charged the *Picayune* with going against the interests of the South and West. "It is not a fair representation of the wishes or interests of Louisiana that the reasonable increase of circulating medium should be censured," its editor argued. "We repeat that Wall Street and State Street have one interest, the planters and laborers in cotton and sugar another and an opposite interest." The *Republican* reminded the Democratic newspaper that among those voting for expansionist proposals were southern Democrats who preferred to safeguard "the property of their constituents, white and colored," rather than "that of the bloated foreign bond holders" and who wished to relieve the

33. Austin *Democratic Statesman*, August 16, 1873, April 26, 1874; Selma *Southern Argus*, February 27, April 17, 24, 1874; Charleston *Daily Courier*, November 5, 6, 1872; Mobile *Register* and Savannah *Advertiser and Republican* quoted in *Congressional Record*, 43rd Cong., 1st Sess., 3894–95; Hampton *Southern Workman*, May, 1874. The hard-money Richmond *Southern Planter and Farmer* was among those who totally ignored the currency debate.

planter of his "dependence upon the factor and country note shaver." Specie payments would come of their own accord: "As the government becomes more and more able to collect its revenues in currency, the currency will approximate specie par. This will satisfy our people who are by no means clamorous for specie payments."[34]

Many other southern newspapers shared the *Republican*'s position. Merrimon claimed that four-fifths of North Carolina's sixty-odd conservative newspapers and a majority of the state's Republican newspapers opposed Grant's veto. According to Gordon, the entire membership of the Agricultural Convention of Georgia, the "most intelligent body of men we have assembled there," favored the "Inflation Bill." During the House debate, Republican Christopher Thomas of Virginia, under questioning by a Democratic colleague, admitted that most, if not all, Virginia newspapers favored an expanded currency supply. Even the Atlanta *Constitution*, long a bastion of financial conservatism, retreated from its criticism of the national banking system and indicated its willingness to accept bank note expansion. The paper had tried to remain optimistic during the September panic, but by November, it was obvious that Atlanta lacked currency to move the cotton crop and Georgians, like people elsewhere, were hoarding money. Believing that the economic crisis could be remedied by "an increase in the currency from time to time to meet the wants of our rapidly growing country, taking care that the increase is not so great as to produce overtrading and speculation," the editor traded sharp words with the Democratic New York *World* on the issue: "We know very well that New England and New York are interested in preserving the national dependence on that locality as the money stronghold of the country. It is to break that dependence that the South and West are now striving, and to achieve which they have united." The *Constitution* predicted defeat for the Republican majority if they failed to expand the currency and charged that Grant had been bought by northeastern financial interests. The veto was particularly harmful to Republican journals which had continually criticized Boston and New York fi-

34. New Orleans *Daily Picayune*, April 2, 1874; *Picayune* quoted in *Congressional Record*, 43rd Cong., 1st Sess., 3894; New Orleans *Republican*, April 4, 5, 8, 10, February 4, December 10, 1874.

nanciers for fighting expansion and urging Grant to veto the inflation bill.[35]

As real as the currency problem was to the South, the issues of race and reconstruction still overshadowed it. Republican and conservative newspapers alike gave far greater attention to pending civil rights legislation and the progress of redemption. The black *New National Era*, obviously interested in the civil rights bill, argued that Congress should have left the time-wasting currency matter alone, but instead it "kept up deafening chatter for six dreary months, and finally produced a measure satisfactory to nobody, and of no benefit to the country." Charles Francis Adams, Jr., no friend of irredeemable paper money, calculated that the currency debate, including over 125 set speeches, covered more than 1,700 columns in the *Congressional Record*. The net result certainly was not commensurate with the effort expended. "The amount of groaning on the part of the mountain which preceded its still born genius was truly portentous," he said. And its benefits to the South were certainly questionable. The Atlanta *Constitution* speculated that it might bring "some relief," but most newspapers declined comment—apparently in the belief that little had changed.[36] Ultimately, Grant's veto could only harm the southern Republican expansionists; the Democrats could and would blame the Republican administration for failing to respond to southern needs.

Grant's veto was one factor contributing to the disastrous performance of his party in the congressional elections of 1874. Although the veto was more critical to party misfortunes in the Midwest than it was in the South, southern Republican losses were no less apparent. Democrats made dramatic gains; Arkansas and Alabama joined the ranks of the redeemed states, the Ames administration in Mis-

35. *Congressional Record*, 43rd Cong., 1st Sess., 3894, 3941; Charleston *Chronicle*, May 5, 1874; K. Cornwallis, "The Crisis, the Currency, and the Resumption," *Southern Magazine*, XIV (1874), 128–44; Atlanta *Constitution*, September 21, October 5, 26, November 2, 30, 1873, March 29, April 1, June 11, 1874; New Orleans *Republican*, April 11, 12, 18, 23, 1874; New Orleans *Louisianian*, April 25, 1874.
36. Washington *New National Era*, October 22, 1874; Charles Francis Adams, Jr., "The Currency Debate of 1873–74," *North American Review*, CXIX (1874), 112, 120; Atlanta *Constitution*, June 23, 1874.

sissippi was on shaky ground, and Louisiana, as usual, remained in political chaos. The southern congressional delegations reflected the turnabout; twenty-nine Democrats and thirty-nine Republicans had served in the Forty-third House, forty-nine Democrats and seventeen Republicans would be seated in the Forty-fourth. In the Senate, the Republicans' 13−6 margin was reduced to 10−9.

Most Republican leaders would have preferred to avoid the divisive currency issue in the lame-duck second session of the Forty-third Congress, which commenced in December, 1874, but it refused to lie dormant. Under the leadership of John Sherman, northern Republicans decided to "hammer out" a compromise measure which would reunite the party in preparation for the campaign of 1876. The result, referred to as the resumption bill, came to the Senate floor with the disparate party factions pledged not to challenge it. The measure authorized the secretary of the treasury to mint additional subsidiary silver coins to replace the fractional paper currency then in circulation and to establish free banking by eliminating restrictions on bank note circulation. At the same time, it provided for greenback redemption equal to 80 percent of the new bank notes issued until the volume of greenbacks in circulation was reduced to $300 million. Finally, by direct purchase and bond sales, the secretary of the treasury was to build a gold reserve to be used to purchase greenbacks presented for redemption on or after January 1, 1879.[37]

Die-hard greenbackers and immediate resumptionists were not pleased with the measure for obvious reasons, but the Republicans among them remained silent. Over the protests of the Democrats, Sherman rammed the bill through the Senate before Christmas. The only Republicans to question it were Liberal Carl Schurz of Missouri, an immediate resumptionist who was not bound by the Republican caucus, and Morgan Hamilton of Texas, who attacked it as inflationist because it did not specify that the redeemed greenbacks could never be reissued. Sherman had earlier agreed to avoid that issue—a sure threat to party unity, and Republicans turned back attempts to cancel and destroy the redeemed greenbacks. Only Hamilton and antiresumptionist William Sprague broke party ranks

---

37. Unger, *Greenback Era*, 249−63; Huntington and Mawhinney (comps.), *Laws of the U.S. Concerning Money, Banking, and Loans*, 233−34.

and opposed passage, but six southern Republicans did not vote. Southern Democrats dutifully lined up against it. In the House, Republican managers successfully prohibited debate and passed the bill over solid Democratic opposition in January, 1875. Only two southern Republicans, Jason Niles of Mississippi, a hard-money advocate, and William A. Smith of North Carolina, a soft-money man, joined a score of their party colleagues in opposition, but fifteen Southerners, most of whom had favored expansion in the first session, abstained. In both the House and Senate, southern Republicans had the greatest number of abstentions or absences of any regional group—an indication of something less than enthusiasm for the measure.[38]

Designed as it was to promote Republican unity, the Resumption Act was susceptible to a variety of contradictory interpretations. As a consequence of its eventual success, it has been viewed as a hard-money measure, yet in some ways it appeared equally generous to soft-money interests. But until its success was demonstrated four years later, it was one of the few economic issues during Reconstruction to evoke a partisan response. After the Democratic Forty-fourth House convened in December, 1875, midwestern, southern, and border state Democrats made several efforts to repeal parts or all of the act over the opposition of several hard-money Democrats from the Northeast and the Republican minority. Late in the first session, they finally mustered sufficient support to repeal that part of the act setting the resumption date, but the Republican-controlled Senate took no action on the matter.[39]

On the surface at least, the issue remained partisan for southern congressmen. Among the Republicans only John A. Hyman of North Carolina and Charles Hays of Alabama consistently supported repeal. The two had little in common other than similar black, agricultural constituencies—not unlike those of other Republicans upholding the act. The reaction of hard-money southern Democrats and the conservative press was frequently inconsistent with their

38. *Congressional Record,* 43rd Cong., 2nd Sess., 186–89, 194–203, 319.
39. *Ibid.,* 44th Cong., 1st Sess., 444, 920, 1074–75, 1815–16, 2862, 5230–32. All ten southern Republicans voting opposed repeal, Democrats favored it 34–5. For a scalogram on the issue, see Terry L. Seip, "Southern Representatives and Economic Measures During Reconstruction: A Quantitative and Analytical Study" (Ph.D. dissertation, Louisiana State University, 1974), 283–84.

avowed principles. The expansionist sentiment of 1874 had cooled considerably, and resumption clearly had substantial support in the South provided the process was gradual and involved little or no contraction. Some opposition undoubtedly stemmed from the fact that Secretary of the Treasury Benjamin H. Bristow had interpreted the act in such a way as to contract the circulation. But the primary problem was that the act was a Republican measure, and most southern conservatives simply could not bring themselves to endorse it—despite their desire for resumption. Their opposition baffled some observers. One of North Carolina Senator Matt Ransom's correspondents exclaimed that "cotton *commands* gold, every where in the world. and the south is not in favor of specie payments. your politicians are speculative philosophers, not statesmen."[40]

But while most southern Democrats supported attempts to repeal or modify the act, many were less than enthusiastic. John Randolph Tucker of Virginia, for example, voted for repeal while reaffirming his hard-money beliefs. A few, including L. Q. C. Lamar of Mississippi, openly favored an even earlier date for resumption, and the Mississippi delegation usually followed his lead. The Texans, now led by John Hancock, Gustave Schleicher, and Samuel Bell Maxey, were also unwilling to abandon the Resumption Act. Irritated that the Republicans had secured the hard-money ground in the forthcoming campaign, Maxey feared repeal and believed the midwestern Democrats' "hue and cry for issue of more paper money as a measure of relief" would "involve the country in still greater financial perplexity." "We should, if possible, get our erring brothers back to the true faith," he advised Senator Thomas F. Bayard in October, 1875. "In some parts of the West and South it will require a deal of moral courage for the average congressman to rise to the supreme necessity of the hour." Like Maxey, Representative Randall Gibson of Louisiana was embarrassed by the demands of western Democrats for repeal. Shortly after the Democratic convention of 1876, he wrote Manton Marble, the editor of the Democratic New York *World*, of his concern that the platform had committed the party to repeal—

40. James Mant (?) to Matt W. Ransom, February 13, 1876, in Matt W. Ransom Papers, SHC.

something he could not support after having "all winter combatted the views of our western friends." Marble reassured Gibson that the repeal clause in the platform was nothing more than "a sliver of one plank" and was "in terms subordinated to the end—resumption."[41]

Perhaps nothing better demonstrated the position of the hard-money advocates than their attempt to quiet John Brown Gordon. Without question the most prominent soft-money advocate in the South, Gordon clung to his expansionist principles and was a constant source of concern. One New Orleans editor assured Marble that "with the single exception of Gordon—and I don't think he can carry Geo. with him—I don't know a prominent inflationist in the South." He believed the South would be a unit, not "for an extreme 'hard money' platform, but against inflation." Others, including Robert Alston, the editor of the Atlanta *Herald*, knew Gordon's power and appeal and despaired of converting him to the specie standard. Alston finally informed Bayard in late 1875 that he and Gordon had "agreed that as far as possible the matter shall be kept out of the canvass."[42] Had the Resumption Act been a Democratic measure, it appears likely that the southern wing of the party would have experienced little difficulty supporting it.

Still, partisanship so clouded the issue that only a handful of conservative newspapers risked public endorsement. The *Weekly Clarion* of Jackson bravely applauded the Mississippi delegation for voting against repeal, but most specie-minded editors, including McKee of the *Southern Argus*, simply ignored it. The Austin *Democratic Statesman* quickly dismissed the act as "purely a party measure, for

41. John Randolph Tucker to Edmund Wilcox Hubard, July 30, 1878, in Hubard Papers; R. Taylor to Tucker, October 14, 1875, James Randolph to Tucker, January 20, 1876, W. Allan to Tucker, January 21, 1876, in Tucker Family Papers, SHC; Murphy, *L. Q. C. Lamar,* 127; Samuel Bell Maxey to Dr. A. Patton, March 27, 1876, in Samuel Bell Maxey Papers, Barker Texas History Center, University of Texas, Austin; Samuel Bell Maxey to Thomas F. Bayard, Jr., October 2, 1875, in Thomas F. Bayard Papers, Library of Congress (hereinafter cited as LC); Randall L. Gibson to Manton Marble, July 5, 13, 26, 1876, Marble to Gibson (draft), July 12, 1876, in Manton Marble Papers, LC.

42. Theodore Saloutos, *Farmer Movements in the South, 1865–1933* (Berkeley: University of California Press, 1960), 46–47; B. to Manton Marble, October 9, 1875, in Marble Papers; Robert Alston to Thomas F. Bayard, Jr., October 27, November 10, 1875, H. V. M. Miller to Bayard, October 26, 1875, J. R. Hawley to Bayard, October 30, 1875, *Letter of Senator T. F. Bayard, November 5, 1875* (pamphlet), in Bayard Papers.

party purposes," and the Atlanta *Constitution* denounced it as "a mockery and a sham." The Little Rock *Arkansas Gazette* informed its readers in late 1874 that Senate Democrats opposed Sherman's bill because "the policy of the bill is to prevent resumption of specie payments before 1879, and because it makes no preparation for resumption at that time." As late as February, 1878, the *Gazette*, like many other southern newspapers, still called for repeal, but by November its editor was forced to admit that the greenbacks might rise above gold in value and resumption would cease to be an issue. He was not, however, willing to concede that the act of 1875 had aided resumption: "It will have completely wrought out its own accomplishment . . . *in spite* of all the resumption laws, which have been but hinderances to that end." In the first days of 1879, the editor briefly noted that greenbacks were favored over gold in New York, and he tauntingly challenged the Republicans to "now let the long promised good times return."[43]

The resumption controversy contributed directly to the beginning of the debate over the place of silver in the monetary system. In accordance with the 1875 act, Secretary of the Treasury Bristow stockpiled some $10 million in subsidiary silver coins to replace fractional greenbacks as the first step toward resumption. He refused, however, to issue the silver coins because he believed they would disappear from circulation as their actual value was greater than the fractional paper notes. Most congressmen disagreed, and in April, 1876, they passed a "silver resumption bill" ordering Bristow to begin the exchange immediately. Along the way, the discussions strayed from matters of subsidiary coinage to proposals to issue additional silver without providing for greenback contraction, and the congressmen discovered that an act passed in 1873 had discontinued coinage of the 412½-grain silver dollar and limited the legal tender power of silver to amounts not exceeding five dollars. That action had effectively demonetized silver, and as the 1876 debate inten-

---

43. Jackson *Weekly Clarion*, March 29, 1876; Austin *Democratic Statesman*, December 24, 1874; Atlanta *Constitution*, December 24, 25, 1874; Little Rock *Daily Arkansas Gazette*, December 30, 1874, January 12, 1875, February 26, November 1, 1878, January 1, 3, 1879.

sified, a growing number of legislators joined a movement to over-
turn the "Crime of '73" and restore the bimetallic standard by re-
monetizing the silver dollar.[44]

The first round of the silver agitation ended in December, 1876,
with House passage of Missouri Democrat Richard P. Bland's bill
providing for the coinage of "silver dollars of the weight of 412½
grains standard silver to the dollar," to "be legal tender for all debts,
public and private, except where payment of gold is required by law."
Southern Democrats offered overwhelming approval 39–3; the Republicans split 3–3.[45] Those voting for the measure may have reflected the wishes of most of their constituents, but in 1876 silver
excited no public response in the South. Republican and Democrat,
black and white, were far more concerned with the disputed presidential election and the fate of the last three southern Republican
governments. The electoral dispute was certainly one element
prompting the Senate to postpone consideration of the question until the Forty-fifth Congress convened in November, 1877.

When President Hayes had called the new Congress into a special
first session, the House immediately repassed the Bland bill by a decisive margin with only four southern dissenters. Republican William Boyd Allison of Iowa, heir apparent to the Senate financial leadership position when Hayes appointed Sherman secretary of the
treasury, reported the bill with several important amendments, but
the upper chamber first turned to the consideration of a concurrent
resolution sponsored by Ohio Republican Stanley Matthews. With
its declaration that the principal and interest on U.S. bonds were
payable in standard silver dollars and "that to pay in Silver dollars is
not a violation of the public faith, nor in derogation of the rights of
the public creditor," the proposal was quite enough to launch the
Senate on a lengthy monetary debate reminiscent of that four years
earlier.[46]

44. *Congressional Record*, 44th Cong., 1st Sess., 2130, 2341–53, 2360, 2389,
2418, 2513; Allen Weinstein, *Prelude to Populism: Origins of the Silver Issue,
1867–1878* (New Haven: Yale University Press, 1970), ch. 1; Walter T. K. Nugent, *The
Money Question During Reconstruction* (New York: W. W. Norton, 1967), ch. 5.

45. *Congressional Record*, 44th Cong., 2nd Sess., 149–51, 163–72.

46. *Ibid.*, 45th Cong., 1st Sess., 241; Weinstein, *Prelude to Populism*, 236–39;
Congressional Record, 45th Cong., 2nd Sess., 87.

In a debate which quickly became repetitious, the silverites, led by Matthews, John Percival Jones of Nevada, and several southern Democrats, raised the specter of the "Crime of '73" and argued that silver as well as gold was "coin of standard value" when the debt was incurred and was therefore a legitimate form of payment. The Southerners were particularly sensitive to the unspoken accusation that they might be viewed as "repudiators" in favoring silver to pay the debt. "Persons, thousands, perhaps millions of them," declared John Tyler Morgan of Alabama, "might think my vote colored by disloyalty to pay the debt for our subjugation." Such was not the case, Morgan maintained: "People of Alabama scorn the repudiation of just obligations as a stain on the national honor." Merrimon added that a vote for silver was "absolutely no repudiation"—sentiments seconded by Maxey, Gordon, and James T. Jones of Florida. But Lamar and Benjamin H. Hill of Georgia served early notice of their belief that gold should remain the solitary standard of value. Lamar, the most vocal monometallist among the Southerners, feared that silver, if remonetized, would quickly drive gold out of circulation. On the final vote on the resolution in late January, 1878, Democrat Matthew C. Butler of South Carolina sided with Lamar and Hill in opposition. The six southern Republicans, while silent during the debate, joined eleven Democratic colleagues to help pass it over the objections of a bipartisan bloc from the Northeast. When the House approved the resolution three days later, Southerners favored it 52−5.[47]

Once the declaratory resolution was out of the way, the Senate spent another month on the Bland bill and the Allison amendment limiting coinage to two to four million dollars a month. Among the Southerners, two Republicans and seven Democrats preferred free and unlimited coinage; the others favored the amendment as did a majority of the Senate. With the exceptions of Lamar, Butler, and Hill, Southerners voted to pass the amended bill. The Allison amendment evoked a similar response in the House. Twenty-nine of the fifty-four southern Democrats opposed the limitation on coin-

47. *Congressional Record*, 45th Cong., 2nd Sess., 92−94, 120, 168, 352, 549, 555, 559, 140−43, 404−10, 433−41, 560−61, 171−72, 519−26, 628.

age, but it was easily approved 203–72, and the measure went to Hayes with the provision that coinage would be restricted.[48]

As many congressmen anticipated, Hayes vetoed the Bland-Allison bill on the grounds that the legal tender, 412½-grain silver dollar was only worth 90 to 92 cents in gold and would therefore drive gold out of circulation as it was issued. "It will be," Hayes declared, "justly regarded as a grave breach of the public faith to undertake to pay these bonds, principal and interest, in silver coin worth in the market less than the coin received for them." Both chambers quickly overrode the veto in alignments nearly identical to those set early in the debate. Southerners voted 56–6 in the House and 16–2 in the Senate to override (see Table 16).[49]

The Southerners were clearly an important element in the silver drive of 1877–1878. Southern representatives had little opportunity to voice their sentiments until a motion by Alexander Stephens allowed them to spread their comments on the *Record* just before the vote to override. All but one of the thirteen who entered remarks favored overriding the veto, and most would have preferred unlimited coinage.[50] Henry Muldrow of Mississippi, for example, declared that the Allison amendment was a "vital stab in the heart of the bill," but the bitterest sentiments came from carpetbag Democrat Gilbert C. Walker of Virginia, who denounced Hayes as "weak; vacilating [sic], wedded to abstract theories. . . . the child of fraud and the maturity of imbecility." Most, however, appeared willing to take what they could get, and several promised to work for unlimited coinage. The disappearance of party lines on the question delighted those who welcomed sectional reconciliation. One northern correspondent was particularly amused that southern Democrats and their old nemesis, Radical Benjamin Butler, saw eye to eye on

48. *Ibid.*, 1076, 1112, 1284.
49. Richardson (comp.), *Messages and Papers of the Presidents*, VII, 486–88; *Congressional Record*, 45th Cong., 2nd Sess., 1419–20, 1409–10; Huntington and Mawhinney (comps.), *Laws of the U.S. Concerning Money, Banking, and Loans*, 579–81.
50. The exception was Louisiana carpetbagger John Leonard, who believed that remonetization "would only aggravate the present distressed condition of our country." *Congressional Record*, 45th Cong., 2nd Sess., Appendix, 37. The only others sustaining the veto were Democrats Gibson (La.), and Schleicher (Tex.), and Republicans Bisbee (Fla.), Jorgenson (Va.), and Cain (S.C.).

Table 16. SILVER SCALOGRAM: FORTY-FIFTH SENATE

Scale Position	NE D	NE R	MA D	MA R	MW D	MW R	SS D	SS R	BS D	BS R	PS D	PS R	Total D	Total R
0	2	10	4	1	—	1	3[a]	—	1	—	—	2	10	14
1	—	—	—	—	—	2	—	—	—	—	—	—	—	2
2	—	—	1	—	—	4	1	1	—	—	—	1	2	6
3	—	—	1	1	1	6	5	3	1	—	—	2	8	12
4	—	—	—	1	3	3	5	2	6	—	1	1	15	6
Not Scaling	—	—	—	—	—	—	—	—	—	—	—	1	—	1
Total	2	10	6	2	4	16	14	6	8	—	1	7	35	41

Coefficient of Reproducibility = .985
[a]Matthew C. Butler (S.C.), Benjamin H. Hill (Ga.), L. Q. C. Lamar (Miss.).

Scale Position   SCALOGRAM ITEMS
            Identification

0

1 To designate time and date for consideration of H.R. 1093, a bill to authorize coinage of the standard silver dollar and to restore its legal tender character. 41–18; + = Yea. *Congressional Record*, 45th Cong., 2nd Sess., 46 (December 6, 1877).

To amend the Matthews Resolution by requiring that all interest and principal of U.S. bonds be paid in gold. 18–44; + = Nay. *Ibid.*, 558 (January 25, 1878).

To pass H.R. 1093. 48–21; + = Yea. *Ibid.*, 1112 (February 15, 1878).

2 To pass the Matthews Resolution. 43–22; + = Yea. *Ibid.*, 561 (January 25, 1878). To amend H.R. 1093 by fixing the number of grains in the standard silver dollar at 420 instead of 412½. 25–44; + = Nay. *Ibid.*, 1100 (February 15, 1878).

3 To amend H.R. 1093 by providing that treasury notes received for gold and silver shall be reissued in exchange for such. 42–25; + = Yea. *Ibid.*, 1110 (February 15, 1878).

4 To amend H.R. 1093 by authorizing the secretary of the treasury to purchase and coin not less than $2 million and not more than $4 million in silver bullion per month. 49–22; + = Nay. *Ibid.*, 1076 (February 15, 1878).

The higher the scale position, the more receptive a senator was to remonetization and free coinage of silver.

the issue. "It was inspiring to see the affectionate embraces of Butler and the Southern Brigadiers," he wrote. "They all seemed to have a heart that beat as one and a number of souls with but a single thought. It was difficult to tell whether Butler was leading the Brigadiers or the Brigadiers leading Butler. We heard nothing about 'old cock-eye' or the 'spoon thief,' but it was 'the gentleman from Massachusetts,' whose gigantic intellect seemed to draw homage from unexpected quarters."[51]

In the Senate, Democrats Maxey and Richard Coke of Texas and carpetbaggers George E. Spencer of Alabama and Simon Conover of Florida led those favoring unlimited coinage, but they acquiesced after the Allison amendment passed. The others, three Democrats and four Republicans, appeared fully satisfied with the limitation. Among the few novel arguments to enter the debate was one first broached by Morgan, who stated that the freedmen "strongly confide in silver" and "will work harder for silver than paper currency." Merrimon and John Warfield Johnston of Virginia agreed, with the latter declaring that blacks "have little appreciation of paper, and . . . they do not understand gold. Silver is the only money that the colored race knows much about or wants." The other arguments were familiar: the South needed additional circulation and remonetization offered an excellent solution.[52]

Of the three southern senators who opposed remonetization throughout the debate, only Butler and Lamar remained devoted to the gold standard. Butler never spoke during the debate, but Lamar's agony was well publicized. Shortly before the final vote, Lamar presented resolutions from the Mississippi legislature instructing him and Blanche K. Bruce to vote to remonetize silver. According to one

51. *Ibid.*, Appendix, 50, 52–53, 23, 36, 39–40, 48–49, 51, 53, 54, 62–65; Horace V. Redfield in Cincinnati *Commercial*, January 26, February 22, 1878, in Horace V. Redfield Clippings, Rutherford B. Hayes Presidential Center, Fremont, Ohio.

52. *Congressional Record*, 45th Cong., 2nd Sess., 143, 822–26, 976–81, 758, 848–54, 932–37, 1066–67. None of the six blacks serving in the 44th House voted for either the unsuccessful effort to remonetize in July, 1876, or for the Bland bill the following December. Lynch (Miss.), Rainey (S.C.), and Smalls (S.C.), all opposed the July effort, with Haralson (Ala.), Hyman (N.C.), and Nash (La.) not voting. Haralson, Lynch, and Nash opposed the Bland bill; the others did not vote. In the 45th House, Rainey and Smalls favored remonetization, while Cain's record was inconsistent. Bruce (Miss.), supported silver in the Senate. See *Congressional Record*, 44th Cong., 1st Sess., 4855, 44th Cong., 2nd Sess., 172, 45th Cong., 1st Sess., 241, 1285, 1419–20.

correspondent, "He spoke feelingly, almost tearfully of the 'great gulf' which separated him and his constituency upon this subject," before voting against remonetization. His stand brought an unusual rebuke from the legislature in the form of a resolution thanking Bruce for reflecting "the sentiment and will of his constituents"—a move which surprised and pleased the ex-slave, who "supposed it was impossible for him to do anything the Democrats of Mississippi would approve."[53]

Hill proved to be not as principled as Butler and Lamar. In his final speech on the question, he was continually interrupted by silverites, including some of his fellow Southerners, and he seemed frustrated and unsure of his position. During the roll call on overriding the veto, he asked for the indulgence of the Senate, presumably to explain why he was going to switch positions and vote to override, but objection was made, and he was not allowed a personal explanation. As his peers were quick to note, Hill's political career had never been marked by consistency. Fellow Georgian Joseph E. Brown, as opportunistic a politician as the South ever produced, characterized him as "a mighty smart man but lacks *judgement*." Hill had apparently taken the monometallist position without first testing the sentiment of his constituents. One journalist probably exaggerated the situation when he declared that nine of every ten Georgians were prosilver, but Hill's mail ran heavily in favor of remonetization, and in the end he caved in to constituent pressures in what the antisilver *Nation* blasted as a "somersault" on the issue.[54]

There is little evidence that silver, particularly unlimited coinage, created the "frenzy" in the South that it did in certain other parts of the country. With the possible exception of Mississippi, where Lamar was subjected to a surprising amount of abuse, the notion that

53. *Ibid.*, 45th Cong., 2nd Sess., 1061; Horace V. Redfield in Cincinnati *Commercial*, February 15, 1878, in Redfield Clippings; New York *Graphic*, February 7, 1878, quoted in Weinstein, *Prelude to Populism*, 293n.

54. *Congressional Record*, 45th Cong., 2nd Sess., 842–48; Horace V. Redfield in Cincinnati *Commercial*, January 26, 1878, in Redfield Clippings; John C. Reed, "Reminiscences of Ben Hill," *South Atlantic Quarterly*, V (1906), 134–49; James Jackson to John B. Gordon, February 8, 1877, in L. Q. C. Lamar and Edward Mayes Papers, Mississippi Department of Archives and History, Jackson; B. B. Lewis to Robert McKee, January 19, 1876, in McKee Papers; Hiram P. Bell, *Men and Things, Being Reminiscent, Biographical, and Historical* (Atlanta: Foote and Davis Company, 1907), 154–55; *Nation*, March 7, 1878, p. 159.

Southerners had wholeheartedly joined the most radical fringes of the free silver movement was largely the creation of the northeastern antisilver press. The resistance of Lamar, Butler, and Hill, mused the Washington *Post*, "had a wonderfully quieting effect on the nerves of that class of people up North who have been lying awake nights, and suffering with cold sweats, for fear of a new rebellion." The antisilver position in fact won open support from such institutions as the New Orleans Clearing House Association, the city's chamber of commerce and cotton exchange, the same two groups in Savannah, and the Charleston Chamber of Commerce. Such actions caused the conservative New York *Journal of Commerce* to breathe a sigh of relief that "the Southern cities hitherto regarded as strongholds of silver are wheeling into line with the defenders of the national honor and good faith."[55]

The monometallists' fears that the South favored remonetization, while exaggerated, were nevertheless true. A few Southerners were enthusiastic. "I'm all for silver, gold & greenbacks, and plenty of it," wrote one of Ransom's North Carolina constituents. Several others requested copies of Indiana silverite Daniel W. Voorhees' speech on the question, and Ransom secured several hundred reprints of other prosilver speeches for distribution. Still, there was no highly organized clamor for free silver if newspapers and the correspondence of political leaders offer a valid sample of public opinion on the issue. For the most part, southern support for remonetization was moderate in tone, widespread, and relatively quiet.[56]

55. "The South and the Silver Frenzy," *Nation*, January 24, 1878, pp. 52–53, January 10, 1878, p. 17, January 31, 1878, p. 69, February 14, 1878, p. 104, February 21, 1878, p. 123; Washington *Post*, quoted in Little Rock *Daily Arkansas Gazette*, February 13, 1878; New York *Weekly Journal of Commerce*, January 17, 24, 1878, quoted in Weinstein, *Prelude to Populism*, 271. For a sampling of Southern antisilver sentiment and the monometallists' fears of the South, see *Tri-Weekly Raleigh Register*, June 5, 19, 1877; Charles M. Fry to Thomas F. Bayard, December 28, 1878, the clippings in the Bayard Scrapbook on the Silver Question, Edward C. Palmer to Bayard, February 5, 1878, in Bayard Papers; R. B. Avery to William E. Chandler, January 10, 1878, in William Eaton Chandler Papers, LC; F. A. P. Barnard to L. Q. C. Lamar, January 29, 1878, Stewart L. Woolford to Lamar, February 8, 1878, Benjamin H. Hill to Lamar, March 7, 1878, Moses D. Hoge to Thomas F. Bayard, February 19, 1878, in Lamar-Mayes Papers.
56. Jo. B. Cherry to Matt W. Ransom, February 18, 1878, Walter Clark to Ransom, February 1, 1879, R. W. Glenn to Ransom, January 29, 1878, John Percival Jones to Ransom, March 11, 1878. in Ransom Papers. For a sampling of prosilver sentiment, see E. John Ellis to Thomas C. W. Ellis, February 28, 1878, in Ellis Family Papers; Rob-

The *Nation* quite correctly saw the South's attraction to silver as a continuation of expansionist sentiment. The hard-money heritage of southern conservatives, coupled with the currency shortage and popular sentiment for expansion, made silver a natural and attractive alternative to either additional irredeemable paper or gold resumption involving greenback contraction. "We believe in both silver and gold for money," the editor of the *Southern Planter and Farmer* declared, "but we want them arranged in a way to prevent any clashing." In his opinion, Congress should have limited the legal tender qualities of silver to $250 and raised the weight of the silver dollar to 420 or 425 grains to approximate more closely the value of the gold dollar. The editor of the *Arkansas Gazette*, one of the few southern journals to offer a running commentary on the silver debates, better reflected regional attitudes with his call for a middle ground between the gold resumptionists and the soft-money inflationists. "Give us the silver dollar," he declared in November, 1877, but "save us on the other hand from a flood of irredeemable paper." During the debate, the editor constantly reminded his readers that "silver advocates are not inflationary minded people" and that "irredeemable paper is one of the worst curses that can be inflicted on a country." He was pleased that carpetbag Senator Stephen Dorsey, who was personally antisilver, planned to vote for the Bland bill "in deference to the wishes of the people of Arkansas," and he regretted Lamar's opposition. As one of the numerous editors pleased with Hayes's southern policy, he was sorry that the president had imposed a veto against the wishes of "four-fifths of the people." When Congress overrode Hayes, the editor "truely rejoiced" that there were now "silver threads among the gold." After having "read 1500–2000 speeches on the question," he proclaimed that it was now time to get on to something else.[57]

---

ert Toombs to Alexander H. Stephens, January 25, 1878, in Ulrich B. Phillips (ed.), *The Correspondence of Robert Toombs, Alexander H. Stephens, and Howell Cobb* (Washington, D.C.: Government Printing Office, 1913), 732–34; and Robert W. Hughes, *A Popular Treatise on the Currency Question, Written from a Southern Point of View* (New York: G. P. Putnam's Sons, 1879).

57. "The South and the Silver Frenzy," 52–53; Richmond *Southern Planter and Farmer*, XXXIX (1878); Little Rock *Daily Arkansas Gazette*, November 18, 29, 1877, January 27, 30, February 1, 18, March 2, 1878.

The passage of the Bland-Allison Act did not curtail the Southerners' interest in monetary policy, but their subsequent activity was anticlimactic. The conservatives continued, for example, to push for repeal of the tax on the issue of state banks but found little support in other areas of the country. Southern Democratic representatives also contributed a nearly solid bloc to the November, 1877, passage of another bill to repeal the resumption clause of the 1875 act. The Senate, however, passed a substitute without the repeal clause, the House disapproved, and repeal died. The one qualified victory in which Southerners participated involved a measure to halt greenback contraction at $346 million in 1878. The handful of surviving southern Republicans quite appropriately lined up with their Democratic colleagues to pass the bill—once again in opposition to the northeastern wing of their party.[58] The South continued to flirt with greenbackism well into the 1880s, and silver resurfaced in dramatic fashion a decade later, but the return to specie payments on January 1, 1879, closed off a tumultuous period in the history of American finance.

Despite a decade of diligent activity, Southerners achieved little in their central effort to secure an adequate circulating medium. Some southern national banks were created, and others received additional bank note circulation as a result of the act of 1870, but the comptroller of the currency effectively stopped the redistribution of $25 million. The South came out of the first session of the Forty-third Congress with the promise of an immediate redistribution of $55 million and out of the second session with free banking, but by that time the profit on national bank note circulation accruing to bankers had been reduced to the point that there was little incentive for expansion of the system. Bank note circulation in the nation actually declined from a high of $354 million in 1875 to a low of $321 million three years later, and there were thirty-nine fewer national banks in 1879 than 1875. By November, 1875, the ten ex-Confederate states had only eighty-three national banks and 4 percent of the nation's total bank note circulation—the latter figure about equal to

58. *Congressional Record*, 45th Cong., 2nd Sess., 2928, 3871.

the circulation of Illinois. The South gained a few national banks in the last half of the decade, but the section would never come close to a proportional share in the system.[59]

The Forty-third Congress also raised the limit on greenback circulation from $356 million to $382 million to give legal sanction to those Secretary Richardson had already released, but thanks to Grant's veto another $18 million was lost. Then the Resumption Act of 1875 began greenback contraction which Congress finally halted at $346 million in 1878—$9 million less than had been in circulation at the time of readmission ten years earlier.[60] Finally, the limited restoration of the silver dollar pleased the South, but this added nothing to the circulation by the time of resumption. The voluminous and often rancorous monetary debates of the 1870s, in fact, had done little but restore specie payments. They remain significant, however, for what they reveal about southern interests and activity and intersectional alignments.

First, it is apparent that the South and its congressmen were hardly "indifferent" to monetary problems or financially passive until after the Panic of 1873, nor did the silver controversy at the end of the 1870s draw the section "for the first time to a prominent place in the postwar financial discussion."[61] Thanks to the Democrats, the emotional issues of reconstruction and home rule remained at the center of the southern political stage for much of the decade, and the section's press and leadership seldom gave monetary problems the attention they would have commanded in less partisan times. But from the time of readmission, southern congressmen were active participants in the monetary debates, and their articulation of sectional interests and voting behavior is worthy of attention.

59. Sharkey, *Money, Class, and Party,* 232; John A. James, *Money and Capital Markets in Postbellum America* (Princeton: Princeton University Press, 1978), 77–78; Sylla, *American Capital Market,* 49, 57, 69; "Report of the Comptroller of the Currency," in U.S. Treasury Department, *Annual Report of the Secretary of the Treasury . . . 1879* (Washington, D.C.: Government Printing Office, 1879), 124, 114, 105; *Annual Report of the Secretary of the Treasury . . . 1875,* 253. See the discussion of southern banking problems in Roger L. Ransom and Richard Sutch, *One Kind of Freedom: The Economic Consequences of Emancipation* (Cambridge: Cambridge University Press, 1977), 106–16.

60. *Annual Report of the Secretary of the Treasury . . . 1879,* 114.

61. Unger, *Greenback Era,* 233, 340–42; Saloutos, *Farmer Movements in the South,* 44–46; Walter T. K. Nugent, *Money and American Society, 1865–1880* (New York: Free Press, 1968), 58–59, 217–18.

Secondly, the southern Republicans' perceptions of sectional needs matched those of their Democratic colleagues, and they did not neglect what they believed to be legitimate economic interests of their constituents. The Southerners were solidly behind the various proposals to redistribute and expand the bank note circulation in 1869 and 1870, and with few exceptions they also supported the largely unsuccessful attempt to augment the currency volume in 1874. A similar unity marked their response to the silver issue. The only major deviation came on the Resumption Act, which southern Republicans, like their midwestern party colleagues, generally supported. Given the ambivalent attitudes of the South toward resumption and the partisan nature of the issue, one would be hard pressed to argue that the act violated southern interests. A more likely supposition is that had it been a Democratic measure, it would have been accorded widespread support in the South.

Finally, and contrary to the behavior supposedly anticipated by northern Radicals, southern Republicans lined up time after time in direct opposition to their party colleagues from New England and most of those from the mid-Atlantic region. With the exception of a few monetary deviants such as Benjamin Butler and William Sprague, no Northeasterners of either party sympathized with southern views on the money questions. The rift between southern and northeastern Republicans opened as early as February, 1869, during the redistribution debate, and with few exceptions, they clashed whenever Congress considered monetary questions for the remainder of the decade. The Southerners' early independence is even more significant because it occurred during the intensely partisan struggle over reconstruction issues.

That Southerners were able to secure some of their objectives was due to the aid of like-minded colleagues from the midwestern and border states. The bipartisan coalition of Southerners and Midwesterners emerged in 1869 when Republicans dominated the southern delegations, rather than during the silver agitation as C. Vann Woodward has maintained, or in the "Inflation Session" of 1874 as Carl V. Harris has more recently argued.[62] When the bank

62.   C. Vann Woodward, *Reunion and Reaction: The Compromise of 1877 and the End of Reconstruction* (Boston: Little, Brown, 1951), 239–41, 243; Carl V. Harris,

note redistribution and expansion measures were under consideration, the southern delegations were almost solidly Republican. They were still 60 percent Republican in 1874, and even though Republican numbers were few during the silver debate, the survivors continued to side with southern Democrats against northeastern Republicans and the Hayes administration. Southern conservatives constantly preached the benefits of a southern-midwestern alliance on economic questions, but both they and subsequent commentators have failed to notice that for most of the decade Republicans provided a sizable majority of the section's manpower in the coalition against the Northeast. If fear of the reaction of southern Democrats to the economic structure erected during the war prompted northeastern Radicals to guarantee that the region would return Republicans to Congress as Howard K. Beale and others have argued, then they were most surely disappointed with the behavior of those Republicans on monetary questions. Differences in this area contributed early and constantly to the serious breach between the northeastern and southern wings of the Republican party.

"Right Fork or Left Fork? The Section-Party Alignments of Southern Democrats in Congress, 1873–1897," *Journal of Southern History*, XLII (1976), 478–84, 502–503.

VII Appropriations, Subsidies, and the Texas & Pacific Railroad

"What then may we not say in behalf of the man who adds a mile of Railroad to the number already in existence in a State like North Carolina, which is remote from the markets of the world, and without the ordinary facilities of reaching them?" a Raleigh editor asked in 1867. "We say this: That he is the true statesman and patriot whose achievement is worth more than a career in Congress, or volumes of speeches upon party politics." Proposals for building railroads and canals, reconstructing levees, clearing rivers and harbors, and establishing rail connections with the North and West elicited widespread and bipartisan support in the early postwar South. It was readily apparent that the warworn and impoverished states could not finance the needed rehabilitation, but during the war northern congressmen had set the precedent of using federal money for such projects. In the years after secession, Southerners watched as northern Republicans granted liberal appropriations for public works and immense subsidies for internal improvements in the North—the supreme symbol of which were the northern transcontinental railroads. Republican notions of active federal involvement in the economy had come south with the carpetbaggers, and that Whiggish philosophy had proven instrumental in attracting native whites to the party. While most southern conservatives retained constitutional reservations, many laid aside their states'-rights sensitivities and joined the chorus demanding federal aid for economic reconstruction. If, after all, an ever-growing federal largess had become established policy, then the South ought to share in it as a matter of simple justice.[1]

1. Raleigh *Register*, September 3, 1867. For a sampling of similar opinion, see Raleigh *North Carolina Standard*, November 18, 1867; Little Rock *Daily Arkansas*

But even before their readmission to the Union, Southerners had an uneasy feeling that the practice of handing out huge federal subsidies was waning—leaving the section without its rightful share. In response to an editorial in the New York *Journal of Commerce* calling for the curtailment of subsidies to railroads, the editor of the Richmond *Whig* insisted in early 1869 that the South had "certain works of vast national importance," but he claimed that the section was "too poor to complete them, and having never received any assistance from the General Government, while other works in other States have been built by government liberality, we are anxiously looking forward to that source for needed assistance. . . . Is the door to be slammed in our faces after having for years been kept open for others?"[2]

The *Whig*'s fears were justified. Throughout the 1870s, southern Republicans flooded legislative hoppers with internal improvements bills and usually voted as a bloc for railroad, canal, and levee projects with southern Democrats, who were only slightly less active in seeking federal aid. The Senate remained relatively receptive to subsidy legislation until late in the decade, but in the House a growing number of Northerners began to rally behind retrenchment-minded Democrat William S. Holman of Indiana to oppose further subsidies. Railroads were their primary target, but the more adamant among them sought to restrict expenditures for civil projects and river and harbor improvements as well. One of the first proposals to greet Southerners after readmission began was a Holman-sponsored resolution to put the House on record as being opposed to subsidies "either in bonds or money, to railroads or other corporations, or to promote local enterprises." Although the resolution had no practical effect other than to sample congressional attitudes, a favorable response indicated a disposition to curtail subsidies. Southerners

---

Gazette, December 24, 1867; New Orleans *Times*, March 3, 1869; New Orleans *Daily Picayune*, March 29, 1868; New Orleans *Republican*, November 26, 1870; Atlanta *Constitution*, January 20, 1869; Jackson *Daily Mississippi Pilot*, December 30, 1874; Vicksburg *Herald*, March 3, 1875; and almost every issue of *De Bow's Review* from 1868 to cessation of publication in October, 1870. Of the newspapers surveyed only the *Constitution*, *Picayune*, Selma *Southern Argus*, and Austin *Democratic Statesman* had difficulties reconciling the idea of federal aid with their states'-rights principles.

2. Richmond *Whig*, January 1, February 16, 1869.

strongly opposed the resolution, but it passed with the support of over 60 percent of the northern Republicans.[3]

The antisubsidy resolutions, usually introduced at the beginning of each Congress, won increasing favor among Northerners as the decade wore on. By 1874, Objector Holman had broadened his resolution to declare that "no subsidies in money, bonds, public lands, or by pledge of the public credit should be granted by Congress to associations or corporations engaged or proposing to engage in public or private enterprises." Southerners opposed it 13–36, but northern and border state Democrats supported it 45–6 and northern Republicans 87–21. The resolution involved suspension of the rules and failed by one vote 149–75, but similar resolutions would easily pass the next two Houses. By the time the Democrats took control of the House in 1875, the odds were heavily against approval of subsidies in any form.[4]

In short, the so-called "Great Barbecue" was over soon after readmission, and Southerners faced increasing northern opposition to their requests for economic aid. The editor of the New Orleans *Republican* wondered in 1874 if any hope remained "that continued appropriations can be extorted from an unwilling Congress." The frustration often turned to outright anger. In reference to an unfavorable northern commentary on a Georgia canal scheme, an Atlanta editor concluded that such remarks were simply more evidence of the Yankees' "customary disregard, if not hostility to the interests and just claims of the South."[5] Despite the often overwhelming opposition, southern congressmen continued to struggle for federal aid for river and harbor improvements and railroad construction—understandably the areas of greatest interest to their region. They experienced some success in the annual intersectional squabbles to secure rivers and harbors monies. But they won little federal help for their numerous railroad proposals, and their unfortu-

3. *Congressional Globe*, 40th Cong., 3rd Sess., 424; Terry L. Seip, "Southern Representatives and Economic Measures During Reconstruction: A Quantitative and Analytical Study" (Ph.D. dissertation, Louisiana State University, 1974), 100–104.

4. *Congressional Record*, 43rd Cong., 2nd Sess., 173-74, 44th Cong., 1st Sess., 227, 45th Cong., 2nd Sess., 626.

5. New Orleans *Republican*, April 1, 1874; Atlanta *Constitution*, January 25, 1874; Carter Goodrich, "The Revulsion Against Internal Improvements," *Journal of Economic History*, X (1950), 145–69.

nate identification with the ill-fated Texas & Pacific Railroad project overshadowed their more critical needs.

The annual rivers and harbors appropriations bills were classic log-rolling affairs constructed in the House Committee on Commerce from petitions and bills submitted by members. After clearing the committee, they were often scrutinized by the Appropriations Committee and then taken to the floor where those who felt slighted attempted to tack their special projects onto the measure. The senators, both in committee and on the floor, could be counted on to eliminate some House projects and add a considerable number of their own. Invariably, House and Senate conferees ended up hammering out a compromise version during the end-of-session rush. Positions or at least friends on the commerce committees were essential. Southerners usually received two seats on the Senate committee (a proportional share), but they were denied the chairmanship in 1875 when carpetbagger George E. Spencer of Alabama, next in line for the position, was bypassed and Roscoe Conkling of New York became chairman. With only one or two of the eleven available seats, Southerners had much less influence on the House committee, and their projects suffered accordingly.

Rivers and harbors appropriations grew steadily during the decade from $3.8 million in 1871 to $8.3 million in 1878. The ex-Confederate states' portion of this largess ranged from 15 to nearly 27 percent, but Southerners were never satisfied that they had received their fair share until the Forty-fifth Congress, when they secured four of the nine seats on the Senate committee and former Confederate postmaster general John H. Reagan of Texas became chairman of the powerful House committee. Reagan then combined with Spencer, still the second-ranking member of the Senate committee, to construct and pass two large measures which were especially liberal to southern projects.

The rivers and harbors acts were extremely important to the South. The section had always relied heavily on the natural network of streams to move its products, but the war and general neglect had rendered much of the system useless. Southern Republicans thought that federal aid to rehabilitate the system would be an essential part of reconstruction; such legislation would certainly provide much-needed evidence that they were doing something for their constituents. "Prosperity to the South, aided by a generous policy of internal improvement," Alabama carpetbagger Alfred E. Buck argued in 1870, "will more firmly cement and bind us in the family of States."[6]

Buck had party interests as well as sectional needs in mind, and southern Republicans echoed his appeal for economic assistance throughout the 1870s. But their pleas fell on deaf ears, and they had to fight to pry even a proportional share of appropriations from reluctant Northerners. They typically found themselves aligned with a sizable majority of the Democrats from their own and other regions on rivers and harbors proposals. They could also count on the support of many midwestern Republicans, but the Midwesterners, in control of the commerce committees until late in the decade, looked after their own interests first and most generously. Northeastern Republicans, especially those in the Senate, consistently blocked major southern proposals such as those for levee reconstruction. The lack of support among northern Republicans stung and baffled their southern party colleagues, who believed that their political survival was at least partially dependent on their ability to secure federal aid for economic reconstruction.

Southern Republicans received an indication of what they were up against soon after readmission. In the final weeks of the Fortieth Congress, the Senate considered a rivers and harbors bill for fiscal 1870 which the House had approved before readmission. The carpetbaggers and scalawags immediately wondered why their region was so ill provided for in the measure. "I should feel a little more liberal toward this whole bill if I could see in it evidence of Reconstruction," Alabama carpetbagger Willard Warner remarked. "From anything I can see in this bill all of the States of this Union that lie around the coast of the Atlantic, from the Potomac to the line of Mexico, are out of the Union." Warner called for appropriations for the lower Mississippi River and Mobile harbor, Alabama's special interest, but northern Republicans reminded him that the secretary of war had not yet conducted surveys of southern needs. This pre-

6. *Congressional Globe*, 41st Cong., 2nd Sess., Appendix, 498.

sented a problem because the Commerce Committee had already eliminated appropriations for surveys and a pending committee amendment proposed to delete a section describing the surveys. As Republican Zachariah Chandler of Michigan, the committee chairman, explained, "The committee thought it best not to incur the expense at this time." Warner and other Southerners promptly added surveys of their projects ranging from the Mobile and Charleston harbors to the Cape Fear River in North Carolina, the Apalachicola in Florida, and the White and Ouachita in Arkansas and then called for a vote to retain the surveys with the idea of later adding appropriations for them. Southerners voted 1–9 against striking the surveys and barely won 23–23. Many northern Democrats abstained rather than support the carpetbaggers and scalawags, but northern Republicans voted 18–6 to eliminate the section, and the Senate sent the bill back to the committee for reconsideration. Chandler, apparently irritated with the Southerners, sat on it until the end of the Congress, and southern Republicans thus went home with nothing to show for their efforts.[7]

With their numbers augmented by the continuing process of readmission, the Southerners fared somewhat better on two bills in the Forty-first Congress, but the sectionalism associated with the issue remained strong. On the first, Buck and others complained of the Commerce Committee's bias against southern projects and charged that Michigan and Wisconsin had received nearly as much as the entire South—thanks to the work of Chandler and Republicans Omar D. Conger of Michigan and Philetus Sawyer of Wisconsin in the House. In the bill's final form, the South's portion was 20 percent of $3.8 million, but over half of that went to improve the mouth of the Mississippi and the channel of the Cape Fear in North Carolina. An amount equal to that of the ten ex-Confederate states was spread over eleven projects in Wisconsin and nineteen in Michigan.[8]

7.   *Ibid.*, 40th Cong., 2nd Sess., 3615, 40th Cong., 3rd Sess., 1171–74, 41st Cong., 1st Sess., 599–600, 624–25. To compensate for the failure of the measure, Congress appropriated $1.5 million in the waning moments of the 40th Congress and another $2 million early in the 41st Congress to be used by the secretary of war for rivers and harbors improvements, but he was not to inaugurate new works. This virtually eliminated the ex-Confederate states from consideration.

8.   Richard Nelson Current, *Pine Logs and Politics: A Life of Philetus Sawyer, 1816–1900* (Madison, Wis.: State Historical Society of Wisconsin, 1950), 65; *Congressional Globe*, 41st Cong., 2nd Sess., Appendix, 497, 499, 690–91.

The South, now at full strength, did not do as well on the second act. Its share of the $4.2 million appropriation fell to 15 percent; Michigan and New York each picked up a matching amount. While others complained that the needs of the lower Mississippi Valley had not been satisfied, Warner became embroiled in a sectional quarrel typical of the debate when he proposed to double the appropriation for Mobile harbor to $100,000. Several northern and western Republicans immediately protested. William Stewart of Nevada suggested that the appropriations for each state should be proportional to the amount of taxes collected therein, and he asked if Warner had a list of taxes paid in Alabama. Warner did not dignify Stewart's irritating query with a reply, but the implication was that the South contributed less federal revenue than other regions and thus should not share equally in internal improvements monies. Others argued that since the surveys Warner had requested the previous year had not been completed he should wait until next year for increased appropriations. Despite the support of nine of the ten Democrats voting, southern Republicans fell far short of passing his amendment primarily because their northern party colleagues voted 1–22 in the negative. Warner glumly took the $50,000 and requested more surveys.[9]

The struggle continued into the Forty-second Congress. The bill approved during the second session generated no roll call divisions in the House, but New York Democrat Samuel S. Cox, sensing the Republican split, initiated a spirited sectional debate by charging that the Commerce Committee had treated southern proposals unfairly. Cox was joined by Texas Democrat John Hancock, who noted that Michigan had again received almost as much money as all the southern states combined. Conger of Michigan, the floor leader for the bill, protested the charges of discrimination and argued that Southerners on the committee were "as talented and as zealous in behalf of the interests of the section as the gentleman from New York could possibly be for them." In the heated exchange that followed, Georgia Democrat Pierce M. B. Young and Louisiana carpetbagger Lionel A. Sheldon denied the existence of any sectional bias

9. *Congressional Globe*, 41st Cong., 3rd Sess., 1889–91, 1976, Appendix, 379–80.

in the committee, but Southerners still scrambled to add as many of their projects as possible before sending the proposal to the Senate.[10]

Senate additions necessitated a conference committee, whose report was accepted by the House but disputed in the upper chamber. Spencer, irritated because of an appropriation for Mobile harbor had been reduced, called for a second conference. Republicans West of Louisiana, Flanagan of Texas, Rice of Arkansas, and Alcorn of Mississippi joined the fray and traded charges with Edmunds and Morrill of Vermont, Buckingham of Connecticut, Trumbull of Illinois, and Conkling of New York over whose projects deserved funding. Although half of the Southerners, all Republicans, opposed the report in the hope of getting a second conference, it passed 41–13. They picked up slightly over a million dollars, about 20 percent of the total, but once again an equal sum went to Michigan and Wisconsin.[11]

The South fared much the same on the bill passed in the third session. Southerners fought for another million dollars, much of which was gained on the House and Senate floor, but their share fell to 16 percent. At one point in the House deliberations, Mississippi carpetbagger George C. McKee, having failed to secure an appropriation of fifty thousand dollars for the improvement of the Yazoo River, moved that it "be considered as lying within the boundaries of Wisconsin and Michigan, for then my amendment would get through." McKee's motion provoked laughter, but some southern Republicans were clearly irritated. A typical division came when Southerners voted 40–2 for improvements on the White and Saint Francis rivers in Arkansas. Democrats from other regions supported the proposal 44–9, but Republicans outside the South reacted sharply against it 18–56. Southerners also voted 41–3 to double the amount for improvements on the Mississippi River between Saint Louis and Cairo, Illinois. Republican opposition was unanimous in the Northeast, and even midwestern Republicans split 20–19 on the proposal. In the Senate, Chandler's committee proposed amendments to strip several southern projects out of the bill, but with the backing of most northern Democrats and a handful of northern Republicans,

10. *Ibid.*, 42nd Cong., 2nd Sess., 1425, 2443–52.
11. *Ibid.*, 4406–4409, Appendix, 814–16.

the carpetbaggers and scalawags were able to defeat several of them on the floor. Still the final distribution was a familiar one—the share granted to Michigan and Wisconsin was greater than that of the ex-Confederate states. There was really little Southerners could do about the situation; northern Republicans appeared deaf to their arguments regarding the pressing needs of the South. Although southern Republicans were loath to recognize the fact, it was clear that most of their northern colleagues saw reconstruction as a purely political process—it would have no economic dimension.[12]

Declining revenues following the Panic of 1873 and what Texas Democrat Asa Willie termed "the economical spirit suddenly springing up" jeopardized rivers and harbors appropriations in the Forty-third Congress. Southerners managed a 22-percent share of a small measure approved in the first session, but it was the act passed in the waning moments of the second session which ultimately proved to be the most beneficial to the South of any during the 1870s. The hotly disputed tax and tariff proposal held up consideration of the bill in the Senate, but on the final day of the session, southern Republicans provided the necessary votes to pass the revenue measure and then furiously added section after section to the rivers and harbors bill. Former Whig James Flanagan of Texas best expressed the mentality of the moment when he declared his support for all additions to the bill: "Boy and man I have always been for internal improvements. . . . This is directly upon that line, consistent and progressive, not going back by any means." In the committee of the whole, southern votes carried an appropriation of $560,000 for the Tennessee River below Chattanooga, $200,000 for North Carolina's Cape Fear, $100,000 for Charleston harbor, and a dozen lesser amounts for other projects.[13]

But this was only the beginning. The big money entered the picture when Alcorn, West, and Powell Clayton of Arkansas rallied the Southerners and a few Midwesterners behind an appropriation of

12. *Ibid.*, 42nd Cong., 3rd Sess., 1463, 1469, 1658, 1643, 1649–50, 1657, 1659, 1758, 2053–66, Appendix, 284–86.
13. *Congressional Record*, 43rd Cong., 1st Sess., 3771, 5370–73, Appendix, 196–201; *The Statutes at Large of the United States of America*, XVII, Pt. III (1874), 237–44; *Congressional Record*, 43rd Cong., 2nd Sess., 2159, 2160, 2163, 2165–68.

$3,420,000 for rebuilding and maintaining the levees of the Mississippi River. A product of Alcorn's select committee which southern Republicans had established to frame levees legislation nearly three years earlier, the proposal had long been the subject of agitation in the Mississippi valley. Clayton viewed it as "the most important measure that can possibly be adopted for the benefit of the South," and Alcorn and West pushed the amendment through the committee of the whole over the protests of Chandler, Sherman, George S. Boutwell of Massachusetts and other northern Republicans (see Table 17: A).[14]

West then proposed an even larger and more unusual appropriation to remove the mud bar which blocked the passage of large ships into the mouth of the Mississippi. The movement to open the river had general support in both chambers, but Southerners disagreed over the best means of accomplishing the task. One group, including most southern Republicans and the New Orleans press, backed a scheme to construct a canal beginning below Fort Saint Philip on the eastern bank and running southeast to the vicinity of Breton Pass. In 1874, however, Captain James B. Eads, to whom one representative referred as "a successful carrier-out of great works," submitted a more radical plan to construct jetties to narrow and extend the mouth of the river into the deep water of the gulf. The confined force of the river current, Eads explained to a host of doubters, would then clear the mud bar. Given a choice between the two proposals,

14.   *Congressional Globe*, 41st Cong., 2nd Sess., 4043, 4078, 5625; Jacob H. Sypher to Henry Clay Warmoth, February 13, 1871, in Henry Clay Warmoth Papers, Southern Historical Collection, University of North Carolina, Chapel Hill (hereinafter cited as SHC); *Congressional Record*, 43rd Cong., 2nd Sess., 2164; James B. Eads, *Address . . . to the Grand Convention for the Improvement of the Mississippi and Its Tributaries* (Saint Louis: George Knapp and Co., 1867); *De Bow's Review*, XII (1869), 837–40; New Orleans *Republican*, March 29, 1874; Jackson *Daily Mississippi Pilot*, January 31, 1875; William C. Harris, *Presidential Reconstruction in Mississippi* (Baton Rouge: Louisiana State University Press, 1967), ch. 10; Lillian A. Pereyra, *James Lusk Alcorn: Persistent Whig* (Baton Rouge: Louisiana State University Press, 1966), 26–30, 113–15, 151, 165–67. The only southern opposition found to Alcorn's levees proposal came from an Austin Democratic journal. "We have always been adverse to the exercise of doubtful powers on the part of the central government even for the apparent good of the people," the editor argued, "but we confess that, in this instance, much may be said for its exercise." Nevertheless, he opposed the measure on principle, and he hoped that the interested states could finance levee construction themselves. This might delay construction, but it would "be better for the people." Austin *Democratic Statesman*, December 13, 1873.

Table 17. SELECTED VOTES ON MISSISSIPPI RIVER LEVEES: FORTY-THIRD SENATE AND FORTY-FOURTH HOUSE

A. To amend H.R. 4740 by appropriating $3.42 million for Mississippi River levee improvement to be divided as follows: Missouri, $320,000; Arkansas, $1 million; Mississippi, $600,000; and Louisiana, $1.5 million.[a]

Region	Yea		Nay	
	Dem.	Rep.	Dem.	Rep.
NE	—	1	—	7
MA	—	1	1	3
MW	1	4	—	8
SS	5	8	—	1[b]
BS	3	1	—	—
PS	1	1	—	3
Total	10	16	1	22
Grand Total	26		23	

B. To suspend the rules and pass H.R. 3430, a bill appropriating $4,202,000 "to repair and rebuild the levees of the Mississippi River."[c]

Region	Yea		Nay	
	Dem.	Rep.	Dem.	Rep.
NE	1	—	8	12
MA	2	4	16	15
MW	10	9	24	22
SS	23	13	10	1
BS	10	—	4	—
PS	—	1	1	1
Total	46	27	63	51
Grand Total	73		114	

[a] Congressional Record, 43rd Cong., 2nd Sess., 2165 (March 3, 1875).
[b] Morgan C. Hamilton (Tex.).
[c] Congressional Record, 44th Cong., 2nd Sess., 2232 (March 3, 1877).

the House passed the canal scheme sponsored by Louisiana carpet-baggers Lionel Sheldon and Jacob Sypher. The Senate, however, preferred the Eads scheme—primarily because he agreed not to accept any pay until he had achieved a depth of at least twenty feet of water, at which time he would receive $500,000. He would then be paid $500,000 for every additional two feet thereafter until the channel reached a depth of thirty feet and $100,000 a year for maintaining that depth for twenty years. The total amount involved was $7.25 million. In explaining the proposal, West emphasized the "no water, no pay" nature of the contract, which the Senate found most attractive and agreed to without the formality of a roll call.[15]

In a short period, Southerners had added a potential obligation of approximately $11 million to a bill which had begun as a routine proposal of about $6 million. Northerners warned that the measure had no chance of passing the House, and when the committee of the whole reported it to the Senate with just a dozen hours left in the session, Alcorn's levees proposal immediately came under northern attack. In response, the ex-Whig contended that the delta states, impoverished by the cotton tax of $57 million, could not afford to finance levee work. The federal government had paid out over $700,000 in aid to flood victims within the past year alone. "Will you feed those poor colored people whose homes are upon the banks of the Mississippi River?" he asked. "You must feed them if you will not protect their homes." Levee reconstruction should have been undertaken "at the end of the war instead of putting an onerous tax on the products of the South," the carpetbagger Clayton argued. There would be "less cause for troops in the South now" if Northerners had undertaken economic rehabilitation instead of trying "to tranquilize" the section. This time, however, midwestern support disappeared and the levees appropriation was eliminated. In retaliation, the southern bloc deleted several northern projects, but the

15. *Congressional Record*, 43rd Cong., 1st Sess., 4566–73, 4624–26, Appendix, 407–10; New Orleans *Daily Picayune*, February 28, 1869, April 8, 1874; New Orleans *Republican*, February 15, 22, 24, 26, 28, March 1, 13, 17, November 16, 1874; New Orleans *Weekly Louisianian*, March 14, April 11, June 6, 18, July 2, 5, 1874, February 25, 1875; Austin *Democratic Statesman*, January 10, March 5, 1875; James B. Eads, *Mouth of the Mississippi: Jetty System Explained* (Saint Louis: Times Print, 1874), 1–38; *Congressional Record*, 43rd Cong., 2nd Sess., 2161–62.

Eads proposal survived. A hastily convened conference committee trimmed other sections of the bill to only $620,000 over the original House version, and with time running out, the Senate and the House approved the conference report. Exclusive of the Eads project, the South received about $1.4 million, its biggest share of any rivers and harbors measure since the war. The jetty plan worked and by 1879 Eads had opened up a channel thirty feet deep. Northerners later showed some reluctance to meet the terms of the 1875 contract, but it could not be violated and the opening of the river's mouth ultimately cost the government about $8 million.[16]

Southern Democrats assumed control of their section's drive for internal improvements in the Forty-fourth House with even less success than their Republican counterparts had previously had. Initially the prospects looked good. They picked up $1.2 million of a $5 million act in the first session after fighting off the efforts of northeastern Republicans and some northern Democrats to cut the appropriations in half. But because of revenue problems, Grant informed Congress in December, 1876, that he and the secretary of war had agreed that only $2.2 million would be spent and that no new works would be launched. Furthermore, Congress failed to produce a rivers and harbors bill in the second session. Much to the Southerners' irritation, Holman applauded the retrenchment accomplished by the first Democratic House since the Civil War and declared "that the lavish appropriations made on the pretense of improving rivers and harbors of late years have been a fruitful source of corruption."[17]

Another levees bill demonstrated what the South was up against. On the last day of the Forty-fourth Congress, Democrat E. John Ellis of Louisiana moved to suspend the rules and pass a bill appropriating

16. *Congressional Record*, 43rd Cong., 2nd Sess., 2169–79, 2265–66; *Statutes at Large*, XVIII, Pt. III (1875), 456–66; Florence Dorsey, *Road to the Sea: The Story of James B. Eads and the Mississippi River* (New York: Holt, Rinehart and Winston, 1947), chs. 11–13; *Nation*, February 25, 1875, p. 124.

17. *Congressional Record*, 44th Cong., 1st Sess., 2359–60, 4536–48, 4568–87, 4919–20, 5121–22, 5173–75, 5254, 5389–98, 5427; Charleston *Journal of Commerce*, July 21, 1876; *Statutes at Large*, XIX (1876), 132–39; *To the Old Whigs of Louisiana*, March 1, 1876 (pamphlet), in J. R. G. Pitkin Papers, Middleton Library, Louisiana State University, Baton Rouge; James D. Richardson (comp.), *A Compilation of the Messages and Papers of the Presidents, 1789–1897* (10 vols.; Washington, D.C.: Government Printing Office, 1897), VII, 408; *Congressional Record*, 44th Cong., 2nd Sess., Appendix, 259–61.

$4,202,000 "to repair and rebuild the levees of the Mississippi River, and to reclaim the alluvial lands thereof, to improve its navigation, and promote and protect its commerce." Six states were to benefit from the appropriation, but $3.5 million was earmarked for work in Arkansas, Mississippi, and Louisiana. Building on the earlier work of the carpetbag and scalawag congressmen, Ellis had had the bill prepared for six months but had not been able to get it before the House. The measure was of tremendous importance to the South, yet it gathered only fourteen Democratic and thirteen Republican votes from the Midwest and Northeast and was resoundingly defeated 73–114 (see Table 17: B). The southern Democrats' 23–10 vote and their sixteen absences was one of their poorer performances, but thirteen of the fourteen southern Republicans supported the bill—a notable response given the partisan atmosphere of the electoral crisis. In some ways, however, it was altogether fitting that the surviving carpetbaggers, scalawags, and blacks should break with their northern party colleagues and vote for the levees appropriation on what was, symbolically at least, the final day of Reconstruction.[18]

With Democrat John H. Reagan heading the House Committee on Commerce, and Spencer, carpetbagger John J. Patterson, and Democrats Matt Ransom and John Brown Gordon on the Senate committee in the Forty-fifth Congress, the South was finally in a position to wield power on rivers and harbors legislation. The basic forces behind the measures were the same as always, but Southerners rather than Midwesterners were now in the commanding position. In 1878 Spencer mustered a bipartisan committee majority, overrode Conkling, the chairman, and added several southern projects to Reagan's bill. He then drove it through the Senate with a bipartisan coalition of Southerners and Midwesterners and over the opposition of such northeastern Republican powers as James G. Blaine, Henry L. Dawes, Justin Morrill, and Conkling. For the first time, Southerners placed three men, Spencer, Ransom, and Reagan, on the six-man

18. *Congressional Record*, 43rd Cong., 2nd Sess., 2232; E. John Ellis to Ezekiel P. Ellis, February 25, 1877, in Ellis Family Papers, Middleton Library, Louisiana State University, Baton Rouge; C. Vann Woodward, *Reunion and Reaction: The Compromise of 1877 and the End of Reconstruction* (Boston: Little, Brown, 1951), 145–47.

conference committee, and Spencer managed the conference report in the Senate. The ex-Confederate states' share increased to 27 percent, but more important, the number of southern projects jumped to nearly sixty and the amount of the bill was considerably larger— over $8.3 million of which $2.2 million went to the South. Since this was the first rivers and harbors appropriation passed in two years, its size was more than justified, but the same coalition pushed through a second act eight months later which gave another $2 million to over seventy projects scattered across the South. Once again Reagan, the ex-Confederate, and Spencer, the carpetbagger, constructed and managed the bill and the conference report. Southern Republicans, now numbering only six in each chamber, provided the strongest support for the two bills of any regional party group (see Tables 18 and 19). The tragedy was that the large appropriations had come too late to be of any value to the party in the South.[19]

Although rivers and harbors improvements commanded a broad base of support in the South, many Southerners pinned even greater hope on the creation of a railroad network as a catholicon for their region's economic problems. Led by Republicans with the support of many conservatives, some reconstruction governments overindulged in funding railway proposals and sometimes committed state resources to projects with little consideration of their merit. The atmosphere naturally attracted less reputable types looking for quick wealth. "The day of old fogyism is past in N.C. and the people must and will rapidly learn to appreciate the end without caring for the means," one of railroad dealer George Swepson's friends assured him in 1868. "All men, even those most Christian, are dictated in their judgment of results by the ways their pockets or personal comforts are affected. . . . Ten years from now the people of N.C. will see so

19. *Congressional Record*, 45th Cong., 2nd Sess., 2713–18, 2737–56, 4358–80, 4421–42, 4641–47, 45th Cong., 3rd Sess., 1488–90, 2191–2222, 2365–68; *Statutes at Large*, XX (1878), 152–63, and (1879), 363–77. See Carl V. Harris' analysis of the final and conference roll calls on rivers and harbors legislation in "Right Fork or Left Fork? The Section-Party Alignments of Southern Democrats in Congress, 1873–1897," *Journal of Southern History*, XLII (1976), 494–99. The region-party alignments on civil appropriations bills during the 1870s were quite similar to those on rivers and harbors legislation.

Table 18. RIVERS AND HARBORS SCALOGRAM: FORTY-FIFTH HOUSE

Scale Position	NE D	NE R	MA D	MA R	MW D	MW R	SS D	SS R	BS D	BS R	PS D	PS R	Total D	Total R
0	2		6		8		2		4		1		23	
		—		4		7		—		1		—		12
1	—		6		4		3		3		—		16	
		4		7		5		—		—		—		16
2	1		1		1		1		1		—		5	
		6		6		2		—		—		1		15
3	1		2		2		4		—		1		10	
		3		4		5		—		—		—		12
4	—		3		5		6		2		—		16	
		1		3		4		—		—		—		8
5	1		8		11		37		10		1		68	
		5		9		36		6		—		3		59
Not	1		3		2		3[a]		7		—		16	
Scaling		3		5		6		—		1		—		15
Total	6		29		33		56		27		3		154	
		22		38		65		6		2		4		137

Coefficient of Reproducibility = .973
[a]E. John Ellis (La.), Auburn L. Pridemore (Va.), and Alfred M. Scales (N.C.) did not scale because of excessive absences.

Scale Position	SCALOGRAM ITEMS Identification

0

1 To adjourn in order to prevent action on H.R. 4236, a bill making appropriations for river and harbor improvements (1878–79). 33–207; + = Nay. *Congressional Record*, 45th Cong., 2nd Sess., 2715 (April 22, 1878).

2 To suspend the rules and pass H.R. 4236. 166–66; + = Yea. *Ibid.*, 2761 (April 22, 1878).

3 To suspend the rules and pass H.R. 6463, a bill making appropriations for river and harbor improvements (1879–80). 173–74; + = Yea. *Ibid.*, 45th Cong., 3rd Sess., 1490 (February 17, 1879).

4 To agree to the conference report on H.R. 6463. 108–62; + = Yea. *Ibid.*, 2367 (March 3, 1879).

5 To adopt the conference report on H.R. 4236. 150–99; + = Yea. *Ibid.*, 45th Cong., 2nd Sess., 4674 (June 15, 1878).

The higher the scale position, the more receptive a representative was to rivers and harbors appropriations.

Table 19. RIVERS AND HARBORS SCALOGRAM: FORTY-FIFTH SENATE

Scale Position	NE D	NE R	MA D	MA R	MW D	MW R	SS D	SS R	BS D	BS R	PS D	PS R	Total D	Total R
0	—		—		—		—		—		—		—	
		3		1		1		—		—		1		6
1	—		2		—		—		4		—		6	
		—		—		—		—		—		2		2
2	—		2		1		1ª		—		—		4	
		2		—		—		—		—		—		2
3	—		—		—		—		1		—		1	
		—		—		1		—		—		—		1
4	—		—		—		1		—		—		1	
		—		—		4		—		—		—		4
5	—		—		1		6		—		—		7	
		2		—		5		3		—		—		10
6	1		—		—		5		2		—		8	
		—		1		4		2		—		1		8
Not	1		2		2		1ᵇ		1		1		8	
Scaling		3		—		—		1ᵇ		—		3		7
Total	2		6		4		14		8		1		35	
		10		2		15		6		—		7		40

Coefficient of Reproducibility = .976

ªJohn Tyler Morgan (Ala.) consistently opposed all appropriations and subsidies for internal improvements.

ᵇAugustus H. Garland (D-Ark.) and Blanche K. Bruce (R-Miss.) did not scale because of excessive absences on H.R. 4236. Both ranked in the most favorable position on a separate scale on H.R. 6463.

Scale Position	SCALOGRAM ITEMS Identification
0	

1 To amend H.R. 4236 by increasing the appropriations for Charleston harbor from $5,000 to $200,000. 41–8; + = Yea. *Congressional Record,* 45th Cong., 2nd Sess., 4378 (June 10, 1878).

2 To amend H.R. 6463 by eliminating the $80,000 appropriation to improve Red Fish Bar to Morgan's Point, Texas. 12–37; + = Nay. *Ibid.,* 45th Cong., 3rd Sess., 2196 (March 1, 1879).

3 To amend H.R. 4236 by appropriating $15,000 for improvement of the French Broad River in North Carolina. 35–17; + = Yea. *Ibid.,* 45th Cong., 2nd Sess., 4377 (June 10, 1878).

4 To amend H.R. 4236 by providing for the expenditure of not more than 75% of the appropriations for this year. 20–37; + = Nay. *Ibid.,* 4441 (June 11, 1878).
 To concur in the conference report on H.R. 4236. 39–22; + = Yea. *Ibid.,* 4647 (June 15, 1878).

5 To pass H.R. 6463. 29–18; + = Yea. *Ibid.*, 45th Cong., 3rd Sess., 2222 (March 1, 1879).
6 To proceed to the consideration of H.R. 6463. 23–34; + = Yea. *Ibid.*, 2173 (March 1, 1879).
The higher the scale position, the more receptive a senator was to rivers and harbors appropriations.

clearly the vast benefit of the present proposed Railroads that they will care very little how or by what means they were built." With such forces at work, it is hardly surprising that much of the corruption and a sizable portion of the sharp increase in some states' bonded indebtedness stemmed from their greed for railroads. Here again, Southerners looked to the federal government for aid.[20]

Almost a third of the 251 southern congressmen had a financial stake in one or more southern lines, and nearly all, Republicans and Democrats alike, were sympathetic to their section's demands for more railroads. During the first half of the 1870s, they carried bill after bill to Washington requesting subsidies in public lands, right of ways, renewals of antebellum land grants, or time extensions for lines already under construction. In the lame-duck session of the Fortieth Congress, for example, with only limited time for consideration and passage, congressmen from the first six readmitted states submitted thirty railroad bills. But in a pattern which was to become increasingly familiar, their proposals disappeared into the railroad or public lands committees never to reappear. The Southerners were not easily discouraged; as late as the Forty-second Congress (1871–1873), they sponsored almost eighty railroad proposals. No more than a handful passed. Those which managed to clear the Senate invariably encountered opposition in the House. If they passed the committee's scrutiny, Holman or some other northern

20. Henry E. Colton to George W. Swepson, November 16, 1868, in George W. Swepson Papers, North Carolina State Archives, Raleigh. Mark Wahlgren Summers provides a thoroughgoing study of the problem in "Radical Reconstruction and the Gospel of Prosperity: Railroad Aid Under the Southern Republicans" (Ph.D. dissertation, University of California, Berkeley, 1980). See also John F. Stover, *The Railroads of the South, 1865–1900: A Study in Finance and Control* (Chapel Hill: University of North Carolina Press, 1955), especially ch. 5, but compare Carter Goodrich, "Public Aid to Railroads in the Reconstruction South," *Political Science Quarterly*, LXXI (1956), 408–38, and Maury Klein and Kozo Yamamura, "The Growth Strategies of Southern Railroads, 1865–1893," *Business History Review*, XLI (1967), 358–77.

Democrat either objected to their consideration on the floor or killed them with delaying tactics.[21]

The steadfast refusal of northern Democrats to permit railroads to feast on the public domain forced their southern party colleagues to depend on Republican support for their proposals. Early in the period, southern Democrats frequently abandoned their party to vote for subsidies for northern lines—probably in the hope that those interests would return the favor.[22] Their support began to wane, however, as their own proposals encountered difficulty. On a series of key roll calls relating to northern and western railroads in the Forty-second House, for example, southern Democrats were notably less receptive than they had previously been to aiding such lines (see Table 20). Southern Republicans continued to back subsidy legislation, but opposition grew among their northern party colleagues—particularly after the Credit Mobilier scandal surfaced in the fall of 1872. The banking panic of the following fall, a depressed economy, and Democratic victories in the congressional elections of 1874 sounded the death knell for subsidy legislation. Convinced that further efforts were useless, most Southerners simply stopped submitting railroad proposals, and many of the ever-increasing number of Redeemers joined the Democratic-led reform movement to curtail subsidies.

Nothing better exemplifies the Southerners' problems than the decade-long effort to establish a transcontinental railroad along the thirty-second parallel to San Diego. The tortuous course of the Texas & Pacific Railroad through the 1870s reveals much about the limits of the northern commitment to economic reconstruction and the emerging colonial economic status of the South. Still, one might write off the whole matter as simply another unsuccessful Gilded Age speculation or view it, as did many Southerners, as a telling example of continuing sectional prejudice were it not for its alleged role in the final act of the reconstruction experiment. Accord-

21. *Congressional Globe*, 40th Cong., 3rd Sess., Index, 42nd Cong., 1st Sess., Index, 42nd Cong., 2nd Sess., Index, 42nd Cong., 3rd Sess., Index.

22. See, for example, the House roll calls and debate on a land grant to the Oregon Central Railroad and on a bill extending construction time for a Wisconsin line, in *ibid.*, 41st Cong., 2nd Sess., 3110, Appendix, 644–45, 42nd Cong., 2nd Sess., 1274–78, 1301–13, 1714–21, 2481–83.

Table 20. RAILROAD SCALOGRAM: FORTY-SECOND HOUSE

Scale Position	NE D	NE R	MA D	MA R	MW D	MW R	SS D	SS R	BS D	BS R	PS D	PS R	Total D	Total R
							Region and Party							
0	2		18		7		10		13		—		50	
		1		—		1		—		—		—		2
1	—		2		4		2		4		—		12	
		2		—		9		—		—		—		11
2	1		1		2		1		1		—		6	
		1		1		10		—		—		—		12
3	—		2		1		4		1		1		9	
		2		1		5		—		—		—		8
4	—		—		1		2		1		1		5	
		2		3		11		4		2		—		22
5	—		2		1		3		1		—		7	
		10		19		11		18		—		2		60
6	—		—		—		—		—		—		—	
		2		4		3		1		—		1		11
Not Scaling	1		5		6		—		1		—		13	
		3		3		2		3		1		—		12
Total	4		30		22		22		22		2		102	
		23		31		52		26		3		3		138

Coefficient of Reproducibility = .957

Scale Position	SCALOGRAM ITEMS Identification
0	

1 To table a bill (H.R. 2199) incorporating the Great Salt Lake and Colorado River Railway Company and granting the company right of way through public lands. 63–105; + = Nay. *Congressional Globe*, 42nd Cong., 2nd Sess., 2547 (April 18, 1872).

2 To table a bill (S. 242) enabling the Atlantic and Pacific Railroad Company to mortgage its road. 63–104; + = Nay. *Ibid.*, 42nd Cong., 1st Sess., 745 (April 18, 1871).

3 To suspend the rules and pass a bill (H.R. 3743) granting the right of way through public lands to the Atchison, Topeka, and Santa Fe Railroad. 98–77; + = Yea. *Ibid.*, 42nd Cong., 3rd Sess., 1577 (February 21, 1873).

4 To pass a bill (H.R. 1553) relating to lands for the Central Pacific Railroad Company. 100–87; + = Yea. *Ibid.*, 42nd Cong., 2nd Sess., 2739 (April 24, 1872).

5 To suspend the rules and pass a bill (S. 1537) granting rights to a right of way for a western branch of the Texas Pacific Railroad Company. 89–79; + = Yea. *Ibid.*, 42nd Cong., 3rd Sess., 2131 (March 3, 1873).

6 To table a bill (H.R. 3483) repealing appropriations to the Central Pacific Railroad Company made in an army appropriations bill for fiscal 1872. 12–163; + = Yea. *Ibid.*, 540 (January 13, 1873).

The higher the scale position, the more receptive a representative was to railroad legislation.

ing to the standard interpretation, southern Democrats, northern Republicans, and the promoters of the Texas & Pacific became embroiled in the political dealing surrounding the disputed presidential election of 1876 and played a pivotal part in creating the Compromise of 1877. The story of the electoral dispute is a familiar one, but the role of the Texas & Pacific in its resolution merits reconsideration—especially when placed in the context of the line's legislative history and the Southerners' reaction to it.

The idea of a southern route to the Pacific was hardly new. In the early 1850s, Texas had chartered two companies, one to build west from Marshall, just opposite Shreveport, Louisiana, through Fort Worth to El Paso, the second to begin at Texarkana in the northeastern corner of the state and build through Sherman to El Paso. Despite generous land grants, neither company had made much progress by 1861. After the war, John C. Fremont purchased the second company, the Memphis, El Paso, and Pacific Railroad, secured a land grant of over eighteen million acres from the Texas legislature, and petitioned Congress for a right of way from El Paso to San Diego. Late in the Fortieth Congress, the House, with the unanimous support of the Southerners, passed a joint resolution complying with Fremont's request, but the Senate took no action. The lower chamber immediately repassed the measure when the next Congress convened in March, 1869. The Senate again refused to take it up. One southern editor suspected that Yankee prejudice against southern projects underlay the Senate decision, but he also reported rumors that the upper chamber feared establishing a precedent of granting no land subsidies other than the right of way. Although there is evidence that some Northerners wished to pass the measure and thus sabotage more liberal subsidies, the rumors had substance. North Carolina carpetbagger Joseph Abbott, for example, was prepared to argue against the resolution and thought it foolish for anyone to believe that "any company is going to build across nine hundred miles of arid desert without any subsidy."[23]

That the southern senators had other plans became apparent in

23. *Congressional Globe*, 40th Cong., 3rd Sess., 1444–45, 1589, 41st Cong., 1st Sess., 196–97, 677; Richmond *Whig*, April 3, 1869; Lewis H. Haney, *A Congressional History of Railways in the United States, 1850–1877* (2 vols.; Madison, Wis.: Democratic Printing Co., 1910), II, ch. 9; Woodward, *Reunion and Reaction*, 70–73. The Memphis, El Paso, and Pacific failed in 1870.

late 1869 when Louisiana carpetbagger William Pitt Kellogg introduced a bill (S. 647) "to aid in the construction of a railroad and telegraph line from Marshall, Texas, to San Diego, California, with branches and connections." As altered by the Committee on the Pacific Railroad, the measure granted the trunk and several branch lines a right of way and twenty alternate sections of public land per mile on each side of the line "in any Territory and ten in any State," as well as the usual rights to resources on adjacent lands. The bill assigned an estimated twenty-six million acres of the public domain to a corporation to be called the Texas & Pacific Railway Company.[24]

The carpetbaggers and scalawags pushed consideration of the measure. The bill's sponsors, justifiably apprehensive of House reaction, killed several southern amendments adding branch lines. More controversial was the committee's stipulation that the Texas & Pacific be built with a gauge of 4 feet 8½ inches, the northern standard, thus making it incompatible with the five-foot gauge of southern lines. The gauge issue was critical. Kellogg, Abbott, Spencer, Warner, and Benjamin F. Rice of Arkansas, all carpetbaggers, endorsed South Carolina scalawag Frederick Sawyer's protest that Southerners did not want a "Northern Pacific railroad" along the thirty-second parallel: "Republican Senators on the floor cannot afford to do this thing in the way to make a show of giving a transcontinental railroad to the southern section of the country, and in fact putting its control absolutely and completely in the hands of northern corporations." If the gauge was not set at five feet, southern port cities would be bypassed and the Texas & Pacific would naturally link with northern lines at Saint Louis and lead to the Northeast. After listening to Northerners argue that the line should conform to their gauge, Abbott declared that he saw "a cat in this meal as big as an elephant." The cat was the Pennsylvania Railroad, which already had connections with Saint Louis and dominated the Southern Railway and Security Company, which controlled many financially troubled southeastern lines. As Abbott put it, none of the Southerners wanted their

24. *Congressional Globe*, 41st Cong., 2nd Sess., 1776, 4553–54, 4638–45. Initially referred to as the Southern Pacific Railroad, the name was changed to the Texas Pacific Railroad in the 1871 act, and to the Texas & Pacific Railway in a supplemental act the following year.

constituents to say that they had "sold out to the Penn Central." With the backing of a few Northerners who agreed that the Texas & Pacific should be a "Southern road," the carpetbaggers and scalawags amended the bill to specify a gauge of five feet, and it passed the Senate without a roll call division.[25]

The Senate bill was not considered at any length in the House until February, 1871, when William A. Wheeler of New York, chairman of the Committee on the Pacific Railroad, reported it with a drastic amendment which cut the land grant in half by eliminating the branch lines. Wheeler appeared especially sensitive to "the growing dislike of the American people to these large grants to corporations," and he assured the House that the "bill grants no solitary acre of land upon which the cereals can be grown without artificial irrigation." Nevertheless some northern representatives quickly proclaimed their opposition to the measure. One Pennsylvania Democrat bluntly declared that "these magnificent endowments to railway corporations by grants and subsidies are undermining republican virtue." Even so staunch a Republican as James A. Garfield refused to support it unless guarantees were given that no money subsidies or government loans would be pledged to aid the trunk line.[26]

Wheeler's amendment and the general northern reaction left the Southerners in a quandary. Some believed that the committee had emasculated the bill by stripping out the branches. Texas scalawag Edward Degener, for example, eventually voted against it because it did not provide for a connecting line to cities in his district. More disconcerting was the amendment's provision that the trunk have a "uniform gauge" and not the standard southern gauge as the Senate had requested. Despite the persistent questioning of Alabama carpetbagger Charles Buckley, Wheeler refused to admit why the gauge was not specified, nor would he allow Buckley to amend the bill to require a five-foot gauge. Frank Morey of Louisiana, another carpetbagger, charged that Wheeler obviously intended the Texas & Pacific

25. Ibid., 4640–45, 4718–22, 4762–77, 4883–85, 4901–15; John F. Stover, "The Pennsylvania Railroad's Southern Empire," Pennsylvania Magazine of History and Biography, LXXXI (1957), 28–38; George Rogers Taylor and Irene D. Neu, The American Railroad Network, 1861–1900 (Cambridge: Harvard University Press, 1956), 3, 43, 79–81.
26. Congressional Globe, 41st Cong., 3rd Sess., 1468–73.

to become a feeder to northern lines, and he estimated that it would cost the South $70 million to change its twelve thousand miles of line to the northern standard.

Outsiders saw the stripped-down version of the Texas & Pacific as a sop to the South. Garfield, satisfied with Wheeler's amendment, dignified the sentiment of most northern Republicans when he declared "that as a great act of commercial justice to the South, Congress should . . . aid the people of the South and Southwest to build a great continental line of road, as we have aided to build a line across the North and the center." In his final arguments, Wheeler justified the bill as "a most important and potent element in the reconstruction of the South" which would bring it "into direct contact with northern men, northern progress, northern ideas and capital, and in the general commingling of interests, in the general prosperity, and in the new enterprises opened to the South, the feelings of antagonism engendered by the late war will be sure to fade out." As it became apparent that the House would not reconsider the branch lines or specify the gauge, the Southerners acquiesced and, with the exception of Degener, voted for the amended bill.[27]

The altered proposal came back to the Senate in the midst of the end-of-session rush. Newly seated Democrat Francis Blair, Jr., of Missouri and North Carolina scalawag John Pool promptly denounced the House's elimination of the gauge specification and the branch lines. Blair declared that the Texas & Pacific was now "a delusion and a snare"—a "road pointing to the north and with a northern gauge"—while Pool called for its defeat rather than to pass it "in the shape in which it has come from the House." Other Southerners, apprehensive that the entire line might be lost, rallied support for a conference committee, which submitted its report to both houses on the last day of the Congress. The gauge remained unspecified, but the conferees had added a branch line from the eastern terminal to New Orleans via the Red River Valley and had authorized the Southern Pacific Railroad to build a line running from Tehachapi Pass through Los Angeles to connect with the Texas & Pacific trunk at or near the Colorado River. The two branch lines, attached at the insis-

27. *Ibid.*, 1468–73, Appendix, 175–76, 177–78, 237–38.

tence of the carpetbagger, scalawag, and Democrat who represented the South on the committee, added between five and six million acres of the public domain to the thirteen million acres granted the trunk line.[28]

Wheeler reassured restless Northerners that most of the additional subsidy was desert land, and after Holman failed to table the report, the House passed what proved to be the last large subsidy for railroad construction. The Southerners were obviously disappointed, but, as was so often the case on economic measures, they had no choice but to accept what they could pry out of reluctant Northerners. With the exception of two Kentucky Democrats, representatives from the southern, border, and Pacific states approved the conference report, but Northern Republicans offered only grudging support 53–46, and northern Democrats opposed it 9–17 with a substantial number of abstentions on both sides.[29]

Southern senators were by no means pleased with the report. Benjamin Rice and Alexander McDonald, the Arkansas carpetbaggers, called for another conference committee to consider adding a right of way for a third branch from Fulton, in the southwest corner of their state, to Dallas. "I know my own success depends upon having it there," Rice pleaded. "I know my people expect it to be there, and they have confidence that I can get it done if I want to do so." The Senate rejected their request and refused to postpone the decision until the evening so that they could continue their arguments. With other appropriations bills pending and less than twelve hours remaining in the Congress, the Southerners swallowed the conference report, uniform gauge and all, and the Senate, "in justice to the South," voiced its approval of the Texas & Pacific subsidy.[30]

There was little doubt at this point that the South desired the

28. *Ibid.*, 1557, 1632, 1682, 1818, 1899. A group of enterprising Louisiana carpetbaggers made a last-ditch attempt to persuade the conference committee to add a branch east of the Mississippi from New Orleans to Chattanooga with connections to Vicksburg and Marshall. See Joseph Rodman West to Henry Clay Warmoth, March 2 (2 letters), March 3, 1871, Lionel A. Sheldon to Warmoth, March 5, 1871, in Warmoth Papers.

29. *Congressional Globe*, 41st Cong., 3rd Sess., 1899–1900. For a scalogram of several votes on the issue, see Seip, "Southern Representatives and Economic Measures During Reconstruction," 172–73.

30. *Congressional Globe*, 41st Cong., 3rd Sess., 1954–61, Appendix, 391–93.

thirty-second parallel route to the Pacific, but reconstruction issues so occupied Southerners that public agitation for the line was moderate and its passage came as a pleasant surprise for some. The editor of the Little Rock *Arkansas Gazette*, for example, declared that the act was "the most important one for the interests of Arkansas" ever passed by Congress. Other southwestern newspapers echoed the *Gazette's* sentiments, and the southeastern press, envisioning the establishment of new connecting lines running back to Norfolk, Wilmington, Charleston, Savannah, and Jacksonville, were equally pleased. Even such states'-rights newspapers as the New Orleans *Picayune* and Atlanta *Constitution*, both previously opposed to federal subsidies, were enthusiastic about the Texas & Pacific grant. "All hail the Southern Pacific railroad," proclaimed the *Constitution.* "It is a momentous thing for the South . . . a mighty step in substantial reconstruction."[31]

In their initial enthusiasm, most Southerners never paused to consider what in fact they had gained. First of all, the Texas & Pacific grant was small in comparison to the earlier subsidies for the Union Pacific, Central Pacific, and Northern Pacific. The company received no bonds or cash, its bond issues were not to be guaranteed by the government, and the public lands were not of the quality or the quantity given to the other transcontinental lines. The northern orientation of the line was unmistakable. Southerners, including several of the congressmen, were among the incorporators, but the real powers on the list were northern railroad men.[32] There was never any question but what the Texas & Pacific would be built on the

31. Little Rock *Daily Arkansas Gazette*, March 2, 1871; Tuskaloosa *Independent Monitor*, July 19, 1870; New Orleans *Republican*, November 26, 1870, March 15, 1871; Austin *Democratic Statesman*, September 19, 1872; Richmond *Whig*, March 26, 1869; Columbia *South Carolina Weekly Republican*, May 14, 1870; New Orleans *Daily Picayune*, March 4, 1871; Atlanta *Constitution*, March 5, April 21, 1871.

32. Carter Goodrich, *Government Promotion of Canals and Railroads, 1800–1890* (New York: Columbia University Press, 1960), ch. 5; *Congressional Globe*, 41st Cong., 3rd Sess., Appendix, 391–93. Among the incorporators were Republican Senators Alcorn (Miss.), West (La.), and Clayton (Ark.), and the brothers, sons, or business partners of at least a dozen other southern congressmen, but only three Southerners were listed on the seventeen-member board of directors in 1872 and only one the following year.

northern gauge; southern lines wishing to connect would be forced to make the expensive 3 ½-inch narrowing of their gauge. Finally, because the Mississippi River was spanned only by the Eads bridge (completed in 1874) at Saint Louis, that city, not Memphis, Vicksburg, or New Orleans, would become the easiest connection to the East, and the Saint Louis roads led naturally to Philadelphia and New York, not Norfolk and points south.

The fate of the Texas & Pacific as an extension of the Pennsylvania system was sealed when Thomas A. Scott of Philadelphia, the energetic vice-president of the Pennsylvania Railroad, took control of the line early in 1872. Among his other interests, Scott had been president of both the Union Pacific and the struggling Atlantic and Pacific, the latter having been subsidized in 1866 to build along the thirty-fifth parallel. In 1870 he organized and became president of the Pennsylvania Company and managed the lines connecting the Pennsylvania Railroad with Saint Louis. The following year he established the dominance of the Pennsylvania in the Southern Railway and Security Company, and he became president of the Pennsylvania in 1874. Scott saw the Texas & Pacific as a means by which the Pennsylvania could become transcontinental and challenge the Union Pacific/Central Pacific line completed in 1869.[33]

Scott started his task quickly. He formed the California and Texas Railway Construction Company, acquired the services of General Grenville M. Dodge, a superb lobbyist and engineer who had been instrumental in the completion of the Union Pacific, and sent him to Texas to begin construction. In the interim, Scott acquired an immense land grant from the Texas legislature and purchased the rights to the defunct Memphis, El Paso, and Pacific, which obligated him to build west from Texarkana as well as from Marshall. By the summer of 1873 Dodge had pushed lines from Marshall to Dallas, connected Marshall with Texarkana to the north, and built west from Texarkana to Sherman (see Map 2). This initial burst of construction proved to be the last significant mileage the Texas & Pacific would lay for some time. The fall panic nearly toppled Scott, who was overextended in the Texas operation, and he lost heavily in

33. Woodward, *Reunion and Reaction*, 68–70.

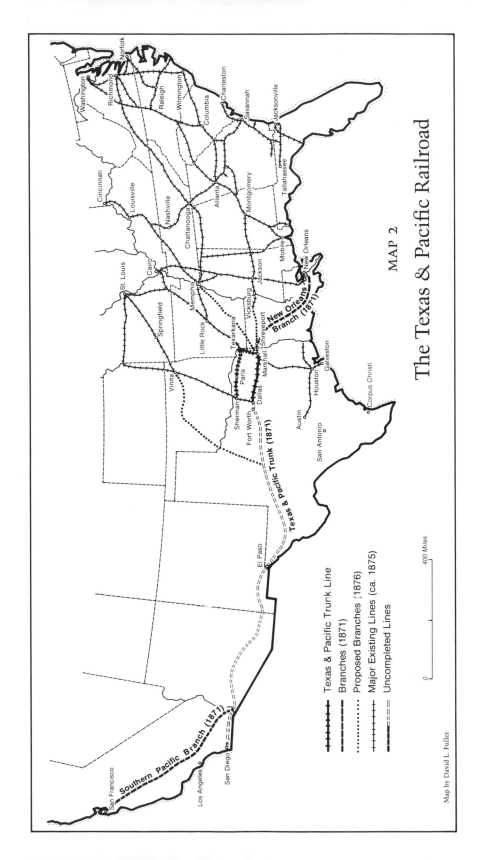

MAP 2

The Texas & Pacific Railroad

Texas & Pacific Trunk Line
Branches (1871)
Proposed Branches (1876)
Major Existing Lines (ca. 1875)
Uncompleted Lines

0   400 Miles

Map by David L. Fuller

Norfolk
Washington
Richmond
Raleigh
Wilmington
Charleston
Columbia
Savannah
Jacksonville
Cincinnati
Louisville
Nashville
Chattanooga
Atlanta
Montgomery
Tallahassee
St. Louis
Cairo
Memphis
Jackson
Mobile
New Orleans
Springfield
Little Rock
Texarkana
Vicksburg
Shreveport
Marshall
Galveston
Corpus Christi
Vinita
Sherman
Paris
Dallas
Fort Worth
Houston
Austin
San Antonio
El Paso
San Francisco
Los Angeles
San Diego

New Orleans Branch (1871)
Texas & Pacific Trunk (1871)
Southern Pacific Branch (1871)

the failure of Jay Cooke & Company. Scott's salvation, and that of the Texas & Pacific, depended upon additional federal subsidies.[34]

Until the panic, Scott had little contact with southern congressmen other than Texas Democrat James Throckmorton, an employee, and those already involved in the project such as carpetbaggers Kellogg and West of Louisiana and Spencer of Alabama. Aware, however, that the North had become increasingly cool to railroad interests, he pooled his resources and turned to rally southern support for further federal aid in 1874. Since southern Republicans had led the fight for the 1871 act, Scott and Dodge were forced to walk a tightrope between the Republicans and Redeemers. They stressed that the line was vital to the whole South and above party divisions. "The great point in this case is to get the united action of the Southern Democrats to act now with regard to its necessity to the South," Scott assured Democratic Senator Matt Ransom of North Carolina. "It has no political bearing whatever."[35]

With a well financed campaign, Scott and Dodge won the enthusiastic endorsement of influential newspapers from Virginia to California and secured resolutions of support from most southern legislatures and the chambers of commerce and economic groups in major cities. Care was taken to cultivate southern congressmen, especially those who were members of the Pacific railroad committees. At stake was a bill requesting the government to guarantee the interest on the railroad's forty-year, 5-percent bonds. In return, the company offered the government a first mortgage on the line, a re-

34. Stanley P. Hirshson, *Grenville M. Dodge: Soldier, Politician, Railroad Pioneer* (Bloomington: Indiana University Press, 1967), 183–85, 189–91, 193–96; Woodward, *Reunion and Reaction*, 72–76; J. M. Daniel to Benjamin H. Epperson, May 23, 1871, B. F. Grafton to Epperson, February 19, March 9, 1872, in Benjamin Holland Epperson Papers, Barker Texas History Center, University of Texas, Austin; Ralph N. Traxler, Jr., "The Texas and Pacific Railroad Land Grants: A Comparison of Land Grant Policies of the United States and Texas," *Southwestern Historical Quarterly*, LXI (1958), 359–70; Frank S. Bond, *The Texas and Pacific Railway Company's Relations to the State of Texas, and the Character of State Legislation in Respect to That Company* (Marshall, Tex.: Jennings Brothers, 1877). Map 2 is based on maps in Texas & Pacific Railway Company, *The Texas and Pacific Railway: Its Route, Progress, and Land Grants* (New York: Texas & Pacific Railway, 1872); G. W. & C. B. Colton & Company, *Map of the Texas and Pacific Railway and Its Connections* (New York: Colton and Co., 1878); and Stover, *Railroads of the South*, 25, 106.

35. Thomas A. Scott to Matt Ransom, December 15, 1874, in Matt W. Ransom Papers, SHC.

turn of public lands, and the right to retain $5,000 of the maximum of $35,000 per mile of bonds issued to finance construction. Scott hoped to push the bill through the lame-duck session of the Forty-third Congress, which opened in December, 1874, because its chances of approval would be sharply diminished in the incoming Democratic House. "This whole fight is to rest solely upon the status of the south in the question," Dodge wrote Throckmorton late in 1874. "If they go there determined to carry this Bill through, it can be done: if they are lukewarm there is no use trying it. I wrote Mr. Scott to have you and all our Southern friends in Washington on or before the commencement of the session."[36]

But the atmosphere in late 1874 was not favorable to the consideration of another railroad subsidy. The Republicans, sobered by their untoward performance in the fall elections, had things other than railroad legislation on their minds—most notably Sherman's resumption bill and the civil rights bill, both of which would have to be pushed through with the party whip. The ongoing depression and declining revenues also forced Congress to face the unpleasant alternative of either raising tax and tariff levels or abandoning various appropriations bills. The northern leadership of both parties seemed obsessed with retrenchment. "The rage and passion of the hour is hatred of extravagance, and of thieves in government," a conservative Austin editor observed. "After gorging itself, Radicalism is almost crazed to practice terrible economy; and Democracy is quite as anxious to grab power. In order to seize it, it would perhaps even sacrifice Texas and the South, and deny the justest demand ever made

36. Texas & Pacific Railway Company, *Resolutions of Legislatures, Boards of Trade, State Granges, Etc., Favoring Government Aid to the Texas & Pacific Railway* (Philadelphia: Review Printing House, 1874); Texas & Pacific Railway Company, *The Press and the People on the Importance of a Southern Line of Railway to the Pacific and in Favor of Government Aid to the Texas and Pacific Railway Co.* (Philadelphia: McLaughlin Brothers, 1875); Grenville M. Dodge to William E. Chandler, May 18, 1874, Dodge to James W. Throckmorton, August 28, 1874, Dodge to Beverly Tucker, December 16, 1874, George E. Spencer to Dodge, October 23, 30, 1871, in Grenville M. Dodge Papers, Iowa State Historical Department, Des Moines; Joseph E. Brown to Alexander H. Stephens, December 27, 1873, in Alexander H. Stephens Papers, Library of Congress (hereinafter cited as LC); undated note on "Expenditures for Political Purposes During the Presidential Campaign of 1872 by General G. M. Dodge," in William Eaton Chandler Papers, LC; Hirshson, *Grenville M. Dodge*, 187–88; *House Reports*, 43rd Cong., 2nd Sess., No. 267, pp. 1–4; Grenville M. Dodge to James W. Throckmorton, November 19, 1874, in Dodge Papers.

by the people and States upon the Federal Government." The editor's apprehensions were solidly based. Two weeks earlier northern representatives had failed by one vote to suspend the rules and pass Holman's latest antisubsidy resolution, which Scott saw as "directed especially at Southern interests." Furthermore, northern newspapers had become sharply critical of Scott's scheme while applauding Holman's efforts to stop all subsidies.[37]

In the House, most Southerners appeared willing to consider aiding the Texas & Pacific, but Scott's proposal was never allowed to reach the floor. Late in February, 1875, a motion to suspend the rules and consider it evoked a Vermont Republican's derisive query, "Is this not what is generally known as the Tom Scott subsidy bill?" By a margin of 118–127, the House refused to hear the favorable committee report. The Southerners, who voted 43–7 for the motion, received solid support only from the border and Pacific states. Northern backing was negligible. Democrats opposed it 16–22; more significant was the Republicans' resounding 30–89 negative response with most of the favorable votes coming from Pennsylvania—Scott's home base.[38]

Scott had even less luck in the Senate where a similar bill failed to clear the Pacific Railroad Committee. Some members simply opposed further aid; others disliked an additional section allowing the Atlantic and Pacific Railroad, which controlled lines from Saint Louis to Vinita in Indian Territory, to connect with the Texas & Pacific west of Fort Worth. This, of course, would allow Texas & Pacific traffic to avoid east Texas on a route through Saint Louis to the Northeast. Still others were under the influence of Collis Huntington, head of the Central Pacific and the Southern Pacific and Scott's chief rival in the West, who was building the line connecting San Francisco with the Texas & Pacific trunk at the Colorado River. Huntington certainly wanted to control all traffic in California, and he had visions of building east from the Colorado River to El Paso

37. Austin *Democratic Statesman*, January 3, 6, 7, 1875; Scott to Ransom, December 15, 1874, in Ransom Papers; *Congressional Record*, 43rd Cong., 2nd Sess., 174; Chicago *Tribune*, December 11, 16, 21, 22, 1874; *Nation*, December 24, 1874, p. 411, February 25, 1875, p. 124; New York *Times*, February 3, 4, 23, 26, 1875; New York *World*, January 16, 1875; New York *Tribune*, December 22, 1874, February 23, March 5, 1875.

38. *Congressional Record*, 43rd Cong., 2nd Sess., 1600–1601.

and thus eliminating Scott from that end of the project. Of the three Southerners on the committee, carpetbagger J. Rodman West of Louisiana favored the measure, scalawag Morgan C. Hamilton of Texas opposed it, and Ransom, the North Carolina Democrat, apparently remained undecided until the last minute. The rabidly Democratic Vicksburg *Herald*, in fact, blamed the North Carolinian for the failure of the measure. Ransom, the editor raged, "has inflicted upon the people of the South an injury that outweighs all the good he can ever accomplish if he should live a thousand years."[39]

In selecting Ransom as the scapegoat, the *Herald* overlooked numerous other obstacles in the bill's path. Measures calling for federal aid of any kind, including the major appropriations bills, were tied up until the last day of the session by the tax and tariff bill. When the Senate finally approved the revenue measure, Southerners and Northerners alike were far more interested in using the last few hours gaining appropriations for their areas. It was highly unlikely that the Texas & Pacific measure would have been considered, let alone passed in this atmosphere. Even if it had cleared the Senate, it would have faced overwhelming opposition in the House. Scott's failure in the Republican-dominated Forty-third Congress is of pivotal importance in understanding just how little support the Texas & Pacific had at this early date—not only among northern Democrats, but among northern Republicans and in the northern press as well.

It is equally apparent that a good many southern congressmen did not rank the Texas & Pacific high among their priorities. Despite Scott's work in the section, a considerable number of Southerners remained skeptical. Morgan Hamilton, for example, had opposed the project from the beginning. Most Texas Republicans disowned the cantankerous scalawag early in his term, and one Republican editor claimed that even the Democrats were "wary of the old gentleman, whose course recently must be very gratifying to them." Hamilton considered the "power and the greed of Railroad Rings" to be the

39. Shreveport *Times*, January 17, 1875; Little Rock *Daily Arkansas Gazette*, December 14, 1874, January 12, 1875; New Orleans *Republican*, December 17, 1874, January 30, 1875; Austin *Democratic Statesman*, December 12, 1874; Lewis B. Lesley, "A Southern Transcontinental Railroad into California: Texas and Pacific Versus Southern Pacific, 1865–1885," *Pacific Historical Review*, V (1936), 52–60; Woodward, *Reunion and Reaction*, 82–85; Vicksburg *Herald*, March 3, 1875.

"greatest danger to the administration and the country." When the Texas & Pacific was first considered in the Senate in 1870, he proposed amendments to strike all references to Texas and let the line begin at El Paso. When it became apparent to Hamilton that "every southern senator except my self will vote for the bill—so they do for everything that benefits the south right or wrong," he gave up and declined to oppose it in debate as "it would not have made the least difference."[40]

A maverick and outsider like Hamilton could be ignored, but the lukewarm attitude of such Democratic powers as Senator John Brown Gordon of Georgia and the outright opposition of Senator John Warfield Johnston of Virginia and a few states'-rights editors worried the Texas & Pacific forces. When Scott was unable personally to impress Gordon with "the necessity of the Southern members taking this question of the Southern route . . . up with vigor" in December, 1874, he asked Ransom to secure Gordon's support and tell him to "bring with him all the friends he can." Scott also turned to Samuel L. M. Barlow, Gordon's friend and creditor, who promptly warned the ex-Confederate general of the dangers of united Democratic opposition to the measure and asked him to sound out other Southerners. After "diligent inquiry," Gordon reported that he was "scarcely prepared to give an opinion as to the fate of the measure." "A large majority of Southern Democrats wish the Road built," he thought, "but whether they can overcome their long settled convictions against subsidies is doubtful." Gordon, in the awkward position of being in debt to Barlow, personally confessed "the greatest reluctance to giving a vote for the Bill." Apparently not wanting to be viewed as one of Barlow's agents, Gordon asked him to come and talk to the Southerners himself, but he reiterated that he could "not promise now to vote for the subsidy."[41]

40.   T. H. Duval to Andrew Jackson Hamilton, August 9, 1867, in Andrew Jackson Hamilton Papers; Andrew Jackson Hamilton to William Wallace Mills, June 1, 1869, in William Wallace Mills Papers; Frank Brown, "Annals of Travis County" (Typescript in Frank Brown Papers); San Antonio *Express*, July 20, 1871 (clipping), Morgan C. Hamilton to James P. Newcomb, June 13, July 2, 10, 17, 24, August 10, 1870, in James Pearson Newcomb Papers. All these collections are in the Barker Texas History Center, University of Texas, Austin.

41.   Scott to Ransom, December 15, 1874, in Ransom Papers; John Brown Gordon to Samuel L. M. Barlow, January 23, 1875, in Samuel L. M. Barlow Papers, Huntington Library, San Marino, California.

After Scott failed to secure additional aid, Johnston offered the most detailed critique of the project from a southern perspective. Because of the gauge and the natural connection to the Northeast, he argued that the Texas & Pacific "was in fact a northern road . . . got up by northern interests and influences," and useless to southern states east of the Mississippi River. A San Francisco merchant, he reasoned, could ship his goods directly to Philadelphia or New York via Saint Louis—completely bypassing the South, even east Texas—without ever having to unload them. If the same merchant wanted to ship to a south Atlantic port, his goods would have to be unloaded at Marshall, transferred to the Cairo and Fulton line which had a gauge of five feet, shipped to Little Rock, transferred onto the Memphis & Little Rock line to the Mississippi, unloaded again, placed on drays to riverboats, unloaded on the Memphis bank, placed on drays again, and taken to the Memphis depot for final shipment to the Southeast. The same procedures would be involved if shipping via Vicksburg or New Orleans. When Johnston advised the Senate committee to drop the Saint Louis branch, he was told that such a move would lose northern votes. When he asked the bill's sponsor, John Scott of Pennsylvania, about the gauge and the problems posed by the Mississippi, Scott advised the South to change the gauge of its lines and either build bridges over the river or place the train on ferryboats. "And this," Johnston fumed, "was said lightly, as if a man would speak of taking his hat and going for a morning walk." The financially troubled railroads east of the Mississippi could not make the expensive gauge change, the ferryboat idea was at best cumbersome and risky, and James Eads informed Johnston that the bridge at Saint Louis had cost $6.8 million. The river at Memphis was twice as wide, and a bridge there would involve a costly fill on the lower west bank. "Can you even make a guess," Johnston wondered, "as to where the money is to come from to build it?"[42]

Johnston's arguments found support in other quarters. Railroad operators George Swepson of North Carolina and William Mahone

42.   John Warfield Johnston to Joseph R. Anderson, June, 1875 (28 pp. draft letter), "The Southern Route to the Pacific" (speech draft), in John Warfield Johnston Papers, and John Warfield Johnston to John F. McMullen, September 30, November 14, 1875, in McMullen Family Papers, both collections in Perkins Library, Duke University, Durham, N.C.

of Virginia saw Scott as a threat to established southern lines. Even before Scott took over the Texas & Pacific, Swepson feared that he was "determined to Rule & monopolize all the [southern] roads & that he will clog everything until he does." Mahone found "nothing of substance for the South in the proposed scheme" and thought it "a wanton fling at the poverty, at the intelligence and at the integrity of her people." The nearest the line came to any southern state was a hundred miles, Mahone wrote angrily to a friend, "and this [is] called a Southern Pacific R.R. Don't you feel outraged?"[43]

But the primary southern opposition began to coalesce around Robert McKee's Selma *Southern Argus.* "It's Tom Scott's job in Congress now," McKee wrote in January, 1875. "And it will take weeks of investigation to ascertain who got the money." McKee was aware that the *Argus* "stood almost alone among southern newspapers in opposition" to Scott's project, but some of the Alabama congressmen began to echo his states'-rights position. "Where is any warrant in the Constitution to loan the credit of the United States to the amount of millions and millions to a private enterprise headed by Tom Scott?" Alabama Representative B. B. Lewis asked in early 1875. Lewis was amazed "that any man claiming to be a Democrat" could support Scott's "mischievous" scheme. "Southern newspapers and politicians who would denounce as flat robbery a subsidy for the Northern Pacific Railroad or an appropriation for the Hennepin Canal . . . see no inconsistency in asking government aid for Tom Scott's Pacific job," McKee argued. "The principle is the same in all the raids accomplished or meditated on the public credit or public treasury." McKee was pleased when the bill failed in the Forty-third Congress, but he knew that Scott would be back. As McKee became a power in Alabama politics, he rallied the state's congressional delegation (with the exception of Spencer, the Republican senator) to

43. Swepson quoted in James W. Throckmorton to Benjamin P. Epperson, December 17, 1871, in James Webb Throckmorton Papers, Barker Texas History Center, University of Texas, Austin; William Mahone to John W. Daniel, February 24, 1876, in John Warwick Daniel Papers, Perkins Library, Duke University, Durham, N.C.; William Mahone to S. L. M. Barlow, February 24, 1872, in Barlow Papers; William Mahone to James H. Williams, January 20, February 23, 1875, in Williams Family Papers, Alderman Library, University of Virginia, Charlottesville; Nelson Morehouse Blake, *William Mahone of Virginia: Soldier and Political Insurgent* (Richmond: Garrett & Massie, 1935), 123.

his position, and the Alabamians became the focal point of opposition to Scott for the remainder of the decade.[44]

Having no alternative, Scott and Dodge went to work on the Forty-fourth Congress with their usual energy. They fought Huntington for control of the Pacific railroad committees, they continued to ply the southern press, and they brought southern railroad promoters, politicians, and civic leaders together in a highly publicized "National Railroad Convention" at Saint Louis in late 1875 to demonstrate support for the project. They found Alabamians to work on McKee, they enlisted former Confederate general P. G. T. Beauregard and others to try to convince Johnston that the line was "not a northern road in disguise," and they employed such well connected men as Beverly Tucker of Virginia to promote the project across the South. According to an Alabama representative, Scott "scandalously supported" Pennsylvania Democrat Samuel J. Randall for the House Speakership in December, 1875—an endorsement which immediately marked him, in the *Nation*'s opinion, as the candidate of the undesirable "jobbing element of the party." After Randall finally won the position a year later, Beverly Tucker informed him that he had personally "imposed" on his brother, John Randolph Tucker, and other Virginia representatives, swung the editor of the Richmond *Whig* to Randall's side, and lined up the Louisiana delegation. In return, Tucker asked for "as much favor as you can possibly grant to our Texas & Pacific, for both at the last time & This, my exertions have been tireless to secure for you their united support." Randall knew that the Texas & Pacific forces had been important in his election, but he later denied that he had ever given Scott "a ray of hope that I would give the least support or countenance to his subsidy."[45]

Just how much support the Texas & Pacific actually commanded among southern congressmen after the failure of Scott's request in

44. Selma *Southern Argus,* January 29, February 19, March 5, 1875; Burwell B. Lewis to Robert McKee, February 24, 1875, in Robert McKee Papers, Alabama Department of Archives and History, Montgomery. The McKee Papers for the last half of the decade are filled with letters applauding his opposition to the Texas & Pacific and occasional ones attempting to win his support for it.

45. Woodward, *Reunion and Reaction,* 80–100; Thomas A. Scott to L. Q. C. Lamar, April 13, 1876, in L. Q. C. Lamar and Edward Mayes Papers, Mississippi Department of Archives and History, Jackson; J. C. Walker to Robert McKee, November 11, 1875, B. B. Lewis to McKee, December 12, 1875, in McKee Papers; S. W. Buck to

the Forty-third Congress is debatable. It is likely that most members from Louisiana, Texas, and Arkansas favored the line. Several, including Throckmorton, Senators Stephen Dorsey and Powell Clayton of Arkansas, and West, the chairman of the Senate Pacific Railroad Committee, had a financial interest in the project. The Mississippians, led by L. Q. C. Lamar, chairman of the House Committee on the Pacific Railroad, probably continued to believe that the line was to their benefit. East of Alabama open support among the congressmen was more limited. Democrats Alexander H. Stephens and Benjamin Hill of Georgia and Gilbert C. Walker of Virginia backed the project to some degree; otherwise, active supporters of the line were few. It is clear that southern congressional support for the line had fallen sharply since 1871.

The Southerners' reaction to Holman's now familiar antisubsidy resolution when the Forty-fourth Congress convened in December, 1875, offers an important indication of their attitudes. The Indiana Democrat had been gaining support for his resolutions since 1869; they were serious business and the subsidy seekers knew it. A year earlier, before Scott's bill failed, 65 percent of the southern Democrats and 81 percent of the region's Republicans had opposed the resolution. This time it passed by an overwhelming margin of 223–34 with southern Democrats voting 28–15 and southern Republicans 6–5 in favor. It was well known that the proposal was directed against the Texas & Pacific; if the Southerners felt strongly about the matter, they might have taken the opportunity to express themselves. Yet the Democrats from Alabama, Georgia, and Louisiana unanimously endorsed the resolution. Only the Virginia Democrats lined up solidly against it—Beverly Tucker had obviously earned his pay. The Virginians were joined by three of the four Texans, two North Carolinians, one Arkansan, and Lamar, who notably failed to

---

Edmund W. Hubard, December 10, 1875, P. G. T. Beauregard to John B. Gordon, Richmond *Dispatch*, September 17, 1875 (clipping), in Edmund Wilcox Hubard Papers, SHC; Albert V. House, "The Speakership Contest of 1875: Democratic Response to Power," *Journal of American History*, LII (1965), 252–74; *Nation*, December 9, 1875, p. 363; Beverly Tucker to Samuel J. Randall, November 24, 26, 1876, in Samuel J. Randall Papers, Van Pelt Library, University of Pennsylvania, Philadelphia; Samuel J. Randall to Chauncey F. Black, May 13, August 14, 1877, quoted in Woodward, *Reunion and Reaction*, 231.

carry the votes of his three Mississippi party colleagues. Only nineteen of sixty-four southern and border state Democrats, supposedly the locus of Scott's congressional strength, opposed Holman's resolution. Their response hardly justifies the conclusion that "the last foothold of the political philosophy of the Great Barbecue was the Redeemed South." If there was any foothold left, it was somewhat ironically among the handful of surviving southern Republicans, who by 1876 were the waifs of American politics.[46]

Men less determined than those whose fortunes were linked to the Texas & Pacific might have seen the proverbial writing on the wall and given up the futile struggle. Even if Scott had the unanimous backing of the South and the border states, and there was unmistakable evidence to the contrary, he needed much more. Those areas had neither the votes nor the committee and floor leadership to push his request through Congress. Not surprisingly, Scott and Dodge failed to get their bill reported in the first session. During the second session, in the midst of the electoral crisis, they reluctantly entered into an uneasy coalition with Collis Huntington, their western competitor, agreed on a compromise proposal beneficial to both, and began a desperate push to get it out of committee. By joining forces with Huntington, Scott resolved one of his problems, but the new bill only compounded the Texas & Pacific's difficulties. The proposal split the rights to build the trunk between Scott and Huntington and provided for five branches (to San Diego, New Orleans, Vicksburg, Memphis, and Vinita, in Indian Territory) for a total of over 2,500 miles of line. The federal government was asked to guarantee the interest on the line's bonds until they were payable in fifty years. The bill could have involved the government in an obligation of nearly $224 million, which, as C. Vann Woodward has noted, was "more than twice the total of all Federal expenditures for railroads, canals, and wagon roads from 1789 to 1873."[47]

46. *Congressional Record*, 44th Cong., 1st Sess., 227; Woodward, *Reunion and Reaction*, 62, 127. With regard to the "persistent Whiggery" thesis, it is worthy of note that ten of the fifteen southern Democrats who opposed the resolution had been Democrats all their lives, at least nine had been secessionists, and thirteen had served the Confederacy in some capacity. Most former Whigs and unionists among the Democrats, including leading Redeemers Benjamin Hill (Ga.), E. John Ellis (La.), David B. Culberson (Tex.), and Alfred M. Waddell (N.C.), favored the resolution.

47. Texas & Pacific Railroad Company, *Statements, Arguments, and Accompanying Exhibits Submitted to the Senate Committee on Railroads and to the House*

To believe, as some of the Texas & Pacific people apparently did, that such a measure would pass either chamber showed an incredible misreading of congressional sentiment regarding subsidy legislation. And yet the Texas & Pacific forces, some southern Democratic congressmen, and certain supporters of Republican Rutherford B. Hayes supposedly became critical parties in the negotiations and decisions which eventually settled the dispute following the election of 1876. According to Woodward, the Compromise of 1877 entailed a number of agreements between northern Republicans and southern Democrats. Some Southerners agreed not to oppose Hayes's interest in the electoral dispute by refusing to support their northern party colleagues' dilatory motions and filibustering after it became apparent that the electoral commission was going to favor Hayes's claim to the disputed states. There was also some loose talk of allowing the Republican party to organize the next House with James Garfield as Speaker. For their part, northern Republicans promised a cabinet position in the Hayes administration to a southern Democrat, and "home rule" for South Carolina and Louisiana—the last two states in which Republicans were still contending for control. More nebulous, but certainly central to Woodward's account, were Republican assurances that they would support subsidies for internal improvements projects in the South including the Texas & Pacific Railroad.[48]

From the perspective of the southern congressional Democrats, the actual importance of several of the "understandings" is questionable. Without doubt, there was some sectional ill feeling in the Democracy stemming from differing economic concerns and other matters dating back to the antebellum period. Some Southerners also had never been fully satisfied with New Yorker Samuel J. Tilden, the Democratic claimant, and they were further angered by his passivity during the electoral crisis. Thus it is not surprising that some of them appeared receptive to Republican overtures during the

---

Committee on the Pacific Railroad on Behalf of the Texas & Pacific Railway Company, 44th Congress, 1st Session, 1876 (Washington, D.C.: n.p., 1876); House Reports, 44th Cong., 2nd Sess., No. 139; "The Texas-and-Pacific Job," Nation, January 11, 1877, pp. 23–25; "The South and the Texas-and-Pacific Job," Nation, February 8, 1877, pp. 82–83; Woodward, Reunion and Reaction, 113–16, 127–42.
  48. Woodward, Reunion and Reaction, 101–85.

dispute, and it is apparent that a few northern Republicans and southern Democrats (or, more truthfully, their self-appointed spokesmen) discussed the benefits each might derive from a compromise. Most southern congressmen did acquiesce in the election of Hayes, but only when it became apparent that Tilden would be counted out by the electoral commission—a mechanism for resolving the dispute to which most Democrats had given their approval—and that his interests could be maintained only by a potentially dangerous partisan struggle whose outcome no one could predict. Hayes did appoint a moderate Tennessee Democrat to the cabinet and, after an interval, ordered the removal of federal troops from the support of Republican governments in Louisiana and South Carolina. But the other elements of the compromise, particularly the talk about railroad subsidies, fell by the wayside so quickly that their support in either North or South is moot. The significance of the Texas & Pacific's role in the resolution of the crisis suffers accordingly.[49]

Particularly questionable are Woodward's estimation of the power of the Texas & Pacific lobby, his belief that those forces had a lock on southern congressmen, his positing of a serious rift on internal improvements legislation between northern and southern Democrats, and his assumption of much stronger support among northern Republicans for subsidies, all of which lie at the base of his analysis of the subsidy "agreements." Despite its image in the press and the minds of its creators, the Texas & Pacific lobby had not even come close to producing any legislation beneficial to the line since 1872. Southern congressional support of the line was at best unreliable for

49. *Ibid.*, 45–50, 127–49, 171–75, 216–29, 229–32; Keith Ian Polakoff, *The Politics of Inertia: The Election of 1876 and the End of Reconstruction* (Baton Rouge: Louisiana State University Press, 1973), 220–23, 240–42; Michael Les Benedict, "Southern Democrats in the Crisis of 1876–1877: A Reconsideration of *Reunion and Reaction,*" *Journal of Southern History*, XLVI (1980), 497–508. See also Chapter VIII below. The notion that southern Democrats would allow the Republicans to organize the incoming Forty-fifth House was little more than wishful thinking on the part of a few northern Republicans. Even Woodward admits that it was probably no more than "a tentative agreement on the part of a few Southerners" and that a great majority of the southern congressmen would have repudiated the idea. Yet he persists in seeing its breach as the important first step in the undoing of the compromise. To have voted for Garfield would have been political suicide for southern Democrats, as Garfield himself suspected. Allan Peskin, *Garfield* (Kent, Ohio: Kent State University Press, 1978), 414, 420–21, 424–26.

the reasons discussed above as well as the fact that Southerners were far more concerned with securing home rule in the winter of 1876–1877 than they were with economic matters. Similarly, Woodward overemphasizes the sectional split in the Democratic party on internal improvements legislation. Southern Democrats were not pleased with the attitudes of Tilden, Randall, and Holman on such issues, and there were disagreements throughout the 1870s between southern and northern (especially northeastern) Democrats on certain types of economic proposals, but no significant party rift existed on railroad subsidy legislation after 1874. On these matters southern Democrats were far more likely to agree with their party colleagues than they were with northern Republicans.[50]

If southern Democrats actually believed that northern Republicans would follow through on their "pledges" to support subsidies for the Texas & Pacific, then their memories were amazingly short. And if northern Republicans thought that they could turn about and vote for the type of financial guarantees Scott demanded, then they had foolishly committed themselves to a policy that they, their constituents, and their press had rejected in the early 1870s. An overwhelming number of Northerners had turned their back on the Texas & Pacific's modest requests for additional aid as early as 1874, and northern Republicans were not about to swallow the massive subsidy requested by the temporary alliance of Scott and Huntington in early 1877. Particularly offensive was the inclusion of subsidies for branch lines even greater than those northern representatives had struck out of the original bill in 1871. As late as December, 1875, northern Republicans voted 76–6 to approve the latest version of Holman's resolution declaring that Congress would grant no subsidies of any kind to public or private corporations. Their response was similar to the northern Democrats' favorable vote of 88–3.

The likelihood that Republicans would defy the northern electorate, their hostile press, and their own record was nil; southern Democrats, no political fools to be sure, were far too perceptive to believe otherwise. If some Southerners remained under the illusion that northern Republicans had had a dramatic change of heart, it

50. See above, and Harris' concise analysis of the section-party voting patterns on economic issues in "Right Fork or Left Fork?" *passim.*

should have been dispelled by their response to Ellis' levees bill on the last day of the Forty-fourth Congress—*after* the "compromise" had been effected. A matter far more critical to southern interests than the Texas & Pacific, the levees appropriation was large but not new—it had been carefully considered in committee since 1873 and had nearly passed the Senate as a part of the rivers and harbors act of 1875. Northern Republicans nevertheless disapproved of it 13–49— a reaction almost identical to that of the northern Democrats. In fact, a greater percentage of northern Republicans than Democrats were willing to go on record against it; nearly 45 percent of the northern Democrats had the good graces to abstain.[51]

Furthermore, the dedication of most southern Democrats to these projects is questionable if their roll call behavior is an indication of attitudes. Unfortunately, the Texas & Pacific project did not generate a roll call during the Forty-fourth Congress (a telling indication of the power of Scott's lobby), but the attitudes of southern Democrats were suggested by their approval of the Holman resolution 28–15 and their half-hearted endorsement of the levees bill by a 23–10 margin with sixteen absences. Although some conservative journals such as W. H. Roberts' New Orleans *Times* and Andrew J. Kellar's Memphis *Avalanche* (both Scott papers) gave much attention to and supported gossip of subsidy agreements in early 1877, others had joined McKee in open opposition to Scott. The Austin *Democratic Statesman*, for example, had come to oppose the Texas & Pacific on states'-rights grounds, and the Jackson *Weekly Clarion* doubted the wisdom of southern congressmen pushing the project "to the peril of more important objectives" and disliked the "favoritism shown to jobs of particular individuals." Most newspapers, however, simply ignored the matter, and it was rarely mentioned in the correspondence of southern congressmen and other political leaders. At best, the idea of pushing for federal aid for a northern-owned and

51. *Congressional Record,* 43rd Cong., 2nd Sess., 2164–65, 2169–79, 44th Cong., 2nd Sess., 2232; Woodward, *Reunion and Reaction,* 62–63, 127, 145–47. See Table 17: B above. Woodward unwisely uses the levees roll call and the earlier vote on the Holman resolution to document the rift between southern and northern Democrats. These roll calls could be used equally well to demonstrate a split between southern Democrats and northern Republicans—a notion counter to Woodward's thesis.

northern-run corporation which offered only dubious benefits to most of the South did not rank high on the congressmen's list of priorities—especially when the more important matter of home rule was at stake.[52]

It is difficult to believe that the overwhelming majority of northern Republicans or southern Democrats attached any significance to the rumors of subsidy agreements. The notion that such talk might actually bear fruit existed in the minds of a few Southerners obsessed with the importance of the Texas & Pacific, a small number of Northerners willing to promise anything to put Hayes into office, and a handful of self-appointed spokesmen for "southern interests" who still believed that the Texas & Pacific lobby had immense political clout in Washington. Although many pretended to know the mind of southern congressmen during the crisis, one is hard pressed to find any significant evidence that more than a handful of the Southerners "negotiated" with northern Republicans—much less that their primary topic was subsidies for the Texas & Pacific. And there was some political peril for Southerners appearing to be involved with their northern adversaries. "Many Republican newspapers and party mongers have been trying to seduce two or three [southern] members of the House and have flattered themselves with hope of success," an Alabama congressman confided early in the crisis. "But they will fail of their purpose, I think; yet if they were to succeed, they could do no harm, as the *supposed influencial* members would have no following should they desert to the standard of Hayes." When it became apparent that the electoral commission favored Hayes and that to continue to press Tilden's case could throw the government into complete chaos (the consequences of an

52. Austin *Democratic Statesman*, undated clipping (*ca.* December, 1875), in Throckmorton Papers; Austin *Democratic Statesman*, January 7, 1877; Jackson *Weekly Clarion*, February 23, 1876. The newspaper clippings in the J. W. Throckmorton Scrapbook, 1875–1877, in Throckmorton Papers, and in the John Henninger Reagan Papers, Barker Texas History Center, University of Texas, Austin, amply document the fact that Texans were not of one mind on the Texas & Pacific. For the Southerners' preoccupation with home rule, see Polakoff, *Politics of Inertia*, 240–45, 297–307, 309–14; George C. Rable, "Southern Interests and the Election of 1876: A Reappraisal," *Civil War History*, XXVI (1980), 347–61; and William Gillette, *Retreat from Reconstruction, 1869–1879* (Baton Rouge: Louisiana State University Press, 1979), especially 311–34.

interregnum for the South were unpredictable, but certainly worth considering), the southern Democratic congressmen simply moved to insure that Hayes would guarantee home rule for their section. That had been their ultimate objective since the end of the war, and that was what they received from the Compromise of 1877. Whatever else they might pry from the Hayes administration through the process of "reconciliation" would be dressing.[53]

Equally illusionary were suppositions that Hayes's policy of reconciliation and nebulous endorsement of "internal improvements of a national character" would foster the development of a strong southern Republican party with a base among "more respectable" conservatives. More than anything these notions demonstrate the continuing naïveté regarding the South on the part of Hayes and many of his close friends and advisors. After twenty years of political warfare with southern conservatives, some northern Republicans had learned very little about their adversaries. They persisted in drawing lines between secessionists and unionists, between old-

53. Taul Bradford to Andrew Cunningham, December 17, 1876, in Robert Joseph Cunningham Papers, Alabama Department of Archives and History, Montgomery. Polakoff rightly argues that Woodward's focus on the relatively small number of Southerners, southern "spokesmen," and Texas & Pacific advocates has led him to overemphasize the importance of the subsidy agreements. Evident too is his neglect of section-party voting alignments on economic issues earlier in the decade and his failure to cover some pivotal episodes in the troubled legislative history of the line such as Scott's defeat in the 43rd Congress. He also relies heavily on northern newspapers and the Hayes, Dodge, and William Henry Smith papers although it should be noted that many southern newspapers and manuscript collections were not readily available when he completed his study thirty years ago. These sources make one especially hesitant to accept the Western Associated Press group or even the Scott editors in the South and the handful of Scott men among the southern congressmen as representative spokesmen for the section. They also make readily apparent the South's obsession with home rule. I certainly agree with Woodward's acknowledgment that home rule was "the supreme objective of the southern negotiators. . . . All else was incidental or contributory." The problem is that the primacy of home rule has been overshadowed by the "incidental and contributory," and the actual power and influence of the Texas & Pacific forces in Congress and in the "negotiations" has been greatly overstressed. The origins of this problem lie in *Reunion and Reaction* despite Woodward's skillful qualifiers and disclaimers both in his book and his later reply to critic Allan Peskin. See Polakoff, *Politics of Inertia*, especially 244–314; Rable, "Southern Interests and the Election of 1876," 347–61; Benedict, "Southern Democrats in the Crisis of 1876–1877," 489–520; Allan Peskin, "Was There a Compromise of 1877?" C. Vann Woodward, "Yes, There Was a Compromise of 1877," *Journal of American History*, LX (1973), 63–75, 215–23; Woodward, *Reunion and Reaction*, 142, 178–79, 183, 204–10.

line Democrats and former Whigs which simply did not exist. The idea of attracting ex-Whigs and perhaps Douglas Democrats to the Republican party with subsidy legislation as a lure was a pipe dream which showed absolutely no understanding of the primacy of the race question and the degree to which party loyalty had become an article of faith in the South. A trip south destroyed the illusion for at least one Northerner who had been privy to the "negotiations" during the electoral crisis. "The 'old Whig' sentiment I spoke of in a former letter petered out before we reached New Orleans," Ohio editor James M. Comly lamented to Hayes in May, 1877. "There is nothing here to hang an old Whig party on." Six months later, North Carolina Governor Zebulon Vance capsulized the situation for another friend of the president. "President Hayes is certainly being deceived by men who claim to know the South about Democrats going to support him," he told his northern visitor. "These men do not know and are simply petting Hayes and deceiving him for the purposes of building themselves up in his good graces."[54]

Even if northern Republicans had renounced all connections with the freedmen, the task of building a new coalition in the South would still have been difficult if not impossible. Most southern Republicans and the bloody-shirt-waving northern "stalwarts" opposed Hayes's southern strategy from the beginning, and it is doubtful that others put much stock in it. It is more likely that moderate to conservative northern Republicans gave the policy lip service because it facilitated slipping out of their party's commitment to a reconstruction which had obviously collapsed. If the new policy met with success, then the party had saved some face; if it failed, as it did, then in reality nothing had been lost.

There was, of course, no further federal aid for the Texas & Pacific. Scott blamed his failure in the Forty-fourth Congress on the logjam of legislation created by the electoral crisis, but his defeat was a mere matter of numbers. After the House refused to consider the bill and it failed to reach the Senate floor, a New Orleans editor main-

54. James M. Comly to Rutherford B. Hayes, May 11, 1877, in Rutherford B. Hayes Papers, Rutherford B. Hayes Presidential Center, Fremont, Ohio; Watt P. Marchman (ed.), "The 'Memoirs' of Thomas Donaldson," *Hayes Historical Journal*, II (1979), 176.

tained that it would have passed "by a large majority" had it been considered—an opinion which reflected the extent of the propaganda job Scott had pulled on some southern newspapers. Nevertheless, Scott continued to push for aid for the remainder of the decade. "Year after year, congress after congress," the editor of the *Arkansas Gazette* lamented in 1879, "we have been deceived, hoodwinked and imposed upon by having this great and important measure thrust aside on the flimsy plea and pretext that to press it would injure the prospects of the democratic party at the north and jeopardize the election of a democratic president." But he might well have extended blame to include the northern Republicans, for it was clear that they were no more receptive to the Texas & Pacific than northern Democrats.[55]

For that matter, the editor would have found ample opposition to Scott in his own region had he bothered to look. When Scott and Huntington squared off for their final clash in the Forty-fifth Congress (1877–1879), a handful of die-hard Texas & Pacific men, Throckmorton, Lamar, Stephens, and James Chalmers of Mississippi, mouthed Scott's well-worn arguments about the line's enormous benefits for the South and raised the specter of a Huntington monopoly of western railroads. In a speech given just two days before Hayes's inauguration, Throckmorton denounced as "utterly false and atrociously slanderous" rumors of "collusion" between supporters of the Texas & Pacific and "friends of the republican candidate for president" and then proceeded to chide southern politicians for their "ancient prejudices" and "stickling about State rights" which prompted them to oppose the Texas & Pacific.[56]

But Scott's southern opponents were now more vocal. Johnston reiterated his belief that Scott intended to take his traffic to the North, not to Vicksburg or New Orleans, and concluded that the Texas &

55. New Orleans *Times*, February 19, 1877, quoted in Woodward, *Reunion and Reaction*, 177; Little Rock *Arkansas Gazette*, February 2, 1879, November 27, December 13, 1877, January 24, 1878.

56. *Congressional Record*, 45th Cong., 2nd Sess., 3653–59, 4129, 3117–23, Appendix, 246, 45th Cong., 3rd Sess., Appendix, 115–19, 44th Cong., 2nd Sess., Appendix, 179–85; Beverly Tucker to Edmund W. Hubard, March 16, April 18, 1878, in Hubard Papers; Thomas A. Scott to Matt W. Ransom, July 3, 1878, in Ransom Papers; James R. Chalmers (comp.), *The Opinions of the Fathers upon the Power and Duty of the General Government to Make Internal Improvements: . . . To Encourage Aid for*

Pacific was "a positive menace to the commercial interests of the South." Alabama Representative Hilary A. Herbert, echoing McKee, denounced the line's northern leadership and stressed that further aid was clearly unconstitutional. John Brown Gordon's lukewarm attitude had also cooled into solid opposition. "I can not vote for it," he bluntly informed Barlow. ". . . Not only my convictions but my constituents are against it." "We of this State don't care much whether the Southern Pacific Railroad is built or not," Vance declared in late 1877. "As it stands at present, it is a scheme to help Tom Scott." Some such as Representative John H. Reagan who had formerly backed the line now demonstrated a new wariness. Hayes's Texas friend Guy M. Bryan explained to a Galveston editor that Reagan, already a leader in the movement to regulate railroads, would still support the line *if* it "would regard southern interests and build up southern ports, and would not in its PRACTICAL operations discriminate in freights FOR THE BENEFIT OF NORTHERN ROADS, and AGAINST southern interests." Bryan's explanation left the editor wondering if the scheme had not been "ingeniously concocted for getting a Pacific road built, in the interest of a Philadelphia and St. Louis Combination, by playing on Southern sentiment with an empty name and delusive expectations."[57]

Opponents rallied around Georgia Senator Thomas Norwood, a counsel for Collis Huntington, who argued that Scott's line was nothing more than another dependency of "the great Pennsylvania monopoly," a "carpet-bag" line (a particularly damning epithet), and a "parasite" feeding on the government's credit. Huntington, Norwood stressed, was ready to push his Southern Pacific east through Arizona without the benefit of a federal subsidy. There lay the most

---

the *Mississippi Levees and the Texas & Pacific Railroad* (Washington, D.C.: n.p., 1878); John Calvin Brown, *Texas and Pacific Railway: A Letter . . . to the People of the South* (Pulaski, Tenn.: n.p., 1878); Logan Uriah Reavis, *The Texas & Pacific Railway; or a National Highway along the Path of Empire* (New York: Baker & Godwin, 1878), especially 26–30. Grenville Dodge, for one, was well aware of the difficulties the line faced; see Dodge to J. F. Baldwin, January 31, 1878, in Dodge Papers.

57. *Congressional Record*, 45th Cong., 2nd Sess., 4123–29, 4210–16; Hilary A. Herbert to Robert McKee, April 5, July 10, 1878, W. Brewer to McKee, May 13, 22, July 5, 1877, in McKee Papers; John Brown Gordon to S. L. M. Barlow, December 13, 1878, in Barlow Papers; Marchman (ed.), "'Memoirs' of Thomas Donaldson," 176; Galveston *News*, November 9, 1877, clipping in Reagan Papers.

compelling argument of all in 1878. Why subsidize the financially troubled Texas & Pacific when a legitimate competitor was willing to build along the same route without federal aid?[58]

Why indeed? Huntington's offer carried Hayes and Congress and doomed the Texas & Pacific. As Scott's request for further subsidies died, McKee and his converts rejoiced. "The T & P is worse than morbid," Norwood informed McKee in early 1879. "It weakened with marvelous rapidity when it did begin to lose & I dont know anyone 'to do it promise' now." After Scott bounced back the following week and then failed again, Norwood again wrote McKee: "I have the honor of conveying to you the gratifying information that the T. & P. Co. is very sick." Norwood believed that the resistance in Alabama "broke the back of the T. & P. Anyway—the Co. will never make another rally in Washt."[59]

Norwood was right; Scott sold his interest in the Texas & Pacific to Jay Gould in 1880. In the interim, Huntington, with federal consent, simply began laying track into Arizona territory, and he did not stop until he linked up with Gould's Texas & Pacific east of El Paso in 1882. He then continued building to the southeast, made a juncture with the Galveston, Harrisburg and San Antonio Railroad, and by 1883 he controlled a through line from San Francisco to New Orleans. But its immediate value to southern states east of the Mississippi remained limited. The gauge problem was not resolved until southern lines were forced to narrow their gauge to the northern standard in 1886. And it was not until 1893 that the railroad bridge at Memphis, the first below Saint Louis, was opened to traffic.[60]

The Texas & Pacific Railroad was both a source and a symbol of the Southerners' problems in their frustrating struggle to secure federal aid during the 1870s. The line's victory in 1871 not only proved empty, but the continuing controversy overshadowed more pressing

58. Thomas M. Norwood, *The Texas Pacific Railway (A Dependency of the Great Pennsylvania Monopoly) Contrasted with a Real Southern Pacific R.R.: . . . A Letter to the People of the South* (Washington, D.C.: n.p., 1878).

59. Thomas M. Norwood to Robert McKee, March 13, 26, 1879, in McKee Papers.

60. Julius Grodinsky, *Transcontinental Railway Strategy, 1869–1893: A Study of Businessmen* (Philadelphia: University of Pennsylvania Press, 1962), 162–65, 169–74; Taylor and Neu, *American Railroad Network,* 79–81.

southern material needs. "Of all the things the South needs, and their name is legion," the *Nation* observed in early 1877, "better communication with the Pacific coast is probably what it needs least." The Texas & Pacific was "ostensibly for the South," but even the *Nation* recognized that the North would reap the benefits.[61] Its potential value to the South aside, the matter harmed the credibility of more legitimate southern claims on the federal treasury for internal improvements—a concern of considerable importance to the southern wing of the Republican party.

One of the ways southern Republicans could demonstrate their value to their constituents was to bring home federal monies. They went to Washington as spokesmen for a section in dire need of aid, but they discovered, much to their surprise and dismay, that most northern Republicans were unwilling to extend the benefits of the federal largess to the South. Just as was the case on other economic issues, they often found themselves in a frustrating fight against their own party colleagues and retrenchment-minded northern Democrats to secure even token federal funds. They were not asking for the type of assistance involved in the later Tennessee Valley Authority or Marshall Plan (although that is probably what it would have taken to rehabilitate some areas)—that was inconceivable given the attitudes of the age. They were simply asking for an equal share and perhaps a little more because of their greater needs. Fuller northern backing for economic reconstruction would not have saved the problem-plagued southern wing, but it might have eased some of the intersectional tension in the party and made the task of those directly involved in promoting Republicanism in the South somewhat easier.[62]

Northern intransigence also created sectional problems in the Democratic party, but the southern Democrats' political survival did

61. "The South and the Texas-and-Pacific Job," 82–83.
62. See the comments of William C. Harris in *Presidential Reconstruction in Mississippi*, 249–50, and those of W. R. Brock in "Reconstruction and the American Party System," in George M. Frederickson (ed.), *A Nation Divided: Problems and Issues of the Civil War and Reconstruction* (Minneapolis: Burgess Publishing Co., 1975), 112. The same difficulties applied to securing civil appropriations and federal funds for southern education. On the latter, see Kenneth R. Johnson, "Legrand Winfield Perce: A Mississippi Carpetbagger and the Fight for Federal Aid to Education," *Journal of Mississippi History*, XXXIV (1972), 221–56; and George F. Hoar, *Auto-*

not depend on bringing home a share of the federal largess—many had never swallowed the Whiggish economic philosophy behind the "Great Barbecue" anyway. They had instead the Lost Cause and the potent mythology of Reconstruction to sustain them in power. As for the Texas & Pacific, in 1885 southern Democrats voted as a bloc, and one suspects with some relish, to force the line to forfeit its remaining land grant of 15.7 million acres.[63] Tom Scott's promises and pleas of the 1870s were now just an unpleasant memory; southern Democrats had long since turned to more important matters closer to home.

---

biography of Seventy Years (2 vols.; New York: Charles Scribner's Sons, 1903), I, 264–66. Similar problems arose from the Southerners' efforts to set up a commission to review the private claims of southern unionists for goods and property furnished to or taken by the Union army during the war. Over the vehement opposition of many prominent Northerners, the carpetbaggers and scalawags managed to establish a commission in 1871, but Northerners hindered its operation for the remainder of the decade. The problem is thoroughly treated in Frank W. Klingberg, *The Southern Claims Commission* (Berkeley and Los Angeles: University of California Press, 1955), especially chs. 3 and 9.

63. *Congressional Record*, 48th Cong., 1st Sess., 787–96, 48th Cong., 2nd Sess., 1877–85, 1887–99, 2032; David Maldwyn Ellis, "The Forfeiture of Railroad Land Grants, 1867–1894," *Mississippi Valley Historical Review*, XXXIII (1946), 41–43.

VIII   North and South in Congress

"The South is a sort of plantation," North Carolina Republican William W. Holden explained to his wife in 1871. "It ruled the North forty years, and now the North is ruling. This explains all."[1] In many respects, the relationships between North and South in Congress throughout the 1870s verified Holden's early impression. At the end of the decade, true reconciliation was still a hope; sectional feeling remained strong in both political parties. Southern Democrats continued to be the objects of distrust even in their own party—a feeling they amply reciprocated, but sectional discord in the Democracy was less important than that among Republicans. The sources of the serious breach in Republican ranks were obviously multiple, but particularly critical were the less-than-harmonious relationship between Northerners and Southerners in Congress and the failure of most Northerners to understand the political and economic needs of their southern colleagues. These and other factors led to waning northern enthusiasm for reconstruction and boded ill for southern Republicanism and the idealistic vision of a society in which the freedmen would share fully.

The parentage of southern Republicanism lay in the reconstruction act of 1867 which extended the franchise to southern freedmen. From its inception, the final plan of reconstruction has been variously condemned as either too harsh or not coercive enough, for being

---

1. William Woods Holden to wife, April 30, 1871, in William Woods Holden Papers, Perkins Library, Duke University, Durham, N.C. Holden, a wartime unionist, was appointed provisional governor of North Carolina in 1865, won the governorship in 1868, and was impeached by a Democratic legislature in 1871 after two years of bitter political strife and Klan turmoil in the state.

launched after two years of indecision or for not being postponed even longer, for being a political solution to what was basically a social and economic problem. Despite these fatal weaknesses, however, both northern contemporaries and many subsequent commentators have shifted the primary onus of failure from those who formulated the policy to the Southerners. The conservatives' obsession with home rule, white solidarity, and the elimination of the black from politics was, of course, critical to the collapse of the experiment. It is equally apparent that southern Republicans contributed to their own demise with corruption, lack of concern for their black electorate, and intraparty factionalism. But while one can object to the conservatives' means and ends, they can hardly be condemned for following their natural instincts and overthrowing what they considered to be an alien political leadership. The plan, after all, ultimately did not prohibit them from doing so. Similarly, the plan and the manner in which Northerners supported it sharply limited the opportunities and power of southern Republicans to effect what Radicals euphemistically referred to as the "regeneration" of the South. The fact of the matter was that the fate of the 129 southern Republican congressmen and their peers was tied to the panacea of black suffrage, which stood unbuttressed as the keystone of the northern solution to the southern problem. Therein lay the primary source of failure.

The congressmen and their colleagues charged with implementing the plan quickly became aware of its shortcomings. Some sensed the odds immediately; full realization for most came during the presidential campaign of 1868. After the experiment failed, most of the 129 congressmen would have endorsed the sentiments North Carolina carpetbagger Albion Tourgee expressed in his autobiographical novel A Fool's Errand, published in 1879. "It must have been well understood by the wise men who devised this short-sighted plan," he reasoned, "that they were giving the power of the re-organized, subordinate republics, into the hands of a race unskilled in public affairs, poor to a degree hardly to be matched in the civilized world, and so ignorant that not five out of a hundred of its voters could read their own ballots." Joining the freedmen were "such Adullamites among the native whites as might be willing to face a proscription which would shut the house of God in the face of their families, together with the few men of Northern birth, resident in that section since the close of the war . . . who might elect to become permanent citizens, and join in the movement." Against these new Republicans were pitted "the wealth, the intelligence, the organizing skill, the pride, and the hate of a people . . . animated chiefly by the apprehension of what seemed now about to be forced upon them in this miscalled measure of 'Reconstruction;' to wit, the equality of the negro race."[2]

In the naïve faith that the franchise was all the freedmen needed, northern Republicans "went farther, and, by erecting the rebellious territory into self-regulating and sovereign States, they abandoned these parties like cocks in a pit, to fight out the question of predominance without the possibility of national interference. They said to the colored man, in the language of one of the pseudo-philosophers of that day, 'Root, hog, or die!'"[3] In the eyes of carpetbagger Comfort Servosse, Tourgee's protagonist and fictional counterpart, the experiment was doomed. "We Republicans of the South will go down with the reconstruction movement," Servosse wrote a northern friend in 1868. "Some of us will make a good fight for the doomed craft; others will neither realize nor care for its danger." Locked into a situation they were powerless to change, southern Republicans would "bear the blame of its failure" when, in fact, "the North, and especially the Republican party of the North, will be responsible for this ruin, for its shame and its loss, for the wasted opportunity, and, it may be, for consequent peril." It was, Tourgee opined, "cheap patriotism, cheap philanthropy, cheap success!"[4]

Tourgee obviously oversimplified a complex situation. He gave lit-

2. Albion W. Tourgee, *A Fool's Errand: A Novel of the South During Reconstruction*, ed. George M. Frederickson (New York: Harper and Row, 1966), 136.
3. *Ibid.*, 137. The "pseudo-philosopher" referred to was undoubtedly Horace Greeley of the New York *Tribune*, who had used the phrase when he informed southern Republicans in 1869 that it was time that they cease "hanging around the neck of the North." Tourgee later referred to "the 'root-hog-or-die' policy of the great apostle of the instantaneous transformation era." New York *Tribune*, May 24, 1869; Tourgee, *A Fool's Errand*, 169.
4. Tourgee, *A Fool's Errand*, 170–71, 137. In many respects Tourgee is the spiritual father of much recent work on southern Republicanism. His influence is particularly apparent in one of the best pieces on the problem, Otto H. Olsen's "Southern Reconstruction and the Question of Self-Determination," in George M. Frederickson (ed.), *A Nation Divided: Problems and Issues of the Civil War and Reconstruction* (Minneapolis: Burgess Publishing Co., 1975), 113–41. See also Olsen's *Carpetbagger's Crusade: The Life of Albion Winegar Tourgee* (Baltimore: Johns Hopkins Press, 1965).

tle attention to the occasional glimmers of hope and minor triumphs which marked reconstruction. Ignored too was the fact that in some states an exceptionally qualified leadership emerged from the ranks of the freedmen. And northern Republicans, "the wise men" he scorned so sardonically, were clearly limited in what they could accomplish. Mounting public pressure demanded resolution of the problem after two years of wrangling among the Southerners, Johnson, and the various elements of the Republican party, and the true Radicals were forced to compromise with their fair-weather friends at every point. A positive requirement of universal suffrage and proposals to give the freedmen a share of southern economic resources—the chief failings of reconstruction according to most revisionists—were simply unattainable. With the exception of a few Radicals and perhaps the masses of blacks themselves, Americans were not about to trample over dearly held beliefs in the privileges and sanctity of private property to guarantee suffrage for propertyless blacks or to confiscate and redistribute land. In short, the nation was simply unwilling to adopt the kind of comprehensive plan of political, social, and economic reconstruction Tourgee and fellow Radicals envisioned as necessary for the true "regeneration" of the ex-Confederate states.[5]

The "might have beens" and the "ifs" of the situation—the alternatives, if any, Republican policy makers had in 1867—are largely irrelevant. The reality was that the plan was put into effect, it gave birth to southern Republicanism, and the southern wing became the instrument of implementation. Most northern Republicans doggedly clung to it at least through the enforcement acts, and an ever-dwindling number continued to side with their southern colleagues in the losing cause until the last reconstruction government was overturned in 1877. What remains important, then, is the manner in which the process unfolded, the nature and extent of northern sup-

5. W. R. Brock, *An American Crisis: Congress and Reconstruction, 1865–1867* (New York: Saint Martin's Press, 1963), 275–76; Hans L. Trefousse, *The Radical Republicans: Lincoln's Vanguard for Racial Justice* (New York: Alfred A. Knopf, 1968), 357–62, 415–20, 430–31; Michael Les Benedict, *A Compromise of Principle: Congressional Republicans and Reconstruction, 1863–1869* (New York: W. W. Norton, 1974), chs. 10–11, 17; Herman Belz, "The New Orthodoxy in Reconstruction Historiography," *Reviews in American History*, I (1973), 106–13.

port, and the relationships which emerged between Northerners and Southerners in the party and in Congress.

It is apparent, first of all, that little personally differentiated the 129 Republicans from other congressmen with the exception that 16 of them were black. They came from a variety of backgrounds and shared the values, the assumptions, and the same range of motivation of most Americans. Their activity and behavior in Congress were on a comparable plane with congressmen from other regions, and they compiled as reputable a record as that of southern Democrats in serving legitimate sectional interests. With few exceptions they worked and voted with southern Democrats to secure economic legislation beneficial to their section—often in the midst of intense partisanship generated by the politics of reconstruction and frequently against the wishes of party members from outside the South. They were not dangerous economic radicals; they posed no menace to bourgeois values. While the rhetoric of the more radical Southerners sounded threatening, they were scarcely more willing than their peers in either party to threaten property rights and seek legislation which might have given their black electorate a real economic foothold. They did, however, support the freedmen's political cause stronger and longer than most others—that, after all, was the plan. And while their survival depended upon it, to have abandoned it meant betrayal of party and principle. To espouse it meant enduring verbal and physical abuse and being stigmatized with an overwhelmingly negative image.

As far as the Republican congressmen were concerned, the image of personal turpitude and political corruption which plagued them was not so much earned as it was created for them. A few contributed to the image, but its primary origins lay in the hatred of conservative Southerners and a good many Northerners for those brazen enough to associate politically with the freedmen. The disparate elements gathered behind the Republican banner in the South certainly added to their problems with an acrid factionalism based on racial, patronage, and policy divisions. Next to their opponents' use of ostracism, intimidation, and violence, intraparty discord was the most serious internal problem southern Republicans faced, and it figured prominently in their failure. There is little wonder that northern observers looked on in bewilderment and distaste at the vehement intraparty struggles as contending factions besieged them for aid and recognition. But Northerners seldom took time to examine and attempt to understand the bases of division and the merits of the various contenders. Thus they all too often compounded the problem by supporting the less reputable elements of southern Republicanism.

The northern Democratic press gladly perpetuated and even enhanced the opprobrious caricatures of southern Republicans, but the receptivity of northern Republicans is somewhat inexplicable. As early as mid-1868 a northern journalist concluded that most of the southern delegates to the Republican National Convention were as "interested in the welfare of the district sending them to Chicago as a traveller is interested in the condition of the road by which he hopes to arrive at fortune or position." Only a few, he thought, had purchased plantations (as if that were the only economic endeavor in the South), and he believed that these men, among whom were fourteen future congressmen, "will not contribute much to the 'regeneration' of the South." The "bad examples" rumored of some carpetbaggers even bothered such a devout Radical as Ben Butler, who thought that the solution was the selection of well established natives to represent the South in Congress. "While many 'good men & true' have gone from the north to aid in the regeneration of the South of whose service the country has a grateful appreciation and in whom it has Confidence," he wrote in June, 1868, "yet it is the part of wisdom for the South to choose as their leaders the true & tried men whose interests, fortunes and heroes are identified with them [and] confirmed by long residence or birth."[6]

Shortly after the first southern Republicans were seated in Congress, they faced unsubstantiated charges that they callously ignored their constituents' interests and functioned as puppets of northeastern Radicals. Early in 1869, for example, the Washington correspondent of the influential Cincinnati *Commercial* published an al-

6. Adams Sherman Hill, "The Chicago Convention," *North American Review*, CXX (1868), 168; undated draft of Benjamin F. Butler to T. J. Mackey, written on Mackey to Butler, June 3, 1868, in Benjamin F. Butler Papers, Library of Congress (hereinafter cited as LC). Mackey had asked Butler's opinion of "rumors" in South Carolina that northern Republicans would view the election of southern unionists to Congress with disfavor.

leged interview with a "Connecticut congressman elected in the South" which was favorably copied in the conservative press. "These gentlemen of the paper collar and extra dickey follow New England, and vote all the time against the interests of their own constituents," the journalist concluded. "I had a long talk with one of these Representatives ad interim last night, and tried to convince him that it would be well, just for the appearance of the thing, to cast a vote now and then for the region he claimed to represent. But no! I found my friend had intense contempt for one half of his people, and a deadly hatred for the other half."[7] The charge of irresponsible representation would plague the carpetbaggers in particular, but was freely extended to scalawag and black congressmen as well. By the early 1870s, such influential northern journals as the New York *Tribune* and the *Nation* no longer questioned the accuracy of associated press dispatches from the South and frequently denigrated southern Republicans in general and the congressmen in particular. Once launched, the negative image quickly snowballed, and southern Republicans found themselves facing a blanket condemnation which was impossible to overcome.[8]

The precipitous decline in northern support and the breach that opened between the northern and southern wings of the Republican party in Congress is one of the intriguing problems of the period. The fate of southern Republicanism was probably sealed with the plan adopted in 1867, but even within that framework, northern Republicans showed little interest in attempting to make the policy work. It would seem that they would have done everything possible

7. Cincinnati *Commercial* as quoted in Richmond *Whig*, January 5, 1869. None of the carpetbag congressmen serving in the 40th Congress or then elected to the 41st Congress were natives of Connecticut, and none viewed that state as their home. The correspondent either erred, intentionally or unintentionally, in identifying the native state of the carpetbagger or fabricated the story.

8. For a sampling, see New York *Tribune*, May 24, 1869; *Nation*, August 6, 1868, p. 101, January 16, 1870, pp. 5–6, January 13, 1870, p. 17, February 22, 1872, p. 114, June 20, 1872, p. 398; "The State of the South," *Nation*, March 28, 1872, pp. 197–98; Chicago *Tribune*, December 21, 22, 1874. Gillette gives much attention to the emergence of northern distrust of and distaste for southern Republicans in his *Retreat from Reconstruction, 1869–1879* (Baton Rouge: Louisiana State University Press, 1979). Northern public opinion, of course, provided exceptional grist for the disciples of William A. Dunning who first shaped the historical image of the Republican congressmen into the now dog-eared stereotypes of ignorant blacks, unprincipled political adventurers, and purchasable opportunists.

to help their southern allies. They were willing, at least for a time, to sanction the use of troops at election time, and, in the negative spirit of the original plan, they passed coercive legislation such as the enforcement acts. Given the frame of reconstruction, such activity was often necessary, but these "aids" became a crutch for some southern Republicans, embarrassed others, and were abused by still others. They further roused the conservatives (if any rousing was needed), contributed to the image of southern Republican regimes dependent upon federal bayonets, and thus provided additional ammunition for opponents of reconstruction in both North and South.[9]

What was lacking was forms of positive support—the types of assistance one would expect within the structure of a national political party. Even early in the period, northern Republicans were reluctant to solicit and share campaign money with their southern colleagues. What little money did go south went in Grant's behalf; otherwise, the southern wing was left to its own meager resources. Similarly, prominent northern congressmen and party professionals steadfastly declined invitations to join southern Republicans on the campaign trail. It is ironic, and yet indicative of northern attitudes, that quite possibly more money and certainly more Republicans went south *after* the election of 1876 to "save" Hayes's claim to the presidency than had been the case in all the previous years combined. By this time, of course, southern Republicanism was for all practical purposes dead.[10]

If anything, the relationships between northern and southern Republicans on Capitol Hill were even less healthy than those outside Washington. Thanks to their northern leadership, Southerners failed

9. See in particular James E. Sefton, *The United States Army and Reconstruction, 1865–1877* (Baton Rouge: Louisiana State University Press, 1967), especially chs. 8–11; and Gillette, *Retreat from Reconstruction*, especially chs. 2–4, 7, 10, 12.

10. As Jack B. Scroggs has noted, southern Republican correspondence with northern Republicans declined sharply after Grant's election in 1868—another manifestation of the party split. See Scroggs, "Southern Reconstruction: A Radical View," *Journal of Southern History*, XXIV (1958), 422–29. William E. Chandler and, to a lesser degree, Benjamin Butler maintained a correspondence with Southerners in the 1870s, especially during campaigns; otherwise southern letters are at best infrequent in the papers of such prominent northern Republicans as Blaine, Dawes, Garfield, Sherman, and Sumner. Letters from northern Republicans are rare in southern collections.

to secure a proportional share of power in the committee structure. To their dismay, they also found northern congressmen and the Grant and Hayes administrations reluctant to relinquish their control over patronage in the ex-Confederate states and simply unwilling to share the immense patronage in executive departments. Even reconstruction policy, potentially a source of unity, widened the sectional rift. The ongoing southern turmoil, bitter disputes over further enforcement and civil rights legislation within each wing of the party, and growing northern disillusionment turned reconstruction policy into a divisive force.

Finally, and perhaps most important, northern Republicans failed to realize that the South needed economic as well as political reconstruction. It was particularly important to southern Republicans that they be the medium through which federal aid and beneficial economic legislation reached the South. Their requests were not unreasonable; they did not defy the economic values and sensibilities of the period by demanding confiscation or massive injections of federal aid. But regardless of whether the request involved tariff adjustments, a refund of the cotton tax, a scaling down of the tobacco tax, an equal share of bank note circulation, a modest increase in greenback volume, remonetization of silver, appropriations, or subsidies for internal improvements, southern Republicans could count on sizable and sometimes overwhelming blocs of opposition among their northern party colleagues.

Furthermore, the Southerners' adamant defense of their economic interests obviously alienated some influential northern Republicans and added to the sectional split in the party. In light of the foregoing, examples of northern Republicans opposing anything calculated to benefit the South economically are numerous, but the not-so-extreme case of Radical Zachariah Chandler of Michigan epitomizes the problem and is worthy of final note. Chandler was perceived as a "friend" of southern Republicans in Congress and, for what it was worth, he readily engaged in bloody-shirt oratory and supported coercive legislation to buttress southern Republican regimes. But as his biographer and his record make clear, he was "insensitive to the South's real needs." He was a hard-money advocate and immediate resumptionist who opposed currency expansion of any kind. He was a devout protectionist, he vehemently opposed refunding the cotton tax, and he offered no support for federal funds for southern education. He fought legislation to reconstruct the Mississippi River levees, and as chairman of the Senate Commerce Committee until 1875 he could be counted upon to block large appropriations for southern river and harbor projects. He was continuously involved in Republican congressional campaign organizations and was party chairman during the 1876 campaign, yet he routinely ignored southern pleas for campaign funds and speakers, and, although frequently invited, he never bothered to enter the section during Reconstruction. He disliked carpetbaggers, he periodically railed against "Southern Unionists," and he regarded blacks as a curiosity. With such "friends" it is hardly surprising that southern Republicans experienced difficulties in Congress.[11]

Southern Democrats quickly capitalized on the Republican split on economic issues. In addition to waving the flag of "black domination," they charged that Republicans cared nothing about the material interests of the South and were interested only in the economic welfare of the North.[12] The carpetbag congressmen had grown up with Republican notions of active federal involvement in the economy, the blacks were clearly aware of that philosophy's potential benefit for their people, and the northern Republican record of liberal appropriations for internal improvements had been a primary attraction for Whiggish southern whites who while less than enthused about black suffrage could live with it. Instead, however, Southerners were denied economic benefits with which they might have partially counterbalanced the stigma of being associated with the freedmen. They were not out to destroy the "economic edifice" northern Republicans had erected during the war, so the arguments of Beale, Woodward, and others regarding their *anticipated* behavior on economic issues are in one sense correct. But southern Republicans (and many Democrats for that matter) did seek to modify it in impor-

11. See Sister Mary Karl George, R.S.M., *Zachariah Chandler: A Political Biography* (East Lansing: Michigan State University Press, 1969), especially 196–217.
12. For a prime example, see the campaign speech of Virginia Conservative John W. Daniel in the Richmond *Whig*, October 9, 1873, clipping in John Warwick Daniel Papers, Alderman Library, University of Virginia, Charlottesville. Daniel gave "political oppression" only passing attention before cataloging the ways in which Republicans were mindful only of northern interests on economic questions.

tant ways, and they fought to have its benefits extended to the
South. The Northerners' neglect of economic reconstruction and
their unwillingness to live up to what Southerners believed to be the
economic philosophy of the party thus became a significant factor in
the failure of southern Republicanism.

Several years after Reconstruction, former Speaker of the House
James G. Blaine, reflecting on southern Republicans in the Forty-
first House, concluded that "their misfortune was that they had assumed a responsibility that could be successfully discharged only by
men of extraordinary endowments." Had they been brilliant orators
or extremely wealthy, he speculated, they might have been able to
cope with their situation, but after surveying the list, he found "not
one who was regarded as exceptionally eloquent or exceptionally
rich; and hence they were compelled to enter the contest without
personal prestige, without adventitious aid of any kind." They were
therefore "doomed to a hopeless struggle against the influence, the
traditions, [and] the hatred of a large majority of the white men of
the South."[13]

Eloquence, wealth, personal prestige, and whatever else Blaine
might have included in the "extraordinary endowments" lacking in
southern congressmen were among the least of their problems. That
they had personal shortcomings and contributed to their own demise is undeniable, but these must be set in the context of what
they were required to do, the nature and resources of their southern
opposition, and the extent of northern assistance. The plan itself,
which undoubtedly went further in the direction of black political
rights than most Northerners were willing to go, probably doomed
the experiment, but within that framework, the failings of northern
Republican leadership were critical. Much attention has been given
to the waning of northern backing for reconstruction, but the experience of the congressmen suggests that northern support had never
included much more than rhetorical endorsement, troops, and coercive legislation, and enthusiasm for these quickly declined. Excluded were numerous positive types of assistance which were well
within the power of Northerners to offer.

13. James G. Blaine, *Twenty Years of Congress: From Lincoln to Garfield* (2 vols.;
Norwich, Conn.: Henry Bill Publishing Co., 1886), II, 448.

In short, even within the limitations of the plan, there were alternatives. A differing scenario of reconstruction, one in which northern Republicans worked closely with their southern counterparts in a positive, constructive relationship marked by mutual aid, respect, and discipline, might have been written and the halls of Congress would have been an appropriate stage. Whether or not such a scenario could have fostered enough understanding to temper the racism of the age and help ease the freedmen into a more equitable situation is at least moot. But even such a modest alternative apparently asked for too much of a continuing commitment from a people weary after decades of agitation over slavery, four years of civil war, and a bitter struggle to determine the requirements of readmission. Racism, an ingrained distrust of all things southern, and an overriding concern with maintaining their hegemony in the North limited the response of northern Republicans to emancipation. The solution was a qualified black suffrage, and the Southerners so inclined were asked to build a Republican party which would bear responsibility for the regeneration of the region. For a time Northerners were willing to buttress the resulting regimes, so initially at least the situation for southern Republicans was not quite one of "root, hog, or die," as Tourgee later characterized it. But it soon became just that. The negative policy of coercion only fueled and gained sympathy for the cause of southern conservatives. Inevitably, northern support faded and the great experiment collapsed. Among the casualties were the 129 southern Republican congressmen.

The intersectional breach in the Republican party naturally delighted southern Democrats. They also experienced some difficulties with their northern counterparts in Congress, especially on economics, but on the issues of reconstruction and race, a source of discord for Republicans, the Democrats remained united. In addition to using intimidation, southern Democrats worked their way back into power by manufacturing a negative image of their opponents, encouraging the factionalism already epidemic among southern Republicans, and exploiting the sectional split in the Republican party—all the while capitalizing on the waning of northern Radicalism. During the electoral dispute following the election of 1876, they secured the removal of the last significant traces of Republicanism from their region in exchange for a conciliatory Republican president. Even if they had less influence at the national level than they would have liked or perhaps deserved, southern Democrats at least controlled their section at the end of the 1870s, and home rule was what really mattered.

The Democracy north and south lay fragmented at the war's end. The northern wing ranged across the spectrum from strong supporters of the war to equally avid opponents. During the war, as Joel H. Silbey has shown, party leadership divided into two main factions exclusive of the so-called War Democrats. On the one hand were the "Legitimists," unionists committed to a northern victory and yet dedicated to providing a viable opposition—a conservative alternative to the dominant Republican party. The "Purists," on the other hand, favored a negotiated peace and were fearful of the revolutionary, centralizing impact of the war on the Union and Constitution. They were further convinced that the Legitimists had compromised party principles and had made more concessions to the war effort than necessary to win favor with the conservative majority in the electorate.[14]

In the South, the Democracy faced internal problems of a different sort. The Whig-Democrat and unionist-secessionist divisions of the antebellum period overlapped and merged into prowar and propeace factions late in the supposedly nonpartisan Confederate congress. Former Whigs who wanted nothing to do with the increasingly Radical-dominated Republican party in the immediate postwar period were understandably reluctant to join forces with their lifelong political enemies. To ease the Whigs' sensitivities, the Democratic organizations in several states dropped the party label and referred to themselves as Conservatives. The adoption of a new name, of course, did not erase memories of past political battles or resolve basic philosophical differences.[15]

Adding to the Democracy's problems was the North-South dis-

14. Joel H. Silbey, *A Respectable Minority: The Democratic Party in the Civil War Era, 1860–1868* (New York: W. W. Norton, 1977), ch. 4 and *passim.*
15. Richard Beringer, "The Unconscious 'Spirit of Party' in the Confederate Congress," *Civil War History,* XVIII (1972), 312–33. See also Chapter II above.

cord fueled by memories of antebellum divisions, the Charleston convention of 1860, the turmoil of the war, and the direction of the party's postwar policy. Upon his return from a northern sojourn in 1868, Georgian Benjamin Hill concluded that "all parties there are unsound as far as we are concerned. There are individual exceptions, but, as a mass, the Northern people have no sympathy, or only disinterested feelings for the Southern people." The former Whig's distrust of the northern Democracy was perhaps stronger and longer lasting than that of most conservatives, but many expressed reservations about renewing associations with their Yankee counterparts. As late as 1870, John Warfield Johnston of Virginia, the first Conservative and ex-Confederate to serve in the Senate, wondered "exactly what a conservative was, and what he would do,—what party he would act with—or whether he would play the role of an independent." When the Republicans invited him and his fellow senator Republican John Francis Lewis to caucus, Lewis accepted but Johnston declined. Given the Republican alternative after 1866, Johnston and other southern conservatives had no real option but to mend fences with the northern Democracy. Still, intersectional strife troubled the party for years after the Civil War.[16]

In Congress, the most visible party divisions occurred on economic issues. Throughout the decade, hard-money northeastern Democrats worried about the inflationists and silverites among their southern and midwestern brethren, and retrenchment-minded Northerners opposed southern "raids on the Federal Treasury." The southern Democrats' best friends on all economic measures were their political adversaries from the South and Midwest. However much the Redeemers might have detested carpetbaggers, scalawags, and blacks, and the likes of Radicals Oliver P. Morton and John Logan, they nevertheless accepted them as economic allies.

During the first half of the 1870s the intraparty factionalism seldom surfaced other than on economic issues. Despite their problems, the Democrats had a common political foe, and the Northern-

16. Benjamin Harvey Hill to Mrs. Fannie Carr Cody, October 30, 1868, in Katherine Mood Chapman (ed.), "Some Benjamin Harvey Hill Letters, Part I," *Georgia Historical Quarterly*, XLVII (1963), 312–13; John Warfield Johnston, "Reminiscences of Thirteen Years in the Senate" (MS in John Warfield Johnston Papers, Perkins Library, Duke University, Durham, N.C.).

ers were willing and enthusiastic allies of their southern colleagues on reconstruction issues. The conservative South could not have asked for more outspoken defenders than Senators Thomas F. Bayard of Delaware and Allen G. Thurman of Ohio and Representatives Samuel S. Cox of New York and Samuel J. Randall of Pennsylvania. While Republicans still controlled or posed a threat in some parts of the South and while Democrats remained the minority in Congress, they remained relatively united.[17]

By the middle of the decade, however, the situation had changed. After the elections of 1874, only four states remained in Republican hands and the faction-ridden party was vulnerable in all four. Mississippi fell to the Democrats in 1875, and Grant's refusal to intervene raised the hopes of conservatives in Louisiana, Florida, and South Carolina, who knew that the "Mississippi plan" could be used to overthrow their Republican governments in 1876. As they prepared to take control of the Forty-fourth House in 1875, the Democrats had every reason to feel confident, but the smoldering sectional divisions began to resurface as they gained power. After having played the role of an opposition for so long, House Democrats had difficulty adjusting to their newly acquired status as the majority party. When they caucused in December, 1875, to choose a Speaker, Southerners faced a difficult choice between leading candidates Randall and Michael C. Kerr of Indiana. Kerr's midwestern origins and free-trade proclivities were more than offset by his contractionist monetary views, his opposition to all types of subsidies, and his support from New York Democrats. Randall's record as a moderate protectionist, opponent of subsidies, and advocate of reduced appropriations troubled Southerners, and his hard-money stance was less than satisfactory to some, but most supported him because of his reputation as an outspoken opponent of reconstruction.[18]

When Kerr emerged as the choice of the caucus, Randall's south-

17. Albert V. House, Jr., "Northern Congressional Democrats as Defenders of the South During Reconstruction," *Journal of Southern History*, VI (1940), 46–71.

18. Among southern newspapers, the Richmond *Whig* was the most enthusiastic in its endorsement of Randall as the "true Northern Representative of Southern sentiment. . . . We trust that every Southern Democrat and Conservative will support him." Albert V. House, Jr., "The Speakership Contest of 1875: Democratic Response to Power," *Journal of American History*, LII (1965), 252–74; Michael C. Kerr to J. S.

ern supporters immediately found themselves "out of the circle of power." Kerr did appoint Lamar to chair the important Committee on the Pacific Railroad; the Select Committee on the Mississippi Levees went to E. John Ellis of Louisiana, a Kerr supporter; and Southerners were allowed three seats on Ways and Means. But Appropriations went to Randall, with the retrenchment-obsessed William S. Holman in the second position, and Southerners received only two seats on Commerce, two on Banking and Currency, and one on Appropriations. They must have been further irritated by the reaction of the northern party press to the appointment of some of their number to head several minor committees. The Independent-Democratic New York *Sun*, for example, characterized North Carolinian Robert B. Vance as "wholly unfit for the trust" of Patents, Alfred Scales of North Carolina as a third-rate lawyer "without the least ability," and Virginian John T. Harris as an "indifferent lawyer" of "small range." Even Lamar, while "able and upright," was disliked for his connections with Tom Scott's "scheme."[19]

The Democrats suffered from leadership problems and general disorganization throughout the Forty-fourth House. Even the Kerr supporters among the Southerners were disappointed; one Alabamian lamented the party's need for "first-class leadership on the floor." Kerr was particularly ineffective due to poor health and he died in August, 1876. Randall became Speaker at the beginning of the second session the following December, but neither exercised the power of the office as effectively as had Blaine, the Republican Speaker in the three preceding Houses. In terms of legislation passed, the Forty-fourth Congress was the least productive of any during the decade. As one northern Democrat proclaimed, "The

---

Moore, November 17, 1874, enclosed in Moore to Manton Marble, November 19, 1874, Kerr to Manton Marble, December 4, 1874, Samuel S. Cox to Marble, December 8, 1874, May 17, 1875, in Manton Marble Papers, LC; Beverly Tucker to Samuel J. Randall, November 24, 26, 1876, William W. Wilshire to Randall, May 21, 1875, in Samuel J. Randall Papers, Van Pelt Library, University of Pennsylvania, Philadelphia; *Nation*, December 9, 1875, p. 363; Richmond *Whig*, December 3, 1875.

19.   Robert B. Vance to Samuel J. Randall, December 9, 1875, in Randall Papers; Burwell B. Lewis to Robert McKee, December 10, 1875, in Robert McKee Papers, Alabama Department of Archives and History, Montgomery; *Congressional Record*, 44th Cong., 1st Sess., 250–51; House, "Speakership Contest of 1875," 272; New York *Sun*, undated clipping in James Webb Throckmorton Papers, Barker Texas History Center, University of Texas, Austin; *Nation*, December 23, 1875, p. 393.

whole country must understand before Dec '75 that the chief duty of the next Congress will be investigation." During the lengthy first session, which lasted until mid-August, 1876, the Democratic majority seemed obsessed with the Louisiana election frauds, irregularities in the War and Navy departments, and the Whiskey Ring scandal. In the lame-duck session, the disputed presidential election overshadowed all other business. Although the Southerners went along with the investigations, they also had material interests, and they watched those slip away in the face of northern Democratic opposition. No major piece of economic legislation emerged from the Congress. Much to the delight of Holman, the House did not even produce a rivers and harbors appropriations bill during the second session. For those Southerners who still supported it, the Texas & Pacific project again failed, and Ellis' levees bill was rejected on the final day of the Congress.[20]

Among the representatives, Randall became the focal point of the Southerners' discontent. Within days after Randall took office, one Alabama congressman declared that he was "running the speakership in utter disregard of the feelings and wishes of the members from the cotton states." To another he was the "slave of Eastern protectionists and bond-holders, the residing begater of Sammy Tilden and against Southern and Western interests." John Goode ran against Randall in the Democratic caucus in 1877—a move which put the Southerners, especially Goode's fellow Virginians, in a bind. John Randolph Tucker, for example, favored Randall because he was the inevitable choice but was compelled to vote for Goode and thereby injured his chances for possible advancement on Ways and Means or placement on the Judiciary Committee. His son warned him in 1879 that he had better go openly for Randall as "a *third* slip on the speakership question" would further retard his progress. The editor of the *Arkansas Gazette* defended Randall in 1878 while ad-

20. Lewis to McKee, December 10, 1875, in McKee Papers; Edward Spencer to Manton Marble, November 5, 1875, in Marble Papers; John Brown Gordon to Samuel L. M. Barlow, June 7, 1876, in Samuel L. M. Barlow Papers, Huntington Library, San Marino, California; *Congressional Record*, 44th Cong., 2nd Sess., Appendix, 260; Beverly Tucker to Samuel J. Randall, November 24, 26, 1876, in Randall Papers. The 44th Congress passed 278 public and 302 private acts and resolutions—a total about half that of the 42nd Congress and about two-thirds that of other Reconstruction congresses.

mitting that "he may be on the wrong side of many of the great questions of the day." A year later, having decided that Randall did not represent even a third of the House Democrats, the editor supported Joseph Blackburn of Kentucky for Speaker. Blackburn made a run for the position in 1879 with some southern support, but he fell far short of unseating Randall.[21]

The Southerners' dislike of Randall reflected the broader sectional split in the party evident in the national campaigns of the 1870s as well as on economic issues. Some "straight-out" southern Democrats roundly blasted their party's timid endorsement of Liberal Republican Horace Greeley in 1872, and most would have preferred a Democratic nominee. Southerners reluctantly swallowed Greeley and concentrated their campaign efforts on combating Republicanism in their section. They probably favored Thomas F. Bayard as the party's standard-bearer in 1876, but they accepted Samuel J. Tilden of New York despite misgivings. His contractionist monetary beliefs and connections with a "reformed" Tammany Hall were less bothersome than his reputation, as one Democratic editor phrased it, for being "a most pitiless foe of the interests of the West and South" on the question of subsidies and an "unscrupulous oppressor of the great struggling industries" in those areas.[22]

21.   Taul Bradford to Andrew Cunningham, December 17, 1876, in Robert Joseph Cunningham Papers, Alabama Department of Archives and History, Montgomery; E. John Ellis to his father, November 20, 1877, E. John Ellis to Thomas C. W. Ellis, October 28, 1877, in Ellis Family Papers, Middleton Library, Louisiana State University, Baton Rouge; John Randolph Tucker to wife, October 14, 19, 1877, Tucker to Henry Saint George Tucker, October 15, 1877, Henry Saint George Tucker to John Randolph Tucker, March 16, 1879, in Tucker Family Papers, Southern Historical Collection, University of North Carolina, Chapel Hill (hereinafter cited as SHC); Little Rock *Arkansas Gazette*, January 26, 1878, March 18, 19, 1879. Randall's committee appointments in the 45th House were only slightly more favorable to the South than those of Kerr. Southerners headed more committees, but their only real gains were the elevation of John H. Reagan of Texas to the chairmanship of Commerce and an additional seat on Ways and Means. They lost a seat on Commerce, and Randall also replaced Ellis as chairman of the levees committee with a less effective freshman from Louisiana—a move for which Ellis never forgave Randall—and southern seats on the committee fell from four to three. *Congressional Record*, 45th Cong., 1st Sess., 197–98; E. John Ellis to his father, November 20, 1877, in Ellis Papers.

22.   Gillette, *Retreat from Reconstruction*, 58–72; *Official Proceedings of the National Democratic Convention Held at Baltimore, July 9, 1872* (Boston: Rockwell and Churchill, 1872), 45–58; Thomas F. Bayard to John W. Daniel, July 8, 1876, in John Warwick Daniel Papers, Perkins Library, Duke University, Durham, N.C.; John Brown Gordon to S. L. M. Barlow, May 31, 1876, in Barlow Papers; *Official Proceed-*

The Southerners nevertheless worked diligently for Tilden. Their only complaint was that the national Democratic leadership seemed immune to their requests for money, northern speakers, or even advice on campaign strategy. As Keith Ian Polakoff has noted, the national campaign committees of both parties acted as though they "would have preferred to feign total ignorance" of the South. Northerners particularly did not want Tilden embarrassed by southern political disorders. Randall thought that northern Democrats should make "assurances to the Southern States that they are to be left undisturbed in all their States rights & privileges—and ask in return a maintenance of perfect order." During the campaign, the Southerners were frequently advised to keep things quiet; Abram S. Hewitt, the party's national chairman, informed Lamar that he wanted "no outbreaks in the South no matter how great the provocation may be, which will tend to impede the steady gain which we are making on the enemy." Beyond this sort of advice, Southerners received little aid—but they perhaps expected little. When the campaign was over they had reason to believe they had insured Tilden's election. He carried only 65 electoral votes outside the ex-slave states, and over half of those came from his home state. The southern and border states, on the other hand, provided a solid bloc of 138 electoral votes although Republicans contested the returns from Louisiana, South Carolina, and Florida.[23]

In the ensuing electoral dispute, Southerners were dismayed when their northern colleagues appeared reluctant to press their party's claims while Hayes's lieutenants actively advanced his interests. Distressed with the prospect of another Republican administration

---

ings of the National Democratic Convention, Held in St. Louis, Mo., June 1876 (Saint Louis: Woodward, Tiernan and Hale, 1876), 89, 144–46; Matthew C. Butler to Matt W. Ransom, June 4, 1876, Matt W. Ransom to Thomas F. Bayard (draft), June 21, 1876, in Matt Ransom Papers, SHC; L. Q. C. Lamar to Thomas F. Bayard, May 1, 1875, in Thomas F. Bayard Papers, LC; Keith Ian Polakoff, *The Politics of Inertia: The Election of 1876 and the End of Reconstruction* (Baton Rouge: Louisiana State University Press, 1973), 77–83; Cincinnati *Enquirer*, June 5, 1876, quoted in C. Vann Woodward, *Reunion and Reaction: The Compromise of 1877 and the End of Reconstruction* (Boston: Little, Brown, 1951), 136.

23. Polakoff, *Politics of Inertia*, 177, 196; Samuel J. Randall to Chauncey F. Black, April 14, 1875, in Randall Papers; Abram S. Hewitt to L. Q. C. Lamar, October 20, 1876, in L. Q. C. Lamar and Edward Mayes Papers, Mississippi Department of Archives and History, Jackson.

and knowing that aggressive opposition to Hayes would have to orig-
inate with northern Democrats, the Southerners protested as Tilden
and his northern managers sat on their hands. Lamar and Bayard met
with the nominee in late December with the hope of receiving some
advice as to their course of action. They left, as Bayard put it, "unin-
formed and uninstructed." John Brown Gordon made a special trip
to New York to warn Tilden that the Democrats "were being robbed
of our victory by our own supineness." "I am a Southern Rebel &
therefore can only say what the people in the South feel," he wrote
heatedly. "There is but one sentiment & that is that Tilden &
Hendricks are fairly, constitutionally elected & ought to be inaugurated." Gordon called for mass Democratic meetings, speeches, resolutions, and use of the press to advance the cause—otherwise "we
only invite aggression from them [the Republicans] & prepare our
own friends for a degrading submission." Another Southerner complained that "the entire democracy of the south feel more than ever
that they are leaning on a bag of mush when they look for aid &
comfort from the north," and toward the end of the dispute, Ellis
wrote his father that "the great New York leader [Tilden] has proven
himself without a place or a policy . . . or brains, or nerve." An Ohio
congressman warned Tilden in December that the sentiment in a recent gathering of "forty or fifty southern members" of Congress
"was to abandon the democracy if there was a failure to maintain
every right in the present contest."[24]

The southern congressmen, of course, did not abandon the Democracy. But as the Northerners' hesitancy to push Tilden's cause
became apparent, and knowing full well the dangers inherent in
their resisting the electoral commission's decisions, Southerners
turned to look after their own interests first. If Hayes was to be the
next president, then they wanted certain reassurances from him, and
some of them conducted a skillful and useful flirtation with his supporters. In the end, the Southerners lost Tilden, through no fault of
their own, but they emerged from the dispute with home rule—
their primary objective since the end of the war. Furthermore, they

24. Polakoff, *Politics of Inertia*, 238, 222, 241–42; John Brown Gordon to Samuel
L. M. Barlow, January 2, 1877, in Barlow Papers; E. John Ellis to Ezekiel P. Ellis, February 25, 1877, in Ellis Papers.

secured a reconciliation-minded president with a new southern policy which posed little threat to their hegemony.[25]

After Hayes was inaugurated, southern conservatives milked his administration for patronage positions and supported him as long as his activity fostered the elimination of southern Republicanism. Arkansas Senator Augustus Hill Garland best expressed the conservative strategy in August, 1877, when he counseled Bayard that even if Hayes "does not do all we want and need," Southerners should "stand by him for that which he does." His actions would add to the "vindication of our principles," Garland declared. "If he tries to do right let us help him." Moderate southern newspapers generally agreed, and the congressmen frequently advised conservative editors to avoid printing anything which might alienate the Hayes administration. "What [is the] use of us trying to conciliate and use these people [northern Republicans] when this ceaseless torrent of abuse flows from our home press?" Ellis asked after a New Orleans newspaper published an attack on Republican Senator Stanley Matthews of Ohio. "Our hope of Spofford & Eustis is in Hays [sic] and Matthews. Our hope of levees & Pacific Roads & Brazilian mail lines is in Hayes. Every consideration of interest dictates that we court and win him. We will do this if the papers will aid us." As long as Hayes tried to do "right" on southern patronage matters, on southern material interests, and in behalf of southern Democrats in electoral contests, they were more than willing to help him.[26]

Hayes's efforts to promote a "new" Republican party in the South proved disastrous in the elections of 1878. Violence, widespread intimidation of black voters, and simple "counting-out" of Republican majorities in some areas created as solidly a Democratic South as the nation had yet seen. Southern delegations to the Forty-sixth

25. Michael Les Benedict, "Southern Democrats in the Crisis of 1876–1877: A Reconsideration of *Reunion and Reaction*," *Journal of Southern History*, XLVI (1980), 489–524. See Chapter VII above.

26. Augustus H. Garland to Thomas F. Bayard, August 3, 1877, in Bayard Papers; E. John Ellis to Thomas C. W. Ellis, November 29, 1877, March 4, 1878, in Ellis Papers; M. P. O'Conner to Francis W. Dawson, April 17, 1879, in Francis Warrington Dawson Papers, Perkins Library, Duke University, Durham, N.C. Henry M. Spofford and James B. Eustis were the Democratic claimants to the Louisiana Senate seats in 1877. Eustis was eventually seated, but Spofford lost out to carpetbagger William Pitt Kellogg.

Congress reflected the region's political temperament. No Republican senators were selected; two continued and as they came up for election, Democrats replaced them. Four Republicans were elected to the House, but only two served full terms. After the election, Hayes caved in to opposition in his party and admitted that his policy had failed.[27] Whether or not it hastened the movement toward a "Solid South" is largely irrelevant. For all practical purposes, northern Republicans had already abandoned their southern colleagues, and it was evident prior to the campaign of 1876 that the conservatives were going to dominate that region sooner or later. There was never any real chance they would split into two parties—that option, if ever viable, had disappeared with the advent of black participation in politics. Hayes's policy may have soothed sectional feelings somewhat, but it roused hostility in his own party and did nothing to stem the tide of redemption.

All of this is not to say that sectional unity had been restored to the Democracy; Southerners continued to complain about their northern brethren. "There are two troubles we suffer from in congress, namely, the impossibility, as a rule, of depending upon a Northern or Western Democrat when the South needs anything done for her, and the better attention given to business by the Republicans than by the Democrats," the editor of the *Southern Planter and Farmer* declared in early 1879. "It appears that the average Republican drinks less whiskey, and keeps closer to his seat than the average Democrat, and so, though in the minority in the House, actually rules it." After reviewing the politics of the 1870s, another Virginian concluded that the South should have avoided affiliation with both national parties after the war and acted with one or the other *pro tempore*. Instead, he lamented, "We are chained to a party organization and made to suffer for its weaknesses and follies. Our alliance with the Democratic party of the North—quite natural under the circumstances—has brought us much evil and continued as party issues much of the exacerbations of the war." Even crusty old Robert

27.   *Senate Reports*, 45th Cong., 3rd Sess., No. 855; William E. Chandler, *Letters of Mr. William Eaton Chandler Relative to the So-called Southern Policy of President Hayes* (Concord, N.H.: Monitor and Statesman Office, 1878); Gillette, *Retreat from Reconstruction*, ch. 14.

Toombs, never one to display much tolerance for Yankees, informed Alexander Stephens at the end of the decade that it was time for Southerners to "reassert principles and cut loose from the Northern Democracy. We have been the servile tools of the knaves and fools, mostly the former, long enough."[28]

The question of whether southern conservatives preferred the economic policies of northeastern or northwestern Democrats—C. Vann Woodward's "right fork-left fork" decision Southerners supposedly faced at the end of the decade—clouds the complex and shifting nature of sectional alignments in Congress. During the 1870s at least, economic alliances varied from issue to issue and none of them approached formality. The idea of a coalition with the Midwest, however, still figured prominently in the rhetoric of most southern Democrats. In an essay written during the silver debate, Alabama Senator John Tyler Morgan, for example, saw the alliance as resulting from the disregard of the "Solid East" for the currency and general economic needs of the agricultural South and West. At the same time, Ellis argued that the South's future lay in a "firm political and commercial alliance" with the West to strike off "the Shackles that the people of *these* sections have so long and so patiently worn in the service of the monopolists and manufacturers and bondholders of the East." For Beverly Tucker, still struggling for the Texas & Pacific in 1878, the objective was the same: "The South & South West must form an alliance offensive & defensive, with the West and North West, to beat down the tyranny of the high protective tariffites, & selfish money hoarding, Democrats—*So-called*—& then we shall have an era of prosperity & success that can never be reached as long as we of the south suffer ourselves to be the lemon, to be squeezed by Sam Tilden, Hewitt, & Co., for another presidential term. And this alliance, should be made an *entente cordiale*, in *fact*, made not for a *term* but for an *epoch*."[29]

---

28. Richmond *Southern Planter and Farmer*, XL (1879), 174; anonymous letter to the editor of the Richmond *Dispatch*, undated clipping (*ca.* 1878), in John Tyler Morgan Papers, LC; Robert Toombs to Alexander H. Stephens, March 10, 1879, in Ulrich B. Phillips (ed.), *The Correspondence of Robert Toombs, Alexander H. Stephens, and Howell Cobb* (Washington, D.C.: Government Printing Office, 1913), 736–37.

29. Woodward, *Reunion and Reaction*, 237–46; Carl V. Harris, "Right Fork or Left Fork? The Section-Party Alignments of Southern Democrats in Congress,

But despite their disagreements with party colleagues from other regions, the Southerners were in the Democracy to stay. At the close of the decade, the editor of a small South Carolina newspaper best stated regional attitudes: "We of the South should not be too hard to satisfy or too prone to find fault with the Northern Democrats. We could not have expected to be the pets of the National government or treasury. Besides, many things we desire and, perhaps, ought to have, it would be impolitic and utterly useless to demand. . . . The Democratic party has higher aims and purposes than to secure appropriations either for any or for all sections." "If we do not admire Northern Democrats personally," he concluded, "we must, nevertheless, admit that we are of the same political household, and if division occurs, the Democratic party will fall."[30]

To southern conservatives at the end of the 1870s, section mattered more than nation; as long as they ruled at home, intersectional party differences could be tolerated. Thanks to their section's acrimonious experience with Republicanism, the Redeemers were able to fashion a solidly Democratic South which would endure well into the twentieth century. Memories of "the horrors of the Reconstruction governments and 'black domination' . . . are in a sense cherished," Gunnar Myrdal noted in 1944. "They serve a vital defensive function to the white South. . . . They are, in fact, symbols of regional allegiance." Furthermore, with like-minded colleagues from the border states, and through the use of the two-thirds rule, the binding party caucus, and the seniority system, the Redeemers came to possess a power in their party and in Congress far out of proportion to their numbers. It was a rather remarkable achievement. Little, in fact, had changed in the southern polity since the late antebellum period.[31]

1873–1897," *Journal of Southern History*, XLII (1976), 471–506; John T. Morgan, "The Political Alliance of the South with the West," *North American Review*, CXXVI (1878), 309–22; E. John Ellis to Thomas C. W. Ellis, October 28, 1877, E. John Ellis to Ezekiel P. Ellis, November 20, 1877, in Ellis Papers; Beverly Tucker to Edmund W. Hubard, April 18, 1878, in Edmund Wilcox Hubard Papers, SHC.

30. Lexington *Dispatch*, October 22, 1880.

31. "The Political Attitude of the South," *Atlantic Monthly* (1880), 817–23; Gunnar Myrdal, *An American Dilemma: The Negro Problem and Modern Democracy* (New York: Harper and Row, 1944), 446; James Tice Moore, "Redeemers Reconsidered: Change and Continuity in the Democratic South, 1870–1900," *Journal of*

Few of the 251 southern congressmen would regret seeing the 1870s pass. The decade proved to be a particularly bitter experience for the Republicans. Abandoned by their northern creators and locked into a situation over which they had little control, the idealists among them quickly discovered the incompatibilities of principle and power. Carpetbaggers, stigmatized from the beginning, were sharply limited in what they could accomplish—regardless of their motivation. Scalawags found themselves seeking an impossible middle ground between their heritage and the proposed new order. The blacks, of course, carried the immense burden of color and all it symbolized to a generation not ready to face the responsibilities of emancipation. Even the Democrats must have been bothered by the frightening human cost of home rule. Paternalistic, well-respected conservatives found themselves sanctioning ostracism, intimidation, and violence while weaving fables of Radical misrule and black domination to justify the extreme means of redemption. By the time the mythmakers completed their work, the enormities of Reconstruction were firmly entrenched in the southern white mind (and favorably received in many northern quarters as well), and the South emerged from the 1870s with a powerful mythology which was as significant in shaping its future as the war itself.

In the interim, the congressmen, who had served their section well under extremely trying circumstances, became something of a lost generation in southern political history. Several of the Redeemers went on to achieve a measure of national recognition, but many simply slipped into obscurity. Almost all of the scalawags remained in the South, a few continued to be active Republicans and accepted patronage positions, but most retired from public life as their tainted record blocked effective participation in politics. Three-quarters of the still youthful carpetbaggers moved on, sometimes involuntarily, to new locations and new pursuits. Some returned north and resumed political activity in their home states; a large number successfully petitioned Republican administrations for patronage positions. Like the scalawags, the blacks stayed in the

Southern History, XLIV (1978), 357–78; David M. Potter, *The South and the Concurrent Majority*, ed. Don E. Fehrenbacher and Carl N. Degler (Baton Rouge: Louisiana State University Press, 1972), especially ch. 2.

South, almost all remained active in the party, and a few were granted minor patronage jobs. They naturally suffered most from redemption; it was their fate to watch disfranchisement and Jim Crow replace the hopes fostered by freedom.

Looking back on his experiences, former senator Adelbert Ames thought that it might be said that southern Republicans "were out of place or had mistaken ideas of their duty," but he wondered "exactly what they should have done—what unquestionably honest men would have done under the circumstances." "The days are many before Christ's Sermon on the Mount will be our practical religion," he wrote historian Dunbar Rowland in 1929. "Mississippi like other states has a weary task before it." Ames, who died in 1933 at the age of ninety-seven, may have had a certain satisfaction in outliving all but two of the congressmen, but it was perhaps fitting that the last survivor of the 251 was his fellow Mississippian, ex-slave John Roy Lynch. Lynch remained active in the Republican party and spent much of the rest of his life attempting to explain what had actually happened during Reconstruction to a generation which had already dismissed it as a blemish on the nation's history. As James K. Vardaman, the "White Chief," spread an even more virulent racism through Mississippi and southern Democrats returned to congressional power with Woodrow Wilson, Lynch left the South for Chicago where he practiced law until his death in November, 1939.[32] A war which was to alter southern society had already begun, and, too late for Lynch, the civil rights revolution—the "second reconstruction"—lay on the horizon.

32.   Adelbert Ames to M. E. Benjamin Andrews, May 24, 1895 (draft), Ames to Dunbar Rowland, March 20, 1929, in Adelbert Ames Papers, Mississippi Department of Archives and History, Jackson; John R. Lynch, The Facts of Reconstruction (New York: Neale Publishing, 1913); Lynch, Reminiscences of an Active Life: The Autobiography of John Roy Lynch, ed. John Hope Franklin (Chicago: University of Chicago Press, 1970); Lynch to the editor, Journal of Negro History, XVI (1931), 103–20.

Bibliographical Essay

In the name of brevity, I have limited the documentation provided in the notes to those primary and secondary sources which I believe to be essential and representative. Similarly, in this essay I have commented only on those sources which proved most pertinent to the congressmen, economic measures, and intersectional relationships during the period. For a complete listing of the sources used in the initial version of this study, see my "Southern Representatives and Economic Measures During Reconstruction: A Quantitative and Analytical Study" (Ph.D. dissertation, Louisiana State University, 1974), 301–26. Readers wishing to sample the wealth of literature on the postwar period should consult the comprehensive annotated bibliography in J. G. Randall and David Donald, *The Civil War and Reconstruction* (2nd ed. rev.; Lexington, Mass.: D. C. Heath, 1969), 703–834; Charles B. Dew's extensive "Critical Essay on New Works" in C. Vann Woodward, *Origins of the New South, 1877–1913* (Enlarged edition; Baton Rouge: Louisiana State University Press, 1971); and the commentary on more recent work in James M. McPherson, *Ordeal by Fire: The Civil War and Reconstruction* (New York: Alfred A. Knopf, 1982), especially 686–94.

Manuscripts relating to the southern congressmen, particularly the Republicans, are disappointingly few, and those that have survived are widely scattered. I examined over 160 collections and have cited 80 in the notes, but a good many of these yielded but few pertinent items. Among those collections held by the Manuscript Division, Library of Congress, the richest in correspondence to and from southern congressmen are those of Thomas F. Bayard, Benjamin F. Butler, William E. Chandler, Henry L. Dawes, Andrew Johnson, Manton

Marble, John Sherman, and Elihu B. Washburne, but only the Butler Papers and Chandler Papers contain many letters from southern Republicans after 1870. The voluminous and neglected Amnesty Papers (Records of the Office of the Adjutant General, Record Group 94, National Archives) are a key source of biographical data on the more prominent conservatives and scalawags and offer an important indication of their attitudes in the immediate postwar period.

The Thomas Settle Papers and the Henry Clay Warmoth Papers (both in the Southern Historical Collection, University of North Carolina, Chapel Hill) are exceptional sources on Republican factionalism in North Carolina and Louisiana, and both contain a significant amount of correspondence from the congressmen. Only slightly less important in this regard are the James Pearson Newcomb, Sr., Papers (Barker Texas History Center, University of Texas, Austin), the Charles William Dustan Papers (Alabama Department of Archives and History, Montgomery), the Adelbert Ames Papers and Governor's Letterbooks (Mississippi Department of Archives and History, Jackson), and the Charles Sumner Papers (Houghton Library, Harvard University, Cambridge). The Grenville M. Dodge Papers (Iowa State Historical Department, Des Moines) are not only notable for his correspondence regarding the Texas & Pacific Railroad, but also for incoming letters from several carpetbagger congressmen. Several important letters from southern Republicans early in the period can be found in the William and Mary B. Claflin Collection, and the Rutherford B. Hayes Papers and associated collections contain a wealth of correspondence from a variety of sources (both in the Rutherford B. Hayes Presidential Center, Fremont, Ohio). The running commentary on the southern Republican problems in the Amos Tappan Akerman Letterbooks (Alderman Library, University of Virginia, Charlottesville) is particularly perceptive.

Primary materials on the southern Democratic congressmen are somewhat more abundant. The Matt W. Ransom Papers, Edmund Wilcox Hubard Papers, and Tucker Family Papers (all in the Southern Historical Collection, University of North Carolina, Chapel Hill) are particularly valuable, and all three contain a considerable amount of constituent correspondence on southern economic conditions and such topics as the tobacco tax. For Texas congressmen and commentary on the Texas & Pacific Railroad, see the correspondence and newspaper clippings in the Benjamin Holland Epperson, James Webb Throckmorton, and John H. Reagan papers (Barker Texas History Center, University of Texas, Austin). Equally useful for political questions are the L. Q. C. Lamar and Edward Mayes Papers (Mississippi Department of Archives and History, Jackson), the Samuel A'Court Ashe Papers (North Carolina State Archives, Raleigh), the John Warfield Johnston Papers and the McMullen Family Papers (both in Perkins Library, Duke University, Durham, N.C.), and the Ellis Family Papers (Middleton Library, Louisiana State University, Baton Rouge). The latter collection is especially important for detailing Ellis' involvement with the levees issue and his blunt and often cynical commentary on national politics.

Meriting special notice are the Robert McKee Papers (Alabama Department of Archives and History, Montgomery). In addition to being the focal point of opposition to the Texas & Pacific, McKee, publisher of the Selma *Southern Argus* and political wheelhorse of the Redeemer Democrats, also had considerable correspondence with congressmen from Alabama and nearby states, and his papers are filled with letters in response to his editorials on economic as well as political matters. Of the various collections outside the South and the Library of Congress, the Samuel J. Randall Papers (Van Pelt Library, University of Pennsylvania, Philadelphia), and the Samuel Latham Mitchell Barlow Papers (Henry E. Huntington Library, San Marino, California) are most noteworthy. The latter is particularly valuable for Democratic party matters, the Texas & Pacific Railroad, and Barlow's correspondence with several Southerners including John Brown Gordon of Georgia.

Newspapers and periodicals were examined primarily for information on the congressmen and their campaigns, southern economic interests, and their reaction to economic measures. Some were clearly more useful than others for my purposes. I have tried to select a cross section of southern newspapers on the basis of influence, area, and political leaning. Unfortunately, very few complete files of Republican newspapers have survived. I have read the available runs in the period from 1865 to 1880 of several newspapers including, most important, the Atlanta *Constitution*, Richmond *Whig*, Selma *Southern Argus*, Austin *Democratic Statesman*, Washington *New National Era*, Little Rock *Arkansas Gazette*, and the New Orleans *Republican, Picayune,* and *Louisianian.* Repetition, diminishing returns, and the distortion stemming from extreme partisanship led to a more selective examination of other southern newspapers—many of which had only short runs or scattered surviving issues. I have examined these newspapers when critical campaigns or controversies were occurring in their area and when important economic issues were being debated in Congress. Most valuable among the special interest publications were the Richmond *Southern Planter and Farmer*, the New Orleans *Price Current, Commercial Intelligencer and Merchants' Transcript,* and *De Bow's Review*, which unfortunately ceased publication in 1870. Few of the other agrarian journals commented on matters of political economy, and such northern publications as the *Commercial and Financial Chronicle* (New York), *Bankers' Magazine* (New York), and the *Railroad Gazette* (Chicago) rarely contained material regarding the South not found in the congressional debates or other government publications. I have used newspapers and periodicals published outside the South such as the *Nation*, the New York *Times*, and the Chicago *Tribune* principally for northern opinion on southern economic interests and the section's congressmen.

I have placed heavy reliance on government documents for this study. Needless to say, I spent more time than I care to recall during the past decade tracing economic bills through the voluminous debates in the *Congressional Globe* (1868–1873) and the *Congressional Record* (1873–1879), but it was time profitably spent. The debates are required reading for economic and political concerns and critical for understanding the intersectional relationships in the two national parties as well as Congress. Important for economic matters are the *Annual Reports of the Secretary of the Treasury* . . . (Washington, D.C.: Government Printing Office, 1865–1879), which contain summary reports from the commissioner of internal revenue and the comptroller of the currency. Other useful compilations include A. T. Huntington and Robert J. Mawhinney (comps.), *Laws*

*of the United States Concerning Money, Banking, and Loans, 1778–
1909* (Washington, D.C.: Government Printing Office, 1910); Robert
G. Proctor (comp.), *Tariff Acts Passed by the Congress of the United
States from 1789–1897 . . .* (Washington, D.C.: Government Printing Office, 1898); and the comparative tables on tariff rates in *Senate
Reports,* 49th Cong., 1st Sess., No. 12. Presidential sentiment on
economic and other matters is conveniently available in James D.
Richardson (comp.), *A Compilation of the Messages and Papers of
the Presidents, 1789–1897* (10 vols.; Washington, D.C.: Government Printing Office, 1897), and the population figures and statistics
on wealth and production were compiled from county-level statistics in Francis A. Walker (comp.), *Ninth Census of the United States*
(3 vols.; Washington, D.C.: Government Printing Office, 1872). The
problem of underenumeration in the 1870 census is discussed in
Robert P. Porter (comp.), *Compendium of the Eleventh Census:
1890. Part I: Population* (Washington, D.C.: Government Printing
Office, 1892), 35–43.

Because a good many of the southern congressmen either testified
or were the subject of testimony, the most useful of the extensive
literature on congressional investigations of the South is the *Report
of the Joint Select Committee to Inquire into the Condition of Affairs in the Late Insurrectionary States* (13 vols.; Washington, D.C.:
Government Printing Office, 1872). The testimony on disputed elections is digested in four compilations of contested elections in
House Miscellaneous Documents, 41st Cong., 2nd Sess., No. 152,
45th Cong., 2nd Sess., No. 52, 47th Cong., 1st Sess., No. 57, and *Senate Miscellaneous Documents,* 49th Cong., 1st Sess., No. 4; but one
is well advised to look at the original House and Senate *Reports* and
Documents on the individual cases.

Several printed collections of primary source material proved especially useful. Blanche Butler Ames (comp.), *Chronicles from the
Nineteenth Century: Family Letters of Blanche Butler and Adelbert
Ames, Married July 21st, 1870* (2 vols.; Clinton, Mass.: Colonial
Press, 1957), offers a rare glimpse into the motivation and mind of a
prominent carpetbagger. At the other end of the political spectrum,
conservative attitudes are well revealed in Ulrich Bonnell Phillips

(ed.), *The Correspondence of Robert Toombs, Alexander H. Stephens, and Howell Cobb* (Washington, D.C.: Government Printing Office, 1913). The most useful and best-edited diaries are Harry James Brown and Frederick D. Williams (eds.), *The Diary of James A. Garfield* (3 vols.; East Lansing: Michigan State University Press, 1967–1973); and T. Harry Williams (ed.), *Hayes: The Diary of a President, 1875–1881* (New York: David McKay, 1964). John Roy Lynch's *Reminiscences of an Active Life: The Autobiography of John Roy Lynch*, ed. John Hope Franklin (Chicago: University of Chicago Press, 1970), is among the least self-serving of the extensive autobiographical literature of the period—most of it produced by southern Democrats and northern Republicans. Of these accounts, only John Sherman's *Recollections of Forty Years in the House, Senate and Cabinet: An Autobiography* (Chicago: Werner Co., 1895), gives much attention to economic issues.

The Senate and House roll call records used in this study were collected and made available in machine-readable form by the Inter-University Consortium for Political and Social Research (ICPSR) at the University of Michigan, Ann Arbor. The data were supplied in partially proofed form, and the ICPSR bears no responsibility for either the analysis or the interpretations presented here. In a few cases, the party affiliation for southern congressmen has been corrected. With the exception of a few Independents in the Forty-fourth and Forty-fifth Houses, members serving under political labels other than Democrat or Republican have been recoded as members of the party with which they caucused.

The ICPSR's OSIRIS III package of computer programs was used to construct the scalograms. The content description of each roll call in the ICPSR data set and the *Congressional Globe* and *Congressional Record* were examined, and all roll calls relating to economic issues in each chamber were listed to form a "preliminary universe of content." This universe was then reordered by subsets relating to specific economic issues and subjected to a program to compute Yule's Q correlation coefficient for each pair of roll calls in each subset. Yule's Q (which ranges from -1 to $+1$) is the generally accepted measure of the scalability of a pair of roll calls; a high value $(+ \text{ or } -)$

of Q between a pair of roll calls indicates that they scale—that is, few (if any) members will be found who reject an easier-to-support item and then accept a harder-to-support item. Every roll call in a given subset was required to have a Q value of about ±.7 with every other measure in that subset to be considered scalable, and the mean Q for most scales exceeded .85. The matrix of Q coefficients for the universe was then examined both manually and with the computer to produce clusters of scalable votes within each subset and the universe. A "positive" position (*e.g.*, favorable to currency expansion, tariff and tax reduction) was chosen for each cluster. Roll calls with Q values opposite that of the positive position were "reflected"—the yeas and nays reversed—to produce the correct response category indicating the desired positive position.

Each cluster of roll calls was then subjected to a scaling program which ordered the items in a rank from largest passing set to smallest passing set and assigned a scale position to each member. Nearly unanimous roll calls were discarded unless they added a significant indication of attitudes at either end of the scale. In most cases, I have consciously limited the number of items in each scale position to those which best exemplify the attitudes of members at that position. Members who were absent or not seated for more than 30 percent of the votes in a scale were excluded, and almost all members in the "Not Scaling" category are there because of excessive absences rather than because of inconsistent voting behavior. Those with more than one inconsistent vote (*e.g.*, voting for a harder-to-accept proposition after rejecting an easier-to-accept proposition) were usually excluded except when the scale size would legitimately accommodate more than one inconsistent vote (referred to as an "error"). When a member had an acceptable number of errors or absences, his scale position was determined by choosing the median score out of his possible scores. Because the scales were designed to be highly unidimensional, errors were relatively rare, and unless an error-producing measure added significant content to the scale, it was simply removed and the scale reconstructed. A customary measure of the adequacy of each scale is its coefficient of reproducibility, which measures the percentage of responses on scale items that could be predicted accurately from a member's position on the scale.

Scales with a coefficient of reproducibility above .9 are generally considered to be satisfactory.

The format used to present the scale results has been adapted from Thomas B. Alexander, *Sectional Stress and Party Strength: A Study of Roll-Call Voting Patterns in the United States House of Representatives, 1836–1860* (Nashville: Vanderbilt University Press, 1967); and John Kent Folmar, "The Depletion of Republican Congressional Support for Enforcement of Reconstruction Measures: A Roll-Call Analysis, 1871–1877" (Ph.D. dissertation, University of Alabama, 1968). The "Scalogram Items" give a brief description of the items in each scale position, the vote, the positive position, and the citation to the *Congressional Globe* or *Congressional Record*. The vote given in the description is the actual number of yeas and nays, but I have included *paired* and *announced* votes as well as those actually cast in my analysis. In a pair, a member who knew he was going to be absent for a series of votes on a particular question (but still wished to make his opinion known) frequently arranged with a member on the opposite side of the issue to "pair" and withhold their votes on that question. As the roll call was taken, the present paired member would announce the pair and indicate how each would have voted. In the more rare announced vote, a colleague of an absent member would simply announce the way in which the absent member would have voted had he been present. The ICPSR roll call records include special categories for "paired or announced yes" and "paired or announced no." Neither practice was extensive, and, of course, such votes are not considered in the final tally, but in order to get the fullest possible response to a particular question, I believe it advisable to count paired and announced votes, and I have done so in both the scale analysis and the cross tabulations of single votes.

Occasionally the alignment on a large number of roll calls on a particular issue was so rigidly dichotomous that scaling procedures revealed few if any interim positions. Similarly, scaling is a less useful form of analysis on issues such as the tariff because of conflicting and often contradictory local interests, and scale analysis, of course, is of no value on measures such as refunding of the cotton tax which did not generate an adequate number of roll call divisions. In these cases, the voting alignment is better revealed by some measure of bloc cohesion or interbloc agreement, or more simply by a carefully selected key vote. For the purposes of this study, I have occasionally chosen the latter to illustrate the nature of roll call divisions that are not receptive to scale analysis.

For a discussion of scaling methods and examples of their application in addition to the Alexander and Folmar studies cited above, see Duncan MacRae, Jr., *Dimensions of Congressional Voting: A Statistical Study of the House of Representatives in the Eighty-first Congress* (Berkeley and Los Angeles: University of California Press, 1958), especially 218–23; Joel H. Silbey, *The Shrine of Party: Congressional Voting Behavior, 1841–1852* (Pittsburgh: University of Pittsburgh Press, 1967), 14–17; and John Lockhart McCarthy, "Reconstruction Legislation and Voting Alignments in the House of Representatives, 1863–1869" (Ph.D. dissertation, Yale University, 1970). Useful guides to the application of scaling include Lee F. Anderson, Meredith W. Watts, Jr., and Allen R. Wilcox, *Legislative Roll-Call Analysis* (Evanston: Northwestern University Press, 1966), ch. 6; and Charles M. Dollar and Richard J. Jensen, *Historian's Guide to Statistics: Quantitative Analysis and Historical Research* (New York: Holt, Rinehart and Winston, 1971), especially 116–21.

The notes give only a general indication of the variety of primary and secondary sources used to compile biographical data on the 251 congressmen. The most basic secondary source is Lawrence F. Kennedy (comp.), *Biographical Directory of the American Congress, 1774–1971* (Washington, D.C.: Government Printing Office, 1971). Only 52 of the men merited inclusion in Allen Johnson and Dumas Malone (eds.), *Dictionary of American Biography* (22 vols.; New York: Charles Scribner's Sons, 1928–1958), and surprisingly few (38 percent) appeared in the less selective multivolume *National Cyclopaedia of American Biography* (New York: James T. White and Co., 1892–). Other contemporary compilations such as James Grant Wilson and John Fiske (eds.), *Appleton's Cyclopaedia of American Biography* (7 vols.; New York: D. Appleton and Co., 1888–1900), were also consulted, but only rarely did their coverage of relevant background information exceed that in the *Biographical Directory*.

More valuable were the contemporary editions of Benjamin P. Poore (comp.), *Congressional Directory* . . . (Washington, D.C.: Government Printing Office, 1868–1878), for each session of each Congress, and the volumes in William Horatio Barnes, *History of Congress* . . . (New York: W. H. Barnes and Co., 1869–1876), which contain biographical sketches of each senator and representative in each Congress.

Other useful sources included the numerous state and regional biographical directories, state and local histories, a handful of autobiographies and memoirs, newspapers, and the data in subject files such as those at the Barker Texas History Center, University of Texas, Austin, the Mississippi Department of Archives and History, Jackson, and the Alabama Department of Archives and History, Montgomery. For those formerly prominent in Confederate leadership or worth more than twenty thousand dollars in 1860, the Amnesty Papers proved to be especially revealing. The manuscript schedules of free population and slave population of the Eighth Census (1860), the population and agricultural schedules of the Ninth Census (1870), and the population and agricultural schedules of the Tenth Census (1880) for the ten states were used on National Archives microfilm. The voluminous schedules contain vital data on family members, size of household, age, occupation, state of birth, and the valuation of real and personal estate. The statistics on margin of victory for representatives were compiled from the county-level election returns for the ten southern states, 1868–1878, which were collected and made available in machine-readable form by the ICPSR.

The quantifiable biographical information, election-return data, and census statistics on each congressional district were coded in machine-readable form for the purposes of constructing biographical profiles of the delegations and for correlation with roll call records. The quantifiable data collected for each congressman included birth state, age (at the beginning of each term served), ethnicity, level of education, Civil War military service and rank, occupation, former slaveholding status, value of real and personal estate (1870), length of residency, congressional district, party affiliation prior to 1860, secession stand, vote for president in 1860, southern party faction, congressional party, prior political experience, margin of victory (each election), contested election status, and number of terms served. The statistics compiled for each congressional district included racial composition (expressed as percent white), per capita wealth, percent agricultural, and land value per acre.

The raw data were coded in accordance with schemes utilizing either dichotomous (two-valued) or geometric-progression codes. Wherever possible, the standardized codes (*e.g.*, for ethnicity) created by the ICPSR were utilized. To help preserve the original range and richness of the data, multidigit codes were used for certain statistical procedures. For example, multidigit codes for age and occupation were used to calculate univariate frequencies and percentages. To facilitate the use of programs for bivariate analysis the multidigit codes were collapsed to single-digit codes. After punching the data on IBM cards (one card for each congressman in each Congress), the accumulated files were subjected to programs to calculate the frequency distributions for each code and case and related statistics and to create cross tabulations classifying selected variables in terms of every other variable. The biographical data were also merged with roll call records to examine the correlations between biographical variables and specific roll call votes or scale positions.

For a discussion of the methods and applications of collective biography, see Richard E. Beringer, *Historical Analysis: Contemporary Approaches to Clio's Craft* (New York: Wiley, 1978), ch. 13; and Richard Jensen, "Quantitative Collective Biography: An Application to Metropolitan Elites," in Robert P. Swierenga (ed.), *Quantification in American History: Theory and Research* (New York: Atheneum, 1970), 389–405. For the codebook used for biographical and constituent data, see Seip, "Southern Representatives and Economic Measures During Reconstruction," 327–34.

A good many valuable studies have appeared since David Donald's 1969 updating of his comprehensive bibliography of the secondary literature in Randall and Donald, *Civil War and Reconstruction*. For my purposes, Michael Les Benedict's thoroughgoing *A Compromise of Principle: Congressional Republicans and Reconstruction, 1863–1869* (New York: W. W. Norton, 1974), has been the most useful of the recent additions to the already extensive literature on the North and the politics of reconstruction through congressional passage of the Fifteenth Amendment in 1869. Of particular value are several fine studies of the South during this period. The reaction of the traditional southern leadership to the postwar political and racial situation has finally been accorded long-deserved treatment in Michael Perman's *Reunion Without Compromise: The South and Reconstruction, 1865–1868* (Cambridge: Cambridge University Press, 1973); and the early chapters of George C. Rable's "But There Was No Peace: Violence and Reconstruction Politics" (Ph.D. dissertation, Louisiana State University, 1978). The final chapters of James L. Roark's *Masters Without Slaves: Southern Planters in the Civil War and Reconstruction* (New York: W. W. Norton, 1977), are particularly excellent for cataloging the postwar economic situation from the planters' perspectives, and Lawrence N. Powell brings a wealth of primary material, much of it previously unworked, to bear in his *New Masters: Northern Planters During the Civil War and Reconstruction* (New Haven: Yale University Press, 1980). Finally, Leon F. Litwack's prizewinning *Been in the Storm So Long: The Aftermath of Slavery* (New York: Alfred A. Knopf, 1979) is an illuminating and poignant study of the black experience from emancipation to enfranchisement.

A balanced and comprehensive survey of the South from the end of the war through redemption would be most welcome; the last such effort, E. Merton Coulter's *The South During Reconstruction, 1865–1877* (Baton Rouge: Louisiana State University Press, 1947), is badly outdated and unsatisfactory in tone and coverage. The historian undertaking that task would have the benefit, as I have had, of drawing on a remarkable body of state and local literature which has mushroomed over the past two decades. My discussion of strife within the southern wing of the Republican party and more generally the political milieu from which the congressmen emerged relies heavily on these studies. To list them all would serve little purpose, but mention should be made of those I found most useful. Especially noteworthy are several fine comprehensive state studies including Joe Gray Taylor, *Louisiana Reconstructed, 1863–1877* (Baton Rouge: Louisiana State University Press, 1974); William C. Harris,

Presidential Reconstruction in Mississippi (Baton Rouge: Louisiana State University Press, 1967); William C. Harris, *The Day of the Carpetbagger: Republican Reconstruction in Mississippi* (Baton Rouge: Louisiana State University Press, 1979); and Jerrell H. Shofner, *Nor Is It Over Yet: Florida in the Era of Reconstruction, 1863–1877* (Gainesville: University Presses of Florida, 1974). For South Carolina, one turns to three standard-setting studies: Francis Butler Simkins and Robert H. Woody, *South Carolina During Reconstruction* (Chapel Hill: University of North Carolina Press, 1932), one of the early revisionist works; Joel Williamson's *After Slavery: The Negro in South Carolina During Reconstruction, 1861–1877* (Chapel Hill: University of North Carolina Press, 1965), a sensitive and thorough treatment; and Thomas Holt's *Black over White: Negro Political Leadership in South Carolina During Reconstruction* (Urbana: University of Illinois Press, 1977), which skillfully unravels the complex and shifting factionalism within the Republican party.

For my purposes, Jack P. Maddex, Jr., *The Virginia Conservatives, 1867–1879: A Study in Reconstruction Politics* (Chapel Hill: University of North Carolina Press, 1970), Elizabeth Studley Nathans, *Losing the Peace: Georgia Republicans and Reconstruction, 1865–1871* (Baton Rouge: Louisiana State University Press, 1968), Sarah Woolfolk Wiggins, *The Scalawag in Alabama Politics, 1865–1881* (University, Ala.: University of Alabama Press, 1977), Martha Ann Ellenburg, "Reconstruction in Arkansas" (Ph.D. dissertation, University of Missouri, 1967), George H. Thompson, *Arkansas and Reconstruction: The Influence of Geography, Economics, and Personality* (Port Washington, N.Y.: Kennikat Press, 1976), Carl H. Moneyhon, *Republicanism in Reconstruction Texas* (Austin: University of Texas Press, 1979), and John Pressley Carrier, "A Political History of Texas During the Reconstruction" (Ph.D. dissertation, Vanderbilt University, 1971) proved to be the most useful of the monographs on those states, but thoroughgoing surveys in the mold of those by Taylor, Harris, and Shofner are particularly needed for Virginia and Alabama. Similarly, there are a number of fine monographs on North Carolina including James Lawrence Lancaster, "The Scalawags of North Carolina, 1850–1868" (Ph.D. dissertation,

Princeton University, 1974), Edward McGee Hobson, "North Carolina Conservatives and Reconstruction" (Ph.D. dissertation, University of North Carolina, 1972), Catherine Silverman, "'Of Wealth,
Virtue, and Intelligence': The Redeemers and Their Triumph in Virginia and North Carolina" (Ph.D. dissertation, City University of
New York, 1971), and especially W. McKee Evans, *Ballots and Fence
Rails: Reconstruction on the Lower Cape Fear* (Chapel Hill: University of North Carolina Press, 1966), but a comprehensive treatment
building on these studies would be especially welcome. It should be
noted, however, that few of these state studies have much to say
about the southern congressmen—except in situations where their
handling of the federal patronage created problems at the state level.

Of the other recent southern studies, Allen W. Trelease, *White
Terror: The Ku Klux Klan Conspiracy and Southern Reconstruction*
(New York: Harper and Row, 1971), and Rable, "But There Was No
Peace," are essential for understanding the political violence of the
period; Richard L. Hume, "The 'Black and Tan' Constitutional Conventions of 1867–1869 in Ten Former Confederate States: A Study
of Their Membership" (Ph.D. dissertation, University of Washington, 1969), provides a valuable assessment of the personnel and activity of the early Republican party; the essays in Otto H. Olsen
(ed.), *Reconstruction and Redemption in the South* (Baton Rouge:
Louisiana State University Press, 1980), lay bare internal factors
in the failure of reconstruction; and Carl N. Degler pulls together
much of the recent work on scalawags in *The Other South: Southern
Dissenters in the Nineteenth Century* (New York: Harper and Row,
1974). A similar study is needed for the more elusive carpetbaggers.
Finally, an important and neglected revisionist article by Jack B.
Scroggs, "Southern Reconstruction: A Radical View," *Journal of
Southern History*, XXIV (1958), 407–29, first raised in my mind the
nature and gravity of intersectional difficulties within Republican
ranks, and Otto H. Olsen's exceptional essay on why southern Republicanism failed, "Southern Reconstruction and the Question of
Self-Determination," in George M. Frederickson (ed.), *A Nation Divided: Problems and Issues of the Civil War and Reconstruction*
(Minneapolis: Burgess Publishing Co., 1975), 113–41, has been instrumental in shaping my own thought on the subject.

Several of the southern congressmen have been the subject of full biographies. The more notable of those on Democrats include James B. Murphy, *L. Q. C. Lamar: Pragmatic Patriot* (Baton Rouge: Louisiana State University Press, 1973), Hugh B. Hammett, *Hilary Abner Herbert: A Southerner Returns to the Union* (Philadelphia: American Philosophical Society, 1976), Ben H. Procter, *Not Without Honor: The Life of John Henninger Reagan* (Austin: University of Texas Press, 1962), and Louise Horton, *Samuel Bell Maxey: A Biography* (Austin: University of Texas Press, 1974). Democrats meriting new biographies with more attention to their postwar political careers are John Brown Gordon, Benjamin H. Hill, Alexander H. Stephens, and James Webb Throckmorton. With the notable exception of Lillian A. Pereyra's *James Lusk Alcorn: Persistent Whig* (Baton Rouge: Louisiana State University Press, 1966), little work has been done on individual scalawag congressmen. The carpetbaggers have also been neglected—largely because of paucity of source material, yet this has hardly deterred the biographers of black congressmen. Within the last decade, four of the sixteen black congressmen have been the subjects of brief but scholarly biographies: Okon Edet Uya, *From Slavery to Public Service: Robert Smalls, 1839–1915* (New York: Oxford University Press, 1971); Peggy Lamson, *The Glorious Failure: Black Congressman Robert Brown Elliott and the Reconstruction in South Carolina* (New York: W. W. Norton, 1973); Peter D. Klingman, *Josiah Walls: Florida's Black Congressman of Reconstruction* (Gainesville: University Presses of Florida, 1976); and Loren Schweninger, *James T. Rapier and Reconstruction* (Chicago: University of Chicago Press, 1978). Although several solid articles, theses, and dissertations have been completed on others among the Republican congressmen, those deserving full scholarly biographies include John Roy Lynch, Blanche K. Bruce, William Pitt Kellogg, George E. Spencer, Willard Warner, Adelbert Ames, Stephen Dorsey, and Charles Hays.

Richard N. Current's call for work on the carpetbagger congressmen in "Carpetbaggers Reconsidered," in David H. Pinkney and Theodore Ropp (eds.), *A Festschrift for Frederick B. Artz* (Durham: Duke University Press, 1964), 139–57, was at least partially answered a decade later by three dissertations: my "Southern Representatives and Economic Measures During Reconstruction"; Janice Carol Hood, "Brotherly Hate: A Quantitative Study of Southern Reconstruction Congressmen, 1867–1877" (Ph.D. dissertation, Washington State University, 1974); and Philip Joseph Avillo, Jr., "Slave State Republicans in Congress, 1861–1877" (Ph.D. dissertation, University of Arizona, 1975). Avillo concentrates on the reactions and attitudes of Republicans from fifteen states toward the issues of political reconstruction. Hood uses collective biography and a limited examination of roll call responses to examine the congressmen from nine ex-Confederate states (Virginia and Tennessee are excluded) up to the time of redemption in each state. This yields a basic group of 150 men—53 carpetbaggers, 43 scalawags, 14 blacks, and 40 Democrats. Our findings are frequently similar, although differences in group size (my population is 60 carpetbaggers, 53 scalawags, 16 blacks, and 122 Democrats) make comparisons difficult, and we arrive at basically different conclusions regarding their reaction to economic measures. In his "Scalawags, Carpetbaggers, and Reconstruction: A Quantitative Look at Southern Congressional Politics, 1868–1872," *Journal of Southern History*, XLV (1979), 63–76, the only other recent piece dealing directly with the congressmen and one which does not draw on the three dissertations mentioned above, Peter Kolchin tentatively suggests that the appearance of scalawags in the delegations to the House was a sign of weakness in the party in their home states. Less analytical but still useful are a variety of collective profiles of the black congressmen ranging from Alrutheus A. Taylor's "Negro Congressmen: A Generation After," *Journal of Negro History*, VII (1922), 127–71, to Maurine Cristopher's *America's Black Congressmen* (New York: Thomas Y. Crowell, 1971). Outdated but of historiographical interest are C. Mildred Thompson, "Carpet-baggers in the United States Senate," in *Studies in Southern History and Politics Inscribed to William Archibald Dunning* (New York: Columbia University Press, 1914), and Samuel Denny Smith, *The Negro in Congress, 1870–1901* (Chapel Hill: University of North Carolina Press, 1940)—one of the last Dunning-inspired monographs.

The reaction of southern and other congressmen to reconstruction issues and the phenomenon of waning northern support is amply detailed in Folmar, "The Depletion of Republican Congressional Support for Enforcement of Reconstruction Measures," Avillo, "Slave State Republicans in Congress," Hood, "Southern Reconstruction Congressmen," the final chapters of Benedict, *Compromise of Principle*, the last chapters of Hans L. Trefousse, *The Radical Republicans: Lincoln's Vanguard for Racial Justice* (New York: Alfred A. Knopf, 1968), and especially in William Gillette's exceptional *Retreat from Reconstruction, 1869–1879* (Baton Rouge: Louisiana State University Press, 1979).

With a few notable exceptions such as Mark Wahlgren Summers, "Radical Reconstruction and the Gospel of Prosperity: Railroad Aid Under the Southern Republicans" (Ph.D. dissertation, University of California, Berkeley, 1980), southern interests in and reaction to economic issues during the 1870s have been neglected. Glenn M. Linden's "'Radicals' and Economic Policies: The Senate, 1861–1873," *Journal of Southern History*, XXXII (1966), 189–99, and his "Radicals and Economic Policies: The House of Representatives, 1861–1873," *Civil War History*, XIII (1967), 51–65, give little attention to Southerners although in his "'Radical' Political and Economic Policies: The Senate, 1873–1877," *Civil War History*, XIV (1968), 240–49, he correctly suggests that voting behavior on economic issues is better explained by geographical region than by party. More sophisticated in methodology are Benedict's *Compromise of Principle* and Folmar's "The Depletion of Republican Congressional Support for Enforcement of Reconstruction Measures." Both focus on political reconstruction and neither has much to say about the South, but Benedict includes some scale analysis on currency questions in the Fortieth and Forty-first Congresses, and Folmar constructs several general economic scalograms for comparison with scalograms on political questions in the Forty-second, Forty-third, and Forty-fourth Houses. Hood, "Southern Reconstruction Congressmen," and Avillo, "Slave State Republicans in Congress," have chapters on the reaction of their specific groups of southern congressmen to selected economic issues, but their coverage is necessarily limited. Neither uses southern newspapers, manuscript collections, or computer analysis of the roll call records. In a class by itself and offering much support for my own findings is Carl V. Harris' concise "Right Fork or Left Fork? The Section-Party Alignments of Southern Democrats in Congress, 1873–1897," *Journal of Southern History*, XLII (1976), 471–506, a telling critique of C. Vann Woodward's interpretation of the economic attitudes of the Redeemers in the ex-Confederate states plus Maryland, West Virginia, and Kentucky.

On the pivotal money questions, only George LaVerne Anderson, "The National Banking System, 1865–1875: A Sectional Institution" (Ph.D. dissertation, University of Illinois, 1933), and Allen Weinstein, *Prelude to Populism: Origins of the Silver Issue, 1867–1878* (New Haven: Yale University Press, 1970), are notable for their consideration of southern interests and the activity of Southerners in Congress. Walter T. K. Nugent's *Money and American Society, 1865–1880* (New York: Free Press, 1968), gives but cursory attention to the South; Robert P. Sharkey's *Money, Class, and Party: An Economic Study of Civil War and Reconstruction* (Baltimore: Johns Hopkins Press, 1959) concludes in 1869 on the eve of full readmission of the ex-Confederate states; and Irwin Unger's *The Greenback Era: A Social and Political History of American Finance, 1865–1879* (Princeton: Princeton University Press, 1964) focuses on the evolution and elements of northern financial thought while inexplicably overlooking the South. All three are otherwise essential for understanding the intricacies of the postwar battles over money.

Much work remains to be done on the postwar southern economy. We know considerably less than we should, for example, about the overall impact of tax and tariff rates and what kind of adjustments might have helped the South. The actual effect of the 10-percent federal tax on state bank currencies is disputed, the extent and value of private banking and deposit banking remain unclear, and there has been no close investigation of the impact of such events as the Panic of 1873 on the South. There is no study of the economic interest groups of the South comparable to those of Sharkey and Unger for the North, nor is there any close analysis of regional attitudes and interests or of how the various proposed congressional solutions might have alleviated southern economic problems. Although I have utilized newspapers, special interest publications, the infrequent commentary in southern manuscript collections, and the congressional debates for my discussion of economic conditions and interests, I make no claim to a full consideration of the problem. My analysis lies primarily at the level of the southern congressmen's remarkably unified perceptions of their region's economic problems. Their perceptions and proposed solutions, of course, are critical because they became the basis for section-party alignments in Congress. But just how closely their beliefs approximated economic realities awaits further work. Much promise lies in the recent work of cliometricians, and it is hoped that they will eventually relate their discussions of economic circumstances in the postwar South to policy making at the state and federal levels. Harold D. Woodman offers an incisive discussion of these studies in "Sequel to Slavery: The New History Views the Postbellum South," *Journal of Southern History*, XLIII (1977), 523–54. Roger L. Ransom and Richard Sutch, *One Kind of Freedom: The Economic Consequences of Emancipation* (Cambridge: Cambridge University Press, 1977), proved the most useful of these works for my purposes.

Finally, I have made clear in the text and notes my research and thoughts regarding the role of the South and economic factors in the end of Reconstruction—the subject of recent historiographical dispute. Without question, C. Vann Woodward's intriguing *Reunion and Reaction: The Compromise of 1877 and the End of Reconstruction* (Boston: Little, Brown, 1951) is a tribute to the craft of its author. The problems that I and other critics face stem in no small part from the skill with which Woodward handles contrary evidence and sprinkles his account with qualifiers and disclaimers while building the overwhelming impression that southern Democrats and the Texas & Pacific forces played a pivotal role in the resolution of the electoral crisis. Still, as is apparent from my account, I believe that the evidence and arguments of his critics necessitate a sharp modification of his narrative. See in particular: Keith Ian Polakoff, *The Politics of Inertia: The Election of 1876 and the End of Reconstruction* (Baton Rouge: Louisiana State University Press, 1973); Allan Peskin, "Was There a Compromise of 1877?" and Woodward's rejoinder, "Yes, There Was a Compromise of 1877," *Journal of American History*, LX (1973), 63–75, 215–23; George C. Rable, "Southern

Interests and the Election of 1876: A Reappraisal," *Civil War History*, XXVI (1980), 347–61; and Michael Les Benedict, "Southern Democrats in the Crisis of 1876–1877: A Reconsideration of *Reunion and Reaction*," *Journal of Southern History*, XLVI (1980), 489–524.

Index